NEW ESSAYS IN POLITICAL AND SOCIAL PHILOSOPHY

NEW ESSAYS IN POLITICAL AND SOCIAL PHILOSOPHY

Edited by

Ellen Frankel Paul, Fred D. Miller, Jr., and Jeffrey Paul

CAMBRIDGE
UNIVERSITY PRESS

Shaftesbury Road, Cambridge CB2 8EA, United Kingdom

One Liberty Plaza, 20th Floor, New York, NY 10006, USA

477 Williamstown Road, Port Melbourne, VIC 3207, Australia

314–321, 3rd Floor, Plot 3, Splendor Forum, Jasola District Centre, New Delhi – 110025, India

103 Penang Road, #05–06/07, Visioncrest Commercial, Singapore 238467

Cambridge University Press is part of Cambridge University Press & Assessment, a department of the University of Cambridge.

We share the University's mission to contribute to society through the pursuit of education, learning and research at the highest international levels of excellence.

www.cambridge.org
Information on this title: www.cambridge.org/9781107604537

First published 2012

A catalogue record for this publication is available from the British Library

Library of Congress Cataloging-in-Publication data
New essays in political and social philosophy /
edited by Ellen Frankel Paul, Fred D. Miller, Jr., and Jeffrey Paul.
p. cm.
ISBN 978-1-107-60453-7

1. Political science--Philosophy. 2. Social sciences--Philosophy.
I. Paul, Ellen Frankel. II. Miller, Fred Dycus, 1944- III. Paul, Jeffrey.

JA71.N477 2012
320.01--dc23

ISBN 978-1-107-60453-7 Paperback

The essays in this book have also been published,
without introduction and index, in the semiannual journal
Social Philosophy & Policy, Volume 29, Number 1,
which is available by subscription.

CONTENTS

INTRODUCTION

Aristotle expressed the view that the political state exists by nature because human beings are political or social by nature. Thomas Hobbes maintained on the contrary that the political commonwealth arises from an artificial covenant, whereby a multitude authorizes a sovereign to rule over it. Whether it is a result of nature, the consequence of a choice to escape the state of nature, or the outcome of some other process of deliberation, the fact of human association gives rise to recurrent themes in political and social philosophy. The character and requirements of justice, the profile of political legitimacy, and the relationship between the powers of government and the rights of the governed are some of the subjects of ongoing consideration and debate in the disciplines of philosophy, political theory, economics, and law. This volume represents a contribution to the investigation of these issues of perennial interest and import, featuring essays whose authors hope to extend, deepen, and, in some cases, move in new directions, the current state of discussion.

The thirteen essays in this collection explore the foundations of political association, the nature of justice, and the character of the rights and liberties that individuals enjoy by virtue of membership in civil society. Some identify and examine misconceptions common in current thinking among political philosophers and laypersons alike. Some seek to clarify the role played in theory and in policy by concepts prominent in political thought such as ownership and property, or those perhaps less well entrenched, such as exploitation and genocide. Others propose new understandings of the work and influence of political philosophers, such as John Rawls, whose ideas are prevalent in ongoing debates. Still others inquire about the nature and justification of government action such as its criminalization of certain individual conduct, its exercise of coercion over the governed, and its restrictions on economic and other freedoms.

The collection opens with the essay "Political Liberty: Who Needs It?" by Jason Brennan. Brennan argues that although many theorists believe that the political liberties of voting and running for office are of special importance, in most cases these liberties prove not to be especially valuable. Philosophers, he notes, have argued that the political liberties are needed or at least useful for several purposes from which their value supposedly derives. These purposes are: to lead a full, human life; to have one's social status and the social bases of self-respect secured; to make government responsive to one's interests and generate preferred political outcomes; to participate in the process of social construction so that one can feel at home in the social world; to live autonomously as a member of society; to achieve education and enlightenment and take a broad view

of the world and others' interests; and to express oneself and one's attitudes about the political process and current states of affairs. Brennan
considers and argues against each of these reasons adduced in favor of
the value of the political liberties. Among his challenges is the argument
that the political liberties are not, as such, needed for or part of flourishing, but that the extent to which they promote flourishing for each individual depends on that individual's particular conception of the good life.
Regarding social status and respect, Brennan argues that it is a contingent
psychological or cultural fact that the political liberties of voting and
running for office are taken to confer status of this sort; he also maintains
that the fact that people tend to make this connection is itself problematic
and so not a source of value. Additionally, the argument that the rights to
vote and run for office are valuable because their exercise provides incentive for politicians to act in such ways that encourage individual voters to
support them fails, according to Brennan, because the impact on election
results of any individual voter is negligible and, thus, cannot serve to
motivate politicians. Brennan further argues that the exercise of one's
political liberties to vote and run for office are neither necessary for nor
the best way to participate in social construction; they are similarly neither necessary for living autonomously nor the best means to promote the
value of autonomy.

In his essay "State Coercion and Force," Christopher W. Morris also
identifies and attempts to dispel what he regards as a misconception
common in contemporary political theory—that governments are necessarily coercive. The importance of the misconception, Morris argues, is
that the coercive nature of states both makes it very difficult to justify
them and constrains the type of justifications suitable to the task. Morris
argues that it is a mistake to think that states are "by definition" coercive
and contends that coercion and force are conceptually distinct from the
idea of a state; that is, the existence of states without coercion is in principle conceivable. Morris considers the possibility that states are viewed
as essentially coercive because laws may be viewed as essentially coercive
by virtue of their conjunction with sanctions. However, since an account
that ties law centrally to coercion by sanctions is problematic in its own
right because it fails adequately to capture the normative character of a
law as a rule rather than a command, and also because there are counterexamples to the conjunction of law and sanctions (such as power-
conferring laws), this conjunction is unavailable as support for an argument
that the political power of states more generally is always coercive. Morris explains that the coercive features of both law and political power in
general serve as incentive to those who might otherwise not be motivated
to comply with the rules, and thereby also serve to assure the governed
that others will more likely conform. The role that coercion plays, however, is decidedly secondary, Morris thinks, to the authority of the state
rather than central as many political theorists have supposed. Morris

contends that legitimate states, therefore, will have less need to employ coercion because they will achieve greater compliance because of the authority connected with their legitimacy. Morris concludes that the importance of state coercion and force has been exaggerated in contemporary political thought while the centrality of the authority of states has been underappreciated.

John Tomasi's contribution to this volume, "Democratic Legitimacy and Economic Liberty," focuses on the implications for private economic liberty of a deliberative or democratic approach to political legitimacy. On this approach, political and social institutions are considered just and legitimate insofar as they are acceptable in principle to those individuals who lead their lives within them. Democratic legitimacy requires basic rights so that the moral powers of citizens can be fully developed. Democratic theorists tend to limit the economic behaviors that count as basic rights, however, and consequently attenuate economic liberties. In contrast, Tomasi argues that democratic legitimacy requires robust economic liberties—liberties of working and owning, and other liberties subsumed under these—that are constitutionally protected to the same extent the political and civil liberties enjoyed by democratic citizens are protected. Tomasi argues that once democratic theorists acknowledge that some economic liberties are basic rights, they are required by parity of reason to admit a broader class of economic behavior under the purview of constitutionally protected basic rights. Thus, for instance, the same reasoning that leads democratic theorists to include the right to own personal *nonproductive* property among the basic rights—namely, that ownership rights can promote personal security, provide for basic needs in the form of food, clothing, and shelter, can be an expression of identity, and so on—also suggests that personal *productive* property should be counted among basic rights. Tomasi's conclusion that democratic legitimacy requires robust economic liberties upholds the value of personal economic liberty characteristic of classical liberalism, while at the same time embracing the democratic or deliberative standards of political legitimacy associated with John Rawls and others.

In his contribution to this volume, "Who Owns What? Some Reflections on the Foundation of Political Philosophy," Lloyd P. Gerson argues that neither a doctrine of rights nor a doctrine of justice can provide an adequate foundation for political philosophy because such doctrines are either justified on the basis of some further doctrine, negating their claim to be foundational, or they depend on intuitions that differ in important ways across individuals. Instead, he argues, all political philosophical theories must rest on the recognition of the existence of moral agents as individual members of a natural kind capable of entering into associations with other moral agents. According to Gerson, moral agency and self-ownership are virtually equivalent, and in order for there to be any political or other associations, there must be a mutual recognition of self-ownership. From moral agency and self-ownership, Gerson deduces property ownership. He defines a state of affairs as just, then, when and only when there is no aggression against moral agents. And the only nonarbitrary right is that of ownership—self-ownership and property ownership. Thus, A has a right to p means: to deprive A of p is unjust. Gerson concludes that rights are founded on justice, justice is founded on property, and property is founded on self-ownership. The recognition of self-ownership is a necessary condition for the mutual recognition of moral agency, the only possible basis for the existence of human associations. Thus, Gerson argues, rights and justice are derivative or dependent concepts; they are not basic or foundational.

While Gerson identifies ownership as central to the foundation of political philosophy, the author of the next essay in the volume, Donald C. Hubin, calls into question the appropriateness of extending the concept of property to controversial issues concerning reproduction and parental rights. In "Human Reproductive Interests: Puzzles at the Periphery of the Property Paradigm," Hubin argues that although the question of ownership and property rights is important in addressing many issues of public policy, the attempt to subsume all questions of rights under what he calls "the property paradigm" exerts a distorting influence on debates about a variety of complex moral issues. More specifically, he regards as problematic the application of the property paradigm to discussion of the nature and basis of parental rights. Hubin notes that the fact that parental rights are not best understood as property rights is now widely acknowledged. However, while the property paradigm no longer exerts much influence in contemporary discussions of parental rights, it still plays a significant role in discussions of reproductive rights and can, consequently, also have additional implications for parental rights and obligations. Hubin believes that focusing on the question of the ownership of gametes, in particular of sperm, tends to warp the moral dialogue concerning reproductive rights in cases such as posthumous reproduction. He further argues that when disputes arise over whether sperm can be used for reproductive purposes in cases in which it has been transferred by intercourse, policy and legal resolutions of such disputes should not be based on pronouncements or assumptions about ownership and the nature of transfers of ownership. Hubin concludes that these sensitive moral debates are better framed in terms of individuals' legitimate interests than in terms of property.

In "Why Free Trade is Required by Justice," Fernando R. Tesón argues that free trade is required by any plausible conception of justice and that it is supported by a host of consequentialist and deontological reasons. Empirically, trade increases global and national wealth, and in particular improves the situation of the poor. Morally, those who benefit from protectionist laws—which can take the form of tariffs, import and export licenses, subsidies, government procurement rules, national security requirements, and so on—are not deserving beneficiaries of wealth redistribution under any defensible conception of justice. Tesón examines both economic theory and evidence, and argues that both amply warrant the view that trade is beneficial. Further, he argues that protectionism by rich countries is harmful, not only to those countries' own consumers, but to producers in poor countries. Given this, and given the fact that protectionism is almost always the result of political pressure by inefficient producers, he concludes that there is no good reason to support it. Tesón notes that protectionism by poor countries is equally harmful. Relying on the institutionalist literature, he shows that protectionism is a problematic institution that contributes to economic stagnation in those countries which practice it. Finally, Tesón suggests that critics who oppose free trade because of the plight of the poor have a mistaken view of the causes of that plight and fail to recognize the evidence that freeing world markets actually improves the lives of the poor.

In his essay "Structural Exploitation," Matt Zwolinski examines the nature of worker exploitation. He notes that it is commonly claimed that workers in sweatshops—understood as places of employment whose working conditions or labor and/or compensation practices are prima facie morally objectionable—are wrongfully exploited by their employers. Economists typically respond to this claim by pointing out that sweatshops provide their workers with tremendous benefits, more benefits than most workers elsewhere in the economy receive. Since the desperate life circumstances that motivate workers to seek employment in sweatshops are very frequently a result of injustice, however, Zwolinski considers whether the wrongfulness of sweatshop exploitation is to be found not in the discrete interaction between a sweatshop and its employees, but rather in the unjust political and economic institutions that form the background structure against which such interaction takes place. He tries to assess what role, if any, considerations of background injustice should play in the correct understanding of exploitation. He concludes that while background or structural injustice is, of course, a matter of import in itself, it does not typically matter for determining whether a sweatshop is acting exploitatively, and it does not typically matter in a way that grounds any kind of special moral responsibility or fault on the part of sweatshops or the multinational enterprises with which they contract.

The next two essays in the collection address issues of interpretation and provide analysis of the deeply influential work of John Rawls on the concept of justice. In "Rescuing Justice From Equality," Steven Wall discusses Rawls's concept of justice in general and one of the two Rawlsian principles of justice—the difference principle—in particular. He argues that the difference principle—roughly, the principle which holds that social and economic benefits should be arranged in such a way that is of greatest possible benefit to a representative person of the least advantaged class in society—presents an interpretive puzzle. The difference principle seems to require both Pareto-efficient improvements that benefit the worst-off and to permit arrangements that fail to maximize social and economic benefits to the worst-off. Wall notes that this puzzle underscores an ambiguity in Rawls's difference principle. On one reading, the principle favors a maximizing injunction which requires opting for the alternative that maximizes the position of the worst-off members of society relative to the other alternatives. On another reading, however, the difference principle seems primarily to embrace an ideal of reciprocity that the better-off should not gain from the arrangement of social and economic benefits unless the arrangement also improves the lot of the worse-off, or at least does not come at their expense. Wall notes that these alternative interpretations of the difference principle will recommend corresponding alternative regime-types and policy prescriptions within regime-types, and so the puzzle invites a rational reconstruction of Rawls's position. Pursuing the reconstructive project, Wall concludes by making a case for the position that the difference principle should be viewed as a maximizing principle of justice that assigns strong priority to the worst-off group, and contains no trace of commitment to equality as a distributive norm.

Christopher Heath Wellman also pursues an interpretive project in his contribution to this volume. In his essay, "Reinterpreting Rawls's *The Law of Peoples*," Wellman argues that critics of John Rawls's *The Law of Peoples* wrongly presume that Rawls sought to offer a comprehensive theory of global justice, when he meant more minimally to respond to a specific practical problem: "How can we eliminate the great evils of human history?" While Wellman concedes that his reading of Rawls is not uniformly supported by all aspects of the text, he suggests that *The Law of Peoples* is a rich and complex work that does not univocally recommend any single reading, and maintains that his construal squares with Rawls's own description of the project. More importantly, he notes that his interpretation is recommended by the principle of charity, insofar as it suggests plausible responses to commonly-voiced objections to Rawls's work. In other words, if Rawls is understood in *The Law of Peoples* as providing a comprehensive theory of global justice, then many of the standard criticisms appear quite damning. However, Wellman concludes, if the aim of the book is the more modest one of recommending how liberal (and decent) societies might permissibly organize their foreign policies so as to help eliminate unjust war, oppression, religious persecution and the denial of liberty of conscience, starvation, poverty, and genocide and mass murder, then Rawls's book is not problematic in the ways that so many have supposed.

In "Responsible Choices, Desert-Based Legal Institutions, and the Challenges of Contemporary Neuroscience," Michael S. Moore examines the ways in which contemporary understandings in neuroscience present challenges to the basic way we think of ourselves in ordinary thought, morality, and the law. He describes the legal institutions, including both the political philosophy these legal institutions enshrine and the commonsense folk psychology they presuppose, that are challenged in this way by neuroscience. Three kinds of data produced by contemporary neuroscience are thought particularly to challenge commonsense views of ourselves in morals and law and Moore describes these in turn. He also distinguishes four major and several minor kinds of challenge that neuroscientific data can reasonably be interpreted to present. The major challenges are: first, the challenge of reductionism, that we are merely machines; second, the challenge of determinism, that we are caused to choose and act as we do by brain states that we do not control; third, the challenge of epiphenomenalism, that our choices do not cause our actions because our brains are the real cause of those actions; and fourth, the challenge of fallibilism, that we do not have direct access to those of our mental states that do cause our actions, nor are we infallible in such knowledge as we do have of them.

In his essay "Genocide and Crimes against Humanity: Dispelling the Conceptual Fog," Andrew Altman clarifies the concepts of genocide and crimes against humanity, taking care to distinguish their legal meanings and their meanings in moral parlance. Altman points out that genocide and crimes against humanity are among the core crimes of international law, but that they also carry great moral resonance due to their link to the atrocities of the Nazi regime and to other egregious episodes of mass violence. Despite their prevalence, Altman observes that the concepts of genocide and crimes against humanity are not well understood, even by the international lawyers and jurists who are most concerned with them. He draws a number of distinctions aimed at clarifying the concepts. He suggests that it is important to maintain the distinction between the legal and moral concepts of genocide because each plays its own distinctive role in social life. The legal concept of genocide must, thus, be useful in ways the moral concept need not be for purposes of guiding behavior whose noncompliance will be met with legal punishment. Altman distinguishes three concepts of genocide—the existing legal concept, the ideal legal concept, and the moral concept—and two concepts of crimes against humanity—the cultural model and the discrimination model. He criticizes the current legal concept of genocide and, using the idea of discrimination, proposes a model for developing a more adequate legal concept and for better understanding the moral concept. Altman also criticizes in his essay the moral concept of crimes against humanity, which, he argues, many thinkers have conflated with the legal concept of such crimes.

The nature of the limits of criminal law is the subject of Gerald Dworkin's essay in this collection, "Harm and the Volenti Principle." Dworkin takes the work of Joel Feinberg as the basis for his discussion and considers the question whether there are any principles that determine what actions should be treated as criminal. He examines Feinberg's candidate principles—a harm to others principle, which regulates conduct on the basis of its harmfulness to other people, and an offense principle, which regulates certain kinds of offensive conduct—as well as a third principle, the Volenti Principle, which states that one cannot be harmed by conduct to which one has consented. Dworkin explores various issues that arise in connection with these three principles. He explores the possibility and implications of criminalizing some types of consensual conduct without appealing to a principle of criminalization that prescribes the prohibition of consensual behavior on the basis that it is in some sense thought immoral. He looks to the Volenti principle as a possible way to address the prohibition of the types of consensual conduct in question.

In the final paper of the volume, "Education and the Modern State," Anthony O'Hear criticizes the nature of contemporary education under the influence of Darwin's evolutionary theory and the views of philosopher John Dewey. He maintains that it is problematic that current trends in education reveal a failure to appreciate the value of exposure to and engagement with the products of a wide range of great thinkers of the past. O'Hear explores the ways in which modern democratic states are likely to be inimical to traditional liberal education. He objects to the creation of educational settings on a model of participatory democracy as well as the ultimate goal of this model, namely, to educate students to be good participants in democratic political life. This approach is troubling in part, he thinks, because it fails to treat education or cultivation of the mind as worthwhile in itself, but also because there seems no reason to think that this sort of educational system generates better citizens or even ones with any interest in politics at all. Drawing on theoretical considerations and recent history, he shows how any attempt to promote traditional educational values through state interventions, such as national curricula or state regulation, is bound to be unsuccessful. O'Hear concludes that the preservation of liberal education will best be served by the wholesale removal of education from the progressive state and its bureaucracies.

Issues in political and social philosophy persist in capturing the interest of contemporary thinkers and inspiring them to enter ongoing debates in novel ways. The thirteen essays in this volume address a constellation of themes in ways which, it is hoped, will contribute constructively to the shape and trajectory of these important discussions.

ACKNOWLEDGMENTS

The editors wish to acknowledge several individuals at the Social Philosophy and Policy Center, Bowling Green State University, who provided invaluable assistance in the preparation of this volume. They include Graduate Research Assistant Christoph Hanisch, Mary Dilsaver, and Terrie Weaver.

The editors also extend special thanks to Administrative Editor Tamara Sharp, for her patient attention to detail, and to Managing Editor Pamela Phillips, for providing editorial assistance above and beyond the call of duty.

CONTRIBUTORS

Jason Brennan is Assistant Professor of Business and Philosophy at Georgetown University. He was previously Assistant Professor of Philosophy at Brown University. He is the author of *The Ethics of Voting* (2011), the coauthor with David Schmidtz of *A Brief History of Liberty* (2010), and the author of a variety of articles on democratic theory, voting ethics, the epistemology of philosophy, and other issues in moral and political philosophy. He is currently working on a liberal, extra-political conception of civic virtue, as well as on a book-length project on political competence and the right to rule.

Christopher W. Morris is Professor of Philosophy at the University of Maryland. He is the author of *An Essay on the Modern State* (2002) and the editor of *Amartya Sen* (2009), a recent collection of papers on the work of philosopher and economist Amartya Sen. Professor Morris's interests range over topics in moral, political, and legal philosophy, as well as the theory of practical rationality.

John Tomasi is Professor of Political Science and Philosophy at Brown University, where he is Founding Director of The Political Theory Project. He has held appointments at Princeton University, Stanford University, and Harvard University. Professor Tomasi has been developing a hybrid theory of liberalism that combines a commitment to private economic liberty with a concern for social justice. He presents his theory in *Free Market Fairness: A Democratic Defense of Capitalism* (forthcoming 2012).

Lloyd P. Gerson is Professor of Philosophy at the University of Toronto. He is the author, coauthor, editor, and translator of about twenty books in ancient Greek philosophy, mainly on Plato, Aristotle, Hellenistic philosophy, and Plotinus. A longstanding interest in political philosophy is currently coming to fruition in a book on the normative foundation of international relations.

Donald C. Hubin is Professor and Chair of the Philosophy Department at The Ohio State University. Professor Hubin specializes in ethics, philosophy of law, and political philosophy. He currently has two primary research interests: first, the nature of practical rationality and the relationship between morality and rationality; and, second, the nature and basis of parental rights and responsibilities. He has authored many articles on these topics in journals such as *Analysis*, *The Journal of Ethics*, *The Journal of Philosophy*, *The Journal of Law and Family Studies*, and *The Cornell Journal of Law and Public Policy*.

Fernando R. Tesón is the Tobias Simon Eminent Scholar at Florida State University College of Law. A native of Buenos Aires, he is known for his scholarship relating political philosophy to international law (in particular his defense of humanitarian intervention), and his work on political rhetoric. He has authored *Humanitarian Intervention: An Inquiry into Law and Morality* (3d ed., 2005), *Rational Choice and Democratic Deliberation* [with Guido Pincione] (2006), *A Philosophy of International Law* (1998), and many articles in law, philosophy, and international relations journals and edited collections. He is currently working on a book on global justice with Loren Lomasky of the University of Virginia. Before joining Florida State in 2002, he taught for seventeen years at Arizona State University. He has served as a visiting professor at Cornell Law School, Indiana University School of Law, University of California Hastings College of Law, the Oxford-George Washington International Human Rights Program, and the Universidad Torcuato Di Tella, Buenos Aires.

Matt Zwolinski is Associate Professor of Philosophy at the University of San Diego, and Co-Director of the University's Institute for Law and Philosophy. His current research interests are in the intersection of ethics, law, and economics, with two specific areas of focus. The first involves the proper understanding and normative status of liberty and political libertarianism. The second concerns the nature of exploitation and its moral significance for individual ethics and political institutions. He has recently published articles dealing with the ethics of sweatshop labor, the significance of the separateness of persons for liberal political theory, the morality of price gouging, and the relationship between classical liberal thought and the universal basic income. He is currently completing work on a book entitled *Exploitation, Capitalism, and the State*.

Steven Wall is Professor of Philosophy at the University of Arizona, where he is also a member of the Freedom Center. Before beginning work at the University of Arizona, he taught philosophy at Kansas State University, Bowling Green State University, and the University of Connecticut. He is the author of *Liberalism, Perfectionism and Restraint* (1998), and the editor of *Perfectionism and Neutrality* [with George Klosko] (2003) and *Reasons for Action* [with David Sobel] (2009).

Christopher Heath Wellman is Professor of Philosophy at Washington University in St. Louis and Professorial Fellow of the Centre for Applied Ethics, Charles Sturt University. He works in ethics, specializing in political and legal philosophy. His most recent books include *A Liberal Theory of International Justice* [with Andrew Altman] (2009) and *Debating the Ethics of Immigration: Is There a Right to Exclude?* [with Phillip Cole] (forthcoming 2011).

Michael S. Moore holds the Walgreen University Chair and is Professor at the Center for Advanced Studies at the University of Illinois. He is also Professor of Law and Professor of Philosophy at the University of Illinois. His previous appointments have included chairs in law and in philosophy at the University of Pennsylvania, the University of Southern California, and the University of California at Berkeley. He has written extensively in the areas of psychiatry, philosophical psychology, and the philosophy of mind, as well as in legal and political philosophy. From 2007 through 2010 he was a member of the Project on Law and Neuroscience sponsored by the MacArthur Foundation, serving as co-chair of the Responsibility Research Working Group. His most recent book is *Causation and Responsibility: An Essay in Law, Morals, and Metaphysics* (2009).

Andrew Altman is Professor of Philosophy at Georgia State University and Director of Research for the Jean Beer Blumenfeld Center for Ethics. Professor Altman is the author of *Critical Legal Studies: A Liberal Critique* (1990), *Arguing About Law: An Introduction to Legal Philosophy* (2000), and *A Liberal Theory of International Justice* [with Christopher Heath Wellman] (2009). He has also authored many articles in legal and political philosophy, including essays that have appeared in *Philosophy and Public Affairs, Ethics, Legal Theory,* and in previous issues of *Social Philosophy and Policy.*

Gerald Dworkin is Distinguished Professor of Philosophy at the University of California, Davis. He is currently a Visiting Scholar at the Department of Bioethics at the National Institutes of Health. He has written extensively on autonomy, paternalism, physician-assisted suicide, and the limits of the criminal law. He is the author of *Euthanasia and Physician-Assisted Suicide* (with R. G. Frey and Sissela Bok, 1998) and *The Theory and Practice of Autonomy* (1988), and is the editor of *Mill's On Liberty: Critical Essays* (1997); *Morality, Harm, and the Law* (1994); *Markets and Morals* (with Gordon Bermant and Peter G. Brown, 1977); *The I.Q. Controversy: Critical Readings* (with N. J. Block, 1976); and *Ethics* (with Judith J. Thomson, 1968).

Anthony O'Hear is Professor of Philosophy at the University of Buckingham and Director of The Royal Institute of Philosophy. He has served as a senior advisor to five British Secretaries of State for Education. His books include *Beyond Evolution: Human Nature and the Limits of Evolutionary Explanation* (1997), *The Great Books: A Journey through 2,500 Years of the West's Classic Literature* (2008, 2009), *The Landscape of Humanity: Art, Culture, Politics* (2008), and *The School of Freedom: A Liberal Education Reader from Plato to the Present Day* [with Marc Sidwell] (2009). He is also editor of the journal *Philosophy.*

POLITICAL LIBERTY: WHO NEEDS IT?

By Jason Brennan

I. Introduction

Contemporary philosophers, including many deliberative democrats, Rawlsian "high liberals," civic republicans, and civic humanists have recently tended to endorse progressively stronger views about the value of the political liberties—the rights to run for office and vote. They tend to hold that citizens' lives will be stunted, and their status as human beings will be diminished, unless they have equal rights to vote and run for office. It has become more common to hold that these political liberties are of special importance, even more important and valuable than the civil or economic liberties.[1]

In this essay, I challenge part of this trend. I argue that for most people the political liberties are of little value for the purposes of achieving the good life, securing their social status, promoting their preferred political outcomes, participating in the process of social construction, acting autonomously, achieving enlightenment and bettering themselves, and expressing themselves.

The claim that the political liberties are not very valuable is easily confused with other claims. Note the distinction between the following two questions:

1. Are an individual's political liberties typically valuable to that individual?
2. Are the political liberties valuable in the aggregate?

Questions 1 and 2 ask different things. Question 2 might have a positive answer even if question 1 has a negative answer. After all, suppose that democracy with universal suffrage produces the best expected consequences of any form of government. If so, then it would be valuable in the aggregate that citizens have the rights to vote and run for office. However, it might still be true that each individual's political liberties are of little value to her. Consider, in parallel, that each of us is free to pursue advances in physics. Most of us are not clever enough to make much use of these scientific liberties, but we benefit from living in a social system where everyone has them. The scientific liberties are, thus, of little value

---

[1] Consider, for instance, that most people believe that political speech demands stronger protection than commercial speech.

doi:10.1017/S0265052511000045

to the typical person who holds them, even though they are valuable in
the aggregate. So it might be with the political liberties. This essay concerns question 1, but not question 2.

Note also the distinction between these two questions:

1. Are an individual's political liberties typically valuable to that
   individual?
3. Does the typical individual value her political liberties?

Question 3 asks whether citizens subjectively value their political liberties. That is a psychological, not a philosophical, question. We could
answer it with surveys. However, question 1 is philosophical. To ask
whether the political liberties are valuable is to ask whether they *ought to
be* valued, not whether people actually value them. Again, this essay
concerns question 1.

Note finally the distinction between these two questions:

1. Are an individual's political liberties typically valuable to that
   individual?
4. Are all adult citizens entitled to the political liberties as a matter of
   justice?

In this essay, I am not asking question 4, which concerns whether citizens
are entitled to the political liberties. The answer to question 4 might be
positive even if the answer to question 1 is negative. A person might be
entitled to a liberty even if it is not valuable to her. After all, in general,
whether someone is entitled to something is not decided by whether it is
valuable to her. For instance, it would be disrespectful for someone to
steal the unwanted junk out of my basement, even if that person knows
I do not want the junk. There is no straightforward relationship between
answers to question 1 and question 4. I take no stand here on what
political liberties citizens are entitled to. I am not discussing whether
anyone should be deprived of political liberty, but am instead asking how
bad the deprivation would be. So, one way of framing this essay is as
follows. Suppose we strip some random person of her political liberties.
How bad for her is this? This question divides into two further questions.
First, how *valuable* are the liberties we have taken away? Second, how
unjust is it to take away these liberties? This essay concerns the first
question, but not the second.

In this essay, I confine my use of the term "political liberties" to the
rights to vote and to run for public office. Some philosophers also
include under the term the rights of political speech, assembly, and to
form political parties, but for the sake of this essay, I am classifying
these as civil liberties, as instances of free speech and free association.
I intend this to be a stipulation, not a point of conceptual analysis. I

want to argue that the rights to run for office and vote are not particularly valuable, but I am neutral here as to whether the rights of political speech, assembly, and to form political parties and special interest
groups are valuable. The reason I am interested in the rights to vote
and run for office is that these rights—unlike the civil or economic
liberties—are rights to exercise (or attempt to acquire) power over others. My right of free speech gives me power over myself; my right to
vote gives me some power over everyone.

Philosophers and others have argued that the political liberties are
needed or at least useful to:

A. lead a full, flourishing, good human life;
B. have one's social status and the social bases of self-respect secured;
C. make the government responsive to one's interests and generate
   preferred political outcomes;
D. participate in the process of social construction so that one can
   feel at home in the social world;
E. live autonomously as a member of society;
F. achieve education and enlightenment and take a broad view of the
   world and of others' interests;
G. express oneself and one's attitudes about the political process and
   current states of affairs.

My strategy for this essay is to examine and challenge each of these
reasons in favor of thinking that the political liberties are valuable. I know
of no general proof of the nonvalue or minimal value of the political
liberties. However, if I can show that considerations A through G fail to
show that the political liberties are valuable, this provides strong evidence that they are not. Thus, in effect, my argument is this:

1. Reasons A–G fail to show that the political liberties are generally
   valuable.
2. There is probably no further reason, H, to think they are.
3. Therefore, the political liberties are not generally valuable.

I will examine each claim (A–G) in turn.

Before turning to reasons A–G, consider one argument for why the
political liberties might be valuable. Let us call it *the Justice Argument*:

1. Justice requires democracy.
2. Democracy requires that everyone have an equal right to vote and
   run for office.
3. For each individual, it is valuable to live in a just society.
4. Therefore, the political liberties are valuable.

This argument claims that each individual has grounds for valuing her individual political liberties, because if even she alone lacked those liberties, this would be sufficient to make her society unjust. In the Justice Argument, the political liberties are not instrumentally or intrinsically valuable, but have constitutive value because they form part of something intrinsically valuable.[2] In this essay, I am putting aside questions of whether democracy is just, and looking only at arguments that do not rely upon premise 1 of the Justice Argument. If premise 1 turns out to be true, then I admit that some version of the Justice Argument would succeed, and thus my thesis would have to be modified: the political liberties are not very valuable for most people except for the purposes of realizing justice. Note, however, that many people argue for premise 1 of the Justice Argument on the basis of some of the arguments I consider and rebut below.[3]

II. THE CIVIC HUMANIST ARGUMENT

Aristotle suggested that holding and exercising the political liberties are essential for living a full, happy, virtuous human life. He articulated a version of the *Civic Humanist Argument*:

1. Virtue, flourishing, eudaimonia, and achieving the good life are valuable to each person.
2. Holding and exercising the political liberties are constitutive of virtue, flourishing, eudaimonia, and achieving the good life.
3. If X is constitutive of virtue, flourishing, eudaimonia, and the good life, then X is highly valuable.
4. Therefore, the political liberties are highly valuable to each person.

In recent years, there has been renewed interest in and debate over this argument.

The debate focuses on premise 2. I do not want to repeat this debate here, nor will I add to it. Without here examining all the possible arguments for or against premise 2, I will summarize what seems to be its main problem: premise 2 overgeneralizes. The political liberties are constitutive of the good life for some people, but not all or even most people.

[2] Something is intrinsically valuable when it is valuable as an end in itself. Something is instrumentally valuable when it is valuable for the purpose of achieving some *other* end. Something is constitutively valuable when it is valuable as a *component* or piece of something valuable. So, for instance, if I have the final end of having an excellent philosophy career, then publishing papers is constitutively valuable to me as a component of that career. In section II, I examine an argument that holds that the political liberties have constitutive value because they are a component of the good life.

[3] For example, John Rawls defends premise 1 of the Justice Argument on the basis of what I call the Status Argument in section III.

Suppose Bob is a politician. He was always on student council or was class president as a youth. He ran for town alderman at a young age, then worked his way up to state senator, and now dreams of being governor.

I would not deny that the political liberties are valuable to Bob. When I say that the political liberties are not of much value, I speak in general terms. Bob is an exception to a general trend. He needs the political liberties to realize his conception of the good life. The political liberties play a central role in Bob's life—they help define who Bob is.

However, most of us are not like Bob. Some people have a passion for democratic participation, but most do not. To some degree, the value of different liberties varies from person to person. For some people, the political liberties are necessary for them to lead good lives. For many others, the political liberties are irrelevant to lives they have reason to lead. The political liberties rightly play only a minor or perhaps no role in many people's lives.

Suppose Amy has always dreamt of owning her own business. After working an entry-level job as a pet groomer, she saves enough money to open her own business—"Amy's Pup-in-the Tub." John Tomasi asks, "What does it mean to Amy to walk in her shop each morning, or to drive by it late at night?"[4] For Amy, exercising the economic or commercial liberties is constitutive of the good life. The political liberties might rightly play no significant role in her life at all. To suggest that she leads a stunted life unless she gets herself to the forum seems not only inaccurate, but offensive.

Different people have different capacities, abilities, dispositions, and desires. What makes for a good life for any given person depends upon these four factors (among others), and so the good life varies from person to person. For instance, given who I am and given what the contemplative life is like, the contemplative life is valuable to me. Yet, that does not make it the highest form of life for everybody.[5] Similarly, a liberty or right might be valuable to one person but not another.[6] The right to worship in the church of one's choice is worthless to me (a strong atheist with little chance of becoming religious), but that right is crucial to a committed

---

[4] This paraphrases John Tomasi, *Free Market Fairness* (Princeton: Princeton University Press, forthcoming 2012), chap. 4. Tomasi is referring to a real person and a pet-grooming business in Warren, Rhode Island.

[5] I sometimes worry that political philosophy suffers from parochialism, because it is written by political philosophers and thus reflects their peculiar concerns and interests. Plato suggested that philosophers should be kings, and Aristotle suggested that philosophizing was the highest form of life. They might be right, but we have to be suspicious, given that they are philosophers. Contemporary deliberative democrats often suggest that societies would be better if everyone acted like amateur political scientists and philosophers. They might be right, but we have to be suspicious when we hear this from political scientists and philosophers.

[6] When I say that the value of a given kind of liberty can vary from person to person, I do not mean to suggest that the value of liberty to a person is purely subjective, i.e., just a matter of that person's opinion.

Christian. The right to write political books is valuable to me, but not to my handyman neighbor.

III. Status and Respect

One prominent, popular argument holds that if a person lacks the political liberties, this tends to undermine her self-respect and the respect others hold for her. The political liberties are thus valuable as means to achieving respect. Let us call this the *Status Argument*:

1. Social respect and self-respect are valuable.
2. Without the political liberties, citizens cannot (or are unlikely to) have social respect and self-respect.
3. Therefore, the political liberties are valuable.

John Rawls, among others, makes a version of this argument.[7]

Regarding the terms used in premise 1: A person has *social respect* when others view her in a favorable light, regarding her as valuable and of sufficiently high fundamental moral standing. A person has *self-respect* when she views herself in a favorable light, regarding herself as valuable and of sufficiently high fundamental moral standing.[8]

Premise 1 seems largely unobjectionable, so the success or failure of this argument depends on premise 2. In this section, I challenge this second premise. While I will not exactly refute this argument—and I take it to be the strongest argument on behalf of the personal value of the political liberties—I will still, in some sense, undermine it.

Premise 2 claims that citizens need the political liberties in order to have social respect and self-respect. One might be tempted to read premise 2 as stating something tautological: A person who lacks the political liberties by definition has a lower status than someone who holds them. They are things others may do that she may not. This is true, but it is true in the same sense that a person who lacks a driver's, medical, hairdressing, or plumbing license has lower status than those who hold those licenses. All things equal, having a hairdressing license gives someone a higher legal status. Yet, no one thinks that lacking a hairdressing license

---

[7] See John Rawls, *A Theory of Justice* (Cambridge, MA: Harvard University Press, 1971), 234; John Rawls, *Political Liberalism* (New York: Columbia University Press, 1993), 318–19; John Rawls, *Justice as Fairness: A Restatement* (Cambridge, MA: Harvard University Press, 2001), 131; Samuel Freeman, *Rawls* (New York: Routledge), 76. For an especially acute response to Rawls, see Steven Wall, "Rawls and the Status of Political Liberty," *Pacific Philosophical Quarterly* 87 (2006): 245–70, at pp. 257–61.

[8] Different versions of the Status Argument could take different stances on what counts as "sufficiently high fundamental moral standing." For example, on Rawls's account, for citizens to have the right kind of status, they need to have a full range of liberal rights, their rights must be equal to others, and some of these rights (in particular, the political liberties) must have their fair value guaranteed. However, someone propounding the Status Argument could hold a less demanding view of what counts as sufficiently high standing.

(and thus lacking the liberty to practice hairdressing) lowers one's fundamental moral status, or removes the social bases for social respect and self-respect. For the Status Argument to succeed, it needs to interpret premise 2 in a robust way, as showing that lacking the political liberties is a great threat to one's fundamental moral status, in a way that lacking the hairdressing liberties is not.[9]

John Rawls holds that when some citizens lack the political liberties, this thereby encourages everyone to see those citizens as inferior. As Steven Wall (who rejects the Status Argument) summarizes Rawls's argument, "The . . . argument begins with the plausible thought that political institutions established in a society bear importantly on the social component of self-respect. Some institutional arrangements do better than others in encouraging citizens to view one another as moral equals. . . . The public expression of . . . the fair value of political liberty is an affirmation of the equal status of all citizens."[10]

As a matter of fact, we human beings do tend to associate political power with a kind of majesty. We do tend to think that people's fundamental moral standing in some way depends upon their political standing, and vice versa. Nation-states are like clubs, and we tend to treat the rights to vote and run for office as signifying full membership in the national club. People who lack these rights are junior members at best. When people lack the political liberties, we look down upon them. They might feel humiliated by their lesser status. It seems true, therefore, that the social bases of self-respect and social respect depend upon political power. But this is only contingently true — it is an artifact of how we happen to think. We do not need to think that way. And we should not think that way, or so I will argue.

Imagine that in our culture, or in the human race in general, we tended to associate being given a red scarf by one's government as a mark of membership and status. You are not fully in your national club until you get your scarf.

Now, suppose the government gives red scarves to everyone, except homosexuals. Homosexuals would rightly be upset — they would rightly claim that the government's refusal to grant them red scarves shows that homosexuals are considered second-class, inferior people. The government's behavior would tend to induce people (including homosexuals themselves) to regard homosexuals as having low status and being less valuable. Homosexuals and their sympathetic allies would have reason to take to the streets and demand that homosexuals be granted scarves. Given how everyone thinks about red scarves, it in some sense becomes crucial to have one.

---

[9] Even libertarians, who regard such licensing as intrinsically unjust, stop short of saying that licenses threaten people's fundamental moral status.

[10] Wall, "Rawls and the Status of Political Liberty," 257–8.

However, at the same time, we can say, "There is no good reason to attach status and standing to red scarf ownership. Human dignity does not actually depend upon scarves. It is just a silly, contingent psychological or cultural fact that people think this way. And they should not think this way." The red scarves are not *really* valuable. They are valuable only as a result of a social construction, and a *bad* one at that.[11]

We can say the same thing about the political liberties and about associating moral standing with political power. (The political liberties are, after all, rights to political power.) There is no intrinsic or essential connection between status and political power. It is a contingent, psychological or cultural fact that people tend to associate human dignity with political power. But we should not think that way. I am not just saying that we have no good reason to think this way. I want to go further: I think it is a vile, contemptible fact about human beings that we associate dignity with political power.

In the United States, new parents sometimes say, "Who knows? Maybe my child will be president!" Implicit in such daydreams is the assumption that holding political power—and holding the most political power—is the most prestigious thing one can do.

Imagine a world otherwise like ours, in which people lack these kinds of attitudes. Instead of viewing the president as majestic, or the office of presidency as deserving reverence, in the alternative world people just think of the president as the chief public goods administrator. Instead of thinking of the rights to vote and run for office as possessing a lesser kind of majesty, and as signifying membership in the national club, they think of them as licenses akin to hairdressing or plumbing licenses. Imagine that people do not associate national status with international political power, and do not associate personal status with power.

This would be a better world than ours. We tie esteem to political power. But we should not; political power has a terrible track record.[12] Just think of the abuses and injustices entire nations, kings, emperors, presidents, senators, district attorneys, police officers, and average voters have gotten away with throughout history, all because we attach standing, reverence, and status to political power, and we defer before such

---

[11] If it turned out that these attitudes toward scarves resulted not from an arbitrary social practice, but from deep features in our evolved psychology, this argument would still stand. Our psychological tendencies would be lamentable, and scarves would be valuable only in light of these lamentable tendencies.

[12] On this point, blogger Will Wilkinson has an excellent post from shortly after the 2008 U. S. presidential election. Wilkinson says that given that we tend to think of the presidency as "the highest peak, the top of the human heap," and given our history of oppressing blacks, the fact that a black man won the presidency is momentous. At the same time, it would be better if we stopped thinking of the presidency as a majestic office and instead thought of it as the "chief executive of the national public goods administrative agency." Wilkinson continues, "I hope never to see again streets thronging with people chanting the glorious leader's name." See Will Wilkinson, "One Night of Romance," *The Fly Bottle*, http://www.willwilkinson.net/flybottle/2008/11/05/one-night-of-romance/.

majestic standing. Moreover, one reason why kings, presidents, and district attorneys commit such abuses in the first place is that they associate status with power. For example, King Henry VIII's wars had no chance of increasing his (or most of his subjects') personal wealth or comfort. He committed these atrocities in large part because he wanted the prestige and status that attach to increased political power. Most people revere power, more than they would admit to themselves. The romance of power and authority partly explains why people have so often been willing to collaborate with government-sponsored injustices.

The tendency to tie status to political power has other bad effects. Because people tend to use political power—and the right to vote in particular—as a way of signifying who is a full member of the national club and who is inferior, political power has tended to be distributed for bad reasons. For example, many countries have denied voting rights to women and ethnic minorities in order to signify the lesser status of members of these groups. If people had divorced standing from power, perhaps they would not have denied others their political liberties on such bad grounds. Also, many countries now give all adult citizens equal voting rights in order to signify equal status. Perhaps unrestricted universal suffrage is just. Perhaps not—perhaps political liberties should be distributed on the basis of competence, or some other basis, rather than merely on birth, citizenship, or permanent residency. However, we can barely entertain the question of whether there are better alternatives because people associate power with status. Associating power with status, therefore, potentially nullifies improvements we could make in the quality of government.

Given our contingent attitudes, the political liberties confer status. We use these rights to signify who is in our club and whom we hold in high regard. We treat the political liberties as if there were red scarves from the thought experiment above. But we should stop using these rights to signify status. We should not regard political power as a sign of worth. It would be a better world if people did not attach such significance to political power.

Since we are doing normative theory in this paper, we need not take contingent psychological or cultural facts about human beings as given. One hundred years ago, it was a contingent psychological or cultural fact that people associated being male and white with moral standing, and so it was contingently valuable to be male and white. But a political philosopher could still say that being male and white are not fundamentally valuable. They are valuable only as a result of a social construction (a construction that is perhaps rooted in our evolutionary past), and a *bad* one at that. Similarly, it is a contingent psychological or cultural fact that people associate political power (even the small amount conferred by the political liberties) with status. But a political philosopher can still say that political power is not fundamentally valuable. Political power is valuable only as a result of a social construction, and a *bad* one at that.

In some sense, my objections to the Status Argument leave its second premise intact. Political power is indeed conducive to obtaining valuable status. On the other hand, if my objections are sound, this also undermines the spirit of that argument. The political liberties are valuable as a means to securing one's status only in light of a disvaluable pattern of behavior.

IV. POLITICAL OUTCOMES

In this section, I examine an argument that claims that the political liberties are valuable, because each individual's exercise of political liberty has significant value in terms of its impact on the quality of government. Let us call this the *Outcomes Argument*:

1. The government will not be responsive to your interests unless you have the right to vote and to run for office.
2. It is valuable to have the government be responsive to your interests.
3. Therefore, it is valuable to have the right to vote and run for office.

At least among laypeople, the Outcomes Argument is a common justification of the claim that the political liberties are valuable. Prima facie, it is the most obvious argument on behalf of the political liberties. The Outcomes Argument casts the political liberties as means to help ensure good behavior from government. Politicians want my vote. To get it, candidates compete in offering me the best package. Also, since I can run for office, politicians do not just need my vote. They need to behave well enough that I will not run against them.

This argument fails in part because individual votes in fact have vanishingly small instrumental value. The Outcomes Argument overstates the value of an individual's political liberties in terms of their ability to make government responsive to her interests.

If we want to know how valuable a vote is, it depends not only on how high stakes the election is, but also on whether the individual vote will make any difference. The right to vote is itself an opportunity to cast votes, and so the instrumental value of the right to vote is in part dependent on the instrumental value of the votes a citizen can cast.

In a large-scale election, such as the U.S. presidential election or congressional elections, the probability that an individual vote will decide the outcome of the election is vanishingly small.[13] Individuals are much

---

[13] One might argue that individual votes matter, even if they do not tip the balance, because if a candidate obtains a large majority, she will be seen as "having a mandate" and this gives her greater ability to pass legislation. However, this simply relocates the problem. The person making this argument needs to find some way to measure how much individual votes contribute to creating a mandate. The logic is in many respects the same as before. For any individual voter, the likelihood that her vote makes a difference in pushing her candidate from simply winning to being seen as having a mandate is vanishingly small. Even if

more likely to win the Powerball lottery multiple times in a row than to cast a vote that changes the outcome of a presidential or congressional election.[14]

The expected utility of an individual vote is tiny even in high stakes elections. Let me illustrate with an example. Suppose there are two presidential candidates, A and B. Candidate A has credibly promised to pay you $10 billion if she wins, while B will do nothing for you. (To be clear: A will pay you $10 billion if she wins, period, regardless of whether you vote at all or regardless of whether you vote for her.) So, it is worth $10 billion to you to have A win. Suppose also that A has only a slight lead in the polls—50.5 percent of voters favor her. Suppose the number of voters in the coming election is expected to be the same as in the 2004 presidential election.

On these assumptions, is it worthwhile for you to vote for A? If you vote for A, you very slightly increase the probability of her winning. Multiplying this increase in the chance of her winning by the value of her winning ($10 billion), yields the expected utility to you of your vote for A. Once we do the calculations, we find that the expected utility is low: even though A beating B is worth $10 billion to you, your vote for A is worth only $1.45 × $10^{-2,651}$, 2,649 orders of magnitude below a penny.[15]

Politicians rarely read the academic literature on the decisiveness of individual votes, but they generally are aware that individual votes do not count for much. A politician thus has little reason to cater to me. He needs votes, but he does not need *my* vote, and he knows it. My having the liberty to vote does little to ensure that politicians or the government will respond to my interests.

Similar remarks apply to the right to run for political office. The probability that a random American, if she tried, could secure a significant public office is low. In part, this is because there are few seats to go around. There are over 1.7 million Americans for every seat in Congress. Even smaller, less important offices (such as town aldermen) tend at best to have ratios of 1 seat for every 2,000 citizens. If offices were distributed randomly at any given time, these would be bad odds. Of course, offices are not randomly distributed—rich, attractive, well-connected citizens have much better odds than others. I might decide to run for office, but politicians are not cowering at the possibility, and it is not keeping them in line.

---

there is a continuum between merely winning and having a mandate, the marginal impact of an individual vote is vanishingly small.

[14] Steven E. Landsburg, "Don't Vote. It Makes More Sense to Play the Lottery," *Slate* (September 29, 2004): http://www.slate.com/id/2107240/.

[15] This calculation uses the formulae from Geoffrey Brennan and Loren Lomasky, *Democracy and Decision* (New York: Cambridge University Press, 1993), 56–57, 119; and Loren Lomasky and Geoffrey Brennan, "Is There a Duty to Vote?" *Social Philosophy and Policy* 17 (2000): 62–82, at p. 65. See also Jason Brennan, *The Ethics of Voting* (Princeton: Princeton University Press, 2011), chap. 1.

A weaker version of the Outcomes Argument might claim that the political liberties are necessary not to help me get preferred political outcomes, but to prevent me from being dominated by others. The worry is that unequal political liberties expose citizens to domination, and we can protect citizens from domination only by imbuing them each with strong political liberties.

There is a grain of truth to this argument. If we deprive all Snuvs of the right to vote and run for office, then this will help facilitate others in exploiting, dominating, and oppressing the Snuvs. However, this does not show that it is valuable for any individual Snuv to possess the political liberties. Instead, it shows that it is valuable to each Snuv that *enough* Snuvs possess the political liberties. An individual Snuv should be nearly indifferent between situations A and B:

A. All Snuvs *except her* have the political liberties.
B. All Snuvs have the political liberties.

If A is not enough to stop the individual Snuv from being dominated, then neither is B.[16]

In the end, it is just not true that I need the political liberties to prevent others from dominating and exploiting me. What prevents me from being dominated is *other* citizens' restraint. If they decide to act badly, my rights to vote or run for office cannot stop them. The moral majority stops the unjust minority, the courts stop them, or they stop themselves. Yet if tomorrow my country decides to dominate me, my political liberties provide me no more protection than a bucket provides against a flood.[17]

V. SHAPING THE SOCIAL WORLD

Thomas Christiano argues that the political liberties can serve each person's fundamental interest "in making the world a home for [herself]."[18] One is "at home in the world" when "one is able to make sense of the world one lives in and have a sense of how one fits in with it and is connected with it."[19] People have an interest in seeing the world correspond to their view of what's right and good. And, to some degree, they want the world to be a product of their own making. They do not just

---

[16] One might try to argue that having the right to vote is, by the very definition of domination, a necessary condition for being nondominated. However, this seems to render domination so defined of no obvious value.

[17] One might try to argue that a citizen is dominated if and only if she lacks the vote. On this view, for a person to have a right to vote automatically means she is not dominated, regardless of what her country does to her. This seems too implausible to merit further discussion.

[18] Thomas Christiano, "Debate: Estlund on Democratic Authority," *Journal of Political Philosophy* 17 (2009): 228–40, at p. 238.

[19] Thomas Christiano, *The Constitution of Equality* (New York: Oxford University Press, 2008), 65.

want the world to *conform* to their judgments (perhaps by coincidence), but to *be responsive* to their judgments.

Reasoning like this often leads to versions of what I will call the *Social Construction Argument*:

1. (In general, with some exceptions,) each person has a fundamental interest in living in a world in which she can feel at home.
2. In order to serve this interest, each person needs her world to be adequately responsive to her judgments, and she needs to take an adequate part in the process of social construction.
3. In order to make the world adequately responsive to her judgments and to take an adequate part in the process of social construction, each person needs to possess the political liberties and be able to exercise them with others as equals.
4. Therefore, each person needs to possess the political liberties and be able to exercise them with others as equals.[20]

I do not mean to suggest that the Social Construction Argument is equivalent to Christiano's own argument on behalf of democracy or of the value of the political liberties.[21] (It is a strand of his argument, but his argument has other strands as well, including strands of other arguments I consider below.) Instead, I present the Social Construction Argument here because it captures one reason both philosophers and laypeople tend to think that the political liberties are valuable.

Premise 3 claims that I need the political liberties in order to take part in the process of social construction and to make the world adequately responsive to my interests. The Social Construction Argument is meant to be distinct from the Outcomes Argument. We should not interpret it as claiming that an individual's right to vote is instrumentally valuable because it has a significant expected utility in terms of its propensity to produce favored political outcomes. As we saw above, this claim is false.

Thus, a more plausible interpretation of premise 3 of the Social Construction Argument might say that when I have the right to vote and run for office, I thereby acquire the power to *help cause* the government to be responsive to my interests. I cannot cause the government to be respon-

---

[20] See Christiano, *The Constitution of Equality*, 61–63, 101, 115, 154, and passim.

[21] Christiano's argument is more complicated. In a nutshell, he holds that justice requires that everyone be treated as an equal and have her interests advanced equally by society. Everyone has three fundamental interests, including an interest in being at home in the world. In order for people to be sure that their interests are being advanced equally, justice must not merely be done, but must be seen to be done. And in light of the various cognitive biases, self-serving biases, and cognitive weaknesses we all have, the only way for justice to be seen to be done is if everyone is given equal political power. This is an argument for why democracy is justified, but it also contains subarguments that purport to show that for each individual, her political liberties are valuable to her. My discussion here of the Social Construction and Status Arguments makes trouble for Christiano.

sive all by myself, but by acting in concert with others, I can still be *part of the cause* of the government being responsive to my interests. If my favored political outcomes occur, I can say to myself, "I helped make that happen."[22] This might make me more at home in the world.

One problem with this claim, though, is that it relies upon controversial views about causation. Suppose that ten of us throw rocks at a window, and our ten rocks simultaneously hit and break the window. Did I cause the window to break? Did you? Did the ten of us collectively cause it to break, while none of us as individuals caused it to break? Metaphysicians continue to debate these questions.[23] The answers are not clear. We do not want the question of whether the political liberties are valuable to depend on a difficult debate in the metaphysics of causation.[24]

There is another plausible interpretation of premise 3, which relies upon less controversial metaphysics. Premise 3 can be interpreted as claiming that by having the right to vote and run for office, I can thereby *participate* in producing preferred outcomes. This interpretation makes a weaker metaphysical claim—even if I do not cause the window to break, or a candidate to be elected, at least I participate in the collective activities of breaking the window or electing the candidate.[25]

Like the Civic Humanist Argument, the Social Construction Argument might explain why some citizens could find their political liberties valuable. A person might *enjoy* voting, or *enjoy* taking part in democratic processes. If one enjoys these enough, then even once opportunity costs are taken into account, it can be worthwhile to vote or run for office. If so, then having the political liberties can be valuable. On this view, to vote is much like deciding to "do the wave" at a sports game. The wave will happen with or without one's own participation, but it can be enjoyable to participate.

However, this does not yet show that the political liberties are particularly valuable. A person need not vote, or have the right to vote or run for public office, in order to help cause or participate in producing an electoral outcome.[26] Voting is not the only, or even the most effective

---

[22] Richard Tuck, *Free Riding* (Cambridge, MA: Harvard University Press, 2008), 30–98, makes a sophisticated argument on behalf of this claim.

[23] For a good overview of these issues, see Jonathan Schaffer, "The Metaphysics of Causation," *Stanford Encyclopedia of Philosophy*, http://plato.stanford.edu/entries/causation-metaphysics/.

[24] For a defense of the claim that all participants and even eligible nonparticipants are causally responsible for electoral outcomes, see Alvin Goldman, "Why Citizens Should Vote: A Causal Responsibility Approach," *Social Philosophy and Policy* 16, no. 2 (1999): 201–17.

[25] In Brennan, *The Ethics of Voting*, chaps. 3–5, and Jason Brennan, "Polluting the Polls: When Citizens Should Not Vote," *Australasian Journal of Philosophy* 87, no. 4 (2009): 535–49, I argue that certain citizens should not vote because they would be participating in collectively harmful or needlessly risky activities. My argument does not require the stronger claim that voters can be said to cause outcomes.

[26] In Brennan, *The Ethics of Voting*, chap. 2, I argue that a person can help to produce good political outcomes even if she does not participate in politics.

means of helping to cause or participate in the production of preferred political outcomes. One can donate money to a campaign, volunteer, write letters or books, tweet on Twitter, blog, make posters, go door to door, and so on. One can try to change people's general political beliefs by changing school curricula. All of these activities can be more interesting, engaging, and rewarding ways of participating in the political process than voting or running for office, and they do not require the political liberties. So, even if a person had a fetish for helping to cause or partici- pate in the production of political outcomes, the political liberties might not be particularly valuable for that person. To infer that if someone wants to participate in producing political outcomes, then the political liberties must be valuable to her, is sort of like inferring that if someone likes fast food, she thereby likes Taco Bell.

In fact, if someone wants to participate in the process of social con- struction, she need not participate in politics at all.[27] In a liberal society, nearly all citizens participate in the process of social construction, of creating and maintaining a society together, but not all do it through politics. Consider artists, entrepreneurs, small-business owners, venture capitalists, teachers, physicians, intellectuals, stock traders, stay-at-home parents, working parents, chefs, janitors, grocery clerks, and others. Each of these kinds of people in one way or another contributes to creating, shaping, and maintaining a worthwhile society. Through their different kinds of work, these individuals engage in the process of social construc- tion. They help make the social world what it is. If you are an Apple employee, you can look for white earbuds in a crowd to see evidence of how you helped to shape the world. One's right to work helps one engage in the process of social construction at least as well as one's right to vote. By sacking groceries, fixing cars, or teaching high school courses, a citizen helps to influence the character of her society, at least as much as she does through voting. In our roles as consumers and producers—even if we are very poor—we still have much more power to shape our shared social world than we do as voters or as potential political candidates.

If someone wants to participate in the process of social construc- tion, therefore, in order to help her feel at home in the world, the political liberties are dispensable. There are other, much better outlets for participation.

Not only are other outlets better, but unless a person has a strong taste for exercising the political liberties, then exercising the political liberties is not even a very good way to engage in the process of social construction. To infer that if someone wants to participate in the process of social construction, then the political liberties must be valuable to her, is sort of like inferring that if automobiles are valuable, then the Ford Edsel is valuable.

---

[27] Here I summarize an argument made in Brennan, *The Ethics of Voting*, chap. 2.

Politics provides a weak outlet for social construction in part because there are no niches. Democratic political decisions apply to all equally, and if one dislikes the outcomes, there is usually no escape. In trying to explain why the political liberties are valuable, Christiano (and Walzer, whom he cites[28]) use the metaphor of "being at home." The political liberties are supposed to help us feel at home. But this is misleading. Our homes are niches. Most of us are at home in our homes because we may unilaterally shape our homes to reflect our preferences. Our homes are governed by principles we endorse. We do not have to deliberate in public and justify our furniture arrangements to others in society. Many of us can shape our work environments to a significant extent as well, at the very least by choosing where we work. And even if we do not feel completely at home in society, we can at least usually find niches within society where we do feel at home. But in politics, there are no real niches. I find the formulaic women's movies on the Lifetime Channel bland and vapid, so I watch something else. I find marijuana criminalization and farm subsidies stupid and unjust, but there is no niche to accommodate me (or it is prohibitively expensive for me to relocate to that niche).

Politics provides a weak outlet for social construction in part because individual citizens are nearly powerless. They have so little power that they are faced with a choice: A) conform to the majority's position, and thus "help to produce favored outcomes," or B) go against the majority's position, in which case the voter has at best helped to signal dissent from the majority's position. (I discuss the expressive power of the political liberties below.) In light of this powerlessness, it is difficult to take seriously the claim that engaging in politics is a valuable way of participating in social construction.

If you vote with the majority, then you participate in producing the electoral outcome. But the empowerment offered by voting is a sham. Consider this metaphor: Suppose you are swimming at the beach. A large wave heads your way. You can choose to stand your ground, or you can swim with it, but you cannot push it back. If you decide to ride with the wave, you might be said to participate in the wave, and you might even *help cause* some of that water to reach the shore. But to think of any of this as sharing control is self-delusional.[29] If you feel at home in the water, it is because you accommodated yourself to the water, not because the water accommodated itself to you.

Also, even if we grant that voters for the winning candidate count as helping to cause that candidate's election, voters for losing candidates do

---

[28] Christiano, *The Constitution of Equality*, 61. Christiano cites Michael Walzer, "Interpretation and Social Criticism," *Tanner Lectures on Human Values VIII* (Salt Lake City: University of Utah Press, 1988), 14.

[29] Someone might object to this metaphor by saying that in a democracy, we the people are the ocean. Each of us is an equally efficacious water molecule. Perhaps. But waves go through this ocean, and each molecule is powerless against the waves.

not even get this benefit. For losers, the right to vote is at best an opportunity to help cause a favored candidate to win in the future. Persistent minorities—people whose favored candidate or position loses year after year—lack even this opportunity. To get a chance to help cause a candidate to win, you need to accommodate yourself to what other voters favor. In the United States, individual voters can choose to ride the Democrat or Republican wave. If they dislike both parties, they cannot do much to change what is in the ocean.

The Social Construction Argument claims that people need to feel at home in the world. To achieve this, they need the world to be responsive to their interests and they need to take part in the process of social construction. The argument then claims that the right to vote and run for office are instrumental to meeting these needs. In response, I have argued that the political liberties are not particularly good instruments for meeting these needs, and that these needs are better met through other means. The Social Construction Argument represents the political liberties as tickets to the social construction game, but the political liberties are only tickets for the nosebleed seats.

VI. Autonomy

Another argument, closely related to the Social Construction Argument, is the *Autonomy Argument*:

1. It is valuable for each person to be autonomous and self-directed, and to live by rules of her own making.
2. In order for each person living in a shared political environment to be autonomous and self-directed, and to live by rules of her own making, she needs to possess the political liberties and make use of them.
3. Therefore, each person living in a shared political environment needs to possess the political liberties and make use of them.[30]

This argument maintains that the political liberties are instrumental to, or perhaps even constitutive of, maintaining one's autonomy. If autonomy is valuable, then so are the political liberties. This argument suffers from some of the same flaws as the Social Construction Argument, but it has other distinct problems as well.

---

[30] Versions of this argument can be found in Jean-Jacques Rousseau, *The Social Contract and Other Later Political Writings,* ed. Victor Gourevitch (New York: Cambridge University Press, 1997) and Carol Gould, *Rethinking Democracy: Freedom and Social Cooperation in Politics, Economics, and Society* (New York: Cambridge University Press, 1988), 45–85. Gould argues that democracy is necessary for the good of autonomous self-government, and then argues that citizens are entitled to democracy.

If the Autonomy Argument is intended to show that a person needs the political liberties in order to be autonomous and self-directed over her own mind, it is clearly unsound. A person who lacks these rights might still be a self-controlled, self-legislating person, just as a person who has them might be slavish and blindly deferential.

If there is a connection between voting and autonomy, it must be something like this: By voting, a person is in part the author of the laws. If she abstains, then she has no partial authorship over the laws, and thus the laws are in some way imposed upon her.

According to this argument, voting confers autonomy on you only if your side wins. However, even then the political liberties do not confer any significant autonomy. The Autonomy Argument appears to overstate the degree of autonomy that the rights to vote and run for office confer.

I have made quite a few autonomous decisions in my life. I have made autonomous decisions over petty things: what to wear each day, what to eat, what color toothbrush to have, what to watch on television. I have made autonomous decisions over important things: what to write about for my dissertation, where to go to college and graduate school, which job offers I would accept. I have made autonomous decisions over momentous things: whom to marry, whether to have a child, what to choose for a career.

Suppose these choices had been subject to democratic decision-making. We would regard that as taking the choice away from me and giving it to the democratic body. Even if I had an equal vote in this body, it would be a severe loss of autonomy. Even if the democratic body did not just vote, but actively deliberated over the best choices (and listened to me give my reasons), having it make the decisions would mean a severe loss of personal autonomy for me.

It is not just that I have more autonomy when I make decisions alone as opposed to when a democratic assembly (of which I am a member) makes the decisions. Rather, when a democratic assembly (of which I am a member) makes the decisions, I do not have much autonomy at all.

Robert Nozick illustrates this point with a story called the "Tale of the Slave." Nozick describes the changing conditions under which a slave lives, and asks his readers to point out when the slave stops being a slave. Here is how the story goes. Let us say you are the slave. At first, you live under a cruel master, who beats you arbitrarily. Then the master posts a set of rules and only punishes you when you violate the rules. The master then starts allocating resources among all of his slaves on kindly grounds, considering their needs, merit, and so on. The master then decides to allow the slaves to spend four days doing whatever they please and only requires them to work three days on his manor. The master then decides to allow the slaves to live in the city or wherever else they like, provided they send the master three-sevenths of their income. The master also continues to regulate many of their activities and can call them back to the manor for defense. The master decides to allow his ten thousand slaves—other than you—to make decisions among themselves about how to regulate their behavior and how much of their income they must send the master. You are bound by their decision, but cannot vote or deliberate.

When the master dies, he leaves all of his slaves, including you, to each other as a collective body, except for you. That is, his ten thousand other slaves collectively own everyone, including you, but you own no one. The other ten thousand slaves decide to allow you to advise them about what rules they should pass. These rules govern both their behavior and yours. Eventually, as a reward for your service, they allow you to vote whenever they are evenly divided—five thousand to five thousand—over what to do. You cast a ballot in an envelope, which they agree to open whenever they are split. Finally, since they have never been evenly split, they just include your vote with theirs all the time.

At the end of the story, many readers think that the slave never stopped being a slave. This is disturbing because by the end of the story, the situation very much resembles modern democracy. One thing we should learn from Nozick's story is that being a member of a rule-making body, especially a large one, does not give one much control. Each slave in the tale of the slave can legitimately claim that *everyone else makes all the decisions* and that *the decisions the body makes would have occurred without her input.* Even when democratic outcomes result from the equal input of all, there can be a feeling of an utter lack of power. Our voices and votes are lost.

In parallel: I went to Mardi Gras one year. At night, the streets were so congested that I could lift my feet and be carried along by the crowd. It took serious effort to move against the current. Everyone in the crowd had the same predicament. We were all equals. Our individual movements equally decided the collective movement of the crowd. Yet, we were each powerless.[31]

One further point about autonomy: We cannot control or have a say over everything that happens in our lives, so we have to choose where we make a stand, where we think it is important to be authentic. Politics is one place to make a stand, but it is not the only or obviously best place.

Consider an analogy. Chris was a punk-rock kid who rode the bus with me in ninth grade. One day Chris complained about my manner of dress: "You wear the Gap just like everyone else. You don't try to be original or true to yourself." Chris, in contrast, had chosen to conform to the punk-rock subculture. I responded with something like this, "I don't care that much about how I dress. So, I go along with how others dress. It's not that important to me, and how they do it is good enough." (In contrast, it was very important to Chris to dress a certain way.) In this case, it is implau-

---

[31] Perhaps people who lived their whole lives this way would develop false consciousness and begin to regard the situation as empowering and free.

sible to say that I was inauthentic or lacked self-control because I deferred
to the crowd on how to dress. Sometimes this deference is a way of being
authentic, or as authentic as it is reasonable to be, because deferring
prevents one from wasting time on unimportant things.

There is no obvious reason why politics cannot be like that. A self-
controlled, authentic, autonomous individual might defer to others on
politics because she recognizes that others will produce good enough
outcomes, and within that range of likely outcomes, the outcomes just are
not that important to her. Or, she might defer because she accepts that she
cannot take control over everything, and she finds more important places
to make her stand.

In summary, the Autonomy Argument fails for many of the same reasons the Outcomes and Social Construction Arguments failed. To succeed, the Autonomy Argument would need citizens to have much more
power than they in fact have. And one can develop autonomy and have
satisfactory levels of self-control regardless of whether one possesses the
political liberties.

VII. Education and Enlightenment

If someone wishes to show that the political liberties are valuable, she
will need to produce an argument compatible with the point that individual citizens have vanishingly little power over the political process.
One such argument, the *Education Argument*, seems promising:

1. Civic and political activity requires citizens to take a broad view of
   others' interests, and to search for ways to promote the common
   good. This requires long-term thinking, and engagement with
   moral, philosophical, and social scientific issues.
2. If civic and political activity requires long-term thinking, and
   engagement with moral, philosophical, and social scientific issues,
   then civic and political activity serve a valuable educative function.
3. The political liberties are needed to engage in civic and political
   activity.
4. Therefore, the political liberties serve a valuable educative function.

Alexis de Tocqueville and John Stuart Mill advanced versions of the
Education Argument.[32] Many contemporary political theorists, such as
Richard Dagger, have advanced this argument as well.[33] The Education
Argument holds that the political liberties are valuable because exercising
these liberties tends to be enlightening.

[32] See Alexis de Tocqueville, *Democracy in America* (New York: Anchor Books, 1969), 243–4
and John Stuart Mill, *Three Essays "On Liberty," "Representative Government," and "The Sub-
jection of Women,"* ed. Richard Wollheim (New York: Oxford University Press, 1975), 196–7.
[33] Richard Dagger, *Civic Virtues* (New York: Oxford University Press, 1997), 102–4.

On the one hand, if premise 1 is interpreted as a *descriptive* claim, it is plainly false. You can vote or run for office despite being narrow-minded, ignorant, and unenlightened. On the other hand, if premise 1 is interpreted as a *normative* claim, then this argument does not show that exercising the political liberties in fact tends to educate and enlighten citizens. At best, it would only show that the political liberties *could* do so if citizens exercise their liberties in the right way. Premise 1 is best replaced with this alternative:

> 1*: Citizens who make use of their political liberties will tend to take a broad view of others' interests, to search for ways to promote the common good, to engage in long-term thinking, and to engage with moral, philosophical, and scientific issues.

Still, even with Premise 1*, this new argument is problematic.

Premise 3 is false. To engage in civic and political activities, one does not need to have the right to vote or run for office. One can debate politics with others, organize campaigns, donate to causes, write letters, and so on, even if one lacks the political liberties. Instead, if citizens are enlightened, this results from deliberating, reading, debating, watching others deliberate, seeking evidence, and the like. Citizens can get all of these benefits without voting or running for office, and without having the right to vote or run for office.

Also, even if it were true that exercising the political liberties tends to enlighten citizens, that would not show that the political liberties are uniquely or particularly valuable means to achieving enlightenment. There are other activities that tend to be enlightening. And perhaps these other activities do a superior job in enlightening citizens. In fact, even if participating in politics tends to educate and enlighten citizens, it is not as if what enlightens them are voting and running for office.

The Education Argument, therefore, needs to be supplemented with the premise that citizens will tend not to deliberate, read, debate, etc., unless they have the political liberties. This is an empirical claim. Perhaps it is true, but anyone asserting it requires supporting empirical evidence. (To my knowledge, no one has any such evidence.)

Let us take a closer look at Premise 1*. Does engaging in politics really tend to educate and enlighten citizens? On the contrary, politics teaches enlightenment in much the same way that fraternity parties teach temperance. While politics provides an opportunity for enlightenment, it is more likely to stultify than enlighten.

People tend to be on some of their worst epistemic behavior when participating in politics. They display high levels of epistemic irrationality when discussing or participating in politics. In part, this is because our brains were designed more for winning arguments and forming coalitions than seeking truth. As psychologist Jonathan Haidt says,

... reasoning was not designed to pursue the truth. Reasoning was designed by evolution to help us win arguments. That's why [Mercier and Sperber] call [their theory of why reasoning developed] The Argumentative Theory of Reasoning. So, as they put it ... "The evidence reviewed here shows not only that reasoning falls quite short of reliably delivering rational beliefs and rational decisions. It may even be, in a variety of cases, detrimental to rationality. Reasoning can lead to poor outcomes, not because humans are bad at it, but because they systematically strive for arguments that justify their beliefs or their actions. This explains the confirmation bias, motivated reasoning, and reason-based choice, among other things." [34]

Confirmation bias is the thesis that we tend to pay strong attention to and accept evidence in favor of beliefs we already hold, and tend to ignore, reject, or be bored by evidence against beliefs we hold. Motivated reasoning is the thesis that we have preferences over beliefs and that we tend to believe what we prefer to be true. For example, I might prefer to think I am smart, I might prefer to think Democrats are good and Republicans are evil, or I might prefer to think God created the earth six thousand years ago. Motivated reasoning occurs when the brain tries to arrive at beliefs that maximize good feelings and minimize bad feelings. "Reason-based choice" refers to the phenomenon of people confabulating or inventing reasons for their decisions when they in fact had no basis for decision.

Exercising the political liberties could be a way of making people more rational, self-directed, and deliberative, if only human beings were not the way they are. Actual human beings are wired not to seek truth and justice but to seek consensus. They are shackled by social pressure. They are overly deferential to authority. They cower before uniform opinion. They are swayed not so much by reason but by a desire to belong, by emotional appeal, and by sex appeal. We evolved as social primates who depended on tight in-group cooperative behavior. Unfortunately, this leaves us with a deep bent toward tribalism and conformity. Too much and too frequent democracy threatens to rob many of us of our autonomy and rationality.[35] Politics threatens to unenlighten at least as much as it promises to enlighten us.

Economist Bryan Caplan notes that average citizens have systematically different beliefs about basic economics than trained economists. (Note that laypeople tend to hold their economic views just as strongly, in fact, more strongly, than economists.) Even once we correct for possible demographic biases (since economists tend to be male, white, and upper-

[34] Jonathan Haidt, "The New Science of Morality," Edge, http://www.edge.org/3rd_culture/morality10/morality.haidt.html. Haidt is summarizing research (which he endorses) by Hugo Mercier and Dan Sperber.
[35] See David Schmidtz and Jason Brennan, A Brief History of Liberty (Boston: Wiley-Blackwell, 2010), 208-33, for empirical support of these claims.

middle class), economists and laypeople still disagree about textbook economics.[36] According to Caplan, compared to economists, laypeople exhibit four basic biases: an antiforeign bias, an antimarket bias, a pessimistic bias, and a make-work bias. That is, laypeople underestimate the value of trading with foreigners, underestimate the efficacy of markets, underestimate how good the future will be and overestimate how good the past was, and underestimate the value of labor-saving inventions and schemes. Now, since the available evidence strongly favors textbook economics, Caplan contends that average citizens most likely have systematically false beliefs about the economy and how it functions.[37]

Caplan claims that people are rationally irrational about politics. Rational irrationality is the thesis that it can be *instrumentally* rational to be *epistemically* irrational. That is, in the sphere of politics, it is not in most people's interest to collect and assess evidence properly, but instead to indulge in whatever beliefs they find flattering or emotionally appealing. If, despite the honking horns, you believe the street you are crossing is clear, you die. But if, despite overwhelming evidence that free trade is good and protectionism is bad, you believe protectionism is good and vote accordingly, nothing happens. So, if advocating trade restrictions helps to serve one's interests—such as feeling patriotic, forming in-groups and out-groups, sublimating racist attitudes, pretending to have solidarity with union workers or the poor—then a person will tend to endorse trade restrictions. For any given voter, the expected cost of maintaining her epistemic rationality in the sphere of politics is greater than the expected benefit.

The existence of rational irrationality is supported by many independent psychological studies. (Many studies on motivated reasoning are also studies in rational irrationality.) For an illustration, I will here recount one of psychologist Drew Westen's experiments on motivated reasoning.[38] Westen's subjects were loyal Republicans and Democrats. Subjects were shown a statement by a celebrity, followed by information potentially making the celebrity seem hypocritical. Then, subjects were presented with an "exculpatory statement." (A test run had a quote by Walter Cronkite saying he would never do TV work again after retiring, followed by footage showing he did work again after retiring, followed by an explanation saying it was a special favor.) In the experiment, the celeb-

---

[36] By issuing surveys which ask citizens both about their demographics and about their opinions on economics, we can determine using regressions how demographic factors correlate with economic beliefs.

[37] See Bryan Caplan, *The Myth of the Rational Voter* (Princeton: Princeton University Press, 2007).

[38] Drew Westen, Pavel S. Blagov, Keith Harenski, Clint Kilts, and Stephan Hamann, "The Neural Basis of Motivated Reasoning: An fMRI Study of Emotional Constraints on Political Judgment in the U.S. Presidential Election of 2004," *Journal of Cognitive Neuroscience* 18 (2007): 1947–58; Drew Westen, *The Political Brain: How We Make Up Our Minds without Using Our Heads* (New York: Perseus Books, 2008).

rities were identifiable as Republicans or Democrats. Democrat subjects strongly agreed that the famous Republicans contradicted themselves but only weakly agreed that the Democrats contradicted themselves. Republican subjects likewise readily accepted exculpatory statements from their favored party, but not the other party. Functional magnetic resonance imaging (fMRI) showed that subjects' pleasure centers were activated when condemning members of the other party, and activated again when subjects denied evidence against members of their own party.

Political scientist Diana Mutz's research provides evidence that politics tends to be stultifying or, at least, that the people who tend to make the most use of their political liberties tend also to be unenlightened. Following Mutz, let us define a "deliberative citizen" as a citizen who has frequent crosscutting political discussion, who can intelligently articulate arguments both on behalf of her own views and on behalf of contrary views, and who has high levels of objective political knowledge. Let us define a "participatory citizen" as a citizen who engages heavily with politics by voting, running for office, participating in political campaigns, joining causes, engaging in activism, and the like. Mutz's work shows that deliberation and participation do not come together. Deliberative citizens do not participate much, and participatory citizens do not deliberate much. The people who are most active in politics tend to be (in my words, not Mutz's) cartoon ideologues.[39] The people who are most careful in formulating their own political views and who spend the most time considering contrary views tend not to participate in politics.

Mutz's research indicates that active, participatory citizens tend not to engage in much deliberation and tend not to have much crosscutting political discussion.[40] Instead, they seek out and interact only with others with whom they already agree. When asked why other people hold contrary points of view, participatory citizens tend to respond that others must be stupid or corrupt. Participatory citizens are often unable to give charitable explanations of why people might hold contrary views. (This is worrisome, I would add, because people who tend to demonize all contrary views tend to be unjustified in their own views.) In contrast, citizens who exhibit high degrees of the deliberative virtues are able to give charitable accounts of contrary viewpoints.

In summary, the Education Argument seems unsound. If the Education Argument simply asserts that politics can serve an educational function,

[39] See Diana Mutz, *Hearing the Other Side: Deliberative versus Participatory Democracy* (New York, Cambridge University Press, 2006), 128.

[40] Ibid., 30. The more people join voluntary associations, the less they engage in crosscutting discussions. What demographic factors best predict that one will engage in crosscutting political discussion? Apparently, being nonwhite, poor, and uneducated. The reason for this is that white, rich, educated people have more control over the kinds of interactions they have with others. People generally do not enjoy having crosscutting political discussions. They enjoy agreement. So those with the most control over their lives choose not to engage in crosscutting discussions. See ibid., 27, 31, and 46–47.

well, sure, it *can*. A lot of things—joining a street gang, taking heroin, dropping out of high school—*can* serve an educational function and help one achieve enlightenment. But if the Education Argument wants to assert that politics is *likely* to serve this function, our evidence points against this. An *Inverse* Education Argument seems more sound: the political liberties are bad because exercising them tends to be stultifying. However, this might be too strong. Some of the work mentioned above supports this claim, but some of it just shows that politically engaged citizens tend not to be enlightened. Whether that is because politics makes them less enlightened or because enlightened people choose not to engage in politics is not clear. In either case, though, the evidence on behalf of Premise 1* is weak, and so the Education Argument fails.

VIII. SELF-EXPRESSION

Another argument holds that the political liberties are important means of self-expression. Let us call this the *Expression Argument:*

1. Generally, it is valuable to each citizen for that citizen to be able to express her opinions about what her country is doing, what values should be promoted, what changes should be made, and so on.
2. The political liberties are valuable means for a citizen to express her opinion on these matters.
3. Therefore, generally, the political liberties are valuable to each citizen.

The Expression Argument suffers from many of the same flaws as the other arguments we have considered. First, exercising the political liberties is not a very good way to express oneself, and second, there are much better alternatives.[41]

The political liberties are ineffective ways to communicate our attitudes to others. A vote is not an expressive instrument. It is like a piano with only four keys and which breaks after playing one note. (We might add that the strings tend to be out-of-tune and rusty.) Suppose that in the last election, I voted for a certain candidate, regarding him as the lesser of two warmongering, paternalistic, exploitative, plutocratic evils. Suppose a colleague voted for that same candidate, regarding him as a truly positive

---

[41] I am not here challenging the expressive theory of voting. The expressive theory of voting is a *descriptive* theory, which claims that many citizens vote in order to express attitudes. The expressive theory claims (roughly) that citizens know that their votes will not change the outcome of an election, and so they vote to express solidarity with certain causes. One person votes Democrat to express solidarity with the poor, while another votes Republican to express concern for personal responsibility. See Geoffrey Brennan and James Buchanan, "Voter Choice," *American Behavioral Scientist* 28, no. 2 (1984): 185–201; Brennan and Lomasky, "Is There a Duty to Vote?"; Geoffrey Brennan and Alan Hamlin, *Democratic Devices and Desires* (New York: Cambridge University Press, 2000).

change he could believe in. Suppose someone else voted for that same candidate because he wanted to fit in with his friends. Suppose a fourth person cynically voted for that candidate because he wanted to hasten his country's demise. What did any of our votes express to others? Just by knowing for whom someone voted, you cannot infer what someone meant to express.

Or, suppose I run for office. What does that communicate? I might claim that I want to change the world for the better, but every politician says that. Regardless of my communicative intentions, running for office tends to communicate that I am power- and status hungry.

Exercising the political liberties is ineffective, then, if we want to communicate with others. Still, sometimes we just want to express our attitudes to ourselves, rather than to others. In private, I might tear up photos of a recent ex-girlfriend. Here, the point is to express finality to myself, and to perform a closing ritual to help me move on. No doubt people can use their votes this way. The cynical voter can express his cynicism to himself by voting for the worst candidate. So, while the political liberties have little value in expressing our attitudes to others, they have some value in expressing our attitudes to ourselves.

Still, we have many other better outlets for self-expression. Even if someone wants to communicate his political attitudes to himself, he can usually best do so without exercising the political liberties. For example, the cynical citizen could donate money to the worst candidate, write a poem, or build and burn an effigy. And if someone wants to communicate with others, then writing letters, joining online forums, creating websites, making YouTube videos, and the like, are much more effective means of communicating than voting or running for office.

IX. CONCLUSION

I have examined a number of arguments in favor of the view that the political liberties generally are of high value to the people who hold them. These arguments have been found wanting. Unless there is some further argument in favor of the political liberties, we can conclude that they probably are not of much value to most people who hold them. The civil and economic liberties are likely to be more valuable to most people than their political liberties.

Again, I am not saying that people *do* value their political liberties less than these other liberties, nor am I claiming that they in fact regard their political liberties as having little value. On the contrary, I suspect most people think their political liberties are quite valuable. Instead, in saying that the political liberties are not of much value, I am saying that they do not deserve to be valued highly.

However, I am arguing for only a general trend. Some people, given their needs, ends, abilities, and circumstances, will have grounds to value their political liberties highly. Since I am arguing for a general trend, to rebut my thesis, it will not be enough to show the political liberties are sometimes of high value to some people, but instead that they are generally of high value to most people.

Again, all of this leaves open whether the political liberties are valuable in the aggregate, or whether anyone is entitled to the political liberties. It might be that democracy is good and just, even if individuals do not usually have grounds for holding that their political liberties are valuable. I take no stands on these issues here.

Business and Philosophy, Georgetown University

STATE COERCION AND FORCE*

By Christopher W. Morris

"Covenants, without the Sword, are but Words, and of no strength to secure a man at all," Thomas Hobbes famously proclaimed.[1] He exaggerated. As I shall point out later, his position is more subtle than that suggested by this famous citation. There is no doubt, however, that he thought the sword to be of central importance to the state. This is one of the very few points about which there is little disagreement today with Hobbes; state power is widely thought to be coercive. The view that governments must wield force or that their power is necessarily coercive is widespread in contemporary political thought. For instance, John Rawls claims that "political power is always coercive power backed up by the government's use of sanctions, for government alone has the authority to use force in upholding its laws."[2] He is not alone in thinking this, as we shall see. This belief in the centrality of coercion and force plays an important but not well-appreciated role in contemporary political thought. However, it is an idea which is to some extent mistaken and quite misleading.

I. State Power Is Coercive

Rawls's belief in the coercive nature of political power appears to be significant for his liberal theory. It is one of two special features of "constitutional regimes" central to his influential conception of political legitimacy. The other feature is that "[p]olitical society is closed: we come to be within it and we do not, and indeed cannot, enter or leave it voluntarily."[3] Indeed, it is these two features that he believes give rise to "the

The predecessor of this essay, entitled "Is the State Necessarily Coercive?" was discussed at Bowling Green State University, George Mason University, Georgetown University, the University of Maryland, the University of Virginia, and the 20th World Congress of the International Association for Philosophy of Law and Social Philosophy (Amsterdam). I am grateful to these audiences for comments, as well as to Marvin Belzer, Alon Harel, and Arthur Ripstein for helpful written remarks. Drafts of this version of the essay were presented at Chapman University and the University of Arizona, and I am grateful to these audiences as well as to the other contributors to this volume for comments. Lastly, Ellen Paul and James Taggart have provided me with valuable comments on the penultimate draft of the essay.

[1] Thomas Hobbes, *Leviathan*, ed. Richard Tuck (Cambridge: Cambridge University Press, 1991 [1649]), chap. XVII, 117.
[2] John Rawls, *Political Liberalism* (New York: Columbia University Press, 1996 [1993]), 136.
[3] Ibid., 136.

doi:10.1017/S0265052511000094

28   © 2012 Social Philosophy & Policy Foundation. Printed in the USA.

question of the legitimacy of the general structure of authority." Rawls
thinks that

> our exercise of political power is fully proper only when it is exer-
> cised in accordance with a constitution the essentials of which all
> citizens as free and equal may reasonably be expected to endorse in
> the light of principles and ideals acceptable to their common human
> reason. This is the liberal principle of legitimacy.

Rawls distinguishes the "special domain of the political identified by the
two features above described" from "the associational, which is voluntary
in ways that the political is not . . . and the personal and the familial,
which are affectional, again in ways the political is not."[4] The political is
marked by the prevalence of coercive power, and this fact is thought to
have special significance.

Rawls, as I said, is not alone in emphasizing the coercive powers of
states and in attributing special significance to them. Contemporary libertarian thinkers, as we should expect, do the same. In his well-known
discussion, Robert Nozick takes anarchist challenges to the state as his
starting point: "I treat seriously the anarchist claim that in the course of
maintaining its monopoly on the use of force and protecting everyone
within a territory, the state must violate individuals' rights and hence is
intrinsically immoral."[5] While some anarchists hope that a stateless world
would be one without coercion, most object to the manner in which states
accumulate, centralize, and seek to monopolize coercion and force.[6]

The apparent consensus that states are essentially coercive needs to be
examined in part because of its significance to contemporary political
thought. As we saw, it is central to Rawls's particular conception of political legitimacy. It seems to be especially important to the thinking of many
contemporary left-liberal theorists as well. Thomas Nagel argues that

> if you force someone to serve an end that he cannot be given ade-
> quate reason to share, you are treating him as a mere means—even if
> the end is his own good, as you see it but he doesn't. In view of the
> coercive character of the state, the requirement [that one should treat

---

[4] Ibid., 137.

[5] Robert Nozick, *Anarchy, State, and Utopia* (New York: Basic Books, 1974), xi.

[6] See Crispin Sartwell, *Against the State: An Introduction to Anarchist Political Theory* (Albany, NY: State University of New York Press, 2008) and virtually all of the authors in Roderick T. Long and Tibor R. Machan eds., *Anarchism/Minarchism: Is Government Part of a Free Country?* (Ashgate, 2008). Michael Taylor's useful characterization of anarchy is in terms of the dispersal of coercion and force, not its absence: "a minimum test, a necessary condition, for the existence of a state is that there is *some* concentration of the means of using force, or equivalently some inequality in its distribution . . . Conversely, in a *pure anarchy* force is perfectly dispersed, not concentrated at all." Michael Taylor, *Community, Anarchy, and Liberty* (Cambridge: Cambridge University Press, 1982), 5–6.

humanity never merely as a means, but always as an end] becomes a condition of political legitimacy.[7]

Revealingly, Nagel notes elsewhere that we think of politics as a domain "where we are all competing to get the coercive power of the state behind the institutions we favor—institutions under which we all have to live. . . ." He is concerned not only about conflicts of interests between people "but conflicts over the value that public institutions should serve, impartially, for everyone." He asks whether there is "a higher-order impartiality that can permit us to come to some understanding about how such disagreements should be settled?"

> This question is part of the wider issue of political legitimacy—the history of attempts to discover a way of justifying coercively imposed political and social institutions to the people who live under them, and at the same time discover what those institutions must be like if such justification is to be possible.[8]

A coercive conception of states seems to play an equally important role in the thinking of Ronald Dworkin. A consideration that he thinks supports his favored principle of integrity in politics is that "a political society that accepts integrity as a virtue thereby becomes a special form of community, special in a way that promotes its moral authority to assume and deploy a monopoly of coercive force." Dworkin argues that

> A conception of law must explain how what it takes to be law provides a general justification for the exercise of coercive power by the state. . . . Each conception's organizing center is the explanation it offers of this justifying force. Every conception therefore faces the same threshold problem. How can *anything* provide even that general form of justification in ordinary politics. What can ever give anyone the kind of authorized power over another that politics supposes governors have over the governed. . . . This is the classical problem of the legitimacy of coercive power.[9]

I wish to examine critically this thesis about the central importance of coercion and force to states. It is, as I said, widely shared and largely accepted uncritically, but I do not think that its significance has been well appreciated. It is an imprecise thesis, but I think it is of some importance in contemporary political thought. The coercive nature of states is thought to have two important implications for political theory, both of which are

---

[7] Thomas Nagel, *Equality and Partiality* (New York: Oxford University Press, 1991), 159.

[8] Thomas Nagel, "Moral Conflict and Political Legitimacy," *Philosophy and Public Affairs* 16, no. 3 (1987): 215–16, 218.

[9] Ronald Dworkin, *Law's Empire* (London: Fontana Press, 1986), 188, 190–1.

well illustrated by the work of the theorists I have cited. The first implication is that states are very hard to justify because of their coercive
nature. It is the state's special power to coerce that makes it so difficult to
justify; state legitimacy is problematic principally because of its coercive
power. And, secondly, only certain kinds of justifications are likely to
succeed as a consequence. It will not, for instance, suffice to ground state
legitimacy on its pursuit of the good if this will, as Nagel argues, involve
treating people as mere means, or, as Nozick argues, violate their rights.[10]
And consent will not help either if it is not available (because, repeating
Rawls for example, "Political society is closed: we come to be within it
and we do not, and indeed cannot, enter or leave it voluntarily."). As
Charles Larmore argues,

> To avoid the oppressive use of state power, the liberal goal has there-
> fore been to define the common good of political association by
> means of a *minimal moral conception*. . . . [T]he terms of political asso-
> ciation must now be less comprehensive than the views of the good
> life about which reasonable people disagree. More precisely, funda-
> mental political principles must express a moral conception that cit-
> izens can affirm together, despite their inevitable differences about
> the worth of specific ways of life.[11]

Left-liberals like Rawls and Nagel may differentiate between the concern owed to members of a particular society and that owed to outsiders
for different reasons. In a particularly illuminating essay, Michael Blake
argues "Coercion, not cooperation, is the sine qua non of distributive
justice. . . ."[12] The "political and legal institutions [members of a particular society] share at the national level create a need for distinct forms of
justification. A concern with relative shares, I argue, is a plausible interpretation of liberal principles only when those principles are applied to
individuals who share liability to the coercive network of state governance."[13] The "tremendous coercive powers of the state"[14] are what
mandates this approach to political theory.

On the view of many important liberal political thinkers, the coercive
nature of states calls for special kinds of justifications. The state's coer-

---

[10] Nozick argues that "the state may not use its coercive apparatus for the purpose of
getting some citizens to aid others, or in order to prohibit activities to people for their *own*
good or protection." Nozick, *Anarchy, State, and Utopia*, ix.
[11] He goes on to argue that "It is in this light that we should understand the traditional
liberal concern for the protection of individual liberty." Charles Larmore, "Political Liberalism" (1990), reprinted in Larmore, *The Morals of Modernity* (Cambridge: Cambridge University Press, 1996), 123.
[12] Michael Blake, "Distributive Justice, State Coercion, and Autonomy," *Philosophy and
Public Affairs* 30, no. 3 (2002): 257–96.
[13] Ibid., 258.
[14] Ibid., 263.

civeness plays an important role in contemporary liberal political theory. I shall explore why we might think that states, especially just ones, are as coercive as contemporary thinkers believe. These thinkers' reliance on the claim that the state is fundamentally coercive, however, threatens instability. They assume that states are very coercive and propose ways of justifying them. There are a number of ways the story could go. On one possibility, the states that are justified will be much less coercive (because they will be just and widely supported). That result would threaten the assumption that states are by nature deeply coercive, since from an alternative baseline perhaps a different type of state would be justified. Another way the story could go is this: the states justified would remain quite coercive. This second possibility would seem puzzling and might suggest that the justification is defective. There is much more to be said here, but I shall move on to an examination of the hypothesis of the state's coerciveness.

II. By Definition States are Coercive

This assumption about the state's coercive nature is mistaken and misleading, I shall argue. How does it come to be so widely shared? Andrew Levine, a Marxist thinker, believes that "States are 'grounded' in force in the sense that, by definition, they are coercive: they coordinate behavior through the use or threat of force."[15] Now, why might we think this to be true *by definition*? We are taught from an early age that we must "define our terms" or at least explain what we mean by them. So when thinking about something as complicated and perplexing as the state, we ought to say at the outset what we mean. In his introductory text, Jonathan Wolff notes that

> Before deciding how best to justify the state, we had better be sure what it is. . . . [I]t has been noted that there are some things that all states have in common. . . . States clearly possess, or claim to possess, political power. The sociologist Max Weber (1864–1920) made a similar point, if in more startling language: states possess a monopoly of legitimate violence. . . . All legitimate violence or coercion is undertaken or supervised by the state.[16]

The search for a "definition" of the state in contemporary political theory invariably refers us to Max Weber's famous claim that "a state is a human community that (successfully) claims the *monopoly of the legitimate use of physical force* [*physischer Gewaltsamkeit*] within a given territory." Weber

---

[15] Andrew Levine, *The End of the State* (London: Verso, 1987), 176.
[16] Jonathan Wolff, *An Introduction to Political Philosophy* (Oxford: Oxford University Press, 1996), 39.

goes on to note that "the right to use physical force is ascribed to other institutions or to individuals only to the extent to which the state permits it. The state is considered the sole source of the 'right' to use violence [*Gewaltsamkeit*]."[17] We may be tempted, then, to say that states are coercive *by definition*.

I think contemporary political thought is mistaken in its view of the coercive nature of the state and that this error has led much of it astray in a number of important ways. I shall briefly argue that Weberian definitions of a state are mistaken and that we should not understand coercion or force to be part of the concept of the state. My main objective is to challenge the centrality contemporary political thinkers accord to coercion.

The so-called Weberian definition of a state is mistaken, first of all, insofar as it is incomplete. There is much more to a state than a claimed monopoly on the legitimate use of physical force or coercion in a territory. As one would expect, Weber himself offered a much more complete characterization elsewhere:

Since the concept of the state has only in modern times reached its full development, it is best to define it in terms appropriate to the modern type of state, but at the same time, in terms which abstract from the values of the present day, since these are particularly subject to change. The primary formal characteristics of the modern state are as follows: It possesses an administrative and legal order subject to change by legislation, to which the organized corporate activity of the administrative staff, which is also regulated by legislation, is oriented. This system of order claims binding authority, not only over the members of the state, the citizens . . . but also to a very large extent, over all actions taking place in the area of its jurisdiction. It is thus a compulsory association with a territorial basis. Furthermore, today, the use of force is regarded as legitimate only so far as it is either permitted by the state or prescribed by it.[18]

This is a much better characterization than the oft quoted passage from Weber's "Politics as a Vocation," which was a public address. It is not clear that one can offer a genuine definition of a cluster concept as complex as that of the state, but at the least its characterization must allude to a large number of attributes, themselves quite complex. Simple definitions like the standard one attributed to Weber are inadequate. (Elsewhere, I offer a general characterization of a modern state in terms of a

---

[17] Max Weber, "Politics as a Vocation," in *From Max Weber: Essays in Sociology*, Hans H. Gerth and C. Wright Mills, trans. and eds. (New York: Oxford University Press, 1946 [1919]), 78.

[18] Weber, *The Theory of Social and Economic Organization* (Part I of *Wirtschaft und Gesellschaft*), A. M. Henderson and Talcott Parsons trans. (New York: Oxford University Press, 1947), 156.

cluster of attributes.[19]) A more serious problem, which I shall not address, is how one can define complex terms with histories: "only that which has no history is definable."[20] It is not clear how an argument from definition for the centrality of coercion can be persuasive.

The incompleteness of Weberian definitions is only part of my objection to them. The second major concern is about understanding coercion or force to be part of the *concept* of the state; they do not seem to be conceptually tied. States without coercion or force are *conceivable*. If that is the case, then coercion and force are not conceptually connected to the concept of the state. I will say more about the antecedent presently. First another thought experiment. Consider a "state" without law or one for which its jurisdiction was not territorial; we would not consider it to be a state. Law and territoriality are essential properties of states, part of the concept of a state. Contrast these properties with coercion or force. We can conceive of a state which does not employ coercion or force. It seems that, unlike law or territoriality, coercion and force are not part of the concept of the state.

This claim may be controversial, and the argument is certainly too swift. I need, in any case, to say more at this point about how we should think about coercion and force. Part of the attempt to understand the relation between states and coercion and force must involve a clearer understanding of these concepts. We may think of coercion and force as ways of getting people to act as they might not act if not so compelled; they are species of *power*. To *coerce* someone is to induce him or her to act by credibly threatening harm if he or she does not comply with one's wishes. To coerce people to act may be to *force* them to do something, but coercion leaves its victims some choice. *Force* usually involves additional constraints, for instance, restraining someone or confining his or her movements, leaving victims little or no choice.[21] *Violence* paradigmatically is a species of physical force, and it may be understood to "violate" its subjects, damaging their bodies. Coercion and force are to be contrasted with other ways of getting people to act. We often seek to *persuade* others to act in ways they would not have otherwise considered, or we make them an offer (which they can refuse).[22] And, as I shall note later, *authority* is an important means of moving people to action.[23]

[19] See my *Essay on the Modern State* (Cambridge: Cambridge University Press, 1998), 45–46, where I characterize a state in terms of a number of interrelated features. See also my "How (not) to Define the State" (unpublished manuscript).

[20] Friedrich Nietzsche, *Beyond Good and Evil*, trans. R. J. Hollingdale and Walter Kaufman ([1887] New York: Random House, 1967) II, 13.

[21] Force can also be used to seize assets or close routes of escape. We are focusing on the uses of force directly against persons.

[22] Persuasion normally presupposes that the persuader may not resort to coercion or force, lest his or her offers be those that cannot be refused. This point is important for the discussion at the end of this essay about the possibility that resorting to coercion or force is always available to states, even if rarely resorted to. I owe this point to James Taggart.

[23] We may also trick, manipulate, or deceive others into doing as we wish.

These characterizations are not complete, and they are less than adequate for many inquiries. (For instance, debates about the possibly coercive nature of certain wage offers or of plea bargains will require a better analysis.[24]) More detailed characterizations of these concepts are quite controversial. The concept of power is itself notoriously difficult to characterize precisely.[25] Much of the recent literature on coercion focuses on the question whether the notion can be understood empirically and non-normatively.[26] If the concept of coercion is necessarily *moralized*—if, for instance, coercive proposals are necessarily wrong—then to think of the state as *coercive* is already to consider it presumptively illegitimate, or at least problematic.[27] I shall not address these difficult questions and shall assume an imprecise, nonmoralized characterization of coercion and force, which I think will not beg any important questions.

To return to the conceptual question: can one conceive of a state that does not coerce, that is, does not seek to induce people to act as they are required to act by credibly threatening harm if they do not comply? Can one coherently think of a state which does not use force to secure compliance or conformity? I should have thought so. Here is the thought experiment: Suppose that a particular state is legitimate, its basic structure and its laws are just, and those subject to its laws are obligated to obey them. Suppose that the latter are always motivated to comply with just laws; they do not, for instance, suffer from any weakness of the will or any other problem which might lead them to fail to do what they ought to do. Then, coercion and force would not be needed to enforce the law. This possibility—admittedly fantastic and utopian—seems perfectly *coherent*. There is nothing in the nature of a law which requires that compliance be assured coercively. It does not seem to be, then, a conceptual truth that states are coercive.[28]

I do not want to make too much of this claim. For one, in order to do so I would need to defend the conceivability test of conceptual truths employed above, and there are difficult questions here about the nature of concepts and conceptual truths. (Was sovereignty once part of the concept of a state but no longer is? Does it remain part of a

---

[24] A specialized physician offers to save a dying infant if its mother agrees to marry him. Is this a coercive proposal?

[25] See, for instance, Keith Dowding, *Power* (Minneapolis: University of Minnesota Press, 1996).

[26] See Joel Feinberg, "Coercion," in *Routledge Encyclopedia of Philosophy*, Edward Craig, ed. (New York and London: Routledge, 1998), vol. 1, 387–90; Alan Wertheimer, "Coercion," in Lawrence and Charlotte Becker, eds., *Encyclopedia of Ethics*, 2d ed. (New York and London: Routledge, 2001), 172–75; and Scott Anderson, "Coercion," *Stanford Encyclopedia of Philosophy*, http://plato.stanford.edu/entries/coercion/.

[27] See William A. Edmundson, *Three Anarchical Fallacies* (Cambridge: Cambridge University Press, 1998), chap. 6, and Alan Wertheimer, *Coercion* (Princeton: Princeton University Press, 1987), chap. 14.

[28] My formulation, in terms of legitimate states, just laws, and the like is intended to sidestep a number of debates about obligations and reasons to obey.

European concept, but not an American one?) Now we might well be able to imagine a state without force or violence, but it may still seem to us that states are typically coercive and that one which did not use force would be something quite different from the states we know. It is also the case that being necessary does not entail being important and vice versa.[29] Coercion may be an important attribute of states without being part of the concept or otherwise linked to it necessarily. The fact that state and coercion are not conceptually connected does not seem to settle any important questions.

The principal claim that I wish to examine and to challenge is that of the centrality of coercion. Contemporary political theorists seem to agree with Rawls that "political power is always coercive power backed up by the government's use of sanctions." I do not think that this is correct; at the least it is very misleading. Whatever we think about definitions and conceptual truths, this claim needs to be examined more closely.

III. LAWS AND SANCTIONS

The thinkers I have quoted also emphasize the state's claimed *monopoly* on the legitimate use of force, and it is clear that this sort of normative power is special and does require special attention. G. E. M. Anscombe notes that "civil society is the bearer of rights of coercion not possibly existent among men without government."[30] I do not, however, wish here to discuss the state's alleged monopolization of force (see my remarks at the end of the essay).[31] Rather, I wish now to argue that the state's use of coercion or force is not, in a certain sense, primary. I will also argue that its use of force is not as prevalent or as important as it is believed to be by contemporary political thinkers.

Rawls says that "political power is always coercive power backed up by the government's use of sanctions." Why then might we think this? Perhaps because of the conjunction of law and sanction. It is not uncommon to associate laws with sanctions. Recall John Austin's well-known account of laws as coercive commands of a sovereign. Austin argued that laws are commands, and that these are distinguished from other "significations of desire ... by the power and the purpose of the party commanding to inflict an evil or pain in case the desire be disregarded." Commands yield duties: "Being liable to an evil from you if I comply not with a wish which you signify, I am *bound* or *obliged* by your command,

---

[29] I owe this point to Leslie Green.

[30] G. E. M. Anscombe, "On the Source of the Authority of the State," in *Ethics, Religion and Politics: Collected Philosophical Papers*, vol. 3 (Minneapolis: University of Minnesota Press, 1981), 147.

[31] See Morris, *An Essay on the Modern State*, 203–4. As I shall argue later, the state's claimed monopolization of coercion is merely an instance of its claimed authority, specifically, its "comprehensive" authority.

or I lie under a *duty* to obey it."[32] This important view is no longer influential in jurisprudence. H. L. A. Hart's well-known criticisms of this account in *The Concept of Law* are conclusive. Many laws do not "order people to do or not to do things"; some laws do not impose duties or obligations but confer *powers* to individuals or to officials or institutions (e.g., courts, legislatures).[33] But the central failure of Austin's account— and of similar reductive stories—is in the attempt to explain the normativity of law in terms of nonnormative notions like commands and threats. While we may speak of "being obliged" to do something when compelled or forced to do so, *obligation* is normative. While it would not be true that one had been obliged to do something if one had not, in fact, done it, the claim that one has an obligation is not falsified by one's failure to comply.[34] Hart emphasizes the importance of the idea of a *rule* to an understanding of law:

> The root cause of failure is that the elements out of which the theory was constructed, viz. the ideas of orders, obedience, habits, and threats, do not include, and cannot by their combination yield, the idea of a rule, without which we cannot hope to elucidate even the most elementary forms of law.[35]

Theories like Austin's, recognizing that not all threats to impose sanctions will be effective, usually formulate their accounts of law in terms of the *likely* application of sanctions. Hart's two-point criticism is definitive:

> . . . where rules exist, deviations from them are not merely grounds for a prediction that hostile reactions will follow or that a court will apply sanctions to those who break them, but are also a reason or justification for such reaction and for applying the sanctions.
> If it were true that the statement that a person had an obligation meant that *he* was likely to suffer in the event of disobedience, it would be a contradiction to say that he had an obligation [to do something and] . . . there was not the slightest chance of his being caught or made to suffer. In fact, there is no contradiction in saying this, and such statements are often made and understood.[36]

It is implausible to understand laws as commands backed by threats, even if many or most (duty-imposing) laws are in fact backed by sanc-

---

[32] John Austin, *The Province of Jurisprudence Determined* (Cambridge: Cambridge University Press, 1995 [1st ed. 1832, 5th ed. 1885]), Lecture II, 21–22.
[33] H. L. A. Hart, *The Concept of Law*, 2d ed. (Oxford: Clarendon Press, 1994 [1961]), chap. 3.
[34] Ibid., 82–83.
[35] Ibid., 80.
[36] Ibid., 84.

tions.[37] This means that it is also unlikely to be the case that "political power is *always* coercive power backed up by the government's use of sanctions" (emphasis added). Political power may often be coercive, but it cannot always be. Not only are some laws not duty-imposing, but some duty-imposing laws are not backed by sanctions—for instance, many laws obligating officials. It is also true that enforcement is usually imperfect in the best of cases. When a sanction is not attached to a law or when a law is not certain to be enforced, we do not say that it ceases to be a law.[38]

IV. The Authority of Law

Even if sanctions are not always in place or necessary, we should ask why many laws are in fact backed by sanctions and why coercion sometimes is necessary. Why must compliance sometimes be assured by coercion? Obviously, people—most of us included—will not always do as they are required to do unless prodded. Presumably, virtually all of us will always refrain from intentional homicide. But we might not put coins in parking meters or adhere to speeding limits or pay all of our taxes in the absence of the threat of sanctions. Legal systems provide for sanctions to offer people special incentives when they are not otherwise motivated to comply.

Why exactly might people fail to comply? There are many circumstances which may contribute to disobedience. Sometimes we violate laws because of ignorance or stupidity. Othertimes we may fail to obey out of weakness of the will or some other form of irrationality. We may, in our youth, simply wish to defy authority. Or we may be fanatics, in the grips of a picture recommending disobedience. And, of course, some laws are unjust and many others are pointless or stupid.

More interestingly—and controversially—there may exist "motivational gaps"; that is, it may be that even reasonable, just people will not always have sufficient reason to obey every law, even every just and good law. That is, sometimes it may be rational, sanctions aside, not to comply with just laws. This will often be due to the complexity of institutions and the differences between the situations of different persons. The ailing chemist may imbibe some illegal drugs, and the skilled racing driver may drive his Porsche above the speed limit on

[37] In addition to Hart, see Hans Oberdiek, "The Role of Sanctions and Coercion in Understanding Law and Legal Systems," *American Journal of Jurisprudence* 71 (1976): 71–94. I regret not being able to discuss Frederick Schauer, "Was Austin Right After All? On the Role of Sanctions in a Theory of Law," *Ratio Juris* vol. 23, no. 1 (2010): 1–21, which I came across too late to include here.

[38] Of course, in common law systems there are principles for treating laws that have not been applied for a long time as no longer being in force. It should be noted that sanctions can function to signal that a rule is a genuine law. And they sometimes can also express the compulsory nature of the state and the status of the state, a point I owe to Alon Harel.

deserted highways.[39] Of course, if the state is illegitimate and the laws unjust, there will be additional reasons for noncompliance, but I am focusing on the case of legitimate states with just laws.[40]

If there are circumstances in which some people will not, in the absence of sanctions, be adequately motivated to comply with laws, then an important additional reason for sanctions is *assurance*. To threaten to impose sanctions for disobedience will assure those who are otherwise disposed to comply that they will not be taken advantage of by the violators. In situations where compliance with certain laws is thought to be conditional on the like compliance of others, enforcement may have as its main purpose the provision of assurance.[41]

What is crucial to note about these rationales is that they implicitly understand sanctions to be *secondary*. Coercion is thus rationalized, but only as a *supplementary* measure. And this is as it should be: the law's primary appeal is to its *authority*. Hart notes this early in his discussion of command theories of law: "To command is characteristically to exercise authority over men, not power to inflict harm, and though it may be combined with threats of harm a command is primarily an appeal not to fear but to respect for authority." [42] The citation from Hobbes with which I opened this essay may encourage an Austinian (mis)reading of his theory. But his account of law is, as I said, more subtle. For Hobbes, law is command, but his particular analysis is interesting: "Law in generall, is not Counsell, but Command ... addressed to one formerly obliged to obey him [who commands]," where command is "where a man saith, *Doe this*, or *Doe not this*, without expecting other reason than the Will of him that sayeth it." [43] Hart interprets Hobbes's account of a command to mean that "the commander characteristically intends his hearer to take the commander's will instead of his own as a guide to action and so to take it in place of any deliberation or reasoning of his own: the expression of a commander's will that an act be done is intended to preclude or cut off any independent deliberation by the hearer of the merits pro and con of

[39] See my "The Trouble with Justice," in *Morality and Self-Interest*, ed. Paul Bloomfield (New York: Oxford University Press, 2008), 15–30.

[40] I formulate this claim in terms of *just* laws but could weaken it to refer only to valid laws of a legitimate state. The point is that *even if* the laws in question are valid, just, *and* reasonable, there may still not be reasons for action for everyone. If one does not accept this controversial thesis and one thinks that valid, just, and reasonable laws always are reasons of the right sort for everyone, one will have one less reason to want states to attach sanctions to laws.

[41] Hart, *Concept of Law*, 198. (The following is a note for those familiar with elementary game theory.) Suppose that everyone in a political society has Assurance Game preferences (i.e., they prefer mutual cooperation to unilateral defection); then information about people's preferences will increase cooperation. Suppose that some people have Assurance Game preferences, but many others have Prisoners' Dilemma preferences (i.e., they prefer unilateral defection to mutual cooperation). Then coercion may be necessary to secure the cooperation of all.

[42] Ibid., 20.

[43] Hobbes, *Leviathan*, chap. xxvi, 183, and chap. xxv, 176.

doing the act."[44] Authorities guide behavior by providing reasons for
action to their subjects. Something is an authority in this sense only if its
directives are meant to be reasons for action.[45]

One does not understand law and, more generally, states if one does
not see coercion and force as *supplementary* to authority. Coercion and
force are needed when the state's claimed authority is unappreciated,
defective, or absent. Unjust states, recognized widely as such, will need to
rely heavily on force; just states presumably need much less force.[46] The
latter will have recourse to coercion or force only when applying the law
against the ignorant, the irrational, and those who may lack a sufficient
reason to comply. If a state—in Rawls's terms, a constitutional regime—is
just (and legitimate) and widely recognized as such, then its need for
coercive power should be considerably less than Rawls suggests when he
states that "[p]olitical power is always coercive power." It is puzzling,
then, that the state's coerciveness is one of the two features Rawls invokes
in defense of a particular account of justification.

We are and should be especially concerned about the justification of
states given their potential for harm, that is, given the wrong that unjust
states have been capable of. But why should our account of justification
or legitimacy be tailored to the particular evils of unjust and massively
coercive states (e.g., Nazi Germany, the Soviet Union)? If just states have
much less need to rely on coercion and force than evil ones, why the
special emphasis on coercion in contemporary liberal theory? The coercive nature of political power is for Rawls one of two features that give
rise to "the question of the legitimacy of the general structure of authority. . . ." Why? If a state is just, especially if justice itself makes allowances
for "the strains of commitment,"[47] the coercion needed should be relatively little, restricted mainly to the unreasonable and teenagers. It is
unclear that left-liberal theorists are entitled to make coercion and force as
central as they do.

Notice that the use of coercion and force that is considered especially
problematic by left-liberal thinkers and in need of special justification is

[44] Hart, "Commands and Authoritative Legal Reasons," in *Essays on Bentham* (Oxford:
Clarendon Press, 1982), 244, 253.
[45] Joseph Raz, *The Authority of Law*, 2d ed. (Oxford: Oxford University Press, 2009 [1979]),
chaps. 1–2, and *The Morality of Freedom* (Oxford: Clarendon Press, 1986), chaps. 2–3. See also
Raz, *Practical Reason and Norms* (Oxford: Clarendon, 1999 [1975]) and Leslie Green, *The
Authority of the State* (Oxford: Clarendon Press, 1988).
[46] The position I have defended elsewhere is that legitimacy is conferred by justice and
efficiency. See Morris, *An Essay on the Modern State*, chaps. 4–6. Justice may, of course, require
consent, or consent may be an independent requirement. I am sidestepping these controversial questions by talking simply of "just states." See my "State Legitimacy and Social
Order," in *Political Legitimization without Morality*, ed. Jörg Kühnelt (Heidelberg: Springer,
2008), 15–32. The starting point for contemporary discussions of these questions should be
John Simmons, "Justification and Legitimacy," reprinted in his *Justification and Legitimacy*
(Cambridge: Cambridge University Press, 2001), 122–57.
[47] As Rawls's account of justice does; see *A Theory of Justice* (Cambridge, MA: Harvard
University Press, 1971), 145, 176ff.

that used against members of one's political society. The use of force (and violence) against external adversaries, presumably, is not equally problematic to the contemporary liberal thinkers whose theories I am considering. If it were, these thinkers would want to require that the concerns of noncitizens or foreigners be addressed by the justificatory account they favor.[48] If it is the problematic use of coercion and force that calls for special consideration, then perhaps the state's powers are not to be understood as justified all together, but rather piecemeal. That is, as I have argued elsewhere, some of the powers of states are justified for some people some of the time. The "some" here may in certain circumstances include most of us much of the time. The state's claims are much more ambitious: all of its claimed powers are justified all of the time, except when they are self-limiting. But these claims may be false, or at the least exaggerated.

V. ALTERNATIVES TO COERCION

I think that contemporary liberal thinkers exaggerate the coercive power of states. Coercion and force are not as important in most liberal, democratic societies as they are often said to be. In the same way that many people often confuse laws with commands, discussions of state coercion often confuse a number of different things. I have talked somewhat casually about (coercive) sanctions and force, but they should not be confused. States affix sanctions to laws, but these rarely involve force directly. Sanctions imposed by liberal states in criminal cases typically consist in the withdrawal of rights or the imposition of duties—for instance, the loss of the right to move about freely (imprisonment or probation), the prescription of certain ownership rights (confiscation of property), the duty to pay a sum of money (a fine). The application of some sanctions can involve force, and some are violent (e.g., flogging, capital punishment). But, for the most part, force when conjoined with sanctions is merely an enforcement measure to ensure compliance with prior sanction-imposing orders and with ordinary law.[49] We should expect the resort to force to be less common than that to sanctions, especially in just states.[50]

---

[48] Famously, Rawls and Nagel do not think outsiders have a right to be consulted. See Rawls, *The Law of Peoples* (Cambridge, MA: Harvard University Press, 1999), and Nagel, "The Problem of Global Justice," *Philosophy and Public Affairs* 33, no. 2 (2005): 113–47.

[49] Handcuffs may be put on the criminal when apprehended and after sentencing. Force, of course, is also used by state officials in matters unrelated to the enforcement of the law and the application of sanctions, e.g., in restraining someone who is mentally ill or at risk of spreading contagious disease. See Grant Lamond, "The Coerciveness of Law," *Oxford Journal of Legal Studies* 20 (2000): 39–62, and "Coercion and the Nature of Law," *Legal Theory* 7 (2001): 35–57.

[50] It is worth remembering that power-conferring laws lack sanctions and do not involve force; if one fails to comply with the legal conditions for valid contracts or wills, one's acts will lack the desired legal effect, but one will incur no sanction.

The reliance of states on force or coercion is often exaggerated. It is consequently worth remembering what resources legitimate states have other than force or sanctions. The most important one may be *authority*. Leaving that aside for the moment, consider what governments may do to motivate individuals without the threat of sanctions or force. States may prod by levying taxes or by imposing fees for different activities.[51] They may also impose various restrictions or requirements on anyone wishing to carry out certain activities—for instance, licenses for those wishing to teach, to practice medicine, or to be a plumber, or insurance for anyone wishing to operate a motor vehicle or run a business. These may modify behavior and motivate without coercion or force (though they may violate rights to freedom).

States may also influence behavior without sanctions or force by providing incentives—for instance, tax exemptions for charitable deductions or business investments, and awards or honors for public service. Most governments influence a large number of people more directly: they employ and pay them (e.g., civil servants or soldiers or contracted employees). As John Stuart Mill points out, governments may also simply seek to persuade, educate, and advise:

> Government may interdict all persons from doing certain things; or from doing them without its authorization; or may prescribe to them certain things to be done, or a certain manner of doing things which is left optional with them to do or to abstain from. This is the *authoritative* interference of government. There is another kind of intervention which is not authoritative: when a government, instead of issuing a command and enforcing it by penalties, adopts the course so seldom resorted to by governments, and of which such important use might be made, that of giving advice and promulgating information; or when, leaving individuals free to use their own means of pursuing any object of general interest, the government, not meddling with them, but not trusting the object solely to their care, establishes, side by side with their arrangements, an agency of its own for a like purpose. . . .[52]

Our governments often succeed in changing behavior by "giving advice and promulgating information"—for instance, recent campaigns against tobacco. States also influence behavior by the simple act of recognizing or establishing standards for action.[53] Without resorting to sanctions or to

[51] We may count these as coercive in certain respects depending on how we understand people's prior property rights. On some views, taxation is always coercive. But note that this would only be the case when taxation was unjust and thus a form of theft. If a state is justified or legitimate *and* has a (limited) right to tax, then imposing taxes would not itself be coercive, even if threatening noncompliers would be.

[52] John Stuart Mill, *Principles of Political Economy*, J. Riley ed. (Oxford and New York: Oxford University Press, 1994 [1848; 1871]), Bk. V, chap. 11, p. 325.

[53] Raz, *The Concept of a Legal System* (Oxford: Clarendon Press, 1980 [1970]), 232–34.

force, states may influence behavior by informing, persuading, educating, advising, or bribing people, or by influencing them in a number of other ways. Admittedly, government activity requires resources, typically revenues derived by taxation, and these may be extracted coercively (but see note 51). The point here, often missed, is that the activity funded by coercive taxation need not itself be coercive.

Insofar as subjects acknowledge state authority or accept principles recommending conformity with the law, states may influence behavior largely by determining and publicizing the law. Sanctions and force need not, under these circumstances, be a significant motivator of compliance with law.

One needs also to recall that force may not be very effective against a large population generally inclined to disregard or to disobey the law. Even popular regimes usually cannot legislate or effectively control certain domains, whatever they wish. (Consider the difficulties most states have with many "victimless crimes," or the American experiment with "prohibition" of alcohol.[54]) Many regimes that are dependent on the massive use of force are unstable and subject to swift disintegration, as they can govern only if most subjects do not resist at once, and collapse when many refuse at the same time to go along.[55]

We should, of course, expect that laws will typically be backed by the threat of sanctions and that force may be needed. One of the reasons, after all, for wanting to have a legal system is to ensure compliance on the part of those not otherwise inclined or tempted to behave in the ways required by social order, thereby providing assurance to the remainder of the population. But recourse to coercion and force, it must be stressed, does not mean that laws cannot provide reasons or motivate without such sanctions or that laws must presuppose them. The law claims authority, and that claim may often be valid. Unless one assumes that norms *per se* cannot be reasons, then there should be no ground to insist that legal rules must necessarily or always be backed up with sanctions.[56] But we should expect sanctions to be an important part of virtually all legal and political orders, given the way humans seem to be. The way Joseph Raz summarizes his discussion of this question seems right:

> Is it possible for there to be a legal system in force which does not provide for sanctions or which does not authorize their enforcement

---

[54] Europeans are often surprised when they come to understand that the United States federal government could not, even if it wished to, disarm the American public.

[55] See Gregory S. Kavka's discussion of "rule by fear" in *Hobbesian Moral and Political Theory* (Princeton: Princeton University Press, 1986), chap. 6.2.

[56] It is, of course, an implication of the received theory of practical reason that all reasons for following a norm must be *forward-looking*. Even this need not, however, entail that sanctions are needed for reasons for obedience, as other forward-looking considerations could provide these.

by force? The answer seems to be that it is humanly impossible but logically possible. It is humanly impossible because for human beings as they are the support of sanctions, to be enforced by force if necessary, is required to assure a reasonable degree of conformity to law and prevent its complete breakdown.[57]

VI. "Ultimately Coercive"

Most governmental activities of liberal states do not require the deployment of force, many that involve the threatening of sanctions do not customarily involve force, and much compliance with law is secured by other means. It may be claimed, however, that the state's influence is *ultimately based* on force. Recall Rawls's words: "political power is always coercive power backed up by the government's use of sanctions, for government alone has the authority to use force in upholding its laws." The fact—if it is one—that the state monopolizes the use of legitimate force is not itself a reason to think that "political power is always coercive power backed up by the government's use of sanctions." Something may monopolize a power but rarely use it. We have also seen why this claim is, at best, too sweeping. But the state's authority is, as Rawls says, *backed up* by the threat of sanctions. So it may be that the state's power is *ultimately* coercive. In the end, "in the final instance," we may say, its power is based on force. This is not an uncommon view.[58]

What does it mean to say that law is *ultimately* backed by sanctions or a matter of force? This claim is different from that asserted by those who say that the state's power just *is* force. Consider the aim of *provocateurs.* They seek to provoke the agents of the state to retaliate with force so as to show state power as it is, without any disguise, as "naked force." They think that the state's appeal to its authority and to justice is a subterfuge; provoking the establishment will force it to reveal its true colors. This view, of course, is false. Such incitements establish no such thing; they merely show that governments sometimes need to use force to secure or

---

[57] He continues: "And yet we can imagine other rational beings who may be subject to law, who have, and who would acknowledge that they have, more than enough reasons to obey the law regardless of sanctions. Perhaps even human beings may be transformed to become such creatures." Raz, *Practical Reason and Norms,* 158–59.

Some think that were humans such that they could do well with sanctionless political systems, then they would most likely not need much, if any, government in the first place. In such a world, "[s]tate interference in social relations becomes, in one domain after another, superfluous, and then dies out of itself; the government of persons is replaced by the administration of things. . . . The state is not 'abolished.' *It dies out.*" Friedrich Engels, "Socialism: Utopian and Scientific" [1880], in *The Marx-Engels Reader,* R. Tucker ed., 2d ed. (New York: W.W. Norton, 1978), 713. This is mistaken as we presumably would need states—e.g., legislative, judicial, and administrative agencies—in order to make general principles determinate and specific and to apply them to new cases. This is an important point that I cannot pursue here.

[58] "The state rests ultimately on force, of course. . . ." Sartwell, *Against the State,* 18.

to re-establish order. Even tyrannical regimes require something more
than force to remain in place. It cannot be only (or even mainly) force. The
claim that the state is ultimately coercive seems to be something else. It is
not to say that state power is always coercive, albeit in disguise. It is to
say something different, that "ultimately" state power is based on force.
"State-power is in the last analysis coercive power . . . 'the political' refers
to a domain in which the use of force *as a final resort* is always present as
a real possibility."[59] What might this mean? How might we determine if
this is true?

The term "ultimate" is one of the most opaque in philosophy and social
theory and should be used with care. In one context, that of an ultimate
authority, it can be made clear. An authority may be ultimate if it is the
highest authority. This idea presupposes that authorities constitute an
ordering (often a strict ordering), and that the highest authority is the last
one in a certain chain or continuum of authorities. Most legal systems are
thought to have such a hierarchical structure, so that we can talk of the
highest or ultimate authority for any such legal order. The reality may not
always conform to this picture, but that point need not detain us.[60] Even
if we can find in all legal systems a hierarchical ordering of *authority*, it is
very unlikely that nonnormative *power* generally will be so ordered. That
is, it is very unlikely that we can order power relations in this way, so that
for any pair of powers one is greater than the other and the set of all
powers is an ordering (i.e., transitive). If this is right, it means that the
concept of an ultimate power will be ill defined. This means that it is
unclear and likely misleading to talk of "ultimate" powers. For there may
never be one power that is so placed that *it* is "ultimate" (or "final").[61]

One may argue that coercion and force are fundamental to maintaining
social order. That is, it may be thought to be more important than any other
factor in maintaining the state. The proof is that no state can do without it.
(Raz: "for human beings as they are the support of sanctions, to be enforced
by force if necessary, is required to assure a reasonable degree of conformity to law and prevent its complete breakdown.") Remove force (and sanctions), and the legal order collapses. But this argument, common and
persuasive as it is, is too swift. Why do we obey the law or, for that matter,
do almost anything? Usually our reasons are *multiple*. And very often our
actions are *overdetermined*. Consider first the case of overdetermined actions.
Removing one consideration favoring the action in question may not change
the balance of reasons. I am supposing that we act, and should act, in most
circumstances on the balance of reasons.[62] The metaphor here is that of
weights and measures. The rationality of an act is determined by the rel-

---

[59] Raymond Geuss, *History and Illusion in Politics* (Cambridge: Cambridge University
Press, 2001), 14, 17.
[60] See my *Essay on the Modern State*, chap. 7 and Raz, *The Concept of a Legal System*, 138–40.
[61] As argued in my *Essay on the Modern State*, chap. 7.
[62] Rational choice theory is a special case of the more general balance-of-reasons account.

ative "weight" of reasons favoring it over other alternatives. If an act is over-determined by reasons, then removing one reason (e.g., the threat of sanctions) may not affect our rational choice. Consider next acts that are not overdetermined. Suppose, for instance, that I decide to put money in a parking meter or to pay my employee's (U.S.) Social Security taxes and that I would not have done so had there been no credible threat of sanctions. Does this show that coercion is *decisive* in determining my action? We might say that it does, but this would be true only in the sense that a number of things are equally decisive. After all, if the act is not overdetermined and is favored by the balance of reasons, virtually any change will alter the balance; anything that "tips the balance" will, on this account, be decisive. For instance, if one becomes a principled anarchist or just less risk-averse, one may defy the parking authorities and the tax agencies in spite of the threat of sanctions.[63]

Coercion and force may be important and even indispensable, but that does not mean they are more important than anything else. A political order which may not hold together without force may also collapse if numerous other factors are not present—for instance, if subjects cease to be patriotic, if they become less imprudent, if they sober up, if they become literate, or if they act together. Our societies are held together by many things. Some may be more important than others, and some of these may be indispensable. But it is not clear that coercion or force are in any interesting sense "ultimate."

VII. Some Brief Remarks about Authority and Coercion

Many political and legal thinkers have thought that laws constrain liberty. Hobbes and Bentham and many others believed this. We are now aware that only duty-imposing laws seem to do this—power-conferring laws do not. If one thinks of restrictions of liberty as forms of coercion, then this thesis would have us understand many laws as coercive. I want to resist this understanding of coercion, and I do not want to endorse Bentham's thesis or any particular account of human liberty.

When law restricts liberty, it is usually not law *per se* but (genuine) authority that restricts liberty. That is, when an agency with (genuine) authority lays down or endorses a duty-creating rule, making it a law, it restricts liberty. (It may also expand liberty, but I am leaving these matters aside here.) To deny this is to deny that the "authority" in question is a genuine authority, that is, has the power to create genuine duties that are reasons for action.

---

[63] It is not easy establishing that a consideration is decisive. Suppose one is deliberating buying a multi-attributive object, such as a car. One hesitates, and the salesperson throws in a great stereo. That is not evidence that the stereo is decisive. If something "tips the balance," then removing many other things will tip it back. Are they also decisive?

Arthur Ripstein, in an important essay, argues that "the state's claim to authority is inseparable from the rationale for coercion." [64] He is arguing against philosophers like myself who view authority as prior to coercion. Ripstein understands coercion differently than I do. For him, following Kant, it is an interference with external freedom. This is not the place to examine and challenge his Kantian account of the nature of authority.[65] Still, one does not need to accept his Kantian account to agree that authority and coercion are connected, at least in several ways.

Authority and coercion are connected in important ways. Coercion and force are authorized by law (as well as by justice). So coercion and force are permissible in circumstances when they are allowed by the law (of a legitimate state).[66] Authority here is prior to coercion.

More importantly, the state's (normative) power includes the right to enforce the law. The (legitimate) state's right to rule includes the right to enforce. Must it? Presumably not in all possible worlds. But return to the hypothetical example I gave earlier of a just state that needed to deploy no coercion or force. I think it would still have the right to use coercion or force if necessary.[67] I am not sure that this is a conceptual connection, but that does not matter. The (normative) powers of a legitimate state seem to include the right to coerce.[68]

When many political theorists highlight the state's coercive nature, they often emphasize its apparent claim to a monopoly of (legitimate) coercion or force. I have said little about this monopolistic power. The state's apparent coerciveness may have three elements. A legitimate state (1) may coerce justly, (2) has the (limited) right to determine when coercion is justified, and (3) has the right to prevent others from coercing. I mentioned earlier that elsewhere I argue that (3) in effect follows from the state's claim to comprehensive authority, the power to regulate any type of activity.[69] As I do not think this claim to comprehensive authority is justified, I think that the state's right to prevent others from coercing may be quite limited. However, I do think that when a legitimate state does justly forbid others from coercing, the source of this power is its authority. So I partially agree with Ripstein that authority and the power to enforce

---

[64] Arthur Ripstein, "Authority and Coercion," *Philosophy and Public Affairs* 32 (2004): 2.

[65] See Arthur Ripstein, *Force and Freedom: Kant's Legal and Political Philosophy* (Cambridge: Harvard University Press, 2009).

[66] Here our understanding of legitimacy and the ways it is different from justification matter. Only the laws of states that meet certain standards will have the normative power relevant here, and I think the standards are those of legitimacy.

[67] I did not see the significance of this point when Mahesh Ananth, Marvin Belzer, Wade Maki, and Sangeeta Sangha pressed it against the predecessor of this essay. Michael Pace more recently also suggested to me that the mere retention of this right could threaten (and, perhaps, could thus be coercive).

[68] Grant Lamond argues in the essays cited earlier that the law's claim to authority includes the right to authorize coercion. I regret not having read these essays until recently.

[69] See my *Essay on the Modern State*, 205–6, and the references in note 80 (on p. 205).

are connected. Much more needs to be said here, but an extended discussion of these issues is beyond the aims of this essay.

VIII. Concluding Remarks

I have argued that influential conceptions of state power as essentially coercive are mistaken. They are mistaken in thinking that states and force are conceptually connected, but much more importantly, they err in attributing too much importance or significance to coercive power. It is not that just states can entirely eliminate the threat of sanctions. It is that coercion and force do not play as central a role as is widely thought, and this fact should affect the role the state's coerciveness ought to play in our accounts of legitimate or just states.

The widespread belief that "political power is always coercive power" has misled political thinkers in a number of ways which I shall mention briefly. First of all, it suggests "bad man" accounts of law or "realist" views of states (and international affairs), and these accounts are one-sided, as has often been argued.

The belief that state power is essentially coercive leads us, second, to neglect other means of getting people to act as we should want them to act. Nagel's depressing conception of politics as a domain "where we are all competing to get the coercive power of the state behind the institutions we favor" is not only misleading; it is dangerous if it discourages us from using noncoercive means to get people to act justly.

Third, this mistaken belief also contributes to the neglect of the large amount of consensus and coordination necessary for states or for any political order, a theme I have barely touched on here.[70] Fourth, it contributes to the neglect of consideration of alternatives to states.[71]

Lastly, the belief that political power is fundamentally coercive also contributes to the neglect in contemporary political theory—but not in legal theory—of the importance and centrality of the state's *authority*. Libertarians and left-liberals put the state's coercive powers at center stage, but these powers are less puzzling or problematic than their claims to authority. Indeed, what is puzzling about the state's coercive powers is not the justification for its use of sanctions or force; rather it is the justification for its claim to *monopolize* legitimate force. It may be this power that Anscombe singles out when she remarks that "civil society is the bearer of rights of coercion not possibly existent among men without

---

[70] Hart's "rule of recognition," central to his account of the constituting of a legal system, depends on agreement; see Hart, *The Concept of Law*. See also Russell Hardin, "Why a Constitution?" in Bernard Grofman and Donald Wittman, eds., *The Federalist Papers and the New Institutionalism* (New York: Agathon Press, 1989), and *Liberalism, Constitutionalism, and Democracy* (Oxford: Oxford University Press, 1999), chap. 3; and Barry Weingast, "The Political Foundations of Democracy and the Rule of Law," *American Political Science Review* 91, no. 2 (1997): 245–63.

[71] See my *Essay on the Modern State*, especially chap. 2.

government." In a certain respect, states are both easier and harder to justify.[72] In my view their use of force may be much less problematic than is usually assumed. Quite often it is not hard to justify the use of force, for instance, against killers and bullies. What is hard to justify are the extraordinarily sweeping powers claimed by states. I tend to be skeptical that these claims can be justified.[73] But the path to justifying them lies through the state's authority.

Philosophy, University of Maryland

---

[72] I bypass questions about the distinction between justification and legitimacy here. See my essay on legitimacy referred to above, as well as Simmons, "Justification and Legitimacy."

[73] See my *Essay on the Modern State*, as well as the works of Leslie Green, Joseph Raz, and John Simmons cited.

DEMOCRATIC LEGITIMACY AND
ECONOMIC LIBERTY*

By John Tomasi

I am developing a hybrid theory of liberal governance that I call market democracy.[1] Market democracy combines insights from classical liberals such as F. A. Hayek with insights from "high liberals" such as John Rawls.[2] Like classical liberal views, market democracy affirms the primary importance of private economic liberty. It sees a wide-ranging right to economic freedom as among the weightiest constitutional rights of liberal citizens. Like views in the high liberal tradition, however, market democracy affirms a robust conception of social justice as the ultimate standard of institutional evaluation. Basic rights and liberties in place, a set of institutions is just only if it is specifically designed to benefit the poor. As a consequence of the scope and weight assigned to economic freedom, market democracy strictly limits the scope of legislative authority in economic affairs. Instead, market democracy emphasizes the use of markets in pursuit of social goals. The distributional requirements of social justice are to be pursued mainly through the forces of spontaneous economic order.

I have long been attracted to the classical liberal and libertarian emphasis on private economic liberty. At its best, I see that emphasis as being based on a robust ideal of agency. Possessing some particular bundle of material goods, for classical liberals, is not nearly as important as possessing those goods because of one's own actions and choices. Free individuals should be aware of themselves as central causes of the lives they lead. It is not just captains of industry or heroes of Ayn Rand novels who define themselves through their accomplishments in the economic realm. Many ordinary people—middle-class parents, single-moms, entry-level workers—become who they are, and express who they hope to be, by the personal choices they make about working, saving, and spending. For classical liberals, diminishing personal agency in economic affairs—no

* For comments on earlier drafts, I thank my fellow contributors to this volume and the members of the *Political Philosophy Workshop* at Brown University. Special thanks to Zack Beauchamp, Jason Brennan, Dave Estlund, Laura Joyce, Sharon Krause, Charles Larmore, Jason Swadley, and, most especially, Ellen Frankel Paul.
[1] John Tomasi, *Free Market Fairness* (Princeton, NJ: Princeton University Press, forthcoming, 2012).
[2] The term "high liberal" was coined by Samuel Freeman, "Illiberal Liberals: Why Libertarianism Is Not a Liberal View," *Philosophy and Public Affairs* 30, no. 2 (2001): 105–51.

doi:10.1017/S0265052511000124

matter how lofty the social goal—drains vital blood from a person's life. When private economic freedoms are curtailed, libertarians claim, people become in some important sense less free. People in this broad tradition also emphasize property rights for instrumental reasons: property rights are linked to other basic rights, promote the creation of social wealth, and mitigate the dangers of concentrated political power. But the claim that property rights protect liberty has always seemed most important to me.

I am also drawn to the classical liberal idea of "spontaneous order." Sometimes social goals are most effectively pursued directly, for example by the creation of a governmental program guaranteeing the delivery of some needed good or service. But classical liberals emphasize that at other times—perhaps most times—social goals are best pursued indirectly. A commercial market is a paradigm of a spontaneous order. The production of the most ordinary commercial good—a lowly pencil— requires the mobilization of a staggeringly complex system of actors: foresters, miners, sailors, metallurgists, chemists, gluers, and more. As Leonard Read observed, there may be literally *"not a single person on the face of this earth"* who knows how to make a pencil.[3] Yet pencils are produced. These complex productive systems typically were not planned: they evolved. These systems are products of human action but not of human design. Friedrich Hayek argues that a free society is best thought of as a spontaneous order. In such a society, people should be allowed to pursue their own goals on the basis of information available only to themselves.[4] Along with the moral ideal of private economic liberty, I find the classical liberal and libertarian emphasis on spontaneous order deeply attractive.

At the same time, I am increasingly attracted to a form of political justification widely associated with the high liberal tradition. While libertarians such as Robert Nozick justify political forms by naturalistic arguments about self-ownership, classical liberals such as Hayek and Richard Epstein ground their institutional recommendations mainly on consequentialist arguments about efficiency or happiness (I elucidate this distinction between libertarianism and classical liberalism below). By contrast, many left-liberal theorists recently have adopted a different approach to political justification.[5] If a set of political and economic institutions is to be just and legitimate, those institutions must be justifiable in principle to the citizens who are to live within them. According to John Rawls, the problem of political justification is to be settled "by working out a problem of deliberation."[6] This approach need not require the

---

[3] Leonard Read, "I, Pencil" *The Freeman*, December 1958.
[4] F. A. Hayek, *The Constitution of Liberty* (Chicago: University of Chicago Press, 1960).
[5] Robert Nozick, *Anarchy, State and Utopia* (New York: Basic Books, Inc., 1974).
[6] John Rawls, *A Theory of Justice* (Cambridge, MA: Harvard University Press, 1971), 17; and John Rawls, *A Theory of Justice*, revised edition, (Cambridge, MA: Harvard University Press, 1999), 16.

literal consent of all the members of society (a requirement that would lead us toward anarchy). It does require, however, that institutions pass a test of acceptability to citizens understood as beings who, in their moral nature, wish to live together on terms that all can accept. As Gerald Gaus has shown, this deliberative approach can be interpreted in different ways and thus can lead to different political conclusions.[7] Still, according to Rawls and many other philosophers on the left, this deliberative or "democratic" approach is closely connected to a further idea: the idea of social, or distributive, justice.

Against the libertarians (and many classical liberals), left-liberals insist that the concept "justice" applies to more than mere individual actions. Instead, the social order as a whole—the pattern in which goods and opportunities are distributed or, better, the set of institutions that generate such patterns—can properly be described as just or unjust. Social justice requires more than the protection of the formal rights of citizens. In Rawls's elegant phrase, justice requires that citizens "share one another's fate."[8] If institutions are to be acceptable to all, those institutions must be arranged so people can look upon the special skills and talents of their fellow citizens not as weapons to be feared but as in some sense a common bounty. There are many formulations of the distributional requirements of social justice within the left-liberal tradition. Here is a general formulation that will do for now: justice requires that institutions be designed so that the benefits they produce are enjoyed by all citizens, including the least fortunate among them. Everyone is the author of a life, and the storyline of that life is fantastically important to each of them. We honor the importance of self-authorship when we insist that our institutions leave no one behind. Like the deliberative approach to political justification, I find this idea of social justice extremely attractive.

In developing a market democratic approach to liberal governance, I seek to combine ideas from these two rival liberal traditions and demonstrate how they fit together into a philosophically coherent whole. Market democracy rests on three theses: 1) economic liberty is among the basic constitutional rights and liberties held by liberal citizens, 2) social justice, on some interpretation to be specified, is the ultimate standard of social evaluation, and 3) as a matter of ideal theoretic analysis, the institutions of market democracy realize the conception of social justice specified in thesis 2) even while affirming the priority of economic liberty set out in 1). Further, if market democracy is to be a philosophically coherent view, this set of theses should be defended in a way that is strongly principled. Let us say that a defense of a set of theses is strongly principled if the

---

[7] Gerald Gaus, *The Order of Public Reason: A Theory of Freedom and Morality in a Diverse and Bounded World* (New York: Cambridge University Press, 2011).

[8] Rawls, *Theory of Justice*, 102. This phrase was deleted from the revised edition. For an interesting discussion of this change see Loren Lomasky's "Libertarianism at Twin Harvard," *Social Philosophy and Policy* 22 (2005): 178–99.

defenses of all the theses are grounded in a common set of foundational ideas.[9]

In this paper, I wish to offer a defense of the first thesis mentioned above: that private economic liberties must be recognized as constitutional essentials by any properly liberal regime. However, given my wider commitment to theses 2) and 3), I approach this task in a slightly unusual way. Unlike the defenses of economic liberty traditionally offered by libertarians and classical liberals, I wish to defend the importance of economic liberty in terms of the same foundational ideas that are commonly used by high liberals to defend social justice.[10] In particular, I hope to show that a powerful right of economic liberty is a requirement of respecting citizens as free and equal self-governing agents committed to a principle of mutual self-rule.

I begin with a few words about economic liberty. I then sketch a map of the ideological terrain, showing how market democracy differs from traditional accounts of high liberalism, classical liberalism, and libertarianism alike. I then turn to my main task, which is to offer a defense of private economic liberty on grounds of democratic legitimacy.

I. Economic Liberty

When I speak of economic liberty in this paper, I shall mean "liberty" in a broad sense to include a variety of elements like those the legal scholar Wesley Hohfeld called "rights-relationships." So economic liberties may refer to *claim-rights*, where a right-holder has a claim on some duty-bearer to act or to forbear from acting in some specified way; or to *liberties* proper, whereby a right-holder is at liberty with respect to others to perform some act or not to perform that act; or to *powers*, where a right-holder is in a position such that he may alter the rights, duties, liberties, or powers of some duty-bearer.[11] Whether used in a moral or legal sense, then, the term "liberty" here is used to cover a wide variety of rights-relationships.

James Nickel helpfully describes the *economic* liberties as involving "a right to independent economic activity" and "a right to own personal and

---

[9] Imagine a classical liberal position that affirms a strong set of private economic liberties on grounds of economic efficiency, but affirms a tax-funded social safety net as a requirement of beneficence. (Milton Friedman is sometimes interpreted as having defended a version of classical liberalism exhibiting this structure.) The justification for this position would not be strongly principled.

[10] Obviously, there are other logically coherent approaches available here. For example, one might seek to justify a concern for social justice in terms of the same foundational ideas by which libertarians or classical liberals commonly defend the priority of economic liberty. That is not my project.

[11] Wesley Newcomb Hohfeld. *Fundamental Legal Conceptions as Applied in Judicial Reasoning* (New Haven, CT: Yale University Press, 1964). See also Lawrence Becker *Property Rights: Philosophical Foundations* (Boston, MA: Routledge & Kegan Paul, 1977), 11–21.

productive property." Nickel then divides the economic liberties into a variety of categories. Simplifying Nickel's schema, we can think of economic liberty as divided into two broad categories: liberties of *working* and of *owning*.[12]

The economic liberties of *working* protect the freedom of individuals to labor and to use labor in productive activities. As Nickel puts it: "This is the liberty to employ one's body and time in productive activity that one has chosen or accepted, and under arrangements that one has chosen or accepted." The other main categories of economic liberty that Nickel describes—those of transacting, holding, and using—can be subsumed under our category of *ownership*. Thus, the liberty of transacting allows individuals to engage in free economic activity: "This is the freedom to manage one's economic affairs at the individual and household levels and on larger scales as well." Transacting involves the liberty to trade in the market place, to create things for sale, and to save and invest. It also covers the freedom of individuals and groups to start, run, and close down businesses such as factories, shops, farms, and commercial enterprises of many sorts. The economic liberty of holding concerns freedom in the realm of several property. "This category covers legitimate ways of acquiring and holding productive property, using and developing property for commercial and productive purposes, and property transactions such as investing, buying, selling, trading, and giving." Finally, there is a range of liberties concerning using. "This is the liberty to make use of legitimately acquired resources for consumption and production." The liberty of using protects the freedom of citizens to buy, use, and consume natural resources, consumer goods, and services. On the commercial level, this liberty protects production-related consumption (such as deciding which parts to use, or which power sources to purchase). On the domestic level, it protects a range of personal economic decision-making, including questions about what to eat and drink, what to wear, what type of housing to have, and a wide range of services—including what forms of entertainment, of cultural experience, and perhaps what educational experiences and which health care services—one might choose to purchase.

These categories of economic liberty overlap in a variety of ways. If a school teacher uses his summer break to remodel the basement of his home, for example, he might be described as exercising a liberty of working or one of owning (for example, that of holding). Nonetheless, this simplified schema gives a sense of the range of activities at play when we speak of economic liberty. Most important, the economic liberties of working and owning can be interpreted in a great variety of ways, both in terms of the range of activities each category of liberty is understood to

[12] James Nickel, "Economic Liberties" in *The Idea of a Political Liberalism: Essays on Rawls,* ed. Victoria Davion (Lanham, MD: Rowman and Littlefield, 2000), 155–76. Nickel lays out his four-category scheme of economic liberty on pp. 156–57.

cover and in terms of the social importance assigned to those activities. To see this, let's look more closely at the idea of ownership.

Anthony Honoré, in a classic article, defines ownership as "the greatest possible interest in a thing which a mature system of law recognizes."[13] By studying a great variety of legal systems, Honoré suggests that the concept of ownership can be broken down into eleven aspects or "incidents." These are: 1) a right (claim) to possess (exclusive physical control of a thing); 2) a right (liberty) to use (in the narrow sense of personal use and enjoyment); 3) the right to manage (the power to determine how and who will use a thing); 4) the right to income (a claim to the benefits from possession of a thing); 5) a right to capital (including the power to alienate a thing and the liberty to consume and/or destroy it); 6) the right to security (an immunity from having one's things taken by compulsion); 7) the right of transmissibility (the power to transfer one's property rights in a thing to another person, as in a bequest); 8) the right to absence of term (ownership is long-lasting, such that a person's claim is immune from expiration); 9) the prohibition of harmful use (ownership includes a duty not to use the property in a way that harms others); 10) liability to execution (owners are liable for their debts and their property may be repossessed in payment for them); and 11) residuary character (rights of ownership sometimes expire, and thus may come to be vested in some other person or entity).[14]

Honoré does not defend these "incidents" as moral requirements of ownership. Rather, he simply observes that when most mature legal systems address issues of ownership, they see ownership as involving most or all of these eleven aspects. Honoré suggests that this de facto convergence on the formal aspects of ownership might be explained by the "common needs of mankind and the common conditions of human life." Nonetheless, as Honoré is quick to point out, each of these aspects can be interpreted in different ways. Thus, while mature legal systems tend to include the same eleven incidents in their concept of ownership, this certainly does not mean "all systems attach an equal importance to ownership (in the full, liberal sense) or regard the same things as capable of being owned."[15] A socialist system, for example, might recognize this full conception of ownership but limit the range of things that can be owned — for example, by not recognizing private ownership rights to productive machinery.[16] Other systems may regard ownership as including the incidents of income and transmissibility, but limit the weight assigned to those aspects of ownership out of concern for other social values (for example, they may subject income and bequests to steeply progressive

---

[13] Anthony Honoré, "Ownership," *Oxford Essays in Jurisprudence: A Collaborative Work,* A. G. Guest, ed. (London, New York: Oxford University Press, 1961), 107–47.

[14] Ibid., 113–24.

[15] Ibid., 109.

[16] Ibid., 110.

rates of taxation in pursuit of some social goal). As Honoré notes, his formal analysis "is not meant to prejudge the issue, how far private ownership should stretch and to what extent it should be modified in the public interest." [17] The economic liberties of ownership, like those of working, can be interpreted in a great variety of different ways in terms of scope and weight.

By scope, I mean the range or number of private economic activities that are to be protected, where "activities" refers to the liberties of working or owning. Thinkers in the liberal tradition interpret the scope of economic liberty in diverse ways. With respect to the economic liberties of *working*, for example, a narrow interpretation of scope might only recognize freedom of occupational choice as meriting protection. A wider interpretation of scope might include freedom of occupational choice, but also include protections for individuals to decide for themselves how many hours they are willing to work each week. The question of the scope of the economic liberties of working also covers issues about what kinds of work might merit protection. Freedom of labor might (or might not) be interpreted to include protections for a great variety of paid activities ranging from surrogate motherhood, controversial forms of entertainment (such as exotic dancing, extreme fighting, or "dwarf-tossing"), and sexual services of various kinds. At its widest interpretation, as affirmed by some libertarians, the scope of the liberty of working might even protect practices such as indentured servitude.[18]

With respect to the economic liberties of *owning*, scope refers primarily to the range of kinds of things that are recognized as being ownable. On a narrow reading, for example, ownership might be interpreted to apply only to personal (nonproductive) property. (An even narrower reading, perhaps, might deny private ownership altogether, as in a forced cooperative where all things are required to be held in common.) Wider readings might extend the range of private ownership to include productive property (businesses, arable land, the means of production). As with the issue of working, further points out on the continuum might include an ever wider and more controversial listing of things identified as subject to the claims, liberties, and powers attendant to (private) ownership: animals, works of art, bodily organs, persons, and more.

Unlike scope, weight refers to the importance assigned to these private economic activities compared to other values and goals. The more important the private economic activities of working and ownership are deemed to be, the stronger the legal protection given to those activities. An important threshold on this continuum of protection concerns whether a given economic liberty—a right of working, say, or of owning—is considered

---

[17] Ibid., 108.

[18] I think of indentured servitude as primarily involving questions of labor, while slavery is more fundamentally an issue of ownership. I am open to alternative ways of categorizing these issues.

weighty enough to merit protection as a basic, constitutional right. Even among constitutionally protected rights, some of those rights can be deemed weightier than others. But all rights deemed weighty enough to be entrenched in the constitution protect activities that are thereby significantly insulated from legislative interference.

Not all rights are constitutionally protected, of course. Legislative bodies can set out economic liberties of various sorts—claim-rights, powers, and immunities—and economic rights and liberties set out that way can vary in their degree of weightiness compared to other sorts of rights and social concerns. Speaking generally, then, economic liberties are treated as more weighty to the degree that they are accorded greater political protection, and less weighty the more susceptible they are to being overridden by other moral values and social goals.

So liberals disagree about the range and importance of protection that should be accorded private economic activity. We can use these distinctions to help us draw a conceptual map of the diverse terrain of contemporary liberal thought.

II. THE CONCEPTUAL TERRAIN

By "classical liberalism," I mean a broad school that includes "libertarianism" as a subset. Classical liberalism is the liberalism of Adam Smith, David Hume, F. A. Hayek, and Richard Epstein as well as libertarians such as Robert Nozick, Eric Mack, and Jan Narveson. High liberalism, by contrast, is the liberalism of John Stuart Mill, T. H. Green, John Rawls, Ronald Dworkin, Martha Nussbaum, Thomas Nagel, Samuel Freeman, Joshua Cohen, Will Kymlicka and a great many other contemporary scholars. One way to distinguish between kinds of liberalism is by their differing conceptions of economic liberty. Classical liberals affirm what I call a *thick* conception of economic liberty; high liberals, a *thin* conception.

Most liberals agree that some rights and liberties are more important than others. These basic liberties merit a high degree of political protection, typically by being entrenched in the constitution. On their lists of basic liberties, most liberals include some economic liberties, such as the right to own property, along with civil liberties, such as the right to a fair trial, and political liberties, such as the right to vote. But liberals differ about the scope of the economic liberties they consider basic. Classical liberals tend to interpret economic liberty as having the same wide scope accorded to the other categories of basic liberty. Just as the recognition of religious liberty requires the general protection of independent activity in the religious realm, economic liberty requires the general protection of independent activity in economic matters. Wide freedom of economic contract and general rights regarding the ownership of property are prominent features of the thick conception of economic liberty affirmed by classical liberals.

A crucial division within the liberal tradition begins with Mill's ambiv-
alent treatment of economic liberty. According to Mill, liberty involves
"framing the plan of our life to suit our own character."[19] While Mill
affirms liberties of thought, association, and religion as protecting liberty,
he sometimes suggests that economic liberties should be treated differently. Decisions people make with respect to questions of labor and ownership in their lives have no intrinsic connection to liberty in Mill's sense.
While economic laws may govern the production of goods, the systems
by which goods are distributed are social creations, subject to collective
choice and control.[20] Since economic activity is not an expression of liberty, rights and powers of ownership and labor should mainly be defined
by the requirements of utility: "Property is only a means to an end, not
itself the end."[21]

Continuing in this high liberal tradition, John Rawls likewise adopts a
platform of economic exceptionalism, according to which economic liberties are singled out for relegation to a lower level of protection. Compared to Mill, Rawls is more forthright in his skepticism about the moral
value of private economic liberty. Regarding freedom of labor, Rawls
recognizes only a limited right to occupational choice as a basic right,
relegating the freedom to engage in self-organized economic activity as
well as the freedom to hire others for productive purposes as issues to be
determined through legislative debates. Regarding ownership, Rawls recognizes only the right to personal property as a basic right, severing off
any rights protecting the ownership of productive property (family farms,
businesses, and other "means of production"). Those wider economic
rights, Rawls states, are not "necessary for the development and exercise
of the moral powers."[22] Since independent activity with respect to those
other economic issues is not an expression of liberty, any rights and
powers regarding those activities should be crafted with an eye toward
the realization of broader distributional requirements, in light of prevailing demographic and sociological conditions, etc. This thin conception of
economic liberty is a hallmark of the high liberal tradition.

Continuing with this approach of demarcating liberal schools in terms
of their treatment of economic liberty, "libertarianism" is identifiable as a
variant within the classical liberal tradition.[23] Like classical liberals, lib-

[19] John Stuart Mill, *On Liberty* (Indianapolis: Hackett, 1978), 12.

[20] "Unlike the laws of Production, those of Distribution are partly of human institution:
since the manner in which wealth is distributed in any given society, depends on the statutes
or usages therein obtaining." John Stuart Mill, *Principles of Political Economy* (Indianapolis:
Liberty Fund, 2006), 21.

[21] Ibid., 223. For most of his career, Mill advocated that governments leave the economy
largely unfettered. However, this was not because he believed citizens had basic rights to
economic liberty. Rather, he thought free economic regimes would tend to produce good
consequences.

[22] John Rawls, *Political Liberalism* (New York: Columbia University Press, 1993), 298.

[23] For a useful survey of the varieties of libertarian thought, see Matt Zwolinski, "Libertarianism," *The Internet Encyclopedia of Philosophy*, http://www.iep.utm.edu/libertar/.

ertarians affirm a thick conception of economic liberty. But while traditional classical liberals affirm economic liberties as on a par with the other
traditional liberal rights and liberties, libertarians affirm those economic
liberties as the weightiest of all rights, and possibly even as moral abso-
lutes. Some libertarians believe that all rights—including rights of free
speech, free association, and sexual freedom—are simply instances of
property rights. (The right to free speech is a right to use one's mouth—
which one owns—in a certain way.) Libertarians such as Nozick see economic liberties as so weighty that the liberal state must enforce most any
contract that citizens enter into—including even ones in which people
sold themselves into slavery.[24] While classical liberals such as Hayek
advocate limited tax-funded support for education and a safety net, the
libertarian approach rules out such programs. Because of these positions,
high liberals such as Freeman claim that ("right") libertarianism should
not even be counted as a properly liberal view.[25]

III. Economic Exceptionalism

Market democracy affirms a thick conception of economic liberty as
among the constitutional rights of liberal citizens. As liberal citizens have
a general right to independent activity and decision-making in the religious, associational, and intellectual aspects of their lives, so too market
democracy recognizes a general right protecting citizens' choices and
actions with respect to economic questions.

This is a fundamental point of moral disagreement between market
democracy and the "left-liberal" versions of high liberalism that dominate the academy today. While affirming general rights of speech and
religious practice as basic rights, high liberals such as Rawls treat the
economic freedoms of citizens differently. Of all the traditional rights of
liberalism, the economic liberties—and only those liberties—are to receive
special definitional narrowing.

Instead of a general right to free economic activity, for example, Rawls
specifies that citizens only have a basic economic freedom regarding their
choice of occupation and the ownership of personal (nonproductive) property. The question of whether it is morally acceptable to single out eco-

[24] Because Nozick altered parts of his view, his critics sometimes claim that he rejected
libertarianism altogether. See Robert Nozick, *The Examined Life* (New York: Basic Books,
1989), 287. There is textual evidence against this claim. See Robert Nozick, *Invariances*
(Cambridge, MA: Harvard University Press, 2001), 281–82, passim. I thank Jason Brennan
for conversations about these passages.
[25] Samuel Freeman, "Illiberal Libertarians: Why Libertarianism Is Not a Liberal View,"
Philosophy and Public Affairs 30, no. 2 (Spring, 2001): 105–51. A more complete map would
include "left-libertarianism," on which see Michael Otsuka "Self-Ownership and Equality:
A Lockean Reconciliation," *Philosophy and Public Affairs* 27 (1998): 65–92; and Peter Vallentyne and Hillel Steiner, eds., *Left-Libertarianism and its Critics: The Contemporary Debate*
(New York: Palgrave, 2000).

nomic liberty to be constrained in this way is a major junction point, perhaps *the* major junction point, within the history of liberal thought. Can this high liberal platform of economic exceptionalism be justified?

Given the importance of this question, it is surprising that high liberal arguments for economic exceptionalism are often presented only obliquely and in an unsustained fashion. Defenses of economic exceptionalism usually take the form of critiques of thick economic freedom. Let us examine these critiques.

One way high liberals seek to undermine the importance of property rights is to claim that property is a legal convention. The economic liberty of ownership exists as a product of regulatory definitions, rules and conventions. Now, the idea that property is a legal convention has been widely accepted by classical liberals at least since Hume.[26] Critics of thick economic liberty, however, add a stinger to this idea. If property is a legal convention, this means that claims to ownership are conceptually posterior to the regulatory rules that define and constrain them. So property rights cannot serve as a basis for limiting those regulatory rules. As Liam Murphy and Thomas Nagel put it: "Private property is a legal convention, defined in part by looking at the tax system; therefore, the tax system cannot be evaluated by looking at its impact on private property, conceived as something that has independent existence and validity."[27]

Against the property-absolutist claims of some libertarians, Murphy and Nagel claim that the system of social rules that potentially impact on property rights is logically prior to those property rights. Thus: "The logical order of priority between taxes and property rights is the reverse of that assumed by libertarians."[28] Murphy and Nagel note that many ordinary citizens believe that they have some kind of right to their pre-tax income, a right that proposals for taxation must overcome. But they argue that these "everyday libertarian" notions are baseless confusions.

Murphy and Nagel direct their argument from legal convention against absolutist conceptions of ownership rights.[29] However, they then proceed as though their critique of pure libertarianism *ipso facto* rules out classical liberal accounts of ownership as well. Libertarians may well object to the way Murphy and Nagel characterize the "absolutism" of their defenses of property rights. This is an important issue, but we can set it aside. For us,

---

[26] "Our property is nothing but those goods, whose constant possession is establish'd by the laws of society; that is, by the laws of justice." David Hume, *A Treatise of Human Nature*, L. A. Selby-Bigge, ed. [Oxford, 1960 (1888)], 491. Milton Friedman says: "What constitutes property and what rights the ownership of property confers are complex social creations rather than self-evident-propositions." Milton Friedman, *Capitalism and Freedom: Fortieth Anniversary Edition* (1962; University of Chicago Press, 2002), 26.

[27] Thomas Nagel and Robert Murphy, *The Myth of Ownership: Taxes and Justice* (New York: Oxford University Press, 2002), 8.

[28] Ibid., 33.

[29] See Gerald Gaus's compact critique in "Coercion, Ownership, and the Redistributive State: Justificatory Liberalism's Classical Liberal Tilt," *Social Philosophy and Policy* (2010): 233–75, at 259.

the important point is that, when applied to non-absolutist defenses of thick economic liberty, this argument from legal convention quickly loses its force. Indeed, applied against the classical liberal conception of economic liberty that I wish to defend, the argument from legal convention is generalizable so as to render it either trivial or circular.

First, let us look at a generalized version of this argument. Consider any legal convention, which we will call "X," where X is defined in part by looking at the surrounding systems of rules and regulations that impact on it. According to the argument from legal convention, systems that impact on X cannot be evaluated by asking whether they impact on X (as though X has an independent existence and validity). But now for X, instead of a libertarian conception of property rights, substitute: 1) the right to vote; 2) the right of bodily integrity; or 3) the right to free intellectual development (such as that protected by freedom of the press). I suggest that any of these rights, and many more besides, could equally well be substituted for X. All basic rights and liberties are socially constructed in important ways.

Consider the right to bodily integrity. We cannot know the content of this right except by reference to the surrounding rules that identify when that right is impinged. Is getting bumped in the hallway a violation of the right to bodily integrity? We answer that question only by looking at the complex system of social rules and definitions (such as those that define various forms of assault and battery) that are relevant to this particular right. So too the right to vote must be given definitional content by rules that set out how often elections will be held and determine how they will be structured.

So the observation that "property is a legal convention" does no normative work specific to issues of property (aside from perhaps blocking the pure libertarian claim). We must evaluate systems that impact on economic liberty the same way we evaluate systems that impact on any other "legal conventions." Namely, we must consider the best substantive arguments that can be advanced to tell us what degree of protection from impingement each of those "legal conventions" merits. Whatever "independent existence and validity" the economic liberties have must come from those moral arguments. The strength (or weakness) of those arguments is unaffected by statements about economic freedom's status as a legal convention. With respect to assertions about the legitimacy of restrictions on economic liberty, the claim that such liberties are legal conventions is trivial.

The only way to make the argument from legal convention undermine the importance of thick economic liberty would be to antecedently assume that the moral arguments supporting such liberty are weak or nonexistent. But, again, the observation that "property is a legal convention" does no normative work to support that assumption. With respect to claims about the legitimacy of restrictions on economic liberty, the legal-convention argument about property is circular.

To avoid these problems, high liberals sometimes offer a supplementary argument against economic liberty. This argument seeks to attach the legal-convention critique uniquely to questions of private economic liberty. With economic liberties, this argument goes, a result of their social protection is that large inequalities will emerge between people. These inequalities are far beyond the inequalities that would have occurred in a Hobbesian state of nature. In the state of nature, as Murphy and Nagel point out, "there is little doubt that everyone's level of welfare would be very low and—importantly—roughly equal. We cannot pretend that the differences in ability, personality, and inherited wealth that lead to great inequalities of welfare in an orderly market would have the same effect if there were no government to create and protect legal property rights . . ."[30]

However, this argument also can be generalized with respect to "legal conventions" besides property. Consider freedom of thought, including intellectual freedom. In the state of nature everyone's level of intellectual attainment would be very low and therefore roughly equal. In society, with rules protecting intellectual freedom, differences in intellectual talent, personality, and ambition will lead to much larger inequalities of learning and intellectual accomplishment. Some will fill their heads with gossip about Hollywood stars and the doings of game show contestants. Others will devote themselves to the study of arcane problems in philosophy (such as the question of what it is like to be a bat).[31] Whether we are considering economic or intellectual liberty, however, the simple fact that social protections magnify inequalities tells us nothing. The important question is the moral one about how we should think about these inequalities. Liberals answer that question first and foremost by examining the moral importance of the activities that give rise to such inequalities in the first place. The observation that economic liberties are social conventions does nothing to undermine the market democratic claim that such liberties should be recognized as basic rights.

Consider a different argument, this one offered by Rawls, against the affirmation of thick economic liberty—though again this argument is presented only obliquely. Recall that in a democratic society, citizens are committed to act in relation to others on terms that they can publically endorse together. Thus one of the central aims of democratic society is to resolve "the impasse . . . as to the way in which social institutions are to be arranged if they are to conform to the freedom and equality of citizens as moral persons."[32] However, Rawls says that the choice between the traditional economic liberties of capitalism (such as private ownership of productive property, and the freedom of individuals to negotiate the terms of their own employment) and the economic liberties of socialism

---

[30] Nagel and Murphy, *The Myth of Ownership*, 16–17.
[31] Thomas Nagel "What Is it Like to Be a Bat?" *The Philosophical Review* 83 (1974): 435–50.
[32] Rawls, *Political Liberalism* 338–9.

(which allow only ownership of personal property and a limited freedom of occupational choice) is too controversial to be decided as matters of political justice. Even a philosophically compelling argument, he says, is "most unlikely to convince either side that the other is correct on a question like that of private or social property in the means of production."[33] In the face of these sharply conflicting views, it is unlikely that an overlapping consensus could be reached on this issue. Rawls says the choice between capitalism and socialism must be to left to later stages of justification "when much more information about a society's circumstances and historical traditions is available."[34] In this way, Rawls denies that the economic liberties of capitalism should be recognized as basic rights.

This is curious argument. For one thing, it is not obvious that socialism affirms economic liberty in a liberal sense at all. For socialists, "economic liberty" involves the right to participate in collective decision-making about the uses of socially-owned property.[35] There are complicated issues here, but classical liberals have good reason to be skeptical: the socialist approach appears to involve a form of *political* liberty rather than one of economic liberty. Imagine a conception of religious liberty under which each citizen was given a say about what religious practices would henceforth be required by all members of the community. Rather than protecting individual freedom in the area of religion, such a system would violate religious liberty in the liberal sense by making religious decisions subject to collective decisions. Similarly, socialism gives primacy to collective decision-making in economic affairs, rather than protecting independent economic decision-making and activity on the part of individuals and voluntary partnerships.[36]

Even if we grant the cogency of the socialist conception of "economic liberty" within the liberal context, this argument faces serious problems. First, Rawls's plea for neutrality on economic issues fits ill with his own later assertion that socialist regimes (such as liberal democratic socialism) realize liberal justice while even tepidly capitalist regimes (such as welfare state capitalism) violate that standard. Further, Rawls bases his ostensible plea for neutrality on this issue on the claim that the choice between socialism and capitalism is too divisive to be settled as a matter of political justice. But such an approach would require that we disfigure the core democratic standard that people should live together on terms that all can

---

[33] Ibid.

[34] Ibid., 298.

[35] For a definition along these lines, see John Rawls, *Justice as Fairness: A Restatement* (Cambridge, MA: Harvard University Press, 2001), 114.

[36] Market democracy makes room for worker-owned firms, and so for whatever forms of economic freedom might be available therein. Against liberal socialism, however, market democracy insists that citizens cannot be compelled to work in worker-owned firms. Nor can workers be compelled to join unions, though individuals may have the right to do so for purposes of collective bargaining. In all these areas, market democracy insists that we protect the private economic liberties of liberal citizens.

accept. As noted earlier, the public reason standard can be interpreted in a variety of ways. Within Rawls's own system, however, that standard requires merely that we seek consensus among citizens who are politically reasonable, rather than among all citizens regardless of the content of their views.

To see the appeal of this approach, consider another example involving religion. Imagine a liberal constitutional democracy within which a large faction of citizens is committed to using the state to impose its preferred religious viewpoint on small factions of citizens holding deviant views. So, as a matter of sociological fact, the status of religious liberty is a matter of controversy in that society. On Rawls's approach to public reason, our commitment to democracy would not allow us (let alone require us) to prescind from philosophical investigations about whether religious liberties should be recognized as among the basic rights of those liberal citizens.

Similarly, even if it were the case that the choice between private and public ownership of productive property was a topic of significant disagreement within the liberal democracies of the west (which it manifestly is not), this sociological fact could not cut off philosophical investigations into the moral standing of thick economic liberty for liberal citizens. With questions of economic liberty, like those of religious liberty, the mere fact of controversy cannot by itself render an issue unfit for public reason arguments. The value pluralism democratic theorists must respect is *reasonable* value pluralism. The mere fact of controversy cannot pull the plug on discussions about the moral requirements of liberal democracy.

So we return to our question: What could justify the high liberal platform of economic exceptionalism? As we have seen, high liberals treat the economic liberties differently than the other traditional liberal freedoms. Rather than including a general right protecting the choice-making of citizens in economic affairs, Rawls's list of basic liberties includes only two narrowly crafted economic liberties: a right to own personal (nonproductive) property, and a limited right to occupational choice. To understand the high liberal platform of economic exceptionalism, we need to take a closer look at the moral powers and their relation to the list of basic liberties.

IV. The Moral Importance of Economic Liberty

Politics is about coercion. Rules against murder, prohibitions against fraud, and policies about the conduct of elections, all require coercive backing. The most basic question philosophers ask about political life concerns the conditions under which the use of such coercion is morally justified. Since Locke, many liberals have given some notion of consent, or justifiability, an important role in legitimating political coercion. The liberal principle of legitimacy is this: the use of political coercion is legitimate only if that coercion is conducted on the basis of principles that can be endorsed by the people subject to that coercion. As Rawls puts it, legitimate political authority requires a "constitution (written or unwritten) the essentials of which all citizens, as reasonable and rational, can endorse in light of their common human reason."[37] The question then arises: Under what conditions might this principle of democratic legitimacy be satisfied?

In order to endorse a set of the political rules, people must first be capable of assessing those rules. To assess political rules, citizens must exercise powers of judgment known as "moral powers." As responsible self-authors, as I describe people exercising the first of these moral powers, citizens are understood to have the capacity to make a realistic assessment of the life options before them and, in light of that assessment, to choose to pursue some course of life as their own. Without this capacity, citizens would not be able to assess what they believe society ought to allow them to do. The other moral power, in my terms, concerns the capacity people have to recognize their fellow citizens as responsible self-authors too. This involves recognizing that their fellow citizens likewise have lives to lead that are important to them. Since they are capable of recognizing this, citizens are capable of committing themselves to abide by just rules of social conduct. Without this capacity, citizens would be unable to evaluate how well the rules of their society square with their commitment to honor their fellow citizens as responsible self-authors.

If people are to be capable of endorsing the rules that are to govern them, they must be free to exercise and develop their two moral powers. The idea that people have special moral powers or capacities in their roles as citizens has a long history, with philosophers defining these powers in various ways.[38] Like Rawls, I will follow tradition by distinguishing two central moral capacities. The first is a capacity for what I shall call responsible self-authorship. By this I mean that all healthy adult citizens, regardless of their particular advantages or disadvantages given by birth, have the capacity to develop and act upon a life plan of their own (whether that plan be individual, collective, or otherwise shared). People are life-agents and their agency matters. As responsible self-authors, they have the capacity to realistically assess the options before them and, in light of that assessment, to set standards for a life of a sort that each deems worth living. The second power is more obviously social in nature. This is the moral capacity to honor one's fellow citizens as responsible self-authors

---

[37] Rawls, *Justice As Fairness*, 41.
[38] Adam Smith described people as simultaneously "self-interested" and "other regarding." Rousseau and Kant offered accounts of the moral powers of citizens. For an illuminating discussion of the idea of moral powers in Rousseau and Kant in relation to that of Rawls, see Thomas A. Spragens Jr., *Getting the Left Right: The Transformation, Decline, and Reformation of American Liberalism* (University Press of Kansas, 2009), 68–71.

too. By this I mean that citizens can recognize that their fellow citizens have lives to lead that are fantastically important to each of them. Whenever they call on the coercive force of the law, they need to be careful to do so in a way that fully respects their fellow citizens as self-authors too.[39]

The role of the basic liberties is to protect those powers. In a society without a general right protecting freedom of speech, a ruling party might allow speech on a wide range of topics but forbid speech by their rivals. Denied access to those forms of speech, the citizens would lack important information about the character of their regime, and perhaps even about the value of political speech itself. Without protection of that general liberty, the evaluative capacities of the citizens would be stunted. Even if they acquiesced to the system of governance, their endorsement would not be as robust as the liberal principle of legitimacy requires.[40] Thus, in drawing up a list of basic liberties, we are seeking to identify a set of liberties that "provide the political and social conditions essential for the adequate development and full exercise of the two moral powers."[41] The basic liberties are those liberties that must be protected if citizens are to develop their evaluative horizons, thus making them capable of truly governing themselves.

Formally speaking, therefore, the stipulation and enforcement of a set of basic liberties is a requirement of political legitimacy. But it is important to note that, while politics is always about coercion, this does not mean that the justification of coercion is the *point* of politics. The liberal commitment to the principle of legitimacy is itself derived from a deeper commitment. At base, high liberals are concerned to respect citizens as free and equal self-governing agents—that is, as members of a cooperative venture who nonetheless have their own lives to lead. It is the commitment to the equal importance of each of those lives that leads liberals to the principle of legitimacy. By insisting that the use of political force be justifiable in principle to all, every person is accounted for as a morally social member.[42] So, the imperative to create a social world in which the moral powers of citizens can be fully developed is a requirement of legitimacy. But that imperative springs from the more basic liberal ideal, rooted in the work of Locke, that political institutions must respect people as free and equal moral beings.[43]

Thus, basic rights are requirements of democratic legitimacy. For this reason, the list of basic rights has a special status within any liberal

[39] For Rawls's discussion of the moral powers, see e.g., *Justice As Fairness*, 18.
[40] Consider another example: Imagine a society that tailored the right of religious freedom to allow the practice of any religion whatsoever—so long as such practice was conducted only in private homes.
[41] Ibid., 46.
[42] See Jeremy Waldron, "Theoretical Foundations of Liberalism," *The Philosophical Quarterly* vol. 37 (1987): esp. 128.
[43] I thank Jason Swadley, Zak Beauchamp, and Jason Brennan for discussion of these ideas.

schema. The protection of the rights on this list is prior to any other social aim—whether that aim be economic prosperity or the pursuit of some distributional goal (such as lessening social inequality, or maximizing the bundle of wealth personally controlled by the poor).[44] Again, democratic theorists can differ about the strength of the priority they assign to basic rights over other social values. Within the orthodox high liberal schema, a basic liberty can only be restricted in order to prevent a more severe restriction to some other basic liberty (or to the scheme of basic liberties as an integrated whole).

The priority assigned to the basic liberties has significant institutional implications. Because the basic liberties are requirements of political legitimacy, high liberals argue that the basic liberties (and the basic liberties alone) should be entrenched in the constitution.[45] The basic liberties are prerequisites for the legitimate exercise of democratic authority. Legislative measures that infringe on those liberties are thus illegitimate. The pursuit of social goals, whether by legislative rule or the exercise of executive prerogative, must not violate the basic rights and liberties enshrined in the constitution.

High liberals claim that some narrowly specified economic liberties should be recognized as basic while other dimensions of economic liberty should be excluded. So high liberals claim that some forms of independent economic activity must be protected if people are fully to develop and exercise their moral powers, while other aspects of personal economic freedom need not be so protected. However, the moral reasoning high liberals use to justify the inclusion of their preferred economic liberties cannot explain why the other aspects of economic liberty must be excluded. On the contrary, the same reasons high liberals offer in support of their preferred economic liberties apply with at least as much force to the aspects of economic freedom they wish to exclude.

Consider freedom of occupational choice. It is easy to see why high liberals affirm this particular economic liberty as a basic right. After all, imagine a society that does not affirm a right to occupational choice. In pursuit of some important social goal, the legislature in this society decides to create a panel of experts (or perhaps a computer program) that assigns an occupation to each citizen. A society organized in this way would not respect citizens as "free and equal self-governing agents." People ordinarily spend a large percentage of their time engaged in their occupation. This is one reason why the choice of occupation is often a profound expression of identity: as Aristotle once noted, what we do influences who we are. By choosing which occupation to pursue, we express our values. We say something about what projects we think are worthy of our

---

[44] On the distinction between these distributive goals, see Derek Parfit, "Equality and Priority," *Ratio* (New Series) X, no. 3 (1997): 202–21.
[45] Rawls, *Justice As Fairness*, 46.

time, how we value the monetary rewards of work compared to the other rewards of work, and about how we balance the value of work with the other parts of our lives.

However, once the right of occupational choice is allowed to be a basic right, it becomes unclear how the other liberties of working can be excluded. Those thicker liberties of working, recall, involve "the liberty to employ one's body and time in productive activity that one has chosen or accepted, and under arrangements that one has chosen or accepted."[46] If the freedom to choose an occupation is essential to the development of the moral powers, the freedom to sell, trade, and donate one's labor looks equally essential for the same reasons. After all, one is defined by one's workplace experience not simply by *what* profession one pursues. One is also defined by *where* one chooses to work, by the *terms* that one seeks and accepts for one's work, by the *number of hours* that one devotes to one's work, and much more besides.

These are not mere details within a person's life. The particular pattern of decisions one makes in response to these questions about working often goes a long way to defining what makes one person's life distinct from the lives of other people. A society that denied individuals the right to make decisions regarding those aspects of their working experience would truncate the ability of those people to be responsible authors of their own lives. Indeed, denied these fuller freedoms of labor, citizens would no longer *be* authors of their own lives. Decisions about matters that affect them intimately would have been taken out of their hands and decided for them by others. The evaluative horizons of those citizens would be narrowed by their experience of life under conditions in which those aspects of liberty were denied. Even if people in such a society acquiesced to these restrictions on their liberty, they would not be in position to endorse the rules of their society in anything like a full or robust manner. Freedom of labor, and to use labor in production, is an essential aspect of a social world that encourages citizens to develop and exercise their moral powers of responsible self-authorship.

A similar argument applies to the economic liberties of ownership. It is easy to see why high liberals affirm that a right to own personal (non-productive) property is important. Ownership rights to such property can provide a person with personal security: citizens with these rights know that they can hold something that cannot be taken away from them. Personal property can include vitally human things such as food, shelter, and clothing. Ownership rights in such things can shelter people from domination by others. The ownership of personal property can also serve as an expression of identity: the things one lives with and attends to on a daily basis help provide moorings to people, providing a kind of stability of life experience through time.

---

[46] Nickel, 156.

However, rights to the ownership of productive property have many of these same features. The ownership of productive property provides security. Ownership of productive property—say, savings in the form of stocks and bonds—provides individuals and families with a measure of independence. (Permitting citizens to hoard cash, while denying them the right to purchase stocks or other securities, would not be a significant concession to the freedom owed to such citizens). Ownership rights in productive property are not only important for entrepreneurs. Such rights free ordinary, working-class people from forced dependence on the state and its agents. People who have ownership stakes in productive property are by that very fact able to stand on their own feet and make important life choices for themselves. Without such rights, people must depend on the decisions of committees or the outcomes of political campaigns. So the independence and security provided by the right to own productive property is not a mere privilege of economic elites: it is a common experience of citizens in societies where such rights of ownership are affirmed.

Further, just as personal property can be bound up with one's identity, for many people the ownership of productive property plays a profound role in the formation and maintenance of self-authored lives. Sometimes the identity-casting relationships people have to productive property are conspicuously material: as with the way a farmer identifies himself with his field, or the owner of a small business identifies with her shop and its customers and employees.

Other times the identity-casting role of ownership is more intellectual, or activity-based. Successful investment bankers, for example, often take an almost professorial approach to their study of financial trends. Through the roles they play as buyers and sellers of productive property, such people often *become* diligent researchers, creative analysts, and fiercely independent ("contrarian") thinkers. This is true of entrepreneurs in other areas as well.

None of this is to deny that the prospect of financial rewards (beyond that needed for bare security) is a strongly motivating factor in people for whom the personal control of productive property plays a central part of their lives. But rights to the ownership of productive property protect projects that are significant to people for reasons that go far beyond the prospect of personal wealth. Societies that protect the ownership of productive property as a basic right can increase the range of projects, and the forms of economic relationships, that are available to citizens.[47] Such societies broaden the evaluative horizons of citizens. The economic liberties make it possible for citizens with diverse values and interests to

---

[47] For example, I am a shareholder in a cooperatively owned ski area (Mad River Glen, in Fayston, Vermont). As a member of that co-op, I participate in deliberations about how we will manage our collectively owned property (such as our policy, enthusiastically renewed each year, of banning snowboarders).

more fully develop and exercise the powers they have as responsible self-authors.

Economic liberty can enhance the freedom of citizens on the output, or consumer side as well. Many people define themselves by the financial decisions they make for themselves and their families. Should everyone in our family pack his or her own lunch this week so that we will have money to go to a movie or restaurant together next weekend? Is it more important to provide our children with separate bedrooms or to add money to college savings accounts opened in their names? What percentage of my earnings should I spend on living now, and what percentage should I save for retirement and for my end-of-life care? Should I take advantage of a sale to purchase a new television or should I build up my savings in case I lose my job? How much should we spend on sport, or on home entertainment, or on culture, or on education, and over what time frame?

Questions about long-term financial planning require that people think seriously about the relation between the person that each is at that moment and the person one will become many years in the future. They call on people to take responsibility now for the person each will later become. The taking up of these responsibilities is a passageway from the dependence of childhood (or late adolescence) and into the more challenging and independent world of adulthood. On Rawls's own description, we must respect citizens as beings who are "capable of adjusting their aims and aspirations in light of what they can reasonably expect to provide for." Economic decisions call on people to do just this. Such decisions require that people assess their most basic values and, in light of that assessment, set themselves on a course of life that is their own. Economic liberty protects these important aspects of responsible self-authorship. Indeed, among the most important protections needed by responsible self-authors are those that empower individuals to act and to make decisions about the economic aspects of their lives.

Charles Murray writes eloquently about the satisfaction ordinary people gain from work. Paralleling Rawls's discussion of self-respect, Murray says that people need to feel that the things they are doing with their lives are *important*. Murray criticizes the model of the European social democracies on these grounds. Programs for the universal provision of social goods "take the trouble out of life." In doing so, Murray worries, the model "drains too much of the life from life." As a result of one hundred years of economic growth, Murray says that a central problem faced by most citizens in advanced societies is not a lack of material resources but the problem of "how to live *meaningful lives* in an age of plenty and security."[48] By insulating people from economic risks, the European model denies ordinary citizens opportu-

---

[48] Charles Murray, *In Our Hands*, 82 (emphasis mine).

nities to feel the special sense that they have done something genuinely important with their lives. The material benefits of social democracies come with a moral opportunity cost.

Murray describes a man who holds down a janitorial job and thereby supports his family (we could as easily imagine a single-mother who takes on a difficult job). Such people, Murray suggests, are doing something genuinely important with their lives. Regarding the janitor, Murray states "He should take deep satisfaction from that, and be praised by his community for doing so." If those same people lived under a system in which they were heavily insulated from economic risks, for example by being assured that they and their children will be well provided for whether or not they themselves contribute, then that status goes away. "Taking the trouble out of the stuff of life strips people—has already stripped people—of major ways in which human beings look back on their lives and say, 'I made a difference.' "[49] The experience of risk seems to be an essential precondition of the sort of self-respect that liberals value.

We should worry about the high liberal platform of economic exceptionalism for all these reasons. A society that denies people the chance to take up questions of long-term financial planning for themselves, or that restricts the ways in which individuals and families can respond to such questions, thereby diminishes the capacity of its citizens to become fully responsible and independent agents. So too a society that limits the freedom of individuals to negotiate the specific terms of their employment, or that makes their ownership of productive property subject to calculations about social expediency, no matter how benevolent their intentions in doing so, thereby creates social conditions in which the moral powers of citizens can be exercised and developed in only a stunted way. Just as respect for the freedom and equality of citizens requires the recognition of religious, associational and intellectual liberty, respect for citizens requires the recognition of economic liberty as well. As a requirement of liberal legitimacy, and to respect the freedom and independence of all classes of citizens, wide-ranging rights of economic liberty should be recognized as among the basic rights of liberal citizens.

When I say that private economic liberties are among the *basic* rights of liberal citizens, I am not suggesting that these rights will play an equally important role in the self-authorship of every citizen. The private economic liberties may be more central to the process by which a small-business owner develops herself as a responsible self-author than they are in the case of someone with a different life plan—say one centrally concerned with political campaigning. So too, the exercise of political liberties may be more central to the life project of the campaigner than they are

---

[49] "The Happiness of the People" *2009 Irving Kristol Lecture,* American Enterprise Institute for Public Policy Research, (Washington, DC: The AEI Press, 2009), 7–9.

to the business owner, just as religious liberties may be more important to the self-authorship of a practicing Catholic (or a committed atheist) than to a person who rarely considers spiritual issues at all. Rather, in recognizing these rights as *basic*, we affirm them as components of a fully adequate scheme of rights and liberties. As a set, basic rights allow citizens to develop their capacities of responsible self-authorship, without requiring that they all conform to any one view of the good life (or even agree about the relative importance of personal decision-making in these different spheres of their lives—political, economic, and religious, for example).[50]

This, precisely, is the problem with the high liberal approach. Rawls makes the protection of private economic liberty a political matter, one to be decided by different liberal societies in different ways in light of cultural conditions. Thus, "liberal (democratic) socialism" would allow only rights to personal (nonproductive) property, while "property-owning democracy" would allow (limited) rights to the private ownership of productive property as well. But this way of accommodating the importance of private economic liberty flouts the requirements of democratic legitimacy. Like political liberty (and religious liberty too), the protection of private economic freedom is a precondition of citizens' extending their evaluative horizons. In seeking the most appropriate specification of the basic rights and liberties, we seek the specification that most fully allows citizens to develop themselves as responsible self-authors and that displays the respect they have for their fellow citizens as responsible self-authors too. As I have argued, private economic liberties have a special role in protecting citizens as they develop and exercise these moral capacities. The platform of economic exceptionalism renders high liberalism a morally impoverished view.

There is an elephant standing within the theoretical framework of high liberalism. For it is not only classical liberals and libertarians who affirm the fundamental importance of private economic liberty. Like most citizens in contemporary western liberal constitutional democracies, I suspect that most contemporary high liberals would affirm a significantly thicker conception of economic liberty than high liberal paragons such as Mill and Rawls. As Jeremy Waldron admits: "nobody these days seriously imagines an economy either at the national or international level in which private property and markets do not loom large."[51] But if left liberals

---

[50] Conversation with Charles Larmore sharpened my understanding of these issues, even though our convictions on these matters diverge.

[51] Waldron, "Socioeconomic Rights and Theories of Justice," working manuscript November 2010, http://www.law.nyu.edu/ecm_dlv2/groups/public/@nyu_law_website__academics__colloquia__law_economics_and_politics/documents/documents/ecm_pro_066908.pdf, p. 3.) Most democratic theorists argue that private property is publically justifiable so long as welfare rights are also guaranteed (typically by the state). See Corey Brettschneider *Democratic Rights: The Substance of Self-Government* (Princeton, NJ: Princeton University Press, 2007), especially 114-35.

abandon the canonical high liberal platform of economic exceptionalism, they immediately begin moving away from a social democratic and toward a more market-democratic interpretation of basic rights. In taking those steps, high liberals do not necessarily have to become full-blown market democrats. They might still claim that some aspects of private economic liberty should be splintered off and denied the protection accorded to the other liberal rights. But then they owe us a moral explanation of how any such narrowing of private economic liberty enhances the status of persons as responsible self-authors. There are reasons why such arguments are unlikely to be forthcoming.

First, any proposal to limit core economic freedoms must not run afoul of the basic liberal concern for the self-respect of citizens. Rawls describes self-respect as having two aspects: a sense of one's own value and a reasonable confidence in one's ability to fulfill one's intentions.[52] With respect to that second aspect, left liberals typically hasten to emphasize that it requires that people be given the material means needed to pursue their goals effectively. But, as we have seen, the mere possession of material means is not sufficient: a person's self-respect is diminished if one is not (and so cannot think of oneself as) the central *cause* of the life one is leading. Having others secure them with "material means" could not provide liberal citizens with that form of self-respect.

There is an analogy with feminism. Before feminism brought about the recognition of women as legal bearers of private economic liberties, women were denied essential preconditions of their self-respect. Having others provide them with all the "gilded material means" in the world could not secure that self-respect for them.[53]

Margaret Holmgren argues that people have a fundamental interest not simply in doing well in life (say in the sense of possessing certain goods) but in doing well *as a consequence of their own activities*. Indeed, Holmgren sees economic agency as a primary good, a precondition of self-respect. Parties in Rawls's original position, therefore, "would want to secure for themselves the opportunity to advance by their own efforts."[54] As Holmgren points out, recognizing this interest does not require that it always trumps all other interests people have: in situations in which people are simply unable to act for themselves, their needs may well be tended to by others without damage to their self-respect. But in the ordinary course of life, she argues, people do have a fundamental interest in seeing themselves as central causes of the lives they are leading. People respect themselves, in part, because of their own genuine achievements. Economic liberties protect this fundamental interest.

[52] Rawls, *Theory of Justice*, rev. ed., 155–7; 386–7.
[53] I develop this idea in "Can Feminism Be Liberated from Governmentalism?" *Toward a Humanist Justice: Essays in Honor of Susan Okin* (New York: Oxford University Press, 2009).
[54] Margaret Holmgren, "Justifying Desert Claims: Desert and Opportunity," *The Journal of Value Inquiry* 20 (1986): 265–78.

Moreover, and significantly, Rawls emphasizes that a condition of the first aspect of self-respect—valuing oneself—is that one be esteemed by others. So Rawls's account of self-respect stresses the importance of status, how we think others value us. Regarding this need for status, crucially, Rawls writes: "the need for status is met by the public recognition of just institutions, together with the full and diverse internal life of the many free communities of interests that the equal liberties allow." Thus, *"the basis for self-respect in a just society is not then one's income share but the publicly affirmed distribution of fundamental rights and liberties."* [55]

And so, with respect to the fundamental economic liberties, market democracy again asks: How can individuals have self-respect if their fellow citizens deny them the right to decide for themselves how many hours they will work each week and under what precise terms and conditions? How can they think of themselves as esteemed by their fellow citizens if those citizens call on the coercive force of the law to impede them in deciding for themselves how much (or little) to save for retirement, the minimum wage they may find acceptable for various forms of work, or to dictate to them the parameters of the medical care that will be available to them?

In emphasizing the importance of economic liberty for responsible self-authorship, I do not deny the other, more instrumental, rationales that classical liberals sometimes offer in defense of property rights and other economic liberties. A robust system of economic liberty—regarding ownership and working—can assist people in making the most efficient use of dispersed knowledge for productive purposes. [56] Economic liberties allow diverse social interests to be peacefully coordinated without recourse to coercive, collective procedures. Property rights can provide bases of resistance against corrupt, oppressive, and fiscally irresponsible uses of political power. [57] The economic liberties are also linked strongly to many other basic rights, in the sense that "blocking them substantially blocks important parts of other liberties that are widely accepted as basic" (for example, economic liberty is linked to freedoms of religion, communication, association, movement, as well as political liberty). [58]

My primary argument for a thick conception of economic liberty, however, is the moral one. Regardless of the orthodoxies we have inherited, open-minded advocates of deliberative democracy should reject the platform of economic exceptionalism. A thick conception of economic liberty is a requirement of democratic legitimacy.

---

[55] Rawls, *Theory of Justice*, rev. ed., 476 (emphasis mine).
[56] F. A. Hayek, "The Use of Knowledge in Society, *American Economic Review* (American Economic Association, 1945).
[57] Milton Friedman, *Capitalism and Freedom* (Chicago: The University of Chicago, 1962), 15.
[58] Drawing on the work of Henry Shue, Nickel calls arguments for economic liberty of this type "linkage arguments" (in "Economic Liberties," 157. For historical discussion, see Richard Pipes, *Property and Freedom* (New York: Alfred A. Knopf, 1999).

V. Kantian Roots

I have been describing market democracy as offering an alternative approach toward private economic liberty taken by contemporary high liberal theorists. But this market democratic approach to economic liberty can claim deep roots in the high liberal tradition as well.[59]

Along with Mill, Immanuel Kant is often mentioned as a founding figure of high liberalism.[60] Kant's political philosophy, like his moral philosophy, is founded on an ideal of autonomy. Freedom, in the sense of being a chooser of one's own ends, is the fundamental right of every person. By virtue of their common humanity, persons have an equal right to this freedom.[61] But freedom also requires that agents be able to choose the means to their ends. Since we are material beings seeking to exercise our autonomy in a material world, we require "external objects of choice" to pursue our ends. For Kant, secure rights to property emerge as postulates of reason derived from our common nature as independent choosers. Reason also shows that the state is required to convert the provisional rights to property in the state of nature into formal rights backed by law. Property rights, for Kant, are among the most important rights of citizens. So Kant is a mixed figure in the history of liberal thought. Because of his emphasis on the moral capacities of citizens and the idea of public authorization of right, Kant can be called an early high liberal. Because of his emphasis on economic liberty and the ideal of formal equality, however, Kant might just as well be described as a classical liberal.[62]

Kant's approach helps highlight the differences between market democracy and the approaches of classical liberals and libertarians working in the Lockean tradition. Following Locke, many classical liberals ground

[59] The account of Kant's theory of property given in this paragraph, as well as the contrast between Kant and Locke developed in the next paragraph, is informed by research done for me over the summer of 2010 by Jason Swadley, as well as by a superb unpublished article manuscript by Swadley entitled "Economic Liberty and the High Liberal Tradition" (draft of August 2010). My understanding of Kant's political philosophy also particularly has been improved by Arthur Ripstein's *Force and Freedom: Kant's Legal and Political Philosophy*, (Cambridge, MA: Harvard University Press, 2009). The applications of these ideas to market democracy are my own.

[60] Freeman, "Illiberal Libertarians," 106. Note that, in a departure from my usual terminological practice, I am here using the term "high liberal" to denote a method of justification, rather than a set of substantive moral commitments. Classified in terms of his substantive moral commitments, Kant is a classical liberal (on which see the following note).

[61] "*Freedom* (independence from being constrained by another's choice), insofar as it can coexist with the freedom of every other in accordance with a universal law, is the only original right belonging to every man by virtue of his humanity." Immanuel Kant, *Practical Philosophy* (Cambridge University Press, 1999), 393.

[62] Allen Wood writes: "Kant's political philosophy or theory of right, considered by itself, is merely a version of classical liberalism." Wood continues: "It is based on two familiar liberal tenets: (1) Competition is nature's means for the development of human faculties; and (2) The state's function is to regulate competition by protecting property and coercively enforcing formal principles of right." (Allen W. Wood, "Kant and the Problem of Human Nature" in Brian Jacobs, ed., *Essays on Kant's Anthropology* (Cambridge Books Online, Cambridge University Press, 2009), 22.

property in some concept of self-ownership. On this approach, property rights emerge as a relation of persons to objects in the world: for example, by the process of self-owners mixing their labor with unowned things. Conceived of this way, property rights are strongly prior to the state. The state exists to protect preexisting rights and so is bounded by those rights.[63] Market democracy takes a more Kantian approach. Rather than grounding a thick conception of economic liberty on self-ownership, market democracy focuses on the moral ideal of citizens living together as responsible self-authors. Market democracy affirms a wide range of individual freedom regarding economic questions for the same reasons it affirms general liberties with respect to religious and associational questions: a thick conception of economic liberty is a necessary condition of responsible self-authorship. Ownership rights, on this approach, are not so much relations between persons and objects as they are relations between persons as moral agents. Rights emerge as a social recognition that honoring the capacity of one's fellow citizens to be self-authors requires that one respects their capacity to make choices of their own regarding economic matters. To restrict the capacity of people to make economic choices or, worse, to treat their economic activities merely as means to the social ends of others, would violate the dignity of such persons and so would be to treat them unjustly. Wide rights to economic liberty, while recognizable without the state, are validated and made fully binding by the political community. For market democracy, the requirements of economic liberty help define the shape and limits of the state, even without being radically prior to it.

Kant's political theory also helps highlight another important difference between market democracy and traditional classical liberal views: while many classical liberals advocate a social safety net funded by taxation, market democracy can provide a rationale for the safety net that is thoroughly principled. (Recall that a rationale for a policy is "thoroughly principled" if the same reasoning that supports the wider features of the view also support that particular policy.) For Kant, the state exists as a requirement of the free and independent nature of the citizens. As an empirical fact, citizens sometimes fall into conditions of abject poverty. Citizens in that position become dependent on the charity of others and so become unable to participate in the united will needed to authorize public law. Kant advocates a tax-funded safety net: "For reasons of state, the government is therefore authorized to constrain the wealthy to provide the means of sustenance to those who are unable to provide for even their most necessary natural needs." [64] Market democracy's affirmation of

---

[63] In the opening lines of *Anarchy, State, and Utopia*, Nozick states: "Individuals have rights, and there are things that no other person or group may do to them (without violating their rights). So strong and far-reaching are these rights that they raise the question of what, if anything, the state and its officials may do." p. ix.

[64] Kant, *Practical Philosophy*, 468 (quoted in Swadley, 12).

tax-funded social safety net programs follows this pattern. The very status of people as responsible self-authors may be threatened by conditions of extreme need. The state must be empowered to act to protect people's moral status as self-authors. But, unlike many traditional classical liberals, market democracy's justification of the safety net is strongly principled. After all, the same reasons that market democracy uses to justify the social safety net also justify the market democratic position against the pervasive encroachments on economic liberty allowed by high liberals such as Rawls. Without constitutional guarantees protecting their independent economic decision-making, people cannot fully exercise their moral powers of self-authorship. For all these reasons, market democracy affirms the importance of economic liberty, and thus rejects the high liberal platform of economic exceptionalism.

VI. Conclusion

At the start of the essay, I said that market democracy rests on three theses: 1) the private economic liberties of capitalism are among the basic rights of all liberal citizens, 2) social justice, on some interpretation to be specified, is the ultimate standard of evaluation for liberal political and economic institutions, and 3) as a matter of ideal theoretic analysis, the institutions of market democracy realize the conception of social justice specified in thesis 2) even while affirming the priority of economic liberty set out in 1).

I have focused on the first thesis, arguing that a thick conception of economic liberty is a requirement of democratic legitimacy. However, that first thesis is entangled with the other two in an interesting way. In particular, people who start with strong commitments to social justice [as contained in thesis number 2)] may well worry that the affirmation of private economic liberties as basic rights may rule out the achievement of social justice [against the assertion made in thesis 3)].

According to Samuel Freeman, for example, an implication of the claim that economic liberties should be treated on a par with the other basic rights and liberties is that "it limits considerably a liberal society's ability to regulate the uses of property, economic contracts, and business transactions and activities." Without such regulations, small numbers of people could establish economic monopolies that would leave many citizens destitute and unemployed. Under these conditions, Freeman continues, many free and equal citizens would be unable to achieve economic independence and so be unable to pursue a wide range of reasonable life plans.[65]

Two points about this worry are worth noting. First, market democracy's claim that economic liberties are among the basic constitutional lib-

[65] Freeman, *Rawls* (New York: Routledge, 2007), 57.

erties is a *moral* claim. The claim stands or falls on the strength of the
arguments that can be brought forth to show that these economic liberties, like the other basic liberties, are essential preconditions to citizens
exercising their moral powers. If that moral argument is persuasive, then
an argument based on the secondary institutional implications of that
claim has little force. It is true that the market democratic interpretation
about the constitutional place of economic liberty would greatly limit the
regulatory power of the state in economic affairs (compared, for example,
to the economic powers granted to the legislative bodies under left-liberal
regimes). But if, as market democracy claims, the protection of thick
economic liberty is a "first principle" concern of legitimacy, this observation might call into question the cogency of market democracy as an
integrated liberal view, but it cannot count as an objection to thesis 1). It
would be akin to objecting to religious liberty on the grounds that such
liberty would greatly limit the power of the state to regulate the religious
affairs of citizens.

The second part of the objection—that the market democratic affirmation of a general right of economic liberty would result in a social world
in which great numbers of citizens were dominated unjustly by a small
group of economic elites—raises more difficult questions. I believe that
this objection, or something like it, plays an important motivational role
in the thinking of many people who are committed to the traditional
institutions of high liberalism. However, this objection rests on controversial ideas about the requirements of social justice, and about the nature
and task of political philosophy itself.

Liberals who work within the deliberative framework can reasonably
disagree about the distributional requirements of social justice. I noted
one dimension of these disagreements earlier: some think social justice is
mainly about equality, while others think it is mainly about giving priority to the interests of the most poor. Rawls's difference principle, which
requires that we prefer social and economic arrangements that benefit the
poor, might reasonably be interepreted as a prioritarian principle. But
even taking that interpretation, we face difficult questions about how to
specify what should count as a "benefit" to the members of the least
well-off class.[66] One approach, which Samuel Freeman has recently attributed to Rawls, sees the experience of workplace democracy as among the
weightiest "benefits" that the difference principle requires us to maximize, even if that requires the reduction of other benefits such as wealth
and income.[67] I call this a "social democratic" approach to social justice
and contrast it with the market democratic approach that I myself prefer.
On that latter approach, the full range of rights and liberties is in place,

[66] Phillipe van Parijs, "Difference Principles" in Samuel Freeman, ed., *The Cambridge Companion to Rawls* (Cambridge University Press, 2002).
[67] Samuel Freeman, "Capitalism in the Classical and High Liberal Tradition," *Social Philosophy and Policy* 28 (2011).

and the morally most appropriate way to "benefit" the least well off is by maximizing the bundle of wealth and income personally controlled by the members of that class. I defend this market-democratic thesis about social justice at length elsewhere, so I will not repeat those arguments here.[68] Setting out this interpretive marker, however, helps us when we turn to thesis 3), and the questions about the nature and purpose of political philosophy that arise there.

As a matter of sociological fact, we must acknowledge that a market-democratic regime that affirms thick economic liberty, however lofty the other aims it announces for itself when affirming such liberties, might well degenerate into an unjust society in which some citizens use their positions to prey upon others. But it is equally true that a democratic-socialist regime, or any of the other regime-types favored by high liberals, could, as a matter of sociological fact, fail to achieve its aims and instead degenerate into a condition of exploitation, fiscal irresponsibility, and injustice. In the real world of social life, problems of feasibility, and the possibility of abject failure, are permanent residents.

The question, however, is what philosophers should make of this fact. Perhaps the objection to market democracy is not simply that its favored institutional regimes *could possibly* degenerate in this way, but rather that they are *more likely* to so degenerate than those favored by high liberals (even allowing each to interpret the distributive requirements of social justice by its own lights). Still, this is an empirical claim. Even if it could be decided, a question of philosophical methodology would remain: In the domain of political philosophy, what is the normative status of this empirical claim regarding the relative *likelihood* of rival regimes achieving or failing to achieve their announced aims? Read as a claim about likelihood, the argument in favor of thin economic liberty would rest on the idea that social-democratic regimes should be identified as morally superior because they are more likely, as a practical empirical matter, to achieve the aims of social justice than are market-democratic ones. Viewed this way, however, the concern about degeneration is not so much an objection to market democracy as it is a challenge to defenders of that view. Such defenders must either dispute the empirical claim that market-democratic regimes are less likely to achieve social justice (as they interpret it) than the left-liberal regime-types favored by high liberals, or they must explain why these concerns about empirical likelihood are not relevant to the task of political philosophy, correctly understood.

I believe the market democratic regimes can be defended on both sets of grounds, empirical and ideal-theoretic. Again simply adverting to arguments I develop elsewhere, I believe that the most important defense of market democracy from a philosophical perspective is the one that runs on the level of ideal theory. In working out his idea of

---

[68] John Tomasi, *Free Market Fairness*, chap. 6 "Two Concepts of Fairness."

"realistic utopianism," Rawls argues that for a candidate regime-type to realize liberal justice, it must aim at liberal justice and also include institutional arrangements that, even if unlikely to achieve justice in some particular set of social conditions, nonetheless could possibly achieve justice. This is the ideal theoretic test that Rawls employs when he identifies his own preferred regime-types—property-owning democracy and liberal socialism—as realizing justice (on his social democratic interpretation of that standard).[69] But employing that same ideal theoretic test, it is not hard to demonstrate that a range of market-democratic regime-types equally realize justice (on our market-democratic interpretation.) Through the lens of ideal theory, regimes that affirm thick conceptions of economic liberty and regimes that adopt a platform of economic exceptionalism are on all fours regarding the question of whether they "realize" the distributional requirements of social justice (as interpreted by each).[70]

I emphasis these points in order to show that market democracy is not merely an *alternative* to the social-democratic conceptions of social justice that have dominated academic discussions for decades. Instead, market democracy is a *moral challenger* to those other more familiar liberal views. Part of the moral challenge market democracy poses to social-democratic approaches resides in the alternative interpretation market democracy offers of the distributional requirements of social justice, such as the difference principle. But market democracy presents a first-level moral challenge to traditional forms of high liberalism as well. A thick conception of economic liberty is a requirement of democratic legitimacy itself. Any account of liberal justice that fails to affirm the economic liberties of capitalism as basic rights is morally defective from the start.

Philosophy and Political Science, Brown University

[69] Rawls, *Justice As Fairness*, 135–40.
[70] John Tomasi, *Free Market Fairness*, chap. 7 "Feasibility, Normativity, and Institutional Guarantees" and chap. 8 "Free Market Fairness."

WHO OWNS WHAT? SOME REFLECTIONS ON THE FOUNDATION OF POLITICAL PHILOSOPHY

By Lloyd P. Gerson

I. Introduction

Works in political philosophy typically build—either explicitly or implicitly—on a foundational concept of rights or of justice; neither of these, however, is satisfactory as a starting point. The concept of rights is unsatisfactory because it is either defined in terms of something else, which is in that case the real foundation, or else it is employed arbitrarily as a matter of intuition. But of course intuitions differ. Presumably, the most plausible candidate for a foundational concept of rights would be natural rights. Natural rights are so called because they are supposedly rooted in human nature. Yet the inherent normativity in the concept of rights is not easily or clearly derived from a nontendentious account of human nature.[1] As for intuitions about rights, few political philosophers seem to limit their accounts of rights to what have been called negative rights.[2] A foundational concept of negative rights faces the intuition problem: which rights, whose rights? But with the introduction of positive rights, the possibility of a conflict of rights inevitably arises and a truly foundational rights theory has, in principle, no resources for resolving these.[3] Founding a political philosophy on a concept of justice has seemed more promising to some. Yet, if "justice" is not merely a formal term like "good," then neither is "injustice." And one is then obliged to provide an

[1] See James Griffin, *On Human Rights* (Oxford: Oxford University Press, 2008), 33, who argues that human rights "can be seen as protections of our human standing or, as I shall put it, our personhood." So, for Griffin, human personhood is basic. Griffin's concept of human personhood, however, is almost entirely derived from his intuitions about human rights. The concept of personhood is designed to generate exactly Griffin's list of human rights. See, e.g., page 51, where Griffin includes in his concept of personhood "minimum provision" for a human life. See also page 101, where Griffin concedes the arbitrariness of much of his account.

[2] One of these is Robert Nozick, *Anarchy, State, and Utopia* (New York: Basic Books, 1974), 10, 118, who seems to rest political philosophy on a Lockean theory of "rights possessed by each individual in a state of nature." These are negative rights.

[3] Since, on a theory of negative rights, conflicts of rights are, at least in some versions, impossible in the way that they are not so on a theory of positive rights, the reason for rejecting the former is slightly different from the reason for rejecting the latter. The very rejection of positive rights in favor of negative rights presumes a criterion for the rejection which in turn requires some moral principle to justify that criterion. Hence, rights are not basic. I emphasize here that my claim is that rights and justice are not basic in political philosophy. I am not here addressing the question of their role in moral theory as basic or not.

doi:10.1017/S0265052511000069

argument for the claim that a certain specific state of affairs is unjust. So, for example, if one holds that justice is equality, then one must explain why inequality is unjust. Appeals to intuitions are obviously irrelevant since there are those whose intuitions lead them to maintain the opposite.[4] Appeals to hypothetical individuals making foundational decisions on the basis of pure rationality are ultimately no different. For, the hypothetical individual usually looks suspiciously like an avatar of the author, thus making "just" anyone who agrees with that author and "unjust" anyone who does not.

I shall argue that in fact the concepts of justice and rights are derivative— the concept of rights is in particular a highly derivative one. More particularly, I shall argue that rights are to be defined in terms of justice and that justice is to be defined in terms of property.[5] That is, the deprivation of property is the only injustice there is. Admittedly, this heterodox conclusion will require some explaining. I begin not directly with a concept of property, but with the necessary ontological subject of property: moral agents. The view for which I shall argue is that only individual human beings are moral agents. I am especially keen to show that groups—such as corporations or states—are *not* moral agents. The relevance of this to discussions about the foundation of political theory will I hope emerge as we go along.

II. Moral Agency

I begin by offering a brief account of what an agent is, and then go on to consider what additional factors could turn agents into moral agents. With the intention of being as uncontroversial as possible (at this stage) I offer this account of moral agency at a rather high level of generality—so high, in fact, that it is shared by many philosophers with radically differing moral theories. Most, if not all, of the controversy in political philosophy springs from the conclusions that are variously drawn on the basis of this account.

An agent is a source of change in another or in itself as other. By "source of change" I mean that which will serve as an explanation of a given change. Both living things like plants and animals, and nonliving things like machines and hurricanes are all examples of agents. Animals, for the most part, differ from the rest because they not only can cause

---

[4] G. A. Cohen, *Rescuing Justice and Equality* (Cambridge, MA: Harvard University Press, 2008), 4, frankly acknowledges that his radical egalitarian concept of justice is founded on his own "deepest normative convictions." This certainly looks like an intuition that dares not speak its own name.

[5] Compare David Schmidtz, "Property and Justice," *Social Philosophy and Policy* 27, no. 1 (2010): 79–100, who provides a somewhat different argument for what is essentially the same claim.

changes in other things but, owing to their self-locomotive power, they can change themselves.

For the sake of simplicity, it is well to distinguish agents from the instruments of their agency. One *could* say that the flying rock was the agent of change in the window or that the boy who threw the rock was the agent. I would prefer to say that the boy was the agent and that the rock was the instrument, largely because attribution of agency is usually part of an explanatory framework. Explanations are conceptually tied to criteria for the adequacy of explanations. In reply to the query about the agent responsible for causing the window to be broken, only the boy would take the attribution of agency to the rock as explanatorily adequate. But owing to the fact that genuine agents typically cause changes in other things by means of instruments, it is possible to layer attributions of agency. Such layering is relatively unproblematic in cases when we are dealing with individual agents, when, for example, we say that the hand turned the doorknob or the woman turned the doorknob with her hand. But the above very general account of agency allows for the possibility that there should be group agents, in which case the layering may be more complex and controversial.[6]

It seems to me that it is perfectly reasonable to say that Italy can defeat Germany in soccer competition, or that one can be fired by a corporation, or that the party upstairs is disturbing my sleep. One may, however, also say that the defeat was owing to the goal made by one player, or that the firing was caused by the words of the personnel manager, or that it was the voice of one reveller that kept me awake. These people would seem both to be instruments of group agency and to be acting as agents in their own right. Someone affecting metaphysical parsimony might maintain that Italy's defeat of Germany in soccer is nothing but the result of the action of the individual agent or, perhaps more plausibly, the complex sum of the acts of multiple individual agents. I find this approach overly fastidious, principally because the explanatory role of the individual agent only makes sense within the framework of the group action. The reduction of group agency to individual agency is no more compelling than is the reduction of individual agency to agency at the microscopic physical level. I take it, though, that one who wished to deny that groups can be agents would, a fortiori, deny that groups can be moral agents. Conversely, one who wants to argue that groups are moral agents is committed to the view that groups are agents.

---

[6] The view I am developing here is a version of what is sometimes called a theory of agent causation as opposed to events causation. The basis for the general view is that agents are irreducible to events in an explanatory framework. Some proponents of agent causation do not distinguish agents from moral agents. See J. Hornsby, "Agency and Actions," in *Agency and Action*, ed. John Hyman and Helen Steward (Cambridge: Cambridge University Press, 2004), 1–23, for an argument for the explanatory superiority of agent causation over events causation.

The concept of a moral agent seems to me to provide the relevant link between the metaphysical concept of person and the implicit normativity of ascriptions of personhood. Moral agents are not logically coextensive with human beings. It is, I take it, an empirical matter whether a particular human being or a particular nonhuman being is a moral agent. It is not similarly an empirical matter, however, whether persons are moral agents, or so I shall argue. Part of what is meant when ascribing personhood is the presence of moral agency. The normativity implicit in the ascription of personhood is revealed in this fact.

As John Locke famously argued, the term "person" is a "forensic one, appropriating actions and their merit; and so belongs only to intelligent agents, capable of a law, and happiness and misery."[7] The forensic dimension of personhood appears in the determination of moral responsibility in law. It is the moral agent who is morally responsible. That we do not typically deny personhood to those who have been determined not to be morally responsible for a particular action is owing precisely to the non-arbitrariness of the ascription of personhood. We suppose that personhood has, at least paradigmatically, *something* to do with humanity and so we are disinclined to deny it to the human being who is declared innocent in court owing to his not having been morally responsible. We believe he *could have been* morally responsible because he is a person.

A claim that we ought or ought not to ascribe personhood to a particular human being is, thus, a function of the ascription of moral agency. A moral agent is, at the very least, one who could be, under suitably defined circumstances, held morally responsible for his or her actions. To be held morally responsible is to be thought to be capable of acting according to some norm. And so a claim about the ascription of personhood, understood as implying claims about how we ought to act in regard to someone to whom personhood is ascribed, is connected to a claim about how that person ought to act as well.[8]

The presence of moral agency or personhood in an individual guarantees at least the intelligibility of the ascription of moral responsibility. Roughly, moral agents or persons are the sorts of thing we suppose could understand the nature and consequences of their actions and have that understanding inform their actions as well. Daniel Dennett has shown

[7] See John Locke, *An Essay Concerning Human Understanding*, ed. P. H. Nidditch (Oxford: Clarendon Press, 1979) Book II, chap. 26.
[8] See John Rawls, "Justice as Fairness," *Philosophical Review* 67 (1958): 166, who includes under the concept "person" nations, provinces, business firms, churches, teams, and so on. He thinks that all of these are subject to laws of justice, though he acknowledges a "logical priority [to] human individuals." In John Rawls, *The Law of Peoples: With "The Idea of Public Reason Revisited"* (Cambridge, MA: Harvard University Press, 1999), 27, he distinguishes "peoples" from states, arguing that it is the former to which a "moral character" may be ascribed. Rawls seems to hold, however, that a state acting in a just way would be indistinguishable from a "people." Immanuel Kant, *Perpetual Peace*, ed. Hans Reiss, 2d edition (Cambridge, MA: Cambridge University Press, 1991), section 1.2, assumes that states or nations are moral persons and, accordingly, fall under (his) moral rules.

with characteristic clarity that the intentionality that is a facet of this understanding is not sufficient in itself for personhood or moral agency.[9] He argues that any object whose behavior can be predicted by assuming the "intentional stance" in regard to it can be considered an "intentional system." Adopting the intentional stance "consists of treating the object whose behavior you want to predict as a rational agent with beliefs and desires and other mental states, exhibiting what Franz Brentano and others call "intentionality." As Dennett proceeds to show, adopting the stance can work perfectly well even for plants or natural phenomena like lightning. Thus, assuming that the plant *wants* to blossom or that the lightning is trying to find the fastest way to the ground, enables us to take steps in response to this in order to achieve *our* goals—in these cases, to get flowers in our garden or to avoid being struck down by lightning.

If the possession of intentional states by plants and lightning just means that it makes sense for us to adopt the intentional stance in regard to them, we should for this reason be wary of supposing that the possession of intentional states is sufficient to constitute personhood or moral agency. What the proponent of the view that nations or corporations are moral agents needs is a sense of "intentionality" such that the putative moral agent with the intentional states—the nation—can be intelligibly classified with unquestioned moral agents and not with plants and natural phenomena. What is that sense?

If we consider for a moment the grounds for our attribution or denial of moral agency, we typically say something like, "he is aware of what he is doing" or "he is no longer aware of what he is doing" or even, "he is no longer aware of who he is." Self-awareness or cognition of one's own states, intentional or otherwise, is surely what we find missing in someone whom we have decided is no longer a moral agent. This self-awareness is to be distinguished from the awareness that consists in behavioral responses to various external stimuli. The response to stimuli may, of course, be attributed to anything capable of what in biology is recognized as a response, like a plant, or even, if we extend the applicability of the term "response," to something like lightning, which can in a sense respond to our strategies employed to divert it from its natural path.

Apart from our typical ordinary-language characterization of what differentiates a moral agent from one who has lost this status, there are many technical versions of this characterization in the literature. Dennett himself characterizes it as a "special sort of consciousness, namely, self-consciousness." Robert Sokolowski uses the term "moral categoriality" to describe it, by which he means, "thoughtful behavior" and "the installa-

---

[9] See Daniel C. Dennett, "Conditions of Personhood," in *The Identities of Persons*, ed. Amélie Oksenberg Rorty (Berkeley: University of California Press, 1976; reprint, *Brainstorms*), 176–78; Daniel C. Dennett, *The Intentional Stance* (Cambridge, MA: MIT Press, 1987), 15–22.

tion of reason into our likes and dislikes."[10] Harry Frankfurt, in a series of justly renowned papers, understands a person—by which Frankfurt means what I mean by a moral agent—as one who is capable of having first and second-order desire, that is, desires about one's own occurrent desires.[11] These second-order desires Frankfurt calls "second-order volitions," desires that the first-order desire be or not be effective in action. Richard Moran uses the technical term "avowal" to describe the fundamental feature of self-knowledge and rational agency.[12] An avowal is a statement of one's belief when that belief is transparent" to oneself.[13] John Martin Fischer uses the term "guidance control" as the basis for the ascription of moral responsibility.[14]

What these views (and many, many other versions) have in common is a recognition that moral agency requires internal complexity of a particular sort, what I shall call "self-reflexivity." It requires that agents have mental states and also that they have cognitive access, at least at some of the time, to those mental states. It is not enough for moral agency that one possesses a desire; one must be able to recognize and somehow respond rationally or cognitively to that desire. Having a desire or ascribing a desire is sufficient grounds for adopting Dennett's intentional stance. But having a cognitive relation to one's own desire is necessary for moral agency. The reason why this fact in itself leaves open the question of whether nonhumans are moral agents is that we have no means of going beyond the intentional stance in our encounter with them. For all we know, a cat *may* be thinking about its own desire for a tasty mouse treat when it sniffs through the bush. But our responses to cats do not presume this and it is difficult to know how, short of having a conversation with the cat, we could ever conclude that it is so.

Can the requisite self-reflexivity belong to a group, specifically, a group of moral agents? Assuming a psychological, as opposed to a biological, criterion for personhood or moral agency, we cannot just assume that the answer to this question is no. One strategy for arriving at the conclusion that groups can be moral agents is to argue for the existence of irreducible

---

[10] See Robert Sokolowski, "What Is Moral Action?" *New Scholasticism* 63 (1989): 23–25.

[11] See, e.g., Harry G. Frankfurt, "Freedom of the Will and the Concept of a Person," *Journal of Philosophy* 68 (1971): 5–20.

[12] See Richard Moran, *Authority and Estrangement: An Essay on Self-Knowledge* (Princeton: Princeton University Press, 2001), especially chaps. 3–4.

[13] Ibid., 101.

[14] See John Martin Fischer, *The Metaphysics of Free Will* (Oxford: Blackwell, 1994), 132–34. "Guidance control" is contrasted with "regulative control." The latter indicates that the agent "could have done otherwise." It is notable that in Fischer's account, the possession of guidance control and, therefore, of moral responsibility does not exclude causal determinism. Cf. 204–5. So, too, on the account of Harry G. Frankfurt, "Alternate Possibilities and Moral Responsibility," *Journal of Philosophy* 66 (1969): 829–39. See Christine M. Korsgaard, "Self-Constitution: Agency, Identity, and Integrity," *The John Locke Lectures at Oxford University*, (2002); Connie Rosati, "Agency and the Open Question Argument," *Ethics* 113 (2003): 490–527, for two similar accounts in terms of "self-constitution."

group intentions.[15] The idea here is to show that any group, even one as small as a group of two, can collectively intend to do something, where the intention is not reducible to the "sum" of each person's individual intention. These shared intentions or "we-intentions", should they exist, might be thought to import with them a form of moral agency. If, for example, you and I have a shared intention to commit a crime, then it might be supposed that you and I bear a shared moral responsibility which, on my accounting, would be a necessary and sufficient condition for moral agency.

Shared agency (as opposed to mere agency) depends crucially on the social practices that give meaning to that that sort of agent. That one football team can defeat another only makes sense in the context of the conventions of the game. Indeed, this is equally the case for corporate legal responsibility. I strongly suspect that the plausibility of the view that groups can be moral agents derives from treating moral responsibility as if it were legal responsibility. This plausibility dissolves if we can track—as we surely can—the moral responsibility of the members of the corporation; we could accomplish such tracking through a process of affirming shared intentions regarding the acts of commission or omission of the corporate body to which we wish to assign moral responsibility.[16]

A crucial property of moral agents is the ability to act voluntarily. Broadly speaking, if such an ability were to be defined negatively, that is, as an absence of constraint or ignorance in acting, then nonmoral agents, including animals, would in fact seem to be moral agents. Agents like animals can act voluntarily, but their volition is nonrational, by which I mean that they are incapable of conceptualizing their desires, so far as we can tell. Such conceptualization is a prerequisite for practical syllogistic reasoning. And it is such reasoning that is the core of the idea of volition in moral agents.

[15] See John Searle, "Collective Intentions and Actions," in *Intentions in Communication*, ed. Philip Cohen, Jerry Morgan, and Martha Pollack (Cambridge, MA: MIT Press, 1990), 401–15; Margaret Gilbert, "Walking Together; a Paradigmatic Social Phenomenon," *Midwest Studies in Philosophy* 15 (1990): 1–14; Michael Bratman, "Shared Intention," *Ethics* 104 (1993): 97–113; David Velleman, "How to Share an Intention," *Philosophy and Phenomenological Research* 57 (1997): 29–50; Philip Pettit, "Groups with Minds of Their Own," in *Socializing Metaphysics,* ed. Frederick Schmitt (Lanham, MD: Rowman and Littlefield, 2003), 167–93. See for a response to this line of reasoning Jan Narveson, "Collective Responsibility," *Journal of Ethics* 6, no. 2 (2002): 180–98; Seumas Miller and Pekka Makela, "The Collectivist Approach to Collective Moral Responsibility," *Metaphilosophy* 36, no. 5 (2005): 634–51.

[16] See Peter A. French, *Collective and Corporate Responsibility* (New York: Columbia University Press, 1984), 37–38, 46–47, 144, who argues that moral agency arises from the distinctiveness of group intention and action. Also, see Carol Rovane, *The Bounds of Agency: An Essay in Revisionary Metaphysics* (Princeton: Princeton University Press, 1998), 137–41, who finds that group moral agency is a sort of unity or concurrence of actions among the individuals in the group. Andrew Vincent, "Can Groups Be Persons?" *Review of Metaphysics* 42 (1989): 712–14 argues in reply to French. French's notion of moral agency is not distinguished from a sense of mere agency sufficient to ground the legal responsibility of corporate entities. In reply to Rovane, the "rational unity" of the group, since it may be adventitious, is irrelevant to the moral agency of the individual.

The ability for voluntary or, if one likes, rational voluntary action, must be sharply distinguished from a supposed ability to act freely. Such an ability typically has as its hallmark the property expressed in the phrase "I could have done otherwise." It is, I think, a confusion to maintain that if one could *not* have acted otherwise, then one is not acting voluntarily. For not being able to do X or not being able to refrain from doing Y can only mean one of two things. Either it means that one was constrained by force (or ignorance), in which case the action was not voluntary, or else it means that, in light of "facts on the ground," including one's desires and beliefs, one thought that it was better not to do X than the opposite or better to do Y than the opposite. If I am not free to go to the movies with you tonight, that does not mean that I do not voluntarily stay home and write this paper. If no one acts voluntarily when constrained, then there is no such thing as moral agency and the normativity that is supposed to come into play in deriving a political philosophy from so-called facts about the constraints under which people act is a fiction.

The standard Marxist complaint that the proletariat has no choice but to sell its labor to capitalists who in turn steal the excess value of that labor rests ultimately on the above confusion. I do not mean to dismiss the Marxist complaint on the grounds that the proletariat always has the choice to starve. I acknowledge that, practically speaking, a poor man has no choice but to sell his labor. Apart from the nonsense of the labor theory of value itself, my point is that the constraints faced by the poor have the same logical status as the constraints faced by any other moral agent. Most of these are less dire than those faced by the poor; some are more so. That which distinguishes moral agents is not an absence of those constraints of which the rich are supposedly free, but rather rational voluntary action.[17]

Another crucial property of moral agency is that all and only moral agents have the ability to enter into what I shall call "associations" with other moral agents. These associations include the full range of interpersonal activities: sexual, familial, recreational, protective, entrepreneurial, religious, intellectual, etc. All associations are, in my account, voluntary, and include only moral agents. Obviously, moral agents enter into associations in order to achieve some goal that they could not otherwise achieve alone or not achieve as effectively. Since these associations are voluntary, they can end voluntarily, when one or more of the parties no

---

[17] See Serena Olsaretti, *Liberty, Desert, and the Market: A Philosophical Study* (Cambridge: Cambridge University Press, 2004), 139, who distinguishes sharply between volition and freedom. But Olsaretti thinks that an action is nonvoluntary if it is performed because there are no acceptable alternatives, where "acceptable" is determined by some objective standard such as well-being. Thus, one is not acting voluntarily if the alternative is, say, starvation. The only way that Olsaretti can distinguish the constraints that justify political coercion from those that do not, however, is to rely on her intuitions regarding some ideal political outcome. That is, she is *not* deriving her political philosophy from a concept of moral agency, but rather the other way around.

longer find the association valuable. An involuntary relation like slavery is not an association. In an association, the voluntariness is revealed in the agreement that the parties enter into to pursue some goal in concert. The agreement may be written or verbal, explicit or implicit. Moral agency is required for agreements because only moral agents can make such agreements, that is, make and understand the terms of the agreement and the commitments that they and the others assume.

The relation between a pet and a pet owner is not an association because there is only one moral agent in the relation acting voluntarily. If it should turn out that, to our great surprise, dolphins are moral agents, then it would be possible for human moral agents to enter into an association with a nonhuman one. Although I think it highly unlikely, nothing in my account would in principle need to be altered if it should come to pass one day that associations between members of different species were to be possible.

I claim that a moral agent is a natural kind. That is, the determination of how many moral agents there are in a given place is an empirical matter. It is not arbitrary or stipulative. Most importantly, it is the only natural kind I know of whose recognition by others involves a normative judgment. Thus, to recognize someone as a moral agent is to recognize that person as capable of entering into associations with other moral agents, including oneself. Since associations are mutually voluntary among the parties who enter into them, the trust each moral agent places in another implies a normative judgment regarding what the other may be expected to do and what the other may be held morally responsible for not doing. Thus, no one would enter into an agreement or association with another moral agent unless he or she expected the other to honor that agreement. I take it that a failure to do so would incite what we would all recognize as a moral judgment: he did not do what he said he was going to do and *therefore* he did not do what he should have done. If we base our concepts of justice and rights on the foundation of the natural kind that is a moral agent, these thereby acquire such nonarbitrariness accordingly. Neither justice nor rights are natural kinds since they are not kinds; they are properties of moral agents and of relations among them.

I add in passing that if a moral agent is a natural kind as described above, it seems wrong to suppose that one can determine a priori that to which the moral agent would give hypothetical consent. Assume that what someone supposedly would hypothetically consent to is constructed or determined on the basis of some theory of practical rationality. That theory must employ a normative criterion of rationality, that is, what one ought to do in the given circumstances. But the sort of rationality that is a necessary and sufficient condition for moral agency is only nonnormative. That is, moral agents, while acting rationally, sometimes act counter to how they ought to act according to some theory or other. It is one thing to speculate on how one ought to act according to a theory; it is quite another to impose one's conclusions on anyone else. For in doing so, one denies the moral agency of those who are supposedly the subjects of the theory. It is only in the associations among moral agents that normative rationality meets nonnormative rationality. For it is here that the former is applied to instances of the latter.

Obviously, *if* it is true that a moral agent is a natural kind, the plausibility of the claim that a group can be a moral agent is severely diminished The claim that the two persons in a marriage constitute three moral agents and so three natural kinds sounds more like a joke than a serious position. There is nothing in the association that is a marriage or in any other association beyond the moral agency of the individuals involved that needs to be posited to account for any normative judgment in politics or in ethics. This is the case even if we wish to acknowledge the agency of the group in various ways. The concept of group moral agency has no independent or unique explanatory role to play.

III. Moral Agency and Self-Ownership

Since the ownership of possessions is dependent on the existence of a possessor, the ownership of self—including one's body, desires, concepts, talents, etc.—is primary. It is not just primary; it is unique, for unlike any other possession, I am the only one who can have self-ownership of me.[18] The substance of self-ownership is identical with moral agency. That is, all and only moral agents are self-owners. Anything that destroys or undermines self-ownership equally affects moral agency. The recognition of someone as a moral agent is at the same time a recognition of him or her as a self-owner. As we saw previously, a moral agent is an agent with the capacity for having second-order or self-reflexive beliefs and desires. Alternatively, we can characterize this as autonomy or self-directedness. We can also express this in terms of self-ownership: a moral agent is one who is authoritative over his first order beliefs and desires.[19] He owns them because he can reject them or endorse them. He can do with them as he likes; that is, he can act or not act on them. As with ownership in general, one who "owns" himself can do with his own beliefs and desires what he wills.

---

[18] Jan Narveson, "Property and Rights," *Social Philosophy and Policy* 27, no. 1 (2010): 105–6, makes a useful distinction between self-ownership and self-possession, in which the latter term is descriptive and the former is normative. I would add that the normative term follows automatically from the existence of any sort of human association. That is, self-ownership is intrinsic to the origin of any political foundation.

[19] Cf. John Stuart Mill, *On Liberty* (Indianapolis: Bobbs-Merrill, 1956 [1859]), 13, for a similar description of self-ownership, "Over himself, over his own body and mind, the individual is sovereign." I am using "authoritative" in the way that Mill uses "sovereign." Perhaps Mill's description is virtually identical to Locke's "every Man has a *Property* in his own *Person*. This no Body has a Right to but himself" (Locke, *Second Treatise of Government*, ed. C. B. Macpherson (Indianapolis, IN: Hackett, 1980), section 27.

The virtual equivalence of moral agency and self-ownership is the
starting point for reflection on the normative basis for politics, whether
national or international. Where self-ownership is denied, the basis for
morality vanishes. Any creature whom we do not recognize as being a
self-owner, such as a pet, is simultaneously and necessarily—on pain of
logical incoherence—denied status as a moral agent. The denial of self-
ownership that is the practice of slavery is abhorrent to those who believe
that the enslaved and the slave masters are both moral agents.[20] Any
limitations on self-ownership or use for which one might argue make
sense only insofar as these limitations are required for the recognition of
the self-ownership and moral agency of others.[21]

The virtual equivalence of moral agency and self-ownership also provides a perspicuous basis for understanding the human associations
that, ultimately, can culminate in the founding of a state. The state is
an association and so, in my terminology, voluntary. If individual moral
agents have agreed to a political authority for the sake of achieving the
good they seek, the starting point is obviously the individual ownership of one's own desires and of the body in which they reside, that is,
self-ownership. To remove these is to cancel the premise of the enterprise, namely, that persons mutually recognize the self-ownership of
the other members of the state. The natural limitation on the pursuit of

[20] Daniel Atlas, "Freedom and Self-Ownership," *Social Theory and Practice* 26, no. 1 (2000):
7, argues that self-ownership does not in itself justify the rejection of slavery because
defenders of self-ownership only condemn involuntary enslavement. What is wrong with
voluntary permanent enslavement given the principle of self-ownership? The answer is that
such an arrangement necessitates the disavowal of moral agency. If it really were voluntary,
then the ongoing possibility of one calling off the arrangement would obtain, and that
would not be permanent enslavement. The only way that permanent enslavement could be
instituted would be by the use of force, in which case it would not be voluntary. Samuel
Freeman, "Illiberal Libertarians: Why Libertarianism Is Not a Liberal View," *Philosophy and
Public Affairs* 30, no. 2 (2001): 131–35, argues that absolute self-ownership entails the licitness
of the complete alienation of the self that is slavery. He takes this as a reductio ad absurdum
of absolute self-ownership. One reply, that of Nozick, *Anarchy, State, and Utopia*, 331, accepts
the entailment but denies the reductio. A better reply is to insist that selling oneself into
slavery is not possible according to any coherent notion of contract law. A contract, if it is
to be licit and so enforceable must specify what each party to the contract must to do fulfill
it and at least implicitly what the sanctions are for nonfulfillment. But the one who enters
into a putative contract to enslave himself to another either expects to get nothing in return
for his slavery or he expects to get something. If the former, there is no contract, but only a
promise, which is perpetually defeasible without penalty; if the latter, then we may well ask
what the difference is between this situation and an employer-employee contract. But no
contract based on wages (however small in amount) for labor is enforceable in perpetuity
because one can only make a defeasible promise to "work forever" for someone. If one
refuses to work, the penalty is loss of wages, nothing more. If one is paid and refuses to
work, the employer or "slave owner" can sue for compensation.
[21] G. A. Cohen, *Self-Ownership, Freedom, and Equality* (Cambridge: Cambridge University
Press, 1995), 234, argues that the appropriation by the state of the fruit of one's own labor
is not slavery because the state, unlike a true slaveholder, is not exercising discretionary
power in doing so. We may agree with Cohen that the state is not a slaveholder just because
the state is not a moral agent. But this hardly absolves the moral agents who run the state
from the injustices committed in transferring by force property from its owners to others.

goods is when that pursuit impedes the attainment of goods by others. To own one's body is also to own its use, where, again, the limit on its use is at the point that it impedes the use by other moral agents of *their* bodies.[22] By "impede" I mean prevent voluntary behaviour, not the imposition of limitations on others entailed by, say, the ownership of a finite resource.[23]

Those who are suspicious of the very idea of self-ownership argue that one does not own one's own body in the same way that one owns, say, a house.[24] A hand is a part of me in a way in which my house is not. Indeed. Yet underlying both the undisputed ownership of the house and the putative ownership of my hand is my being in a position of "control" or "sovereignty" as Mill put it, over each. I can do with each as I please. And the fact or the claim that there are limitations on what I can do with each does not gainsay the ownership any more than the constraints or limitations on our choices gainsay our voluntary agency.

Some who endorse the idea of self-ownership would distinguish this sharply from ownership of the products of one's activity. If I own my body and talents and desires, it does not follow that I own that which I make of them.[25] If the consequences of self-ownership are to be restricted beyond the prohibition of interference with the self-ownership of anyone else, on what principle is this to be done?

I can use my own body and its powers to satisfy my desires in countless ways. Say I use my body to sing for passing individuals who, enamored of my remarkable voice, offer me money. If I own the use of my body in this way, it would seem that I also own the money voluntarily given to me in exchange for my service. To interfere with my ownership of the money is to interfere with my use, provided that I used my body in order to get money.[26] More to the point, to interfere with my ownership of the money

[22] See Eric Mack, "Self-Ownership, Marxism, and Egalitarianism: Part 1," *Politics, Philosophy, and Economics* 1, no. 1 (2002): 75–108 and "Self-Ownership, Marxism, and Egalitarianism: Part 2," *Politics, Philosophy, and Economics* 1, no. 2 (2002): 237–76, on the primacy of self-ownership and for a refutation of arguments against this.

[23] Do threats constitute an impediment to voluntary behavior? I would say that they do, but only if they are threats of physical aggression, not, say, the threat involved in blackmail. Only physical aggression negates the moral agency of another.

[24] See e.g., Atlas, "Freedom and Self-Ownership," 16–18.

[25] See e.g., Peter Vallentyne, "Self-Ownership and Equality: Brute Luck, Gifts, Universal Dominance, and Leximin," *Ethics* 107, 2 (1997): 321–43.

[26] Some, e.g., Barbara Fried, "Wilt Chamberlain Revisited: Nozick's 'Justice in Transfer' and the Problem of Market-Based Distribution," *Philosophy and Public Affairs* 24 (1995): 226–45, question the right to the "surplus" value of one's labor, owing to scarcity. I deny that the notion of surplus value makes any sense whatsoever. For the value of something is exactly what someone is prepared to pay for it. Hence, something has infinite values. What anyone is prepared to pay for something is *always* circumstantial, that is, he or she is prepared to pay so much for something here and now. Hence, nothing can have surplus value. Attempts to distinguish a "fair" price for something from the price that constitutes surplus value fail for the same reason. A fair price could only be something like the average among values at a certain time. But this average, like all averages in real life, is fictitious. Why is it not fair that I am willing to pay more than the average for something?

would mean to interfere with the ownership of the money by my customers who voluntarily transferred it to me.

A more contentious example is this. I use my body to go prospecting in the remote Arctic, where I discover gold. Do I own the gold in the way that I own the money in the previous example? Some would say that the second example is significantly different from the first because the second example involves my appropriation of a natural resource of which I do not have and cannot have exclusive ownership.[27] That is to say, unlike my body, since I obviously did not own the gold before I existed and my mere existence is only trivially different from my stumbling on it sometime after I began to exist, I do not own it now.

IV. FROM SELF-OWNERSHIP TO PROPERTY

More generally, let us consider the following question: who today owns the nickel and other base metals at the bottom of the Atlantic Ocean? Logically, there are three possible answers to this question: (a) no one; (b) everyone (all moral agents); and (c) more than no one but less than everyone. In order to answer this question in a nonarbitrary way, we need to look more closely at the notion of property itself, that is, we need to generalize from the case of self-ownership and consider how property generally is related to moral agency.

In this section of my paper, I raise the question of the normativity of the concept of property.[28] On the one hand, it seems that the normativity of the concept of property is reflected in our distinction between property and mere possession. Someone who steals my property possesses it, though she does not own it. The mere fact of possession no more entails ownership than does the mere fact of homicide entail murder.[29] Implicit in this distinction between possession and property is the claim that if x is the property of S, then it would at least be prima facie wrong to deprive S of x against her will.[30] On the other hand, there is nothing more common in political theorizing than to maintain that property claims are defeasible. For example, one might defend the imposition of estate taxes on one's property. The claim here is not that, like the thief, it was not that person's

---

[27] Nozick, *Anarchy, State, and Utopia*, 150–53, similarly distinguishes between justice in acquisition, justice in transfer, and justice in rectification. An unjust acquisition would taint a transfer, making it unjust. It would also mean that the restoration of property was not just. If I did not acquire the gold justly, I could not justly transfer it.

[28] Cf. Bernard A. O. Williams, *Ethics and the Limits of Philosophy* (Cambridge, MA: Harvard University Press, 1985) on "thick" ethical concepts like treachery, promises, brutality, and courage.

[29] I use the verb "own" and the noun "ownership" to indicate a relation between a subject and that subject's property. As I shall argue below, the only subjects who own property are moral agents. Accordingly, all property is owned by moral agents.

[30] It would seem that if property is a normative concept, then so is possession when used in contradiction to property. I will henceforth distinguish "mere possession" used normatively from "possession" used neutrally or descriptively.

property in the first place, but merely in his possession. Rather, the claim is that in this case property is to be treated nonnormatively, just like possession. Since there is apparently no theoretical upper limit to an estate tax, there is no inviolable property within an estate and the normativity of the concept of property seems to evanesce. But then we are left to wonder about the difference between the thief who merely possesses something and the owner of property in the face of an impending estate tax. To make the normative claim that someone's property may be or ought to be confiscated seems to be not much different from making the normative claim that the thief ought not to be prevented from acting as if he owned what he possessed. If, returning to the first alternative, we should conclude that the concept of property is irreducibly normative, what will the political consequences be?

Some maintain that the concept of property is inseparable from a political matrix.[31] Hence, the determination of what property is and of whether there is a distinction between property and possession cannot be made apart from the articulation of general political principles. I agree that the normative concept of property requires some sort of association wherein the members or participants recognize possession as property. But this does not entail that only in the particular association that is a state does property exist. More to the point, it does not entail that an association, the hallmark of which is having coercive powers, is the determiner of property.

Political associations are constituted by moral agents. Hence, the capacity for reciprocal recognition of other moral agents is another attribute of moral agency. The conceptual connection between being capable of entering into a political association, being a moral agent, and owning property is fairly clear. Rabbits are not moral agents; therefore, they are not capable of entering into a political association. Since they are not moral agents, they are incapable of the reciprocal recognition of moral agency that is a necessary condition for any contractual relationship. Since they are not moral agents, they cannot own property. They cannot own property precisely because there is in regard to them no distinction between property and possession. Even if I freely gave a rabbit all the lettuce in my garden, that lettuce would not be its property; it would simply be in its possession. To claim that there is a distinction between the rabbit who possesses the lettuce against my will and the rabbit who "owns" the lettuce because I gave it to him is to insist that the mode of acquisition of the lettuce alone entails a distinction between possession and property.

The mode of acquisition is indeed crucial for the distinction between possession and property, but only in regard to moral agents. In order to see this point, imagine a single moral agent alone on the proverbial desert island. There is in this case no basis for a distinction between that which

---

[31] See Liam Murphy and Thomas Nagel, *The Myth of Ownership: Taxes and Justice* (New York: Oxford University Press, 2002), especially pp. 8–10, and passim.

is in his possession and that which is his property because there are no other moral agents present. The presence of rabbits or other animals would make no difference. The presence of other moral agents immediately makes possible reciprocal recognition, hence the possible recognition of property that is not merely a possession. It is reciprocity, that is, an agreement about what is property and not mere possession that makes property a normative concept. It may be wrong to deprive an animal of its food, but not because that food is its property as opposed to being its possession. I presume that if it is wrong to deprive the rabbit of its lettuce, it is wrong whether or not I freely gave it the lettuce. However, the deeper point is that if one wanted to insist that the way the rabbit obtained the lettuce makes a moral difference such that in one case it merely possessed the lettuce but in the other it owned it, then I suggest that one is thereby attributing moral agency to the rabbit. If the moral difference is that depriving the rabbit of its property is wrong, whereas depriving it of its possession is not wrong, then one would again be employing the concept of property normatively. I don't believe that rabbits are moral agents, but that is neither here nor there in regard to the conceptual connection between moral agency and the normativity of the concept of property.

The fundamental issue underlying questions of ownership in political discussions is whether it is the case that if no person owns something, then everyone owns it or else if when no person owns something, then, simply, no one does.[32] The question about the ownership of the nickel at the bottom of the Atlantic Ocean is in principle the same as the question about self-ownership. The range of logically possible answers is the same in each case. The view that all the people in the world today own a fractional share of the nickel is so far as I can see no different from the view that all the people in the world today own a fractional share of me.[33]

[32] See Matthias Risse, "Does Left-Libertarianism Have Coherent Foundations?" *Politics, Philosophy, and Economics* 3, no. 3 (2004): 344, who usefully distinguishes between an original state of non-ownership in which case what is needed is a theory of acquisition and an original state of group ownership (whether joint or common) in which case what is needed is a theory of privatization.

[33] The position known as left-libertarianism maintains both a commitment to self-ownership and a denial of the thesis that resources are unowned until they are owned by someone. See Michael Otsuka, *Libertarianism without Inequality* (Oxford: Oxford University Press, 2003). See Richard J. Arneson, "Self-Ownership and World Ownership: Against Left-Libertarianism," *Social Philosophy and Policy* 27, no. 1 (2010): 168–94, for a critique of both left-libertarian claims. Arneson basically argues that self-ownership and access to world ownership on fair and equal terms are incoherent positions taken together because the differences among people will always undercut access on fair and equal terms. All of these views seem to spring from Jean-Jacques Rousseau, *Discourse on the Origin and Foundations of Inequality Among Men*, ed. Helena Rosenblatt (New York; Boston, MA: Bedford Books, 2010), Part Two, ab initio "The first man who, having enclosed a piece of ground, bethought himself of saying *This is mine*, and found people simple enough to believe him, was the real founder of civil society. From how many crimes, wars and murders, from how many horrors and misfortunes might not any one have saved mankind, by pulling up the stakes, or filling up the ditch, and crying to his fellows, 'Beware of listening to this impostor; you are undone if you once forget that the fruits of the earth belong to us all, and the earth itself to nobody.' "

Somewhat less extreme views would take it that national boundaries are
the limit of the group ownership of resources within those boundaries,
whether known or not.[34] Over against these views is the view that ownership is the result of a transfer of a good from a state of being unowned
to one of being owned. In the case of self-owners, this view amounts to
the claim that self-ownership arises when moral agents claim it, that is,
when they act as moral agents.

I have never encountered anyone who has argued that some but not all,
the persons in the world own the nickel at the bottom of the ocean, for
example, all the persons living in countries that begin with the letter "N."
It is clear why this is so: such a claim would be purely arbitrary, to say
nothing of the fact that the determination of what moral agent is to
determine who owns the nickel and who does not is purely arbitrary, too.
But the reason why this answer to the question about ownership is arbitrary is exactly why the answer that everyone in the world owns the
nickel is arbitrary, too. For the arbitrariness of holding that X, Y, and Z
own the nickel is the same whether X, Y, and Z are all or some of the
moral agents in the world now. For if they are "all," they are reduced to
being merely "some" by the appearance of new moral agents. If the new
moral agents have a claim on the nickel, then X, Y, and Z did not own it
in the first place, or at least they did not own that portion on which the
new moral agents now have a claim. In addition, since no potential member of a "future generation" is a moral agent, these members' putative
ownership of anything is highly doubtful.

When ownership is claimed for a group such as "society," the word
"ownership" is used in a special sense. For normally, when we say that X
owns something, that means that X is free to use it or dispose of it as he
pleases. By contrast, social ownership is never represented in these terms.
No one supposes that each individual owns a fraction of the sum of what
is socially owned and that he or she can use and dispose of that fraction
at will.[35] Rather, "social" or "public" ownership is always represented as
consisting of a right to use or derive benefit from that which is owned.
Since this right is more or less a creation of those in power, it can be
adjusted to meet some goal or other. That is, the right can be limited in
whatever way the rulers judge is appropriate for achieving the aims of the

---

[34] See Lawrence C. Becker, *Property Rights: Philosophic Foundations* (London; Boston:
Routledge and K. Paul, 1977), 25; Cohen, *Self-Ownership, Freedom, and Equality*, chaps. 3 and
4; Will Kymlicka, *Contemporary Political Philosophy: An Introduction* (New York: Oxford University Press, 1990), 117–18; Hillel Steiner, *An Essay on Rights* (Oxford: Blackwell, 1994) for
arguments on behalf of the position that with respect to resources, there is no such thing as
a state of being unowned. Cohen, 103–4, recognizes that a regime of self-ownership plus the
left-libertarian principle of the equal ownership of resources will potentially have anti-
egalitarian results. Hence, Cohen, committed to egalitarianism, wants to deny self-ownership.
Cf. Kaspar Lippert-Rasmussen, "Against Self-Ownership: There Are No Fact-Insensitive
Ownership Rights Over One's Body," *Philosophy and Public Affairs* 36, no. 1 (2008): 86–118.
[35] In this regard, social ownership is as much a fiction as a social contract.

state. Thus, the benefits deriving from the right can be variously distributed, say, through taxation or rent.[36]

I would contend, however, that deriving the benefits of ownership from
rights is to get things backwards. A right, if it is not arbitrarily conjured
up, must rest on some principle of recognition of some attribute possessed by those who therefore possess the right. When those who derive
ownership from rights are asked for the relevant principle, the one most
widely acknowledged is egalitarian. Everyone has a right to x because
everyone is equal. This is specious. For one thing, it is never equality that
governs the terms of distribution; rather, it is some perceived *inequality*.
More fundamentally, the notion of equality itself is not the sort of real
attribute that could ground a right. People are equal and unequal in
countless ways, where "equal" and "unequal" must be glossed as "same"
and "different." However, the equality that supposedly grounds some
right to property is nothing but the patently circular equal right to that
property. Indeed, equality is frequently represented as a *goal* derived from
a right or from a principle of justice.[37]

Those favoring some sort of group ownership of resources, like to talk
about "social ownership" or "the world's resources" as if the world owned
them. But "the world" is not even a group. It is held that because these
resources were not created by anyone in particular (in the way that my
music is), they are owned by everyone. This is manifestly a nonsequitur
and it is in fact a false claim precisely for the same reason that the claim
that some arbitrarily selected group of people owns the world's resources
is false. Most typically, the claims made for group ownership of resources
are made on the basis of some principle of justice.[38] Not surprisingly, it
would be an egalitarian principle that concludes in equal ownership of
these resources by all the members of the relevant group. My contention,
by contrast, is that the notions of justice and rights are derivative and that

---

[36] See e.g., John Rawls, *A Theory of Justice* (Cambridge, MA: Harvard University Press,
1971), 101–2; Ronald Dworkin, "What Is Equality? Part 2: Equality of Resources," *Philosophy
and Public Affairs* 10 (1981): 283–345.

[37] John Christman, "Self-Ownership, Equality, and the Structure of Property Rights,"
Political Theory 19 (1991), 37–39, distinguishes between "control rights" and "income rights,"
applying the former to self-ownership and the latter to the fruits of one's labor. He claims
that income rights are subordinated to an egalitarian principle of justice whereas control
rights are to be justified by principles of individual interests such as autonomy and liberty.
Christman does not explain how constraining or regulating the value I put on the labor of
others is not an infringement on my autonomy and liberty. He does not do so, I think,
because the egalitarian principle of justice always trumps individual rights, if not in regard
to my body itself, certainly in regard to what I accomplish with my skills, efforts, etc. It is
odd that Christman says, at p. 35, that "[income rights] cannot be said to be a manifestation
of the individual's autonomy and liberty, since income is a product of things over which an
agent can claim no independent sovereignty." What is the argument for the claim that a
self-owner cannot "claim sovereignty" over his talents and the benefits from the value put
on them by other self-owners?

[38] See, e.g., Philippe Van Parijs, *Real Freedom for All: What If Anything Can Justify Capitalism?* (Oxford: Clarendon Press, 1995); Cohen, *Self-Ownership, Freedom, and Equality.*

there is no nonarbitrary way of determining a just distribution of resources without having *already* established ownership; for justice, basically, looks to the restoration and maintenance of ownership.[39] There are no grounds whatsoever for holding that everyone owns a bit of all the gold in the world *because* that is what justice demands. Justice demands nothing unless and until we know the factors in the equation, namely, where exactly a balance has been disrupted. But the principal factors in the equation concerned with property and ownership are *who* owns *what*.[40] Justice cannot determine that. That is why when philosophers speak of group ownership of the world's resources, they are really claiming that all the members of the relevant group *should* own a fraction of those resources. They therefore have no special theory of ownership, though they do have a theory about the results they would like to achieve and which they believe can only be achieved if the members of the group own the resources.[41]

If we decline the temptation to try to derive ownership from justice, what limitations on the ownership of resources might independently be determined? One of the most influential attempts is found in John Locke's theory of acquisition.[42] The theory actually contains two parts, the first of which maintains that ownership of something is established by the mixing of one's labor with that something; the second part, the so-called Lockean proviso stipulates that in order for this initial acquisition to be just, there must be "enough and as good left in common for others." The proviso has been universally understood by both defenders and opponents of Locke to be a condition of justice. If what is left over after the initial acquisition is not enough and as good left in common for others, then that acquisition was unjust. What Locke must mean here is that a theory of justice is prior to a theory of ownership, for he is evidently

[39] Cf. Jan Narveson, *The Libertarian Idea* (Peterborough, Ontario: Broadview Press, 2001), 82–85. For a contrasting view, see Gerald Gaus, "Property, Rights, and Freedom," in *Property Rights*, ed. Ellen Frankel Paul, Jeffery Paul, and Fred Miller (Cambridge: Cambridge University Press, 1994), 209–40.

[40] As Cohen, *Self-Ownership, Freedom, and Equality*, 98, realizes: "It looks as though the suggested form of external resource equality, namely, joint world ownership, renders nugatory the self-ownership with which he [the advocate of the joint ownership regime] had hoped to combine it. Self-ownership is not eliminated, but it is rendered useless, rather as it is useless to own a corkscrew when you are forbidden access to bottles of wine." What Cohen calls "joint ownership" is what I mean by "group ownership" of the world's resources, which is not fractional ownership. Group ownership undercuts, if not eliminates, self-ownership, if self-ownership includes ownership of the fruits of one's own labor.

[41] Edward Feser, "Classical Natural Law Theory, Property Rights, and Taxation," *Social Philosophy and Policy* 27, no. 1 (2010): 35, argues that "the concept of ownership *presupposes* the notion of rights" since to recognize someone as an owner of property is to acknowledge his right to it. Feser's mistake, I believe, is in supposing that if "X owns P" and "X has a right to have others refrain from appropriating P against his will" are coextensive, then someone's rights get to be logically prior. But the coextension itself cannot entail logical priority. In fact, if, as I have argued, moral agency is prior, we are then in a position to show that ownership is prior to rights even if it is in some sense coextensive.

[42] See Nozick, *Anarchy, State, and Utopia.*, 174–78.

maintaining that if property was acquired in a way that violated the proviso, it is in fact not owned. Or at least that portion of the acquisition that violates the proviso is not owned. Interpreting Locke in this way, however, obscures the reasoning behind the first part of the theory. If my labor mixing establishes ownership, why is it the case that my ownership, assuming it violates the proviso, is defeasible? If I must relinquish the putative ownership, I take it that I did not in fact own it in the first place. In short, on Locke's theory of ownership unjust initial acquisition of property does not seem even possible.[43]

The problem with Locke's theory is the intrusion of considerations of justice into the definition of ownership.[44] I say this is a problem because nowhere does Locke tell us why violation of his proviso is unjust, unless we take seriously his theological assumptions; indeed, I would maintain that there is no non-question-begging way that he *could* tell us. My point is not, however, that violation of the proviso is never unjust. My point is that in those cases in which it is unjust we must show that this is so already having established ownership. In that case, however, the injustice does not reflect on the initial acquisition, but on the relation between an owner of property and someone else.[45]

Another way of making the same point is to distinguish the establishment of ownership as a case of treating someone else unjustly from a case of depriving someone else of an opportunity. Every single object over which I establish ownership is thereby unavailable for someone else to own. If, like Alexander the Great, we lament the fact that all the really lovely places on earth have already been conquered, the unavailability to us of such opportunities is not thereby an injustice. The point is that if we confuse the necessary constriction of opportunities owing to the establishment of the ownership of anything with an injustice done to someone else, we shall be less likely to see that the establishment of ownership does not entail injustice to anyone.[46]

---

[43] The notion of "mixing one's labor" is notoriously vague, though it should be noted that *any* labor added by X gives X a prima facie claim to ownership greater than a claim by any Y who mixes *no* labor. Cf. John Sanders, "Justice and the Initial Acquisition of Property," *Harvard Journal of Law and Public Policy* 10, no. 2 (1987): 388–99, for criticisms of the "labor-mixing" condition and qualified support for it.

[44] See Fried, "Wilt Chamberlain Revisited: Nozick's 'Justice in Transfer' and the Problem of Market-Based Distribution," 230 and n.14, who expresses the problem in this way. If I were to mix my labor with land and so acquire ownership of it, everyone else is deprived of the scarcity value of the land, and so it is not the case that "enough and as good is left in common for others." I do not think that Locke's proviso has to be read in this narrow way. "Scarcity" value is as meaningless as "surplus" value. Everything valuable as property is scarce. If any ownership is to exist, the owner is bound to benefit from the relative scarcity created by the ownership.

[45] See Sanders, "Justice and the Initial Acquisition of Property," 376–87.

[46] See Leif Wenar, "Original Acquisition of Private Property," *Mind* 107, no. 428 (1998): 799–820, who assumes that the acquisition of property produces burdens on others, including duties. That is because he thinks of the acquisition of property as the establishment of a right. He assumes that matters of right and justice can be established independently of and

It may be urged that preventing someone from acquiring property in a specific locale by retaining all the property for oneself is far more than a limitation on another's opportunities. It is, in fact, a direct threat to one's moral agency. Assume that someone owns an entire island and when someone else washes ashore, the owner forbids him access to his property. The unfortunate visitor faces almost certain death if he leaves. In my view, the most important feature of this well-known example is that neither justice nor rights are here at issue. But in saying this, I am not claiming that the one who possesses the property (let us not call it "ownership") and who refuses to allow his visitor to stay has not done something immoral. I am not even claiming that the visitor would be immoral if he used violence in order to remain. Rather, I am claiming that matters of justice and rights are functionally related to the mutual recognition of moral agency. Such recognition would be constitutive of any agreement that the owner and the visitor came to in regard to the terms of the visitor's stay. To suppose that a refusal by the owner to allow the visitor to stay is an injustice or a violation of some right is to assume that justice and rights are features of the world that exist prior to moral agency. But to do this is to forego the only nonarbitrary means for articulating what justice and rights are in any situation. For the supposed "features" of the world are nothing more than the intuitions various persons hold about how they would like to see the world go. Incidentally, resting a political philosophy on a supposed lesson to be drawn from such an extreme situation of dispute over initial acquisition of property is, to say the least, not promising since the vast majority of property disputes are not over initial acquisitions.

An attempt to link a revision of the Lockean proviso to a principle of justice in initial acquisition is made by Michael Otsuka.[47] He argues that the Lockean proviso needs to be replaced by an "egalitarian proviso" according to which "enough and as good left in common for others" is interpreted to mean "equality of opportunity for welfare." This in turn is defined as "a state of affairs in which the levels of welfare that people have attained differ only as the result of choices for which they can be held morally responsible."[48] The idea is that those who through no fault

---

prior to the establishment of property ownership. See also Barbara Fried, "Left-Libertarianism: A Review," *Philosophy and Public Affairs* 32, no. 1 (2004): 74–75, who, too, assumes that "all property rights necessarily infringe the liberties of others." The word "liberty" here is set up for equivocal use: liberties which can and cannot be infringed according to some standard geared-to outcome, such as "general welfare."

[47] See Otsuka, *Libertarianism without Inequality*, chap. 1 which is a revised version of Michael Otsuka, "Self-Ownership and Equality: A Lockean Reconciliation," *Philosophy and Public Affairs* 27, no. 1 (1998): 65–92.

[48] Otsuka, *Libertarianism without Inequality*, 25, n. 39. I take it that the "initial" acquisition is not intended by Otsuka as an absolute historical moment, but only relative to subsequent distributions. That is, "initial" means the state of property ownership before an egalitarian redistribution is enacted. I have no idea, however, how Otsuka supposes that the "world's" resources are to be distributed across national boundaries. See Richard Arneson, "Luck

of their own are less able than others to convert worldly resources into welfare are entitled to acquire additional resources (relative to others) in order to compensate for their lesser ability. The idea of compensation here suggests that a principle of justice is being employed. Apart from the obvious objections that the measurement of abilities other than by achievement is problematic, to say the least, and that one might calculate that evincing a relative lack of achievement in order to be "compensated" might be a desirable substitute for achievement itself, my main issue with Otsuka is that his egalitarian principle of justice is nothing more than an assumption. That *any* principle of justice obtains apart from an association entered into by individual moral agents is itself an assumption. More particularly, that an egalitarian principle of justice obtains assumes that assigning ownership is a means for compensating individuals for an injustice, in this case, the injustice of different abilities.[49] But nowhere does Otsuka tell us who committed the injustice. And I fail to see how compensation for injustice has any meaning if no one committed an injustice. Furthermore, of course, if groups, such as society, are not moral agents, then that group *could not* commit an injustice on the individual to be putatively compensated. Otsuka, unlike Gerry Cohen, thinks that the subordination of the ownership of property to the satisfaction of a principle of egalitarianism does not entail (even if it practically leads to) the subordination of *self*-ownership to the satisfaction of such a principle.[50] Insofar as self-ownership or moral agency encompasses property, however, it is difficult to see why claims to compensation for imaginary injustices do not compromise the moral agency of those from whom compensation is to be extracted.

When we speak of the moral responsibility or the duty of society, specifically, in the compensation for injustices, we typically use the concepts of responsibility and duty in a normative way. The normativity of these concepts is, of course, contingent upon their use in reference to moral agents. If states are not moral agents, then states do not, for example, have a moral responsibility to help the poor, *even if it could be shown that every single member of that state has such a moral responsibility.* Without there being such a group moral responsibility, the justification for all of the welfare or redistributionist policies of the modern state is eliminated.

Egalitarianism: Interpreted and Defended," *Philosophical Topics* 32, nos. 1 and 2 (2004): 1–20, for a defense of "luck egalitarianism" with ample references. The idea of "luck egalitarianism" is that inequalities that are merely a matter of luck should be eliminated. An analysis and a lengthy criticism of various forms of luck egalitarianism can be found in Elizabeth A. Anderson, "What is the Point of Equality?" *Ethics* 109, no. 2 (1999): 287–337.

[49] As pointed out by Risse, "Does Left-Libertarianism Have Coherent Foundations?" 343, Otsuka's egalitarian assumption is actually more arbitrary than Locke's, since Locke, unlike Otsuka, assumes a theistic account of the origin of the world's resources; Locke's proviso, therefore, observes the prima facie claim that anyone has to these resources.

[50] Ibid., 20–21, and n 26. Also see Christman, "Self-Ownership, Equality, and the Structure of Property Rights," 39–44.

Since such policies practically entail the use of force or the threat of the use of force against those who do not subscribe to the putative moral responsibility of the group, it is difficult to see how the force or the threat of it does not negate moral agency. And, as I have already argued, once moral agency is compromised or negated, there is no nonarbitrary foundation for a state at all.

Otsuka's left-libertarianism aims to combine a principle of self-ownership with a principle of egalitarian justice that determines subsequent property ownership, both initial ownership and the ownership that results from transfers.[51] Cohen thinks that a principle of egalitarian justice would eliminate self-ownership. I maintain that self-ownership is virtually equivalent to moral agency and that without moral agency there is no political foundation possible. In my view, a principle of justice depends on a prior principle of self-ownership.

Self-ownership is, of course, negated by involuntary servitude. And though it is probably the case nowadays that there is not much enthusiasm for a theoretical defense of slavery, other forms of involuntary servitude such as military conscription do have ardent defenders. I am not here concerned with the substantive issue of whether military conscription violates someone's property, but rather with the question of the conceptual relation between property in general and moral agency. Those who defend military conscription and other putative violations of property agree that property may belong to all and only moral agents, but they also believe that society or the state or the government is a moral agent. And, though the claim that the entire human race owns my body is absurd, the claim that the state is a part-owner of my body is not so obviously absurd. As part-owner of my body, presumably, sometimes the state's ownership claim trumps mine; sometimes it does not. The point is perfectly general, of course, and would apply equally to any property that I own, whether it be my body or my land or my chattels, and so on.

Now here we do have a really big problem. Grant that all and only moral agents own property (at least their own bodies). If there really are other legitimate claimants to ownership of one's property, then the issue is clouded, to say the least. Some would argue that the state is the foremost such claimant. In order to make good this claim, however, one would first need to show that the state is a moral agent, it having been agreed that only moral agents own property. One would attempt to show this, presumably, by showing either that an aggregate of moral agents is a moral agent or that the state is a moral agent over and above the aggregate of moral agents. The first alternative seems unintelligible given that the aggregate could include simultaneous contrary exercises of moral agency (e.g., I want to do x and you want to do not-x). The second

---

[51] Cf. Vallentyne and Steiner, eds., *Left-Libertarianism and Its Critics: The Contemporary Debate* (London: MacMillan, 2000).

alternative either amounts to the anthropomorphizing of the state or, more typically, to the claim that the expression of the will of some members of the state requires us to postulate a moral agent above and beyond the sum of moral agents within the state. It is important to see that if it is the expression of the will of one member of the state, whoever that may be, there is no plausibility whatsoever in claiming that this expression of will belongs to any moral agent other than the one individual who expresses it. So, somehow the expression of the will of some requires the postulation of a moral agent over and above the moral agents who express their will. The state is this supposed hypothetical moral agent. And it is the state as a moral agent that may at times have a legitimate claim on what would otherwise be my property.

An alternative to this line of reasoning is to deny that only moral agents own property, and to insist that the state, though it is not a moral agent, is the sort of entity that can own property and not just possess it. Someone defending the idea of public property might want to concede that the "public" is not a moral agent, but that the public can indeed be said to own property where "property" is used normatively. Whether we say "public" here or "state" or "society" seems to make little difference. The idea of public or state property is so ubiquitous that it seems preposterous to maintain that there is no such thing, if indeed "property" is being used normatively. Consider a public park or a public building. Are these not owned by the public or the state in a robust sense of "own"? My contention is that they are not the state's property, but only its possession, and the question of whether they are mere possessions depends entirely on whether they have been stolen from someone whose property they were. Thus, the impossibility of the state owning property is analogous to the impossibility of, say, a corpse having the right to free speech.

The reason why it is natural to suppose that the state owns property despite the fact that the state is not a moral agent is that there is a legitimate concept of collective property ownership with which the putative state ownership of property is easily confused. The thought that more than one moral agent can jointly own a piece of property is unproblematic. The simplest case is when two persons, for example, jointly own a house. The hallmark of joint ownership is that it is possible to attribute fractional ownership. Say two persons each own 50 percent of the house. Ownership of 50 percent of the house means that, as in the case of every other piece of property that a moral agent owns, the owner has authority over the use of the fraction of the property that he owns (up to and including 100 percent). A more complex situation arises when there is fractional ownership in a corporation. But the principle is identical. If S owns 1/1,000,000 of the shares in the corporation, then S has authority over the use of this fraction of the property, which, practically speaking, is of course expressed in money, not chattel. This is exactly why corpo-

rations, which are not moral agents, do not own property in the normative sense of "property."

Group ownership of public property is most like group ownership of a
corporation, but with the crucial difference that there is in fact no fractional ownership. Even if a public "asset" is priced, there is no way for me
to cash in my share in this asset, even assuming I am willing to forgo
further use of it. So, I do not own the hypothetical fraction. And if the
state is not a moral agent, as I have argued, the state does not own it
either.[52]

This conclusion is, admittedly, a surprising one. If property is a normative concept and if normative concepts are intelligibly applicable only
to moral agents, and if groups cannot be moral agents, then groups cannot own property, except in the specific sense in which individual members of a corporation have fractional ownership of the corporation and its
property. Neither the state nor the government nor society nor the public
nor the pernicious collective "we" own anything; only moral agents own
anything, in particular that which was acquired in the course of exercising their moral agency. Consequently, the involuntary use of my owned
resources or, indeed, myself, for purposes other than those I specifically
endorse, is unjustifiable. The differences among regimes in the extent of
their appropriation of my property is only a matter of degree.

V. Conclusion

I have argued that the correct, indeed, the only nonarbitrary foundation
for political philosophy is the natural kind concept of moral agency. From
moral agency flows self-ownership, including property ownership. Justice is a state of affairs in which persons are exercising moral agency,
including participation in associations. Injustice is the deprivation of property, where "deprivation" implies involuntary transfer of property from
the owner. For S to have a right is for it to be unjust to deprive S of that
to which she has a right. Thus, a right is a concept derived from justice.
Since injustice is the deprivation of property, the only rights are property
rights.

I have argued that making rights or justice foundational concepts is
arbitrary or reduces to the bare assertion of one's own intuitions. Intuitions, however, differ. Some theorists may claim that the intuitions of
some concocted majority may be authoritative, but these are no less intu-

---

[52] Thus, I would disagree with Jeremy Waldron, "What is Private Property?" *Journal of
Legal Studies* 5 no. 3 (1985): 326–33, who thinks that private property is only one type of
property. He calls "collective property" that which I am denying is possible for a state or a
corporation. According to Waldron, collective property is distinguished by access and use of
material resources by all the members of the collective. But access and use are not, I think
sufficient for property ownership. If I give access and use of my property to someone else,
they do not thereby own it. It is not use, but the authority over use that determines property.

itions for all that. One may reasonably wonder how minority rights fare when they are in conflict with the intuitions of a majority. Certainly, one cannot appeal to these intuitions as justification for such rights. But if the justification is going to sidestep the appeal to majority intuitions, one may also wonder whether what establishes the rights also undercuts or makes altogether irrelevant the majority intuitions.

If moral agency is the necessary and sufficient foundation for a political association, then it is of the utmost importance to determine the range of the concept of moral agency. I doubt very much that cats or dolphins or chimpanzees are moral agents, but nothing in my argument logically precludes such a possibility. My argument does, however, conclude that groups are not moral agents. In particular, neither the state nor society nor some indeterminate "we" constitutes a moral agent. Consequently, they do not possess moral properties including responsibility or rights or duties. "We" do not have a duty to the poor simply because "we" are not the sort of entity that can have duties. In saying this, I am prepared to concede that it is possible that each and every moral agent has a duty to the poor. I have no problem with the claim if this duty arises from a particular injustice that a particular moral agent has brought on another. Nor do I suppose that it is absurd to claim that this duty entails the practice of charity, though in this case the duty is presumably something like a duty to God to be charitable to the poor. But, of course, the fact that charity is voluntary and, in this case, so too is the recognition of the duty, means that an appeal to universal charity ("sell all that you have and give it to the poor") is politically irrelevant.

I do not claim to have addressed, much less settled, all of the issues concerning the foundation of a political association. I am claiming, however, that an ordered set of concepts—moral agency, self-ownership, property, justice, and rights—is the only non-question-begging matrix within which to address them.

Philosophy, University of Toronto

HUMAN REPRODUCTIVE INTERESTS: PUZZLES AT THE PERIPHERY OF THE PROPERTY PARADIGM*

By Donald C. Hubin

I. Introduction

The question of ownership—property rights—is important in addressing many issues of public policy. The ownership of an object does not answer the question of how that object should, morally speaking, be used, but it often answers—or helps to answer—the question about who has the right to decide how the object will be used within rather wide limits. Answering this question does not settle all issues of public policy with respect to a thing. Even if an object is privately owned, there may be good grounds for encouraging or discouraging certain uses of it or for imposing limitations on its use. Obviously, however, issues of public policy are quite different with respect to privately owned objects than with respect to public or communally owned property.

What I will call "the property paradigm" (and describe more fully in Section II) is extremely useful with respect to many moral questions that we encounter and, in particular, with respect to moral questions concerning public policies. I will argue in Section III, however, that it exerts a distorting influence on debates about a variety of complex moral issues. More specifically, I will argue that the application of the property paradigm deformed discussion of the nature and basis of parental rights. The claim that parental rights are not best understood as property rights is not a novel one; it is now widely acknowledged. However, while the property paradigm exerts only vestigial influence on contemporary discussions of parental rights, it still exerts a significant distorting effect on discussions of reproductive rights. More specifically, I will argue that focusing on the question of the ownership of gametes, in particular of sperm, tends to warp the moral dialogue concerning reproductive rights. Those sensitive moral debates are better framed in terms of individuals' legitimate interests than in terms of property, as I will show in Section IV.

* For very helpful comments on an earlier draft of this paper, I'm grateful to Dan Hubin, Piers Norris Turner, and the other contributors to this volume.

doi:10.1017/S0265052511000070

II. The Property Paradigm

To understand what I am calling "the property paradigm," we must begin with the concept of property. There is, of course, continuing controversy over this concept. I will not enter this debate in any detail. Rather, I'll declare the meaning I attach to the term so that merely verbal disputes are not mistaken for substantive ones. That meaning, while not universally endorsed, is far from idiosyncratic. With a clear understanding of what I take the property paradigm to be, we can see how it still exerts some residual influence over discourse concerning parental rights and how it significantly distorts discussions of reproductive rights.

I understand "property" in the relevant sense, to refer to objects in virtue of a cluster of Hohfeldian rights an agent holds over them and other "incidents" that pertain to them.[1] These rights and other incidents that give shape to the concept of property were given their modern, canonical formulation by A. M. Honoré in the seminal paper "Ownership."[2] Honoré identified eleven incidents of ownership, including most importantly for present purposes: the rights to possess, use, and manage an object, the right to income and capital from the object, the duty to avoid harmful use of the object, transmissibility, and the absence of term. When, with respect to a given object, these incidents are instantiated in one individual or group (at least when the rights in question are fairly extensive), it is proper to say that the object is the property of that individual or group. This is an instance of what has come to be referred to as "full liberal ownership." It is our paradigmatic case of ownership.

The concept of property is multidimensionally vague; it is defined in terms of a paradigmatic cluster of rights[3] that are conceptually and often empirically separable from one another—hence multidimensional—and many of these elements are vague in the philosophical sense of admitting of borderline cases and tolerating minimal changes. Property's multi-

---

[1] See Wesley Hohfeld, *Fundamental Legal Conceptions as Applied in Judicial Reasoning and other Legal Essays*, Walter Cook, ed. (New Haven: Yale University Press, 1919). Hohfeld provides an analytical tool for understanding various rights in terms of four "incidents": privileges (sometimes called "liberties"), claims, powers, and immunities. The view that property is to be understood in terms of a cluster of rights is not uncontroversial. See for example Lloyd Gerson's "Who Owns What? Some Reflections on the Foundation of Political Philosophy" in this volume.

[2] A. M. Honoré, "Ownership," in Anthony G. Guest, ed., *Oxford Essays in Jurisprudence* (Oxford: Oxford University Press, 1961), 107. Honoré's analysis presents a plausible proposal for understanding relatively modern conceptions of property and ownership in European and Anglo-American societies. Western conceptions of ownership and property have changed over the millennia. See, for example, Richard Schlatter's *Private Property: the History of an Idea* (New Brunswick: Rutgers, 1951).

[3] For ease of exposition, I will often speak only of the cluster of rights of ownership, omitting explicit mention of those incidents of ownership that are not rights. Unless otherwise indicated, I mean throughout to be speaking of all of the incidents of ownership, not merely those that are properly considered rights.

dimensional vagueness entails that individual instances of putative property can constitute borderline cases in two distinct ways. First, while all of the elements are, perhaps, necessary for *full* liberal ownership, that concept is a creature of philosophers and it is clearly stronger than our ordinary concept of property. In ordinary contexts, an object is comfortably considered property even if some of the incidents of full liberal ownership are missing. As Honoré noted, not all of the incidents of property are equally significant.[4] Our ordinary concept of property would clearly survive a failure to literally satisfy the "absence of term" requirement. So, one source of borderline cases arises from situations where most, but not all, of Honoré's incidents are instantiated in one person or group.[5]

Another source of vagueness arises because many of the incidents of ownership exist in degrees. This is nicely illustrated by Honoré himself in his discussion of his ninth incident of ownership: the prohibition on harmful use. He says:

> An owner's liberty to use and manage the thing owned as he chooses is subject to the condition that not only may he not use it to harm others, but he must prevent others from using the thing to harm other members of society. There may, indeed, be much dispute over what is to count as harm, and to what extent give and take demands that minor inconveniences between neighbours shall be tolerated. Nevertheless, at least for material objects, one can always point to abuses which a legal system will not allow.[6]

Clearly, the prohibition on harmful use can impose a variety of more or less severe limitations on the use of an object by its owner. As the restrictions on the individual's use of the object become more severe, we become less comfortable describing the object as the property of the individual. But it would be silly and simplistic to believe that there is a sharp line dividing those instances where the incidents of rights to use and manage are sufficiently met for an object to be the property of an individual and those where they are not so met.

---

[4] Honoré calls the right to possess "the foundation on which the whole superstructure of ownership rests." See Honoré, "Ownership," 113.

[5] This seems to be Honoré's considered opinion. For example, he says, "the listed ingredients are not individually necessary, though they may be together sufficient, conditions for the person of inherence to be designated 'owner' of a particular thing in a given system. As we have seen, the use of 'owner' will extend to cases in which not all the listed incidents are present." Ibid., 112–13. He does, though, insist that they are "necessary ingredients in the notion of ownership, in the sense that, if a system did not admit them, and did not provide for them to be united in a single person, we would conclude that it did not know the liberal concept of ownership, though it might still have a modified version of ownership, either of a primitive or sophisticated sort." Ibid., 112.

[6] Ibid., 123.

So, there is vagueness with respect to which elements of the cluster of full liberal ownership rights must be present in order for something to be properly considered property and there is vagueness along each (or at least most) of the elements of the cluster. There is much that could be profitably disputed about the ordinary concept of property, but it is foolish and fruitless to look for sharp lines of division between property and nonproperty.

For our purposes, the details of the correct account of property—whether or not the specific incidents of ownership that Honoré identified are correct and correctly characterized—are not crucial. We are trying to understand the nature and function of what I have labeled "the property paradigm." The details of how "the property paradigm" is understood will, of course, depend on the details of how "property" is understood. But these details need not concern us here. In whatever way the specific rights of ownership are understood, one important feature of the property paradigm is that it is *object-oriented;* that is, it is *objects,* either abstract or concrete, that are property. Not everyone uses the term in this way. Jeremy Waldron, for example, understands "property" as referring to "the *rules* that govern people's access to and control of things like land, natural resources, the means of production, manufactured goods, and also (on some accounts) texts, ideas, inventions, and other intellectual products" (emphasis added).[7] While the system of property is certainly a system defined by social and, in modern societies, legal rules, it is more consonant with common usage to reserve the term "property" for the *objects* that one has access to or control of under those rules rather than to apply it to the rules themselves. That "property" refers to the objects that are owned is part of our ordinary understanding of the term. (Police property rooms are, after all, not rooms filled with rules.)

This object-oriented focus is one part of the property paradigm. A second part has to do with the extent of the rights over these objects. We think of the objects which we count as property as being ones over which we have broad, though (as I have claimed) vaguely defined, rights. The third element I want to point to is this: having focused on objects over which we have rather extensive rights, we tend to think that this bundle of rights is largely the same for a wide variety of different objects we might own. We are inclined to think, perhaps without a great deal of reflection, that ownership of diverse objects involves roughly the same set of rights with respect to those objects.[8]

---

[7] Jeremy Waldron, "Property," in Edward N. Zalta, ed., *Stanford Encyclopedia of Philosophy* (Stanford, CA: Center for the Study of Language and Information). http://plato.stanford.edu/entries/property/ (accessed August 28, 2010).

[8] This is overly simplistic. Clearly, to the degree that we recognize intellectual property, we recognize that the rights that determine that the rights of ownership of this form of property are quite different from those of physical property. I am inclined to infer from this that intellectual property is, itself, a bit toward the edge of the property paradigm; it is not

The property paradigm is characterized, then, by object-orientation, and assumptions concerning the extent and similarity of rights over objects. When our thinking is governed by the property paradigm, we tend to focus on the question of *who* owns *what*—in the expectation that this will resolve, or help to resolve, questions of public policy in the way I have suggested above.

The property paradigm works like a conceptual analogue of the computer aided design (CAD) function of "snap to grid." Computer aided design programs assist those engaged in drafting and design by straightening and aligning with a grid of specified granularity lines that are drawn with a mouse or touchpad. The property paradigm is the conceptual analogue in the sense that it takes situations that are intrinsically different from one another and "snaps" them to a predetermined template. Doing this sometimes involves shoehorning and it always involves loss of detail. This is not a bad thing. One purpose of theories is to reduce information overload—to filter out irrelevancies and trivialities to allow us to understand general features of situations. We lack the mental resources requisite to understand the world in all its particularity. Problems arise, though, when the grid that we snap these cases to is too coarse or otherwise poorly defined. And these problems show up as puzzles for the paradigm.

III. PUZZLES

A. An old puzzle

Puzzles for the property paradigm arise nowhere more prominently than with respect to reproductive issues. Perhaps the most familiar example of this lies in the well-known problem of parental rights. Parents have, most believe, rather extensive rights over their children—especially over young children. A now quaintly obsolete approach of treating these rights as property rights provides a historical case study in the errors to which one can be led by the hegemony of the property paradigm. While the treatment of parental rights as property rights is largely a relic of the past, it bears a brief excursion as a prelude to the examination of more current controversies.[9]

In his 1680 defense of political authority, *Patriarcha; of the Natural Power of Kings*, Sir Robert Filmer conceived of parental rights, the "fountain of

the central case of our concept of property. But, in any event, my puzzle cases concern physical property and, so, my claim need only be about our tendency to think of all physical property as involving roughly the same sort of rights.

[9] David Archard explores some of implications of the proprietarian model of parental rights in "Do Parents Own Their Children?" *The International Journal of Children's Rights*, 1, no. 3 (1993): 293–301.

all *Reagal Authority*," as absolute property rights.[10] Filmer's defense of monarchy relied infamously on an extreme form of patriarchy according to which fathers hold full liberal ownership rights over their children. Indeed, the right that Filmer alleged fathers have over their progeny is "absolute dominion,"[11] which, if anything, is even more extreme than full liberal ownership.

In his response to Filmer, *Patriarcha non monarcha*, James Tyrrell raised several objections to Filmer's argument.[12] He challenged the gender exclusivity of this argument—pointing out that the procreative process would, contrary to what Filmer thought, result in mothers having a greater right than fathers.[13] Tyrrell also noted that, since the alleged paternal right would not exist in the absence of marriage, it cannot be grounded solely on a father's role in generation.[14] Moreover, in what strikes me as a rather modern move, Tyrrell proposed that it is not generation, but the education, sustaining, and "breeding up" of the child, that grounds parental rights.[15] Tyrrell specifically identified the limits of parental rights and authority by reference to his proposed grounding of parental rights in rearing, and sharply distinguished parental rights from property rights:

[10] Robert Filmer, *Patriarcha: of the Natural Power of Kings* (London: Richard Chiswell, 1680), 12.

[11] Ibid., 13.

[12] James Tyrrell, *Patriarcha non monarcha* (London: Richard Janeway, 1681).

[13] Tyrrell says: "Some Writers therefore think they have done sufficiently when they tell us, that the Father hath an absolute Dominion over his Child, because he got it, and is the cause of its being. By this Argument the Mother hath greater Right over the person of the Child, since all Naturalists hold the Child partakes more of her than of the Father; and she is besides at greater pain and trouble, both in the bearing, bringing it forth, nursing and breeding it up." Ibid., 14.

[14] Ibid., 14–15.

[15] Tyrrell proposes that:

... the highest Right of Parents in their Children, doth arise merely from their discharge of this great Duty of Education, as may appear from this Instance, Suppose the Parents not being willing to undertake the trouble of breeding up the Child, do either expose it, or pass over their Right in it to another, as soon as it is born; I desire to know if the person that finds this Child, or he to whom it is assigned, breed it up until it come to have the use of Reason, what Duty this Child can owe his Parents, if they are made known to him? Certainly, all the obligation he can have to them, must be upon the score of their begetting him; which how small that is, you may observe from what hath been said before: nor can the Parents claim any further Right in this Child, since by their exposing and granting it away, they renounced all the Interest they could have in it; so that the Duty and Gratitude he should have owed them, had they taken upon them the care and trouble of breeding him up, is now due to his Foster-Father or Mother, who took care of him until he was able to shift for himself. From whence it is evident, that the highest Right which Parents can have in their Children, is not meerly natural, from generation; but acquir'd by their performance of that nobler part of their Duty. And so the highest Obedience which Children owe their Patents, proceeds from that Gratitude and Sense they ought to have of the great obligation they owe their Parents, for the trouble and care they put them to in their Education. (Ibid., 14–15)

Since therefore the Father's greatest interest in his Child proceeds
from his having bred it up, and taken care of it, and that this Duty is
founded on that great Law of Nature, that every Man ought to endeav-
our the common good of Mankinde, which he performs, as far as lies
in his power, in breeding up, and taking care of his Child; it follows,
that this right in the Child, or power over it, extends no farther than
as it conduces to this end, that is, the good and preservation thereof:
and when this Rule is transgressed, the Right ceases. For God hath
not delivered one man into the power of another, merely to be tyr-
annized over at his pleasure; but that the person who hath this Authority, may use it for the good of those he governs. And herein lies the
difference between the Interest which a Father hath in his Children,
and that property which he hath in his Horses or Slaves; since his
right to the former extends only to those things that conduce to their
Good and Benefit; but in the other he hath no other consideration,
but the profit he may reap from their labour and service, being under
no other obligation but that of Humanity, and of using them as
becomes a goodnatur'd and merciful man; yet still considering and
intending his own advantage, as the principal end of his keeping of
them.[16]

It is probably fair to say that Tyrrell saw parental rights as fiduciary
rights—rights one has in virtue of a duty to act for the benefit of another.
This view is, I believe, very attractive to many today.[17]

In the *First Treatise*, John Locke (who corresponded with Tyrrell on
these issues), offers an extended discussion of Filmer's position.[18] Like
Tyrrell, he challenges the conclusion of patriarchy arising from the argument from generation.[19] In response to Filmer, Locke challenges the
assumption that the process of generation of human beings is of the sort
that will generate rights over the object created. Here, Locke must tread
carefully so as not to undermine the very premises he requires for his
labor theory of acquisition of objects, since he clearly believes such objects
can be owned as a result of our labor to create them. As Robert Nozick
notes, however, Locke appears to fail.[20] Locke seems to commit himself to
the idea that, as Nozick puts it, "one owns something one makes only if
one controls and understands all parts of the process of making it"[21]—a
criterion that would undermine much of the property that Locke wants to
endorse in the *Second Treatise*.

---

[16] Ibid., 15–16.
[17] See Donald C. Hubin, "Parental Rights and Due Process," *Journal of Law and Family Studies*, 1, no. 2 (1999): 126.
[18] John Locke, *Two Treatises of Government* (New York: Cambridge University Press, 1960).
[19] Ibid., section 55.
[20] Robert Nozick, *Anarchy, State, and Utopia*, (New York: Basic Books, 1974), 288.
[21] Ibid., 288.

Although the property paradigm has not completely disappeared from discussions of parental rights, I know of no serious contemporary defenses of the view that parental rights are instances of property rights; indeed, that view seems to have achieved the status of being the conclusion of a reductio ad absurdum argument, even if typically a specious one. That is to say, though no one I know seriously embraces the view that parental rights are property rights, various parties disputing custody issues *allege* that their opponents are treating children like property—sometimes in cross-complaints of the same alleged moral mistake.

In the philosophical literature, Susan Moller Okin uses the problem of parental rights to construct what she asserts is a reductio of libertarian theories—a reductio, she alleges, that was obscured by the history of political philosophy as a largely male discipline.[22] Libertarian theories, at least those along the lines of Robert Nozick's, will, she alleges, entail that everyone owns himself or herself exclusively and that everyone is owned exclusively by his or her mother as a result of the mother's labor in creating the child.[23] Since I do not wish to pursue this particular topic, which has been discussed by others,[24] I'll leave it with the simple observation that the obvious response seems to be the correct one—and it is one that Nozick alludes to and, for all Okin says, is not barred from presenting. That is, it is something about the nature of the *product* of human reproduction that bars ownership of that product in virtue of whatever labor the producer has put into the process; it is not the process itself (as Locke suggested) or the status of the raw materials from which the product is produced. This view is easily acceptable to those who deny the permissibility of even fully voluntary slavery. But it is also admissible by those who accept the permissibility (in principle) of fully voluntary slavery if they accept, as Nozick suggests he does, that "some things individuals may choose for themselves, no one may choose for anoth-

[22] Susan Moller Okin, *Justice, Gender, and the Family* (New York: Basic Books, 1989), 74–88. Her suggestion that it is a problem that was obscured by the degree to which political thought was male dominated is undermined, I think, by the fact that the issues were treated with some seriousness by the 17th-century philosophers mentioned above as well as by Nozick himself. Nozick's treatment is quick and breezy, of course, but given the style of *Anarchy, State, and Utopia,* that is no indication that Nozick does not take the matter seriously.

[23] In deducing the latter claim, Okin relies on the claim that a woman's labor in gestating and bearing a child is a clear case ("a paradigm" she says) of the sort of labor that the theory acknowledges gives one ownership in the product of the process. (See Okin, *Justice, Gender, and the Family,* 83.) And, furthermore, it is the woman alone who does this, employing sperm that she has acquired through a legitimate transfer—either as the result of a gift or a purchase. This latter claim will occupy us anon.

[24] See, for example: Anna-Karin Andersson, "An Alleged Contradiction in Nozick's Entitlement Theory," *Journal of Libertarian Studies,* 21, no. 3 (2007): 43–63; Ludvig Beckman, "Rights, Rights-Talk, and Children," *Journal of Value Inquiry,* 35, no. 4 (2001): 509–15; Roy W. Perrett, "Libertarianism, Feminism, and Relative," *Journal of Value Inquiry,* 34, no. 4 (2000): 383–95; Diane Jeske, "Libertarianism, Self-Ownership, and Motherhood," *Social Theory and Practice: An International and Interdisciplinary Journal of Social Philosophy,* 22, no. 2 (1996): 137–60.

er."[25] This is true, at least if we expand, as I suspect Nozick would, the dictum to say that some things individuals may choose for themselves, no one can choose for another, or *otherwise bring about for another* (without that other's choice).[26]

In setting aside here the issue of parental rights, I don't mean to suggest that they do not raise interesting problems for many political and moral theories—including, and maybe especially, libertarian theories.[27] Providing a justification for the set of rights and responsibilities that we believe, on reflection, parents have with respect to children can be a significant challenge—more so for some theories than others. And, *a fortiori*, I do not mean to diminish the importance of providing an adequate grounding for these rights and responsibilities, regardless of what implications such a grounding might have for extant theories. I am simply recognizing that, in the three centuries since the debates by theorists like Grotius, Pufendorf, Bodin, Filmer, Tyrrell, and Locke, the discussion of parental rights has largely moved away from the property paradigm.

This is not to say that the property paradigm does not influence people's reasoning with respect to parental rights. Here is an example of what we might call "remnants of the property paradigm" with respect to parental rights. Anna-Karin Andersson argues, quite reasonably, that parents do not have property rights over their children. She goes on to draw out what she takes to be an implication of her theory as follows: "Since parents do not own their children, other agents are morally permitted to confiscate other's offspring, provided they offer the child at least the same opportunities to develop autonomous agency as would the biological parents."[28] But, of course, unless we are thinking that the only sort of rights biological parents could have over their offspring are rights of ownership, no such thing follows. Progenitors or, more likely, procreators can have rights against such confiscation without having property rights over their offspring.[29] Even if the rights of progenitors and procreators against such confiscation are not acknowledged, virtually everyone would concede that parents who have reared, and are continuing to rear, their children have a right that the children not be confiscated by any strangers who can "offer the child at least

[25] Nozick, *Anarchy, State, and Utopia*, 331.
[26] This is roughly the line taken by Anna-Karin Andersson, "An Alleged Contradiction in Nozick's Entitlement Theory."
[27] I suspect that they are especially problematic for many standard libertarian theories that wish to limit government interference to actions that prevent force and fraud against moral agents.
[28] Anna-Karin Andersson, "An Alleged Contradiction in Nozick's Entitlement Theory," 62.
[29] For a discussion of the distinction between the status of progenitor and procreator, see: Peter Vallentyne, "Equality and the Duties of Procreators," in David Archer and Collin McCleod, eds., *The Moral and Political Status of Children* (Oxford: Oxford University Press, 2002), 195-211; and, Donald C. Hubin, "Daddy Dilemmas: Untangling the Puzzles of Paternity," *The Cornell Journal of Law and Public Policy*, 13 (2003): 61-69.

the same opportunities to develop autonomous agency" as would the parents. And few would ground this on the view that parents who rear those children *own* them. It is, then, implausible to think that *only* a person's ownership of a child can ground a right against confiscation of the child by another equally able potential parent.

Still, despite reverberations of the property paradigm in our reasoning about parental rights, the property paradigm has largely exited the scene as a ground of parental rights. Not so in all matters reproductive. While the property paradigm's role in discussions of parental rights has receded, it is still prominent in discussions of a variety of reproductive issues, including discussion of rights over frozen embryos and gametes. It is my contention that it distorts, rather than illuminates, these debates. I will try to make this case by focusing on certain reproductive issues for men—in particular, men's interest in their sperm.

B. A new puzzle: Sperm as property

Making sperm is a big job; adult human males produce as many as 250 million sperm cells per day. (Still, we are slackers compared with our grandfathers; seventy years ago, the normal sperm production rate was twice what it is now.) And it takes between sixty-five and seventy days for each sperm cell to mature. That is a lot of work, though fortunately it is all at the subpersonal level; that is to say, all of this happens without any conscious effort, or even awareness, on the part of the man. As a result, in typical cases, (Monty Python sketches to the contrary notwithstanding[30]) sperm is not considered by most people to be sacred or a "precious bodily fluid." In many contexts, it would seem to be treated more like a waste product than an object of value. But that is not always true.

Usually, our interest in sperm arises in connection with human reproduction. Of course, we also take a strong interest in sperm when certain crimes have been committed. In these cases, we are clear, I think, that sperm plays only a persuasive evidentiary role in identifying the criminal. That is to say, it is merely evidence of some further fact that is constitutive of the criminal act.[31] Another forensic interest we have in sperm concerns its reproductive role. We use sperm to identify paternity for purposes of establishing a child support obligation. Here, sperm *should* play the same role it does in criminal investigation. That is, it should be probative, but defeasible, evidence of a further fact that serves as the actual ground of a child support obligation. Unfortunately—probably

---

[30] "Every Sperm is Sacred," http://video.google.com/videoplay?docid=9002085385 040727366# (accessed August 30, 2010).
[31] I mean by this that the presence of a man's sperm is, like the presence of a fingerprint, typically good evidence that the man was present. It is also typically good evidence he ejaculated. Both conclusions are, of course, defeasible. However, if not defeated, they can be evidence that the man committed a criminal act in relevant contexts.

because of the current ease with which the producer of sperm can be identified and the difficulties of establishing the other factors that are relevant to whether a man has a morally justifiable obligation to support a child—courts in the United States have often treated a man's being the source of sperm either as constitutive of or as conclusive evidence of paternity in a sense relevant to the establishment of a duty to support a child. Paternity, though, is better thought of as a cluster concept; being the progenitor is only one element in the cluster and not, I think, a plausible candidate on which to rest most of the rights and duties of paternity. That a man's sperm produced a child is typically good evidence that he engaged in an action that can reasonably serve as a basis for assigning a paternal duty to support a child. However, the cases of posthumous impregnation, stolen sperm, and rape of a man by incapacitation all demonstrate that it is not conclusive proof of such an action.[32]

But forensic use of sperm is not the realm where the property paradigm perverts our understanding of the moral issues at stake.[33] The cases of interest are ones in which individuals assert a legally cognizable interest in how sperm is used. In these situations, where people have a strong interest in some specific sample of sperm being used, or *not being used*, in a particular way, it is natural to ask: "*Who* has the right to decide whether the sperm will be used in that way?" And, under the property paradigm, this is taken to be the question of ownership: "Who owns the sperm?" Sperm is treated as property, over which the owner has extensive rights and which can be bought, sold, stolen, given as a gift, obtained by fraud, trespassed, or converted.

Here's one way in which the property paradigm plays out with respect to sperm that is used for reproductive purposes. Susan Moller Okin arrives at her rather surprising (alleged) reductio against Nozick—the claim that his libertarianism implies a form of *matriarchy*—on the grounds that "women, and only women, have the natural capacity to produce *people.*"[34] And she arrives at *this* surprising proposition by assuming that human procreation is a process that is conducted by fertile females from sperm that is "freely given" or, in some cases, purchased.[35] She seems to think that it is obvious that, in a completed act of intercourse without a condom, the man has freely given his sperm to the woman in a sense relevant to the ownership of the sperm. As a result, after the gift, the woman has the extensive rights of ownership.

---

[32] For a sustained development of these arguments, see, my "Daddy Dilemmas: Untangling the Puzzles of Paternity," 50–61.

[33] The practice of various U.S. courts of treating a man's being the source of the sperm that resulted in the creation of a child as constitutive of (or conclusive evidence of) paternity in a sense relevant to the establishment of a duty to support, can be seen as a fallacy that results from what we might label "the paternity paradigm." For a detailed discussion of this matter, see my "Daddy Dilemmas: Untangling the Puzzles of Paternity."

[34] Susan Moller Okin, *Justice, Gender, and the Family*, 76.

[35] Ibid., 83.

The view that sperm is property, the title to which is voluntarily transferred in typical acts of voluntary sexual intercourse is neither unique to
Okin nor restricted to abstract philosophical discussions. In several court
cases in the United States, litigants have asserted the same proposition.
And, those opposing them, while denying that the transfer of sperm in
the act of sexual intercourse is a free gift, have themselves relied on the
property paradigm to assert their claim. The dispute is over *who* owns the
sperm, not over whether it is property.

For example, in New Mexico in 1998, Peter Wallis sued Kellie Smith for,
among other things, conversion of property for using his sperm in a
manner that he did not authorize after he had transferred it to her in an
act of voluntary intercourse.[36] According to Wallis's complaint, prior to
having intercourse, he and Smith engaged in a serious discussion of
possible reproductive consequences. Wallis, who did not want to become
a father, agreed to engage in sexual intercourse with Smith only if she was
on birth control pills. Smith represented to Wallis that she was. Wallis
alleged in his complaint that after their sexual relationship began and
without informing him, Smith stopped taking birth control pills and,
subsequently, became pregnant.

In 2003, in an Illinois case that raised similar issues, Richard Phillips
sued Sharon Irons for conversion of property (again, among other things).
Phillips alleged that in 1999, Irons "intentionally engaged in oral sex with
[Phillips] so that she could harvest [his] semen and artificially inseminate
herself," and that she "did artificially inseminate herself" with his sperm.[37]
At first blush, if the facts are as Phillips alleged, conversion of property
seems like a reasonable thing to allege—*provided the sperm was, even after
it was physically transferred, Phillips's property.* "Conversion of property,"
after all, is "[a] distinct act of dominion wrongfully exerted over another's
personal property in denial of or inconsistent with his title or rights
therein, or in derogation, exclusion, or defiance of such title or rights."[38]

Both sides in these disputes accept the property paradigm. The male
plaintiffs assert that their property has been wrongfully converted. The
female defendants allege that the property was freely transferred and so
their use of the property did not meet the legal definition of conversion
of property. As Sharon Irons put it in her pleadings: "when plaintiff
'delivered' his sperm to defendant it was a gift—an absolute and irrevocable transfer of title to property from a donor to donee."[39] I will not
venture an opinion as to whether, viewing sperm as property, the use
these women have made of the men's sperm that was transferred to them
through a voluntary act constitutes conversion of property as it is legally
defined. It is worth pointing out in passing, though, that the voluntary

---

[36] *Wallis v. Smith*, 22 P. 3d 682, 683 (NM: Ct. App. 2001).
[37] *Phillips v. Irons*, 354 Ill. App. 3d 1164 (Ill. App. Ct. 1st Dist., 2005).
[38] *Ballentine's Law Dictionary*, 3d ed. (Lexis Law Publishing, 2010).
[39] *Phillips v. Irons*, 16.

transfer of physical possession does not (generally) constitute voluntary transfer of property rights. As I have pointed out elsewhere,[40] if it did, parking valets would own far more, and probably far nicer, cars than they do. Given this obvious point, even if we accept the property paradigm with respect to a man's sperm, it certainly does not follow that he has freely given *ownership* of it to the woman in the act of voluntarily transferring it during intercourse.

The U.S. courts in these cases have agreed with the women, at least to the extent of denying that the facts alleged by the men in these cases constituted the crime of conversion of property. In doing so, they have, so to speak, denied the "conversion part" of the legal definition of the crime, not the "property part." I mean by this, that they have not questioned the allegation that the sperm was, initially, the property of the man; they have agreed with the women that in the transfer of the sperm, the man transferred his property rights in the sperm to the woman or, for other reasons, the women's use of the sperm did not meet the legal definition of conversion of property. In *Phillips v. Irons,* the court identified the four elements of the tort of conversion as: "(1) plaintiff's right in the property; (2) plaintiff's right to immediate, absolute, and unconditional possession of the property; (3) defendant's unauthorized and wrongful assumption of control, dominion, or ownership over the property; and (4) plaintiff's demand for possession."[41] The court rejected Phillips's appeal of the trial court's rejection of his conversion suit with this reasoning:

> In this case, no set of facts could be proved under the pleadings that would entitle plaintiff to relief for conversion, as he cannot satisfy the requisite elements. Cases from other jurisdictions have recognized the existence of a "property right" in materials derived from the human body . . . ; however, plaintiff cannot show he had the "right to immediate, absolute, and unconditional possession" of his sperm. Plaintiff presumably intended, and he does not claim otherwise, that defendant discard his semen, not return it to him. "The essence of conversion is the wrongful deprivation of one who has a right to the immediate possession of the object unlawfully held." Plaintiff is unable to satisfy the second element needed to state a claim for conversion. In light of the foregoing, the third and fourth elements of conversion need not be addressed.[42]

While the court did not explicitly hold that Phillips's sperm was initially his property, its reliance on the alleged absence of the second element, together with its explicit abstention on the final two elements suggests

---

[40] Donald C. Hubin, "Daddy Dilemmas: Untangling the Puzzles of Paternity," 52.
[41] *Phillips v. Irons,* 17.
[42] *Phillips v. Irons,* 17–18.

that it did not question this aspect of Phillips's suit. That is to say, it did not question the property paradigm's application to this case.

The property paradigm with respect to sperm also holds sway in cases where sperm has been frozen and could be used to fertilize an embryo either in vitro or in vivo. Sometimes the issue concerns posthumous reproduction. In an interesting, but all too brief, paper aptly titled, "Sperm as Property," Bonnie Steinbock, motivated by the case of bequeathal of sperm for posthumous reproduction, challenges a particular way that the property paradigm is employed in these cases.[43] Steinbock focuses on the California case of *Hecht v. Superior Court*,[44] in which the court had to decide whether the sperm of a deceased man could be bequeathed to his former lover for purposes of reproduction. Steinbock challenges the reasoning the court apparently used in resolving the case. The court seems to have reasoned that the key question to answer in determining whether the deceased man, William Kane, had the legal power to bequeath his sperm to Deborah Hecht, was whether the sperm was Kane's property. If it was, he could bequeath it; if not, he could not. Steinbock believes that this gets the order of justification exactly backwards:

> Cases like *Hecht* require judges to ask whether sperm is property because, if it is not, then it cannot be bequeathed by will. This suggests that we should first decide what property is, determine whether sperm is that sort of thing, and then conclude whether sperm can be bequeathed. However, this approach is backward. Whether sperm is property depends on what we think may permissibly be done with it. If there is a strong moral argument against allowing individuals to store sperm for the purpose of posthumous reproduction, then sperm should not be considered property for that purpose. If there is no such argument, sperm is rightly regarded as an asset that can be bequeathed by will.[45]

It is worth separating two questions here. First, there is the question faced by the court in *Hecht*, which had to do with how to apply the law to this case. With respect to this question, I have considerable sympathy with the court. It may well be that the law requires reasoning of this form. But there is another question that arises here, one that involves taking a legislative stance—the stance not of a court applying a law but of a legislature considering the rationale for proposed legislation.[46] From this

[43] Bonnie Steinbock, "Sperm as Property," in John Harris and Søren Holm, eds. *The Future of Human Reproduction: Ethics, Choice, and Regulation* (Oxford: Clarendon Press, 1998), 150–61.
[44] *Hecht v. Superior Court* 20 Cal. Rptr. 2d275 (Ct. App. 1993).
[45] Bonnie Steinbock, "Sperm as Property," 161.
[46] Two important caveats are needed here. First, if the clear meaning of the statutes in question did not answer the legal questions put by *Hecht*, then (one might argue) the court is placed in the role of adopting a legislative stance within the discretion allowed it by

stance, I think Steinbock is exactly right in her criticism of the order of justification. Regarding this question, I think, the judgment that something is property represents a summary of potentially independent arguments about the various rights involved in the notion of ownership. The various rights, powers, and other incidents involved in ownership must stand on their own, so to speak. When a sufficient number of them stand, we are comfortable calling the thing in question the property of the agent holding those rights and powers.[47]

While I have great sympathy with Steinbock's approach here, I think it grants too much to the property paradigm. In criticizing the court's reasoning as getting it backwards, she suggests that, while we cannot ground the judgment that Kane had the right to bequeath his sperm to Hecht on an independently grounded judgment that Kane owned the sperm, we can ground the judgment that Kane owned his sperm on the independently grounded judgment that he had the right to bequeath it. To be sure, Steinbock inserts an important qualification. She says, "[i]f there is a strong moral argument against allowing individuals to store sperm for the purpose of posthumous reproduction, then sperm should not be considered property *for that purpose.*" And, presumably, she means this qualification to apply to the next sentence as well. That is, she means to conclude, "[i]f there is no such argument, sperm is rightly regarded as an asset that can be bequeathed by will" *for purposes of reproduction.*

But the omission exemplifies the problem with the property paradigm. It is all too easy to move from a demonstration that an individual has some of the most central rights and powers of ownership to a conclusion that the individual owns the object in question. This is our moral consciousness "snapping to grid"; and it leads us into errors. It leads us to conclude, without warrant, that individuals have the full bundle of rights and powers usually attached to objects we are willing to call property when we have justified only a proper subset of these rights and powers. If we are serious about restricting the property right we are asserting to "that purpose," what is added by calling the thing "property"? Why not just stop at saying that the individual has a right to perform the act in question?

Indeed, Steinbock herself goes far too quickly from the absence of a strong moral argument against allowing individuals to store sperm for the purpose of posthumous reproduction to the existence of a right of bequeathal by will. Consider the following situation. We have determined

---

statute and other governing legal standards. Second, the order of justification that is relevant here is that of an ontological grounding, not a mere epistemic grounding. Surely, one should not deny that if it were known (or reasonably believed) on some independent basis, that Smith owns some object, one would be justified in drawing conclusions about what rights Smith had over that object.

[47] Recall that I am using this phrase as shorthand to include all of the relevant incidents of property, some of which are not, in fact, rights or powers.

that there is no "strong moral argument against allowing individuals to store sperm for the purpose of posthumous reproduction." Suppose, though, that we have also determined that there *are* strong moral arguments against each of the following: allowing individuals the right to destroy the sperm; allowing the sperm to be stored for this purpose beyond a very brief period of time, at which time it must be destroyed regardless of the wishes of the donors; allowing individuals to choose when, how, where, or by whom the sperm will be stored; and, importantly, allowing individuals to determine who may be and who may not be inseminated with the sperm. In this case, we *could* still say that the sperm is the man's property for the purpose of posthumous reproduction, but there is little point in invoking the language of property at all. So few of the incidents of property arise in the case that it is rather silly to think of this as the man's property in any sense. It is as if I said, pointing to the watch on my wrist, "This watch is your property for the purpose of looking at for the next several seconds." And, importantly, in our imagined case, the incident of property that allows for bequeathal by will is absent—indeed, it is undermined by the strong argument we have found against that individual choosing who may use the sperm and who may not.

I believe that Steinbock's seemingly seamless move from a mere right to store sperm for purposes of reproduction to the right of bequeathal reflects a lingering influence of the property paradigm.

IV. INTERESTS

Property is defined in terms of rights. If property is best understood along the lines of Honoré's account of ownership—and even if the details turn out to be wrong—in thinking about property, our attention is turned to the cluster of rights (and other incidents) that define property. And, if these are separable elements, then the determination that something is property will depend on how many and which of these elements are present and the degree to which they are present.

I agree with Steinbock that, in thinking these matters through from the foundation, we must place the question of what set of rights (and other incidents of ownership) are justified prior to the determination that an object is the property of some agent. And, then, the determination that the object *is* the property of that agent is really just a shorthand way of talking about the cluster of rights and powers in question. In my view, the discussion of what rights are justified depends crucially on what legitimate interests individual agents have. It is, I believe, the function of rights—their *raison d'être*—to protect certain important interests. But there are long-standing controversies about the relationship between rights and interests and I do not intend to try to resolve, or even to weigh in on, these disputes here. Rather, I hope to show that the moral problems to which I have pointed earlier are better framed in terms of balancing competing interests than in terms of whether or not an individual has enough of a bundle of rights to be reasonably considered ownership.

People care deeply about their own reproduction; they often have strong desires to reproduce under certain conditions or strong desires not to reproduce under others. These desires are important in people's lives, often central to their life plans. These desires are not, in general, morally suspect in the way that malevolent desires—or even desires for positional goods (goods the value of which depends on the status they confer relative to others)—might be thought to be. Because of this, they generally give rise to legitimate, morally significant interests. And, furthermore, they are interests that ought, prima facie, to be recognized by legal systems.

These legally cognizable interests in reproduction generate legally cognizable interests in the use to which our gametes are put. A couple pursuing offspring using in vitro fertilization has an interest in the fertility clinic combining the proper sperm and egg and implanting it in the proper uterus. Because of the artificial nature of assisted reproduction and the requirement for third-party involvement, these interests are generally protected by explicit contracts. Couples engaging in acts that could lead to reproduction have similar interests but, for a variety of reasons, explicit contracts are extraordinarily rare. Instead, we rely on custom and typical practice to set expectations. There may be no contract between a couple engaging in oral sex that the sperm not be used to try to produce a pregnancy, as was alleged in *Phillips v. Irons* and other cases,[48] without advanced notice. Nevertheless, such a use of the sperm is not reasonable for anyone to expect absent what we should surely consider the wrongful conduct of some other person. Furthermore, that conduct risks producing, and sometimes does produce, an outcome that is contrary to the legitimate interests of the man.

To retain the language of property, one *could* agree with the plaintiffs in *Phillips* and similar cases that the man has property in his transferred sperm for the purpose that it not be intentionally used for reproduction. But, here again, it is not clear what is added by the language of property. Certainly the defendants in these cases are right that with respect to any nonreproductive manner of using or disposing of the sperm, the woman is at complete liberty to do with it as she pleases. If one considers the full range of actions that might be taken with respect to the use or disposal of the sperm transferred by this act, surely the woman has a far broader range of dispositional control than does the man. But we overlook a very

[48] See, for example, *Louisana v. Frisard*, 694 So. 2d 1032, 1034 (La. Ct. App. 1997) in which the court found that a man whose sperm was allegedly recovered from a condom after oral sex and used by the woman he had engaged in oral sex with to impregnate herself was not entitled to relief from paternal obligations even if the facts were as he alleged.

important interest if we allow the property paradigm to lead us to the conclusion that the sperm is a "gift—an absolute and irrevocable transfer of title to property from a donor to donee."[49] If we allow our moral perception to be snapped to that gridline, the property paradigm has created a serious distortion of the moral situation.

What of the ownership of sperm transferred in voluntary genital intercourse? In this case, typically there is no subsequent future wrongful action that results in harm to the man's legitimate interests in not reproducing.[50] It would be a mistake, though, to think that in order for it to be true that the man has not transferred the right to use the sperm for reproductive purposes, the wrongful action has to be a subsequent act. Of course, contraception sometimes fails and when it does so through no fault of either party, each consenting party, having assumed the risk of such failure must assume the responsibility for the costs of the failure. However, if there is an intentional misrepresentation of one's use of contraceptive measures and the corresponding likely consequences of the sexual act—if, that is to say, one party intentionally leads the other to believe that the act of coitus has a much lower probability of producing a pregnancy than it would otherwise be reasonable for the other partner to expect it to have, and than it actually has—this is an intentional violation of that second party's serious reproductive interests. It is best not to view the transfer of sperm during sexual intercourse as a free gift of property.

And, if the transfer of sperm in voluntary genital intercourse is not a gift—a transfer of title of property from the man to the woman—then there is yet another problem with Okin's reductio of Nozick's argument. Mind you, it would be reductio enough if one showed that Nozick's theory implied that everyone is owned exclusively by *both* parents. It would contradict the claim of exclusive self-ownership and it would be a morally repugnant conclusion. But it would not be the conclusion that Okin advertises. Perhaps, in the way that Okin alleges that previous political philosophers have approached reproductive issues with gendered lenses that have obscured some legitimate interests, Okin herself has approached this issue with her own gendered lenses. Typically, males who engage in potentially reproductive behavior have legitimate interests in the reproductive uses of their sperm—interests that are ignored if we treat the transfer of sperm as the transfer of *full ownership rights.*

---

[49] *Phillips v. Irons,* 16.
[50] There could be. Suppose that the woman has had a tubal ligation—a fact that is known to the man and on which his voluntary genital intercourse is conditioned. If that woman, without the man's knowledge or permission, retrieves the sperm and combines it, in vitro, with an egg that was surgically removed from her ovaries, then implants it in her uterus resulting in a successful pregnancy (assuming all of this is possible), there would be precisely the sort of subsequent wrongful action of just the sort alleged in *Phillips* and *Frisard.*

Finally, Steinbock's concern with sperm as property is provoked by the case of the bequeathal of sperm for purposes of reproduction. If we admit posthumous interests at all—or even interests in posthumous treatment—I think it is highly plausible that a man has a legally cognizable interest in posthumous reproduction. This seems especially true when the situation is one in which a man's life has been cut short. And a woman may have a legally cognizable interest in being impregnated with a dead husband's or boyfriend's sperm. Now, of course, in any case of reproduction, we have to remember that "baby makes three!" That is to say, in balancing interests affected by choices of whether or not to reproduce (or to allow or facilitate reproduction), we must also consider the interests of the potential products of procreation. As Steinbock notes, in light of the apparent disadvantages to children raised in single-parent families, one might have concern about facilitating, or even allowing, the intentional decision to bring into existence a child who will have no living genetic father.[51] But, of course, some posthumous reproduction will involve a family situation for the child that is indistinguishable from other artificially assisted reproduction procedures that are relatively noncontroversial. There may well be a fully engaged second parent in the child's life. In any case, we have not, as a society, shown much interest in effecting even slight discouragements to intentional single-parenting.

There are difficult issues here that have implications for a much wider range of cases. And, of course, in making these procreative decisions (and the related decisions about what procreative acts to allow or facilitate), we always face the dicey comparison between scenarios that involve different people and different numbers of people.[52] There can be reasonable disagreements about the strength of the various interests involved. But the debate is put on better grounds when it moves from a dispute over who *owns* the sperm to one about which legitimate interests are advanced and which are impeded by the various choices that we could make—that is to say, when we approach the basic underlying moral issues, leaving behind the property paradigm.[53]

---

[51] Steinbock, "Sperm as Property," 155.

[52] The problems with the moral evaluation of population-affecting decisions were recognized early in utilitarian literature—at least as early as 1907 with the original publication of Henry Sidgwick's *The Methods of Ethics* (New York: Dover Publications, 1966), 414–16. Derek Parfit's *Reasons and Persons* (Oxford: Clarendon Press, 1984) provoked a great deal of philosophical literature on the normative and conceptual conundrums involved in the moral evaluation of decisions affecting the identity and size of future populations. See Parfit, *Reasons and Persons*, part four, generally.

[53] I do not mean to suggest that it is never appropriate to subsume gametes under the property paradigm. Absent special restrictions, human sperm and eggs that have been donated for research to one lab could, I would assume, be sold by that lab to another for research purposes. I am grateful to Jason Brennan and Matt Zwolinski for encouraging me to indicate this way in which my conclusion is a limited one.

V. Conclusion

The way in which we are led to think about complex moral questions when we subsume them under the property paradigm is just one instance of a very common and generally useful pattern of reasoning: reasoning from stereotypes. It may frequently involve some distortion, but it is a cognitively efficient approach to complex problems. I have argued, though, that in some cases the distortions are of significant import and give us good grounds for declining to employ the property paradigm to address the moral issues at stake. Attempts to understand the nature of parental rights in terms of property rights provide a historical example of where the paradigm produces distortions that are too significant to tolerate. And, I have argued, we also see distortions produced by the property paradigm in our considerations concerning human gametes.

The moral of these ruminations is not that the property paradigm should be rejected wholesale. With respect to the watch around my wrist or the 1968 Cougar in my garage, I urge that we keep using the property paradigm—especially with respect to my Cougar. It is a useful simplification of the moral situation, I think, and it does not do much harm there. With respect to parental rights over children, it produces terrible distortions, as even its early critics saw. And, I think, it also distorts our discussion of moral and legal issues concerning reproductive uses of sperm. It invites us to avoid the nuances that are necessary for a sensitive moral evaluation of the situation. This is an invitation we should decline.

Philosophy, The Ohio State University

WHY FREE TRADE IS REQUIRED BY JUSTICE*

By Fernando R. Tesón

I. Introduction

In this essay I argue that free trade is required by justice. Protectionist laws are indefensible on two grounds. First, they are indefensible in *principle* because they coercively redistribute resources in favor of persons who are not deserving beneficiaries under any plausible theory of domestic or international justice. Second, protectionist laws have objectionable *consequences* because they harm persons generally (they cause more harm than good), and they particularly tend to harm the poor. Resting on a robust consensus in the economic literature, I claim that liberalizing trade would contribute significantly to global and national growth and, mainly for that reason, would help in reducing poverty. An important corollary of my argument is that protectionist laws are indefensible, not just under a classical-liberal view of politics, but under *any* plausible moral-political theory.

Protectionist laws assume various forms: tariffs, import licenses, export licenses, import quotas, subsidies, government procurement rules, sanitary rules, voluntary export restraints, local content requirements, national security requirements, and embargoes. All these trade barriers, while different in a number of respects, have this in common: they raise the cost (sometimes prohibitively) of importing goods and services.[1] Protectionist laws are artificial, coercive obstacles placed by governments on voluntary transactions across borders. Citizens, and especially the poor, are doubly harmed by trade barriers. On the one hand, protectionist barriers erected by governments of *poor* countries harm their own people. Seen from this perspective, interference with trade is one more instance of the market-unfriendly policies that have caused much of the stagnation in the developing world.[2] Protectionism in developing countries goes hand in hand with unproductive public spending, corruption, ineffectual regulations—all features of economically and socially burdened societies. But on the other hand, when governments in *rich* countries enact protectionist laws, in addition to harming their own citizens, they harm the world's poor by

* I am heavily indebted to Jonathan Klick of the University of Pennsylvania, who did the research summarized in Section II. Many thanks also to the Social Philosophy and Policy Center of Bowling Green State University. The summer I spent there in 2008 as a Visiting Scholar allowed me to conduct part of the research for this essay.

[1] Trade barriers differ in their restrictive effect. See James E. Anderson and J. Peter Neary, *Measuring the Restrictiveness of International Trade Policy* (Cambridge, MA: MIT Press, 2005).

[2] See the discussion below, Section VII.

doi:10.1017/S0265052511000112

denying them access to wealthy markets. This *is* an injustice done by governments of wealthy countries to the world's poor. This particular injustice is a harmful, coercive interference with voluntary transactions—an unwarranted interference in the pursuit of personal projects in order to benefit persons who, as I shall show, are not deserving beneficiaries.

I proceed as follows. First I summarize the economics of trade presented by the most reliable *corpus* of research on international economics. The professional consensus is that free trade contributes to national and global economic growth and, mainly for that reason, helps the poor. I then examine the possible justifications for protectionist laws enacted by *rich* countries and find them wanting. I continue by examining the possible justifications for protectionist laws enacted by *developing* countries and conclude that those, too, are untenable. I end by discussing objections to my arguments.

II. The Economics of International Trade

In this article I assume the accuracy of the general consensus in the economic literature on the beneficial effects of international trade.[3] When trade opens between nations, in all practical situations joint gains occur and no country (considered as a unit) loses. In most situations, the gains of trade are split, so each of them gains. Therefore, not only does trade enhance aggregate wealth (that is, the wealth of both nations added together) but, in virtually every case, it also enhances the national wealth of each nation. This improvement occurs because the resources in each country are used more efficiently, as predicted by the law of comparative advantages. This law predicts that even if a country can produce one of the goods more cheaply than a trading partner, it still may import that good if doing so frees up its resources to produce a good in which its trading partner has an even greater cost disadvantage.[4]

---

[3] Economic models of international trade generally fall into two categories: the law of comparative advantages, which in turn has two versions, the Ricardian original version (see next note) and the Hecksher-Olin version; and the endogenous-growth model. The first model supports the view that liberalized trade is good for general economic growth and for the poor in particular. The second model is a version of the infant-industry argument and, while conceding that open trade is generally beneficial, it makes the case (I think unconvincingly) for sometimes supporting trade barriers in developing countries. For a full discussion of these trade theories, see Fernando R. Tesón and Jonathan Klick, "Global Justice and Trade: A Puzzling Omission," FSU College of Law, Public Law Research Paper No. 285; FSU College of Law, Law and Economics Paper No. 07-24. Available at SSRN: http://ssrn.com/abstract=1022996.

[4] The first proponent of the theory was David Ricardo. See David Ricardo, *On the Principles of Political Economy and Taxation*, section 7.15 (3d. ed. 1821), available at http://www.econlib.org/library/Ricardo/ricP.html. Country 1 has a comparative advantage in the production of good A relative to Country 2 if its opportunity cost of producing good A (i.e., how many units of good B it can no longer produce if it produces an additional unit of good A for a given stock of resources) is lower than Country 2's opportunity cost of producing good A. Or, more succinctly, Country 1's marginal rate of transformation between Good A and Good B is lower than that of Country 2. Ricardo offers an example in which England and

Even under models that defend some trade barriers in specific situations (like the endogenous-growth model) restraints on trade generate short-term losses. Moreover, in this model long-term gains from the restraints are highly uncertain and depend, implausibly, on the foresight and predictive ability on the part of rulers. In particular, those models overlook the potential susceptibility of such actors to rent-seeking activities on the part of those industries seeking protection.[5]

The theoretical and empirical evidence shows that a country benefits even when it liberalizes trade *unilaterally*.[6] In that situation, all countries improve; moreover, the growth is most pronounced in the liberalizing country[7]—an insight that contradicts the folk belief that the country that liberalizes unilaterally is the naive loser in the international trade game.

The finding that trade is a positive-sum game when nations are considered as units contradicts the claim that the country that erects trade barriers helps itself and hurts other countries. We routinely hear this claim from politicians and others not trained in economics, and it is based on a serious economic mistake: that exports are good and imports are bad. The view is known as mercantilism.[8] Mercantilism views trade as a

---

Portugal both produce wine and cloth. If it takes 100 English workers one year to produce quantity X of cloth and 120 English workers one year to produce quantity Y of wine, and it takes 90 Portuguese workers to produce X units of cloth and 80 Portuguese workers to produce Y units of wine in the same time period, Ricardo claims that Portugal will import its cloth from England and export wine to the country. To see this, if Portugal allocates its 90 cloth workers to wine-making, in principle, it can ship 9/8 Y units of wine to England. In turn, England can now allocate its wine workers to cloth production, sending 6/5 X units of cloth in return to Portugal. After this trade, employing the same total amount of workers as before, Portugal has 20 percent more cloth than it previously produced (and the same amount of wine), and England has 12.5 percent more wine than it previously produced (and the same amount of cloth). While the exact split of the surplus generated by the trade will differ depending on the relative demands for wine and cloth in the two countries, in Ricardo's example both countries have the potential to expand their consumption of both goods without using more resources. Joint consumption of both goods across the two countries is guaranteed to rise even though Portugal can produce both goods more cheaply than England can. That is, economic growth occurs even if Portugal has an absolute advantage in the production of both goods. Earlier, Adam Smith had argued the case for free trade when a nation has the opportunity to trade with a country exhibiting an absolute advantage in desired goods. By specializing in the good in which its comparative advantage lies, trade effectively allows both countries to shift their production possibility frontiers outward. I owe this explanation of the law of comparative advantages to Jon Klick. For a full treatment, see Fernando R. Tesón & Jonathan Klick, "Global Justice and Trade: A Puzzling Ommission."

[5] Gene Grossman and Elhanan Helpman, "Protection for Sale, *American Economic Review* 84 (1994): 833 present their rent-seeking model as a plausible way to look at trade policy. An individual engages in rent seeking when he tries to obtain benefits in the political arena, as opposed to trying to obtain them in the market. See David Henderson, "Rent-Seeking," in the *Library of Economics and Liberty*, at http://www.econlib.org/library/Enc/RentSeeking.html.

[6] See the collection of essays in Jagdish Bhagwati, ed., *Going Alone: The Case for Relaxed Reciprocity in Freeing Trade*, (Cambridge, MA: MIT Press, 2002).

[7] See Dan Ben-David and Michael B. Loewy, "Knowledge Dissemination, Capital Accumulation, Trade, and Endogenous Growth," *Oxford Economic Papers*, 52 (2000): 646.

[8] Mercantilism was refuted more than 230 years ago, notably by Adam Smith, *An Inquiry into the Nature and Causes of the Wealth of Nations*, R. H. Campbell and A. S. Skinner ed., vol. 2 [1776]; (Indianapolis: Liberty Fund, 1981), 642–66.

zero-sum game where one country's gains come at the expense of other countries. It rests on the false assumption that a surplus in international trade must be a deficit for other countries.[9] Mercantilists claim that exports, believed to benefit domestic producers, should be encouraged, while imports, believed to hurt domestic producers, should be discouraged.[10] But national well-being is based on present and future increased consumption. Exports are valuable only indirectly: they provide the income to buy products to consume.[11]

Mercantilism is so obviously wrong that one wonders why it continues to enjoy political and, in some circles, even academic success. The endurance of mercantilist beliefs stems from the discursive pathologies of politics. First, trade theory is *opaque and counterintuitive*. The public cannot easily see that the country that protects hurts its own citizens. Instead the public tends to adopt simpler zero-sum explanations of social outcomes.[12] Second, protectionists use the imagery of nationalism. We need to protect "us" against "them"; our local industries against the invading products; our culture against immigrant invasion.[13] People use vivid imagery for political gain. To see the advantages of trade, people need to see that the government that protects *hurts its own people*.[14] This is concealed by the notion of "protecting" *something that is ours*, in our country, against *something that comes from the outside*. Because that "something" is alien or external, politicians and rent-seekers can easily portray it as a threat. All one can say is a trivial truth: that the government can protect *specific* producers and workers by shielding the industry from foreign competition (or, for that matter, from domestic competition.) But trade barriers do not "protect" the employment rate in one's country because they have high opportunity costs. They artificially divest resources toward inefficient endeavors. Nor do trade barriers "protect" the real value of wages. Conversely, trade barriers positively harm *all* consumers, that is, everyone. When the rhetorical smoke clears, trade barriers benefit inefficient producers who prey, courtesy of the government, on defenseless consumers.

---

[9] See Thomas A. Pugel and Peter H. Lindert, *International Economics*, 11th ed. (McGraw-Hill, 2000): 33.

[10] Ibid.

[11] Thus, "imports are part of the expanding national consumption that a nation seeks, not an evil to be suppressed." Ibid. Equally problematic is the claim that imports reduce domestic employment. See Laura LaHayes, "Mercantilism," *Concise Encyclopedia of Economics,* http://www.econlib.org.

[12] Guido Pincione and I analyze this phenomenon in *Rational Choice and Democratic Deliberation: A Theory of Discourse Failure* (Cambridge, UK: Cambridge University Press, 2006).

[13] This rhetorical argument was criticized more than a hundred years ago by Henry George. See Henry George, *Protection of Free Trade: An Examination Of the Tariff Question, with Special Regard to the Interests of Labor,* chap. 6 (1886), Library of Economics and Liberty, http://www.econlib.org/library/YPDBooks/George/grgPFT6.html.

[14] As Jagdish Bhagwati writes: "The fact that trade protection hurts the economy of the country that imposes it is one of the oldest but still most startling insights economics has to offer." Jagdish Bhagwati, "Protectionism," in *The Concise Encyclopedia of Economics,"* http:www.econlib.org/library/Enc/Protectionism.html.

One way to encapsulate the mercantilist mistake is this. Mercantilists see protectionism as an *unsuccessful coordination game:* "Our country must protect because we know *they* will protect. If only they made a credible commitment to repeal their protectionist laws, we would do the same." However, protectionism is best characterized as a *successful rent-seeking game:* industries affected by foreign competition seek and obtain protection from their governments in exchange for political support and other benefits.[15] Two further facts explain the political success of protectionism notwithstanding the well-known fact that open trade benefits the great majority of the population. The groups that benefit from free trade, such as consumers, are *diffuse* and have high organizational costs; while the groups that benefit from protection are *concentrated* and have low organizational costs. Further, while trade theory predicts that in the long run many of the workers and firms now hurt by foreign competition will be better off because free trade creates higher-paying jobs and higher returns to capital, workers and owners have trouble grasping these benefits.

The theoretical prediction is that freer trade causes global and national growth in *aggregate terms.* Critics of free trade have long argued that the beneficial aggregate effect of trade is consistent with the bad effect of leaving the poor out, as it is possible that the gains of trade fall on the rich or the middle class of both trading partners.[16] Nations must be disaggregated to find out who wins and who loses with open trade. On this view, when we take *persons or families* as units, free trade may well lead to losses for the poor.[17]

This objection finds no support in theory or evidence.[18] An analysis of the effect of trade on poverty centers on a simple two-step argument:

---

[15] I owe this insight to Jon Klick.

[16] This is what critics of globalization mean by the cliché that "trade helps big business." Even philosophers of the stature of John Rawls echo such sentiments. Referring to the European Union, Rawls writes:

> The large open market including all of Europe is aim of the large banks and the capitalist business class whose main goal is simply larger profit. The idea of economic growth, onwards and upwards, with no specific end in sight, fits this class perfectly. If they speak about distribution, it is [al]most always in terms of trickle down. The long—term result of this—which we already have in the United States—is a civil society awash in a meaningless consumerism of some kind.

John Rawls and Phillipe van Parijs, "Three Letters on The Law of Peoples and the European Union," *Revue de Philosophie Économique* 8 (2003): 9. Phillipe van Parijs approvingly calls this passage Rawls's "most explicitly 'anti-capitalist' text."

[17] As an aside, all theories of justice have difficulty identifying the appropriate entity (class, family, individual) that should benefit from redistribution of resources.

[18] The specialized research converges on this point. See L. Alan Winters, "Trade and Poverty: Is There a Connection?" (2000), www.wto.org/English/news_e/pres00_e/pov3_e.pdf; T. N. Srinivasan and Jessica S. Wallack, "Globalization, Growth, and the Poor," *De Economist* 152 (2004): 251; David Dollar and Aart Kray, "Growth is Good for the Poor," *World Bank Policy Research, Working Paper,* no. 2587 (2001).

trade enhances growth, and growth reduces poverty.[19] Even if openness to trade *at first blush* does not help the poor more than it helps others, why assume that the poor will end up worse off than before? When a country grows, good things happen. More industries are created, more jobs are available, and so the opportunities for the poor expand. Further, when a country grows, so do societal resources that can be used to alleviate poverty. The more resources a country has, the more resources the government will have. And the more resources the government will have, the more effectively it will address the country's poverty. So whether a country's economic policies are laissez-faire or redistributive, the poor will benefit from access to global markets as producers and consumers.

In general, empirical studies have found that "in most cases, trade reform increases the income of the poor as a group and that the transition costs are generally relatively small relative to the overall benefits."[20] However, a country may liberalize trade yet simultaneously pursue policies that are counterproductive for either growth or wealth distribution. This conflict of forces occurred in Argentina, where the liberalizing measures of the 1990s were accompanied by massive unproductive public spending and political corruption.[21] Under those circumstances, it is of course fallacious to attribute the cause of the country's collapse (and the corresponding increase in poverty) to trade liberalization. It is therefore crucial to control for non-trade variables when assessing the effects of trade on the poor. Specialists recommend that governments accompany the country's adaptation to the law of comparative advantages, for example, by easing industrial adjustment or helping the country diversify its exports, always in the light of its comparative advantages.[22]

But even if the gains from trade were partially skewed against the poor, trade would still be beneficial. For consider: The main goal of development policy is to get poor countries to *develop*, even prior to computing distributional effects. So it is a bit strange for trade skeptics to reject a practice that concededly makes a poor country grow by saying: "no, not *that* kind of growth." At the very least, they should

---

[19] The evidence for this proposition is overwhelming. For a nontechnical account, see Jagdish Bhagwati, *In Defense of Globalization* (Oxford, UK: Oxford University Press, 2004), pp. 51–67. For a more technical analysis, see Neil McCulloch, et al., *Trade Liberalization and Poverty: A Handbook* (Centre for Economic Policy Research 2001), and Jagdish Bhagwati and T. N. Srinivasan, "Trade and Poverty in the Poor Countries," *American Economic Review* 92 (2002): 180. As these authors show, the argument that free trade helps the poor are static (freer trade should help in the reduction of poverty in the poor countries which use their comparative advantages to export labor-intensive goods), and dynamic (trade promotes growth; and growth reduces poverty).

[20] Geoffrey J. Bannister and Kamau Thugge, "International Trade and Poverty Alleviation," *Finance and Development* 38 (2001): 50.

[21] See Jean-Cartier Bresson, "Economics of Corruption," *OECD Observer* (May 2000), www.oecdobserver.org/news/fullstory.php/aid/239; and Joseph Contreras, "Argentina's Fiasco," *Newsweek*, December 21, 2001.

[22] See, e.g., Bhagwati, *In Defense of Globalization*, p. 55.

welcome free trade and then propose measures to correct the undesirable distributional effects.

To be sure, trade liberalization will produce winners and losers, and many of those losers will be poor. But my claim here is not that *each* poor person will improve as a result of trade liberalization; in fact, no policy can do that. The claim is that, in virtually every instance, the poor *as a class* will improve. On the issue of cost of goods, trade liberalization will help the poor in the same way it helps all consumers: by lowering prices of imports and keeping the prices of substitutes for imported goods low, thus increasing people's real incomes. On the question of wages, the evidence seems to show a number of things. Labor markets need flexibility to adjust to comparative advantages. If firms are too constrained by labor laws from reducing their work forces, then the poor may suffer as a result. This is ironic, given that supporters of strict labor regulations claim to act *on behalf* of the poor.[23] Also, the gap between the wages of skilled and unskilled workers may increase, but this is hardly an objection to the claim that the poor as a class benefit from trade liberalization. The objection that liberalizing trade will reduce government revenues, and thus its ability to fight poverty, is also misplaced because it ignores the dynamic effects of trade liberalization. If trade liberalization produces growth, taxable incomes will grow as well, and government revenues will grow with them. And independently of whether the poor are able to export (that is, independently of whether or not foreign markets are open to the goods they produce), the poor *benefit from having a wider variety of available goods to consume*, either because the imported product is not available domestically or because trade lowers the price of the product, bringing it within the reach of the poor.

In sum, trade liberalization (1) increases *aggregate* wealth, that is, wealth measured aggregatively in both trade partners; (2) increases wealth in *each* of the trade partners, and (3) *at the very least*, within each trade partner, such growth is most often shared by the poor in various ways. The burden of proof is on those who deny the beneficial effects on trade. That burden is heavy indeed.

It is important to note the claims I do *not* make in support of free trade. Free trade does not necessarily reduce *inequality* among trade partners or among different groups or individuals within the trade partners. Further, free trade is not a panacea for economic success: countries with bad institutions are less likely to reap the benefits of trade. In particular, nations need to recognize well-defined property rights, freedom of contract, and the rule of law.[24]

---

[23] Thus, for example, critics of sweatshops claim that, due in part to lax work conditions, "clothing companies benefit from free trade through BIG profits, and garment workers lose out." See http://www.sweatshopwatch.org/index.php?s=36

[24] The literature on the importance of good governance is extensive. A seminal work is Douglass C. North, *Institutions, Institutional Change, and Economic Performance* (Cambridge, UK: Cambridge University Press, 1990).

III. The Injustice of Trade Protection by Rich Countries

Rich nations are, in general, less protectionist than developing nations.[25] However, they have enacted strong protectionist laws for targeted sectors—in particular agriculture. The United States periodically reenacts the Farm Bill, which obligates the government to buy surplus from farmers in order to keep prices artificially high.[26] The European Union has long maintained the Common Agricultural Policy, a euphemism denoting, too, a vast system of subsidies that keeps inefficient European farmers in business.[27] In addition to these subsidies, rich nations have enacted a host of (mostly) phony regulations, such as quality control, sanitary rules, government procurement rules, and so on, the effect of which is often to virtually ban imported agricultural products. These restrictions certainly harm *consumers* in rich countries who have to pay more for agricultural products. Without these barriers, consumers would simply buy the cheaper (and usually better) agricultural products from developing nations, while the resources now artificially channeled toward agricultural protection would be freed to produce goods and services where the rich nations are comparatively efficient.

These laws, of course, harm local consumers, and are objectionable just for that reason, since, as we shall see, the government has no moral justification for interfering with a voluntary transaction in this way. But crucially, these laws harm *producers* in developing nations as well, because they lose wealthy markets for their products. I have little to add to the extensive literature documenting this fact.[28] Farmers in developing countries experience catastrophic losses as a result of Northern subsidies.[29] Unless these laws can be morally justified, they inflict an injustice on the world's poor by coercively interfering with their means of subsistence and growth.

Can these restrictions be nonetheless justified? Here we face an interesting problem for global justice. In rich countries, these agricultural subsidies are redistributive: they transfer wealth from domestic consumers and foreign farmers to domestic farmers. Supporters of these laws may

---

[25] See the *2010 World Index of Economic Freedom*, published by the Heritage Foundation and the Wall Street Journal, at www.heritage.org/index/. The study evaluates economic freedom generally, not just trade openness. However, trade openness is one of the components, and the ratings can be found in the section "Executive Highlights" of the report.

[26] The Food, Conservation, and Energy Act of 2008 (Pub.L. 110-234, 122 Stat. 923, enacted May 22, 2008, H.R. 2419, also known as the 2008 U.S. Farm Bill) is a $288 billion, five-year agricultural policy bill that was last passed into law by the United States Congress on June 18, 2008. This bill has been roundly criticized from right and left. See "A Disgraceful Farm Bill," *The New York Times*, May 16, 2008.

[27] For a useful description and summary of criticisms, see "Common Agricultural Policy", at www.economicexpert.com/a/Common:Agricultural:Policy.htm

[28] See Thomas Pogge, *World Poverty and Human Rights* 2d ed. (Polity, 2010): 17–19.

[29] See "The Farmers Ruined by Subsidies," *The Times Online*, www.timesonline.co.uk/tol/news/world/africa/article1629405.ece.

invoke reasons of distributive justice. Let us assume, implausibly, that farmers in rich countries are, under appropriate principles of distributive justice, the rightful beneficiaries of societal subsidies. Still, those subsidies hurt *foreign* farmers, and in particular farmers in developing nations. This means that even if the protectionist could successfully argue that the transfer is *domestically* justified, he cannot possibly maintain that the protectionist laws meet any test of global justice that focuses on alleviating world poverty. For protectionist laws interfere with voluntary transactions between consenting sellers and buyers in such a way as to hurt the most vulnerable. By enacting these laws rich countries *worsen* the situation of the world's poor.

This is a serious problem for mainstream theories of distributive justice, for they were originally designed to evaluate a basic *domestic* institutional structure, the goal of which is to benefit the *domestic* worst-off groups in society.[30] When those theories add global reach, however, it turns out that the domestic redistributive policies they favor often hurt the distant poor, who almost always are considerably worse off than the domestic poor. The startling conclusion is that enforcing redistributive programs in the name of *domestic* justice may well violate *international* justice or, at least, international duties of humanity or charity toward persons elsewhere that are struggling for survival. For example, in the United States some support imposing a tax on corporations who move their operations to developing countries. They justified this tax by proclaiming the need to "keep jobs at home." Yet, should this policy succeed, it will deny significant employment opportunities to poor persons in developing countries.

This incompatibility between domestic and international justice has led some influential philosophers to reject a justice-based global duty to redistribute wealth.[31] Under this view, justice mandates redistribution of resources only within state borders. These writers argue that preferring compatriots is morally acceptable as long as we do not violate the rights of foreigners. Our farmers (farmers in rich countries) hurt by foreign competition are entitled to our solicitude and help; distant others are not. The Farm Bill is simply an instance of moral solicitude toward those who are closest to us and share a common project. As long as our government doesn't *directly* harm foreigners it is empowered to enact policies in accordance with its best understanding of domestic distributive justice. The government is not a global charity agency. It has been appointed by the citizens of the state to serve their needs and advance their interests, as long as in doing so it does not violate the rights of foreigners. Raising the

---

[30] Loren Lomasky and I explore this issue in *Justice at a Distance* (unpublished manuscript).
[31] See Richard Miller, "Cosmopolitan Respect and Patriotic Concern," *Philosophy and Public Affairs* 27 (1998): 202; John Rawls, *The Law of Peoples* (Cambridge, MA: Harvard University Press, 1999), pp. 113–20; and Thomas Nagel, "The Problem of Global Justice," *Philosophy and Public Affairs* 33 (2005): 113. There are important differences among these authors, but all favor a preference for compatriots in tax-based help (as opposed to voluntary charity.)

cost of imported goods is not a violation of a right that the foreign producer holds. True, the foreign farmers' clientele has been reduced, but no one has a vested right in a clientele. If one is willing to export goods, one has to expect that foreign governments will sometimes intervene in markets in order to realize (domestic) social justice. On this view, given the fact that governments are the normal agents for realizing justice in their own societies, this is a risk that exporters in developing countries should assume. So, the argument concludes, we must concede that compatriots are entitled to our help, and that therefore we cannot condemn protectionist laws just because they harm the distant poor.

This superficially attractive objection fails for several reasons. First, trade barriers *actively interfere* with the rights of persons, namely the rights of buyers (the domestic consumers) and sellers (the foreign producer). So it is incorrect to describe the situation as remote or indirect harm. A protectionist law coercively interferes with contract and directly harms the parties. The innocent description of a protectionist law as mere help to local producers misses the coercive nature of those laws. They help the producer by coercively interfering with a contract between the foreign exporter and the domestic importer, thus harming both. If the protectionist concedes that our duty toward foreigners is a negative duty of noninterference (as opposed to aid), then protectionist laws violate that duty. Particularly significant is the fact that a protectionist barrier violates a right of producers in developing nations: their right to freely dispose of their property, a right that is very important because it is intimately tied to their subsistence.

Second, the inefficient local producer does not have a right to foist his products on the public who no longer wants them. If consumers no longer demand the product it is hard to see what principle of justice, or any other principle, authorizes the producer to enlist the government in force-feeding his products to consumers. A law that grants the producer a monopoly can hardly be justified with public reasons. Nor do the workers in that industry retain a right to their job, given that their employer does not need them anymore. I cannot identify any principle that can justify state coercion to help people produce things that consumers no longer want.

The point can be put differently. We all suffer setbacks and disappointments in our lives. If I lose my job, or if someone rejects me, I can say I have suffered a setback.[32] What kinds of setbacks can the state legitimately prevent or compensate? Certainly, the state should prevent unjust setbacks, such as those to which the criminal law reacts. But it is not the state's job to redress all setbacks. This would be absurd because most of what people do in their everyday lives affects others. For example, if Joe decides to marry Kirsten instead of Meredith, and Meredith loves Joe,

---

[32] I avoid the word "harm" here because it prejudges the issue.

Meredith will be disappointed because her interests will be set back. If enough consumers decide to buy Apple computers because they judge them better, makers of PCs will suffer. If two persons compete for the same job, the interests of the one who is not chosen will be set back. Perhaps a necessary condition for legitimate state intervention is that the setting back of an interest be wrongful. That is, A *harms* B when (1) A sets back B's interest, and (2) A does this in a manner that violates B's rights.[33] Since in the above examples no rights are violated, those setbacks ought not to be compensated.

In the realm of international trade the loss of a job due to foreign competition is not an unjust setback of interest because it is purely *competitive*. The worker suffers because consumers are no longer interested in buying what he produces. Here I follow John Stuart Mill's lead in *On Liberty*:

> In the first place, it must by no means be supposed, because damage, or probability of damage, to the interests of others, can alone justify the interference of society, that therefore it always does justify such interference. In many cases, an individual, in pursuing a legitimate object, necessarily and therefore legitimately causes pain or loss to others, or intercepts a good which they had a reasonable hope of obtaining. . . . Whoever succeeds in an overcrowded profession, or in a competitive examination; whoever is preferred to another in any contest for an object which both desire, reaps benefit from the loss of others, from their wasted exertion and their disappointment. But it is, by common admission, better for the general interest of mankind, that persons should pursue their objects undeterred by this sort of consequences. In other words, society admits no right, either legal or moral, in the disappointed competitors, to immunity from this kind of suffering; and feels called on to interfere, only when means of success have been employed which it is contrary to the general interest to permit—namely, fraud or treachery, and force.[34]

Competitive setbacks of interests do not violate rights (notice that in this passage Mill does not even use the word "harm.") A free society should not redress competitive disadvantage for three reasons. First, as Mill says, competition creates wealth and benefits society as a whole. Second, the setback of someone's interest by a competitor is not wrongful because it is the result of a *fair contest*.[35] And third, the attempt to *redress*

---

[33] Joel Feinberg, *Harm to Others* (Oxford, UK: Oxford University Press), p. 65.

[34] John Stuart Mill, *On Liberty* [1859] in John Stuart Mill, *Utilitarianism, Liberty and Representative Government* (New York: Dutton 1971), 72.

[35] Here I follow Arthur Ripstein, "Beyond the Harm Principle," *Philosophy and Public Affairs* 34, no. 3 (2006): 215. Writes Ripstein: "[I]f you defeat me in a fair contest, you do not deprive me of any of my powers. I merely failed at something that I was trying to do. That

competitive disadvantage in turn seriously harms third parties, usually the more vulnerable, by coercively interfering with their voluntary transactions. Whatever the general justification the government of a rich nation may have for interfering with contracts, surely harming poor persons to benefit richer persons cannot be part of it. These deontological and consequentialist reasons should be extended to our present globalized economy. Protectionism is a particularly unjust form of coercive redress of competitive disadvantage.[36]

The protectionist could reply that workers have acquired certain expectations that the government must try to preserve. It is not the worker's fault, he may argue, that his industry is now inefficient. He got this job, started a family, bought a home; in short, made life plans that are now frustrated by events he cannot control. For that reason, the worker disadvantaged by foreign competition is a proper beneficiary of societal help. On this view, trade barriers are justified, not so much to enrich the local employer (although they do that), but to preserve jobs. And it is appropriate for consumers to pay for this: society (the consuming public) subsidizes fellow citizens (the workers of the affected industries) who are suffering hardship. It is no different from other forms of wealth redistribution.

Responding to this argument leads to the final and conclusive refutation of the protectionist view. Even if we assume, contrary to what I have suggested, that the government is generally empowered to interfere with trade, protectionist measures are indefensible because they fail to achieve their goal: they do not and cannot effect just redistribution of wealth.[37] When a government protects an industry it *aborts the creation of jobs in other industries*. This occurs because as the economy is unable to adjust to the efficiencies of production, resources are artificially directed to the less efficient endeavors. The government assists workers in those inefficient industries by erecting trade barriers. But what should we say about the person who is now unemployed *because new industries* that would have employed him have been aborted by the strangling effect of protectionist laws? Seen in this light, producers and workers who benefit from protection are *not* deserving of transfers of wealth in their favor, because protection is harming *other* persons in that society. Since those persons are the unemployed,

---

failure may disappoint me, but it doesn't deprive me of means that I already had, it only prevents me from acquiring further ones. My defeat may change the context in which I use those powers in future: if you win the championship, other people may no longer hire me to endorse their products. But I had no entitlement against you to a favorable context or to have those other people enter into cooperative arrangements with me." (At pp. 238–39.)

[36] A useful discussion of competitive harm can be found in Richard A. Epstein, "The Harm Principle—And How It Grew," *University of Toronto Law Review* 45 (1995): 369.

[37] Mill makes exactly the same point: "Restrictions on trade, or on production for purposes of trade, are indeed restraints; and all restraint, *qua* restraint, is an evil: but the restraints in question affect only that part of conduct which society is competent to restrain, and are wrong solely because they do not really produce the results which it is desired to produce by them." *On Liberty*, Section V, "Applications."

they are worse-off than the protected workers. Just as the firms obtaining protection get rich at the expense of foreign firms, so the workers in protected industries keep their jobs at the expense of the poor, *in their own countries*. Because this harm really consists of the opportunity costs of inefficient laws, it can only be gauged by asserting counterfactuals and is, for that reason, opaque. The public cannot easily see it.[38]

So, even assuming the nationalist premises of the argument, protectionist laws in developed countries are objectionable because: (1) they violate the rights of foreign producers by interfering with their voluntary transactions; (2) they do not benefit persons or groups that, on any plausible theory of domestic or international justice, are entitled to a transfer of wealth in their favor, and (3) they hurt the domestic poor (by aborting the establishment of efficient industries) and domestic consumers (by raising prices). When we add the fact that protectionist policies, far from being the outcome of a quest for justice, are ordinarily the reaction to political rent-seeking and other forms of predatory behavior, the argument from domestic justice vanishes. Well-organized protected industries hire powerful lobbyists who essentially "buy" the protectionist legislation from politicians interested in incumbency.[39] If protectionist barriers in rich countries are objectionable even without considering their effects on foreigners, they become particularly offensive when they harm the distant poor.

IV. The Injustice of Trade Protection by Developing Countries

Some people who criticize protectionism by rich countries are nonetheless reluctant to condemn protectionism by developing countries. This is a mistake. The arguments against protectionist laws apply equally to developing nations. Powerful local monopolies enlist the government in protecting them against foreign competition, thus hampering economic growth and perpetuating economic stagnation. The debate, once again, suffers from a fatal rhetorical glitch caused by the public's failure to understand the economics of trade.

Critics of rich-country protectionist barriers correctly see that those barriers hurt producers in developing nations, thus hampering those nations' growth. But they do not believe that poor-country protectionist laws will hurt producers in rich countries much, and even if they did, it wouldn't matter much from the standpoint of global justice, since the

---

[38] There is yet another reason to oppose protectionism: even if the protectionist is right that the state can legitimately aid workers disadvantaged by trade, erecting trade barriers is a bad remedy. Domestic transfer policies such as industrial retraining are more efficient and fair ways to help those workers.

[39] The politics of protectionism are well summarized in John O. McGinnis and Mark L. Movsesian, "The World Trade Constitution," *Harvard Law Review* 114 (2000): 521–31. See also Gene Grossman and Elhanan Helpman, *Protection for Sale* cit.

critics' moral concern is to alleviate the plight of the world's poor. Protectionism in developing countries, they claim, is at worst morally neutral because it doesn't harm foreign persons in a way that global justice should care: producers in rich countries have vast markets at their disposal, in particular their own wealthy domestic markets. In fact, some have gone further and insisted that protectionism by developing countries *benefits* those countries. This approach enjoyed considerable vogue during the 60s and 70s mainly as a result of the promotion by the United Nations Economic Commission for Latin America and the Caribbean (CEPAL, an acronym of the Spanish name.) It recommended a nationalist economic policy based on import substitution and massive public spending as prescriptions for growth and development. This policy ("Cepalism") was implemented in Latin America and Africa with disastrous results.[40] Vastly discredited today, this theory is still sporadically invoked by populist demagogues to justify nationalist policies.[41]

The view that protectionism by poor countries is benign ignores the central premise of international economics, which bears repetition: the government that erects trade barriers *hurts its own citizens*. Protectionism is self-destructive. In developing countries, the problem is not that these laws hurt producers in rich countries, but rather that they prey on *domestic* consumers in two ways. First, those laws force them to forego the economic choices generated by international trade; second, they abort the creations of new industries by redirecting resources toward inefficient activities. As I indicated, this harm is opaque. Tragically, the unemployed person in my native Buenos Aires cannot *see* that a main reason for his predicament is that inefficient producers and their powerful unionized workers have successfully lobbied the Argentine government to get protection against foreign competition. In this way, the labor unions have improved their situation vis-à-vis our unemployed person, because the latter now will not be employed by an industry that was *aborted* by the perverse incentives created by protectionist laws. Because understanding this requires, not only knowing the complex and counter-intuitive law of comparative advantages, but also positing a *counterfactual* that is itself hard to grasp, the victim of this governmental depredation does not see himself as such and, sadly, continues to support the populist demagogues in the hope that he, too, will benefit from some subsidy or other. A society of producers, sadly, has become a society of beggars.

When we think about who benefits from these laws in developing nations, we realize that the redistribution of wealth resulting from pro-

---

[40] For Latin America, see Hernando de Soto, *The Invisible Revolution in the Third World* (New York: Harper & Row, 1989); for Africa, see George B. Ayittey, *Africa Betrayed* (New York: St. Martin's Press, 1992).

[41] For the example of Hugo Chávez in Venezuela, see Álvaro Vargas Llosa, "The Rise of Hugo Chávez," *The Independent Institute*, September 19, 2007, www.independent.org/newsroom/article.asp?id=2028.

tectionist laws cannot possibly be supported by moral reasons. The crude reality is that more often than not the industries that benefit are close allies of the regime in place. In exchange for protection those industries consolidate the rulers' power by helping them win elections or enabling them to persist in their undemocratic ways. But even ignoring this political reality, even assuming that trade protection is not a corrupt deal between government and industry, the redistribution of resources is a *reverse subsidy* in favor of the better-off members of society. This occurs in two ways. First, the owners and workers of protected industries benefit at the expense both of local consumers (who, remember, in these nations are overwhelmingly the poor). Second, the protectionist laws *abort* the creation of new, efficient industries, thus hurting those persons who *would* have been hired in those industries but is now unemployed. No political theory I know of can justify these transfers.

A final point. It is no mere coincidence that, with some exceptions, the wealthier countries have *less* trade barriers than the developing countries. If protectionist barriers were so good for developing nations we should see some evidence of this in the numbers. Not so. Nations who defeated poverty did so mostly by establishing market-friendly institutions and fixing their non-economic institutions, such as the judiciary. Trade openness is a component of economic openness, and the correlation between market-friendly institutions and economic prosperity is undeniable.

V. Trade and Coercion: The Problem of Stolen Goods

International trade takes place mostly between private agents. A private producer in state A attempts to sell his product to private consumers in state B but the government of state B interferes by placing trade barriers, thus raising the cost for the consumers. Governments, I have argued, should not interfere with these voluntary transactions. But sometimes this voluntariness has been vitiated. Trade presupposes legitimate ownership over the traded goods, but sometimes the traded goods are stolen. How should the international trade system address the problem of stolen goods? The view that condemns trading in stolen goods has two versions: the Imperialist Thesis and the Dictator-Thief thesis. According to the Imperialist Thesis, rich people in developed nations presently hold resources that they obtained in the past from people in developing countries through theft, force, and deception. Trading with the poor the very resources that the owner stole from him is deeply wrong. According to the Dictator-Thief thesis, despots stole resources from their subjects and sold them to foreigners (usually in rich nations) mostly to advance these despots' own interests and consolidate their power. Both theses recommend corrective measures even before opening trade. We must return the stolen goods to their rightful owners; only then we could start talking about free trade. I discuss each thesis separately.

I have two replies to the Imperialist Thesis. The first is simply that its factual premises are, for the most part, wrong. The reasons why some nations are rich and others are poor have little to do with theft. Rather, they have to do with different equilibria between productive and predatory forces in society, as reflected in the quality of institutions and in particular on the success or failure of market-friendly practices. But there are surely some instances (some colonial cases come to mind) where perhaps some of the resources currently held by persons in rich countries are ill-gotten. However, even if ideally compensation would be sometimes justified, the practical difficulties of determining what part of the current wealth held by individuals should be returned to their rightful owners would be daunting. Surely not all wealth, not even its greatest part, is stolen.

But the Imperalist Thesis is misconceived in another sense. It recommends *not* liberalizing trade on the grounds that rich countries have no title over the goods they trade. Yet international institutions should help *reduce poverty, here and now*. If corrective measures are infeasible either because the theft took place too far back in time, or because we cannot possibly know the percentage of wealth that was stolen, or because the amount of coercion needed to restore the *status quo ante* is morally prohibitive, or simply because international politics pose insurmountable practical obstacles, or for some other reason, then that should not be a reason to refuse to liberalize trade, here and now, as a way to alleviate the world's poverty.

The Dictator-Thief thesis is harder to answer.[42] A defense of free trade rests on the moral worth and beneficial effects of voluntary transactions. Yet dictators in some developing countries often appropriate the resources from the people and then sell them to foreigners, most of the time for their own enrichment.[43] In these cases the international transaction was *coerced* at some point, namely when the tyrant appropriated the resources at gunpoint. The case evinces an egregious failure of *domestic* institutions, aggravated by a defective rule of international law—the so-called principle of effectiveness.[44] Under international law, whoever politically con-

---

[42] The argument is made by Mathias Risse, "Justice in Trade I: Obligations from Trading and the Pauper-Labor Argument," *Politics, Philosophy, and Economics* 6 (2007): 356, and more fully by Leif Weinar, "Property Rights and the Resource Curse," *Philosophy & Public Affairs* 36 (2008): 2.

[43] See Leif Wenar, "Property Rights and the Resources Curse."

[44] Under traditional international law, any government (with some exceptions) with effective political control over a territory is deemed to be, internationally, the legitimate government of the state. Moreover, international law is generally indifferent about how the resources of the state are internally distributed: they may be in private hands, or they may have been expropriated by the government in whole or in part. See, e.g. UN General Assembly, *Declaration of Principles of International Law Concerning Friendly Relations and Co-operation Among States in Accordance with the Charter of the United Nations*, 24 October 1970, available at: http://www.unhcr.org/refworld/docid/3dda1f104.html [accessed 25 April 2011], especially the principle that (e) "Each State has the right freely to choose and develop its political,

trols the country has a right to sell its resources. This rule is obviously unjust, not only from the standpoint of basic human rights, but from the standpoint of market rules themselves. The result is objectionable in principle because it countenances the sale of stolen goods, and in terms of its consequences because it aggravates poverty, since the tyrant does not utilize the resources to benefit the people but to increase his own power and wealth. Because the gains from trade are achieved at the expense of the victims of theft and oppression, these persons arguably have a fairness complaint against the trading partner, that is, the buyer of stolen goods.[45] An evaluation of free trade from the standpoint of justice must therefore recommend, as Leif Wenar does, abolishing the rule of effectiveness and substituting the principle that resources belong to the rightful owners and not to the rulers.[46] I think, therefore, that Wenar's general point is essentially correct and that the international trade system should be reformed to require that exported goods belong to their rightful owners.

There are a couple of difficulties with the argument, however. Wenar claims that material resources *collectively* belong to the people. This principle, he says, is compatible with either private or public ownership of the resources. According to Wenar, for the government to be legitimately entitled to sell the resources, the process of public acquisition must meet democratic strictures.[47] But the idea of the *people* collectively owning the resources does not sit well with private property rights. My house belongs to me, not to the people. Wenar attempts to solve this problem by requiring that any transfer of resources to the government be sanctioned by democratic procedures. Yet many "socialist" governments are not very different from our Dictator-Thief. The majority is no more entitled than the dictator to steal from the private owner *just because it is a majority.* So, in order to specify the rightful owners of the traded goods, Wenar must add a plausible *substantive* theory of justice that shows when the government may redistribute resources in its favor (or in its friends' favor.) This is not the place to discuss this large issue in political philosophy. Suffice it to say that grotesque dictators are not the only ones who steal resources from their rightful owners. Many democratically-elected governments

---

social, economic and cultural systems." This rule allows governments to expropriate private property and do exactly what Wenar criticizes: sell them. Even more explicit are the principles in the Declaration on Permanent Sovereignty over Natural Resources, G.A. res. 1803 (XVII), 17 U.N. GAOR Supp. (No.17) at 15, U.N. Doc. A/5217 (1962), cited approvingly by Weinar: "4. Nationalization, expropriation or requisitioning shall be based on grounds or reasons of public utility, security or the national interest which are recognized as overriding purely individual or private interests, both domestic and foreign."

[45] Risse, "Justice in Trade I," 362.

[46] This same point was made by Thomas Pogge, "Recognized and Violated By International Law: The Human Rights of the Global Poor," *Leiden Journal of International Law* 18 (2005): 717; Peter Singer, *One World : The Ethics of Globalization* (New Haven: Yale Univeristy Press, 2004), 96–105; and, in general terms (not specifically in reference to the trade system,) in my book *A Philosophy of International Law* (Boulder: Westview, 1998), 1–2.

[47] Wenar, 20–21.

(governments that would satisfy Wenar's proviso) systematically steal from their citizens as well.

Moreover, dictators of the world believe that placing the collective ownership on "the people" entitles them, the dictators, to dispose of the resources. As I indicated, the standard interpretation of the international instruments that Wenar cites (such as the Declaration on the Permanent Sovereignty of Natural Resources) endorses the governments' power to expropriate resources. This is why dictators support the principle that the "people" collectively own the natural resources: they claim to represent the people, *l'état, c'est moi!* In other words: Weinar's interpretation of the principle of permanent sovereignty over natural resources departs from the (objectionable) common understanding in international law that undemocratic governments, too, are deemed to represent the people. This means that Wenar cannot just invoke the people's ownership of natural resources without adding a theory of international representativeness that is diametrically opposed (although of course better) than the theory presupposed by the international instruments on which he relies.

Finally, it is entirely unclear that the government in the country where the prospective buyers reside will cure this injustice by erecting protectionist barriers. The Dictator-Thief problem dramatically underscores the fact that most injustices are homegrown, as I have indicated. While opening international trade alone will not remedy those injustices, closing trade will not do the job either. Here as elsewhere, protectionism is an ill-suited remedy to cure the problem. Something different is required, namely establishing a corrective procedure for restoring the stolen goods to their owners while maintaining free trade. The Dictator-Thief objection accurately identifies a problem in international trade, the problem of predatory rulers. *This* problem, however, cannot be solved or alleviated by protectionist laws.

These difficulties are not fatal to Wenar's thesis. He can simply claim that the global trade system must address the difficulty of stolen goods, *whatever* our thesis may be about when the goods are in fact stolen. Yet, the fact remains that, grotesque cases aside, liberal egalitarians will often disagree with classical liberals about when traded goods are indeed stolen goods.

VI. The Pauper-Labor Argument

Some authors believe that domestic workers in rich countries are entitled to protection if the imported goods arrive in our shores, not through oppression or theft, but as a result of lower labor standards in the countries of origin. This is the Pauper-Labor argument, usually advanced with considerably stridency in labor circles. Mathias Risse has given a qualified defense of this argument. For him, if labor laws in rich countries are established for moral reasons, then for the sake of consistency workers harmed by imports deserve compensation from the government.[48] The idea is that the moral reasons that underlie labor standards are universal, so while the government cannot enforce those in the country of origin, it should acknowledge the universality of those reasons by compensating domestic workers harmed by imports. The domestic workers' competitive disadvantage is the direct result of a morally objectionable act.

It is doubtful, however, that many labor standards are always or often enacted for moral reasons. The overwhelming evidence is that governments enact them for a host of political reasons, including protectionist reasons.[49] However, perhaps labor standards are *supported* by moral reasons, even if the government had other reasons for enacting the standards. This will largely depend on the labor standard in question. Take minimum wages: It is unlikely that high wages in rich countries are supported by moral reasons. These salaries are the result of self-interested bargaining by workers, either individually or through unions, at a time where world labor markets were highly segmented. With the rise of globalization, it became obvious that labor in developing countries was more competitive. Understandably, labor leaders in rich countries speak of sweatshops and slave labor, thus implying that workers in developing countries are in the same moral category as the oppressed, that they are coerced into working for miserly salaries, almost at gunpoint.[50] This rhetoric conceals the fact that unionized workers in rich countries have been simply out-competed. Assuming voluntary relationships, including a right to terminate the contract, one does not have a right to an ongoing high wage if the employer finds someone that can perform the same work at a lower wage.[51] In fact, my intuition is exactly the opposite to Risse's: domestic workers in rich countries are acting *immorally* when they demand protection against cheaper imports, because in doing so they are knowingly enlisting the state in the aggravation of world poverty.[52]

---

[48] Risse, "Fairness in Trade I," 366–69.

[49] See Risse's example of the 1930 U.S Tariff Act, ibid., 367. Horacio Spector has identified labor standards precisely along these dimensions, and concluded that most of them do *not* reflect moral principles but rather rent-seeking, desire to avoid competition, etc. See Horacio Spector, "Philosophical Foundations of Labor Law," *Florida State University Law Review* 33 (2006): 1119.

[50] For a refutation of these arguments, see Matt Zwolinski, "Sweatshops, Choice, and Exploitation," *Business Ethics Quarterly* 17 (2007): 689–727.

[51] Of course, parties must abide by their contracts, so employers could be contractually committed to paying higher wages even if cheaper labor is available elsewhere.

[52] Quite apart from this, the evidence does not support the view that trading with developing countries has depressed wages in rich countries. Rather, trade with poor countries may well have improved wages, in the sense that it has moderated the decline that might have occurred due to non-trade factors, such as labor-saving technological change. Jagdish Bhagwati, *In Defense of Globalization*, 124–25.

But perhaps *some* labor standards, such as occupational safety rules, are morally required in the sense that the workers have a *right* to those standards.[53] Even then, Risse's argument fails for two reasons. First, if workers in a developing country have a right to a labor standard, the employer who denies it harms those workers. It is entirely unclear why workers in the *rich* country should be entitled to compensation, especially considering that the taxpayers of the rich country, who have done nothing wrong, must foot the bill. Maybe the argument is that the failure of the developing country to secure the standard creates a "right" by workers in the rich country that their government ban the import (or place trade barriers against it.) This has the peculiar effect of enriching parties who were not wronged (were not denied the labor standard in question) and who are already much better off by global standards, while at the same time harming the people who have already suffered the alleged injustice.[54] Surely this cannot be right.

Second, the argument assumes that labor standards are *inalienable*. This is highly dubious. Imagine that the government of a developing country offers a choice to workers in a particularly successful industry. The government offers to enforce the standards, but workers must understand that this would make their product more expensive and hence less competitive overseas. Because the market for this particular product is largely foreign, enforcement of the labor standards will adversely affect the workers' own welfare. Alternatively, the government offers to relax the standards to keep the industry internationally competitive and thus continue to benefit workers. If the workers accept this offer they *consent* to lower standards in exchange for their overall economic welfare. They trade the risk of a workplace injury or illness for their enhanced prosperity. I cannot see why this would be objectionable unless one thinks, implausibly, that individuals are morally forbidden from making trade-offs of this kind. Accepting a higher occupational risk in exchange for a better economic prospect seems far removed from the standard cases of inalienability, such as consenting to being tortured, or even selling an organ. In this case workers in rich countries have no claim to protection.[55]

---

[53] I am even unsure about the claim that safety standards are morally required. Why not think of different levels of safety as labor benefits offered by businesses, so that workers can freely choose between various combinations of accident risk and economic welfare? But I don't pursue the matter.

[54] I owe this point to Matt Zwolinski.

[55] Matt Zwolinski and Ben Powell make a similar point in "The Ethical and Economic Case for Sweatshop Labor: A Critical Assessment" (unpublished, 2011). Here again, the evidence does not support the much feared "race to the bottom", i.e., the view that allowing imports from countries with low standards will cause governments to relax theirs, thus creating a desperate race to lower production costs. Rather, the evidence shows exactly the opposite, a race to the *top*. As incomes rise in poor countries, their growing middle class expects and demands improvements in the workplace conditions. See Bhagwati, *In Defense of Globalization*, 127–34.

VII. Is the Current Trade System Unjust?

Given the advantages of free trade, the role of the World Trade Organization (WTO) in liberalizing trade has been positive.[56] By enforcing the most-favored-nation clause, the WTO system has dramatically lowered tariffs and other trade barriers in the last fifty years or so, with the corresponding global economic growth.[57] However, while the current WTO regime is preferable to a generalized protectionist regime, it has a number of imperfections from the standpoint of justice and efficiency. First, current arrangements allow governments to over-protect, thus hampering the chances that the poor will participate in the world economy. One problem with the WTO treaty, therefore, is that it *does not liberalize trade enough*.[58] In particular, the WTO rules that allow protection of agriculture by rich countries are highly objectionable, as I have already pointed out. The WTO should enforce the most-favored-nation clause without exceptions if it is to be consistent with global justice.[59] Second, although generally structured to gradually lower trade barriers, the WTO regime is partly predicated on outdated mercantilist notions: governments seek to secure foreign markets access for exporters, thus treating access to *their* markets as a bargaining "chip." Because imports benefit consumers, the notion that granting access to one's markets is a *concession* to other countries is false. A government that lowers tariffs helps its own citizens. This fact is, yet again, concealed by the nationalist rhetoric of protectionism. So the WTO is suboptimal from the standpoint of global justice, and it is certainly inferior to more liberal alternatives, like unrestricted trade.[60]

Still, however bad the present system may be, protectionism is worse. Current critics of the WTO, while rightly criticizing protectionism in rich countries, wrongly claim that developing nations can sometimes help

[56] The World Trade Organization was created in 1995, and it is the international organization that deals with trade rules among nations. It is the successor to the General Agreement on Tariffs and Trade, which had been in place since 1947. See http://www.wto.org/english/thewto_e/thewto_e.htm.

[57] See McGinnis & Movsesian, *The World Trade Organization*, 529–47.

[58] For an earlier appraisal of the protectionist features of the WTO (then the GATT), see Jagdish Bhagwati, *Protectionism*, in *The Concise Encyclopedia of Economics*, (1988), available at http://www.economlib.org. My criticism of the WTO is diametrically opposed to the criticism by the anti-globalization forces, who blame the WTO for being too biased toward free trade. I believe, on the contrary, that the WTO does not do enough to promote free trade.

[59] The most favored nation clause is the centerpiece of the international trade system. It prohibits discrimination among trade partners by obligating members to extend any trade concession they make on a product to the same product exported by everyone else. Article 1 of the GATT 1947 (one of the constitutive agreements of the WTO), reads: "any advantage, favour, privilege or immunity granted by any contracting party to any product originating in or destined for any other country shall be accorded immediately and unconditionally to the like product originating in or destined for the territories of all other contracting parties."

[60] See Amartya Sen, "How to Judge Globalism," *American Prospect* (Winter 2002): 2 ("Global interchange is good; but the present set of global rules needlessly hurts the poor.").

their economies by enacting protectionist measures. The institutional solution that could bring the world closer to the ideal of unrestricted trade is a WTO-like organization whose sole purpose is to ensure that nations liberalize trade. On the other hand, excessive international regulation *restrictive* of trade, even if meant to address a genuine market failure, is often counterproductive with regard to the poor.

The main contrary view is represented by the work of Thomas Pogge.[61] He claims that the global order, and especially the world trade system, is *directly responsible* for poverty.[62] According to Pogge, the global order, established and dominated by rich countries, systematically confines millions of persons to extreme poverty. This happens through a variety of mechanisms, of which three are salient. First, rich countries refuse to liberalize agriculture. They protect their own rich farmers, thus harming farmers in the developing world. Second, rich countries have succeeded in enforcing intellectual property rights on pharmaceuticals, which exacerbates health problems in the developing world. And finally, the global order controlled by rich countries is too deferential to sovereignty. This allows corrupt and tyrannical elites in the developing world, in complicity with the West, to exploit their subjects.

Pogge deserves credit for having awakened new audiences to the awful reality of world poverty; for having called attention to the objectionable protectionist policies by rich countries; and for having challenged the prevailing notion of sovereignty upon which the international order relies. On the latter issue, the sanctity of borders and its political incarnations, nationalism and national interest, have harmed many persons in history and done much to undermine justice in the world at all levels. Economic relations, no less than political relations, often proceed without sufficient scrutiny of the moral credentials of governments. Global institutions such as the World Bank and the International Monetary Fund are subject to criticism on this score, because they assist developing countries without pausing to consider whether they are thereby consolidating bad governance and, eventually, perpetuating poverty as well.

The problem with Pogge's theory is that his *causal* claim is wrong. The global order, far from being the cause of poverty, is responsible for the vast amelioration of extreme poverty over the last one hundred years or so. As Mathias Risse explains, according to Pogge's own benchmarks, the global order "has caused amazing improvements over the state of misery that has characterized human life throughout the ages."[63] Once one controls for domestic institutions, Pogge's attempt to blame rich countries loses much of its superficial appeal. Rich countries got rich for quite

---

[61] See Thomas Pogge, *World Poverty and Human Rights*, 2d ed. (Malden, MA: Polity, 2008).

[62] Ibid., 1–32.

[63] Mathias Risse, "Do We Owe the Global Poor Assistance or Rectification?" *Ethics & International Affairs*, 19 (2005): 9–10.

diverse reasons, usually anchored in Europe's embracing of capitalism and technological innovation. The literature points to two of such reasons: the emergence of good, stable institutions, and the establishment of efficient markets.[64] Even when those institutions were morally objectionable to our modern eyes, they were nonetheless hospitable to growth and innovation. As David Landes put it:

> The economic expansion of medieval Europe was . . . promoted by a succession of organizational innovations and adaptations, most of them initiated from below and diffused by example. The rulers, even local seigneurs, scrambled to keep pace, to show themselves hospitable, to make labor available, to attract enterprise and the revenues it generated.[65]

This is known as the institutionalist thesis, the view that poverty and stagnation are caused by deficient institutions, including, but not limited to, insufficient protection of private property and freedom of contract. Pogge's attempt to dismiss the massive evidence in favor of the institutionalist thesis is, I think, unsuccessful.[66] Some of his more specific empirical claims are dubious as well. For example, Pogge cites the rich countries' protectionist agricultural policies as evidence that the global order (which allows these practices) causes poverty. While those unjust practices exacerbate the problem, they are far from being the main cause of world poverty. The explanation understates the importance of domestic institutions, as explained.[67] It suggests that stagnation in the developing world derives mainly or only from what *others* do, and thus fails to control for the ruling elites' contribution to that stagnation.[68] Further, whether the West's protectionist policies harm farmers of a given developing country

[64] Mathias Risse develops a full (and I think definitive) response to Pogge in his article "How Does the Global Order Harm the Poor?" *Philosophy and Public Affairs* 33 (2005): 349-76.

[65] David Landes, *The Wealth and Poverty of Nations*, (New York: Norton, 1998), 67-68. See also his description of the ideal wealth-creating society, 239-40.

[66] Pogge is aware that his views are contradicted by mainstream economic research. That is why he, uncharacteristically, dismisses economists *in totum*. He writes that we should take the economists' findings with a great deal of caution, because "while economists like to present themselves as disinterested scientists, they function today more typically as ideologists for our political and economic 'elites'—much like most theologians did in an earlier age." Thomas Pogge, "Real World Justice," *Journal of Ethics* 9 (2005): 29.

[67] See Kym Anderson, Agriculture, Trade Reform, and Poverty Reduction: Implications for Sub-Saharan Africa, http://www.unctad.org/en/docs/itcdtab24_en.pdf. The author shows that while trade liberalization in the agriculture sector can bring important gains, developing countries need to change their "anti-agriculture, anti-export and anti-poor bias of current policies." The extremely complex empirical issues are set forth in M. Ataman Aksoy & John C. Beghin, eds., *Global Agricultural Trade and Developing Countries* (Washington, D.C.: World Bank, 2004).

[68] At several points Pogge suggests that this emphasis on domestic factors, which he calls *explanatory nationalism*, may be self-serving. See *World Poverty*, pp. 4, 6, and 15.

depends on the size of the market for that country's exports. Argentina, for example, sells her beef and grain mostly to Russia, China, India, and Egypt. Given that the rising demand for agricultural products (at the time of this writing) comes from non-Western countries, farmers in developing countries might be in a particularly advantageous situation, as they do no longer depend on exporting those products to Western markets. They are certainly less likely to be harmed by the West's trade policies. Of course, this is an empirical issue and will vary for particular countries and products, but the truth is that protectionist policies harm first and foremost the country's *own* consumers. Of course Pogge is correct in calling for the dismantling of the West's protectionist policies. As I argued, that call is part of the general call to liberalize trade for *moral* reasons. But saying that liberalizing agricultural trade will help is not the same as saying that the current protectionist policies of Western powers are the main cause of poverty.

VIII. A Curious Case Study: Export Subsidies

I said that the government that enacts protectionist laws hurts its own people. However, economists have identified an apparent exception to this. It is the case of strategic export subsidies. Imagine two firms from different countries, A and B, who export a homogenous product (say, sugar) to a third country, C. C imports all the sugar it consumes. If the two exporting firms cannot collude to fix prices, then in the absence of any subsidies there is a state of equilibrium where each firm would choose its own output to maximize profits (they cannot alter the competitor's output.)[69] Now suppose that A subsidizes its firm's exports. The subsidy will displace the competitor's sugar from C's market. It will shift profits from B's firm to A's firm. If the gains for A exceed the amount of the subsidy, then A will gain. In this specific case it seems to be in the national interest for citizens of A to subsidize its sugar industry. The idea is that "it is to the advantage of a country to capture a large share of the production of profit-earning imperfectly-competitive industries."[70] In this case, where a duopoly competes for a third market, the country that subsidizes reaps net benefits. This finding, in short, would be an exception (albeit a partial and narrow one) to the principle that the country that protects hurts itself.

These findings generated an important literature.[71] In general, economists have been skeptical of the validity of the argument. The problem is that if the assumptions of the models are slightly changed the conclusion

---

[69] The seminal paper is James A. Brander and Barbara J. Spencer, "Export Subsidies and International Market Share Rivalry," *Journal of International Economics* 18 (1985): 83.

[70] Id. at 84.

[71] For a full discussion of the strategic-subsidy debate, see Douglas Irwin, *Against the Tide: An Intellectual History of Free Trade* (Princeton: Princeton University Press, 1996): 207–16.

that the country benefits from the subsidy collapses as well. The following changes in the assumptions would drastically alter the original finding: (1) the possibility of subsidy wars and the their negative effects on the subsidizing country, (2) the possibility of entry of multiple firms in the market, which approach perfect competition and thus prevent appropriation of profits, (3) the possibility of competing firms using a common resource such as research and development, which significantly alters the results, and (4) the possibility of foreign ownership of the domestic firm, which again alters the conclusion.[72]

Let us assume that sometimes it is at least prima facie plausible that the export subsidy helps the country that subsidizes. Is it still *fair*? The strategic trade theory rests solely on the supposition that national interest is the yardstick for measuring the desirability of trade policy. In any country, if a subsidy helps that country, then it is appropriate and rational for that country to enact the subsidy. But this is not enough for global justice. Policies pursued in the national interest may unfairly harm foreigners. I already mentioned *internal* subsidies and how they affect foreign producers. In the United States and Europe governments pay inefficient farmers to keep them in business and thus price foreign producers out of domestic markets. This practice harms the world's poor and is for that reason objectionable (an internal subsidy by a developing country will be objectionable as well since it will harm domestic consumers.)

But, unlike the internal subsidy, the export subsidy is an economic benefit bestowed by a government to a producer for exporting his products. It may consist of monetary payments, tax exemptions, or payments in kind, but in all cases the payment is tied to export performance in the sense that facilitates exportation by lowering exporter's production costs. Like internal subsidies, export subsidies have an effect on the country of importation, albeit a bit different effect. Consumers in the importing country buy the subsidized product which displaces the like product available locally. There is no question that the subsidy is inefficient. It creates what economists call a *deadweight loss*, that is, an aggregate loss that no one recoups. But aside from that, does an export subsidy inflict an injustice on persons in the country of importation (or in third countries)?

Let us evaluate an export subsidy in a rich country from the standpoint of the welfare of the world's poor. Let us consider first the case of firms from rich countries competing for the market of a poor country. Rich country A subsidizes a sugar producer so it can successfully export to poor country C. Country C *does not* produce sugar: it imports all the sugar it consumes. Country A does this to compete with a firm from country B, another rich country. A's and B's firms are competing for C's sugar mar-

---

[72] See the discussion in Irwin, *Against the Tide*, See also Paul Krugman's criticism, "Does the New Trade Theory Require a New trade Policy," *The World Economy* 15 (1992): 423.

ket, and this competition does not displace C's sugar producers since there are none.

It seems clear that no injustice is done by A to persons in C, the poor country. On the contrary, the citizens in A are bestowing a *gift* on C's consumers by paying their sugar supplier so that those consumers can pay less for their sugar and thus increase their welfare. Moreover, C *welcomes* the competition between A and B, even if it takes the form of a subsidy war. In fact, this may be an imaginative and better alternative to development aid provided by the governments of A and B to the government of C. The only injustice is suffered by A's taxpayers, who are coerced by their government into helping the sugar producer. But we can avoid this complication by imagining that A's citizens pay *voluntary* contributions to the sugar producer, and thus indirectly help C's consumers. Here it is clear that, from an economic standpoint, A's citizens are providing a *benefit* to C's citizens. Moreover, the poor country welcomes this subsidy war! But what about B's citizens, the rich country whose firm gets displaced? Aren't they the victims of an injustice? Hardly. No one has a right to maintain its competitiveness in the face of the improved situation of one's competitor. If A's subsidy to its firm can be interpreted as A's citizens giving money to its sugar producer to help it compete against B's firm in C's market, it is entirely unclear that B has any moral claim. Moreover, the assumption is that B is also a rich country. So this is a transaction where A is bestowing a benefit on C, the poor nation. Other things being equal, arranging world trade so that poor countries benefit is a good thing. And this benefit is preferable to direct governmental aid for a number of reasons, including the fact that the benefit is experienced directly by C's consumers without governmental interference.

The situation changes if C, the poor country, has sugar producers. By operation of comparative advantages, C's sugar producers will suffer. They can no longer profitably produce sugar and will have to direct their resources (capital, labor) to a different endeavor. However, C will experience a net *benefit*, since the savings by the sugar-buying public normally will exceed the losses by the local sugar producers. Here everything depends on the ability of C's economy to accommodate to the efficiencies of production, but at any rate, as explained earlier, erecting tariffs is not the adequate response to the subsidy. This is because, quite simply, the tariffs will hurt C's own people. Working families will have to pay more for their sugar. So the verdict is uncertain. If a major goal of international arrangements is to alleviate poverty, then subsidies by wealthy countries to gain access to markets in poor countries, in cases where the subsidizing country is competing against other rich producers, do not wrong others. Subsidizing exports can be seen as a creative way to replace the usually unproductive foreign aid. However, this is true *only if* the subsidized imports do not predictably harm the

developing country otherwise. This occurs in the case, already discussed, of the *internal* subsidies granted by rich countries to their farmers, which displace the more efficient producers from developing
countries from the rich countries' domestic markets.

IX. CONCLUDING REMARKS

With few exceptions, the literature on global justice has been indifferent
or hostile to free trade. Yet anyone who cares about justice should support
free trade for empirical and moral reasons. The benefits from trade to the
poor are denied both by protectionist measures in developed countries
and by local monopolies and foreign interests allied with those in power
in developing nations. Few things have done as much to cause the economic stagnation in the developing world as the policies of import substitution and similar protectionist devices (perhaps only *political* failure
ranks higher in the list of such causes.)[73] Trade barriers cannot possibly
be justified by a theory of justice, domestic or international. Domestically,
trade barriers transfer resources from the worse-off (local consumers) to
the better-off (workers and owners of protected industries). Internationally, trade barriers in rich countries transfer resources from poorer foreign
producers and workers to richer local owners and workers. And this,
assuming the best scenario: More often, trade barriers allow governments
to transfer resources in favor of rent-seekers and other political parasites.

Developed countries deserve scorn for not opening their markets to
products made by the world's poor by protecting their inefficient industries, while ruling elites in developing nations deserve scorn for allowing
bad institutions, including misguided protectionism. International reform,
then, should try to *create those effectively functioning institutions* that best
secure economic growth while helping the poor. Because trade relies on
mutual advantage and not on altruism, there is little doubt that liberalizing global voluntary exchanges will go a long way toward that goal.

Critics of free trade simply do not believe that the poor can compete in
world markets. They conjure up the image of a poor and uneducated
peasant immersed into a whirlwind of overwhelming economic forces
which he cannot possibly shape or control. Yet only by allowing this poor
peasant to participate freely in a global free market will he regain the
freedoms he *does not* currently have: the freedoms to produce, work, and
trade at will. The evidence unequivocally shows that freeing world markets improves the lives of millions of persons. Our poor peasant is the

---

[73] For the effect of import substitution policies in Latin America, see Joseph L. Love, "The
Rise and Decline of Economic Structuralism in Latin America: New Dimensions," *Latin
American Research Review* 40 (2005): 105, ("it is universally agreed that ISI has not been a
viable policy for some time.") For a useful account of the debate, see generally Henry J.
Burton, "A Reconsideration of Import Substitution," *Journal of Economic Literature* 36 (1998):
903.

victim, not of free trade, but of one or more of the following: oppressive political conditions, in particular denial of human rights; collusion of the government with local monopolies or foreign producers; lack of protection of property and contract; lack of labor mobility; and stifling cultural structures. These institutional failures cause poverty, not the other way around.

Law, Florida State University

STRUCTURAL EXPLOITATION*

By Matt Zwolinski

I. Introduction

One of the most common criticisms made by activists and scholars opposed to sweatshop labor is that it is wrongfully exploitative.[1] The economist's standard response to this charge is to point out that sweatshop labor provides tremendous benefits to workers—a fact demonstrated both by quantitative data on sweatshop wages and by the preferences of workers as revealed in their voluntary, indeed often eager, acceptance of sweatshop jobs.[2] Such a response does not exactly *defeat* the charge of exploitation—an exchange can be mutually beneficial and nevertheless wrongfully exploitative.[3] But it does seem to *deflate* the charge. Sweatshops, even if acting exploitatively, are at least doing something that provides substantial benefit to people in desperate need. By

* Thanks to Ellen Paul for her generous editorial suggestions, Anne Slagill for her research assistance in the preparation of this paper, and Kevin Carson, Robert MacDougall, Lori Watson, and Alan Wertheimer for helpful comments on earlier drafts.

[1] "Wrongful exploitation" will appear to some to be a redundant phrase. I explain why it is not in footnote 5. "Sweatshop" will appear to some to be a term that conveys moral opprobrium but little in the way of semantic content. Though sympathetic with the complaint, I attempt to define the term more precisely in Section IV. For a sampling of scholarly criticism of sweatshops, see Denis G. Arnold, "Exploitation and the Sweatshop Quandary," *Business Ethics Quarterly* 13, no. 2 (2003); Denis G. Arnold and Norman E. Bowie, "Sweatshops and Respect for Persons," *Business Ethics Quarterly* 13, no. 2 (2003); Robert Mayer, "Sweatshops, Exploitation, and Moral Responsibility," *Journal of Social Philosophy* 38, no. 4 (2007); Iris Marion Young, "Responsibility and Global Justice: A Social Connection Model," *Social Philosophy and Policy* 23, no. 1 (2006); C. D. Meyers, "Moral Duty, Individual Responsibility, and Sweatshop Exploitation," *Journal of Social Philosophy* 38, no. 4 (2007); Jeremy C. Snyder, "Needs Exploitation," *Ethical Theory and Moral Practice* 11, no. 4 (2008); and "Exploitation and Sweatshop Labor: Perspectives and Issues," *Business Ethics Quarterly* 20, no. 2 (2010).

[2] For evidence that sweatshop wages tends to exceed—sometimes greatly—wages in non-sweatshop jobs, see Ian Maitland, "The Great Non-Debate Over International Sweatshops," in Tom L. Beauchamp and Norman E. Bowie, ed., *Ethical Theory and Business* (Engelwood Cliffes: Pretence Hall, 1996; reprint, 2001); Paul Krugman, "In Praise of Cheap Labor," *Slate* (March 21 1997); Benjamin Powell and David Skarbek, "Sweatshops and Third World Living Standards: Are the Jobs Worth the Sweat?" *Journal of Labor Research* 27, no. 2 (2006).

[3] I shall have more to say about this point in Section II of this essay, but it is one that is compatible with and explicitly accepted by almost all contemporary theories of exploitation. See, for instance, Allen W. Wood, "Exploitation," *Social Philosophy and Policy* 12, no. 2 (1995): 148–49; Alan Wertheimer, *Exploitation* (Princeton: Princeton University Press, 1996), 14–16; Ruth Sample, *Exploitation: What it is and Why it's Wrong* (New York: Rowman and Littlefield, 2003), 4; Snyder, "Needs Exploitation," 390; Mikhail Valdman, "A Theory of Wrongful Exploitation," *Philosophers' Imprint* 9, no. 6 (2009): 1.

doi:10.1017/S026505251100015X

contrast, the vast majority of us—including companies that do not out-source their production overseas—do nothing to provide any compara-ble benefit. If this is exploitation, then how bad can exploitation be?[4]

To some critics of sweatshops, however, this analysis appears to vin-dicate the moral status of sweatshop labor only by ignoring the very factors that make it morally abhorrent. It is a mistake, such critics con-tend, to focus so narrowly on the nature of the exchange between a particular sweatshop and a particular worker, and to note that the exchange is beneficial to the worker relative to the position in which she stood prior to the exchange. For it is precisely in the conditions that lie in the *back-ground* of the exchange that the real injustice of sweatshop labor is to be found. People choose to work in sweatshops only because their situation is desperate, and the desperation of their situation is often—or, depend-ing on one's theory of justice, almost always—a result of serious injustice in the background political and economic institutions against which their decision is made. The choice to accept sweatshop labor might be a smart move for workers, but it is the game itself, and not the particular moves that players make within it, in which the true nature of workers' exploi-tation is to be found.

My goal in this essay is to assess the adequacy of this response. What role, if any, should consideration of background injustices play in the correct understanding of exploitation?[5] My answer, in brief, is that it should play fairly little. Structural injustice matters, of course, but it does not typically matter for determining whether a sweatshop is acting exploitatively, and it does not typically matter in a way that grounds any kind of special moral responsibility or fault on the part of sweatshops or the MNEs (multinational enterprises) with which they contract. My argu-ment shall proceed as follows. In Section II I will present a brief account of the concept of exploitation. In Section III I will discuss the way in which the dominant contemporary analysis of exploitation has seen it as a feature of discrete transactions, and will survey three ways in which some theorists have argued that a greater focus on structural issues is needed. I will provide an overview of the moral and empirical issues concerning sweatshop labor in Section IV. And in Section V, I assess the arguments introduced in Section III in order to determine the ways in

---

[4] I have argued this point at somewhat greater length in Matt Zwolinski, "Sweatshops, Choice, and Exploitation," *Business Ethics Quarterly* 17, no. 4 (2007): 704–10.

[5] I will address this question in this essay with reference to the specific issue of sweatshop labor, but it is worth noting that the question is perfectly general and relevant to a number of other issues of practical concern such as those illustrated in recent debates over organ sales and prostitution, and not-so-recent debates over the legitimacy of interest. See James Stacy Taylor, *Stakes and Kidneys: Why Markets in Human Body Parts are Morally Imperative* (New York: Ashgate, 2005); Peter de Marneffe, *Liberalism and Prostitution* (New York: Oxford University Press, 2009). On the legitimacy of interest, see the debate between the classical liberal economist Frédéric Bastiat and the socialist-anarchist Pierre-Joseph Proudhon, avail-able online at http://praxeology.net/FB-PJP-DOI.htm.

which structural injustice does, and does not, matter for our thinking about exploitation. I conclude in Section VI with a discussion of the implications of structural injustice for the debate over sweatshop labor.

II. WHAT EXPLOITATION IS

In the most general sense, to wrongfully exploit someone is to take advantage of him in a way that is unfair or degrading.[6] Characteristically, exploiters interact with their victims in such a way that they derive some benefit from their victim, either by advancing their self-interest narrowly construed or by advancing their non-self-interested goals or projects.[7] The victim, in turn, might be harmed in the sense that she suffers a setback to her interests relative to how she would have fared in the absence of any interaction. But this is not necessary. For, even if the victim benefits relative to this baseline, the interaction might still be degrading or unfair to her. Imagine someone in danger of drowning who is offered rescue by the only nearby boat only if she agrees to sign away 75 percent of her future earnings. Intuitively, the rescuer's offer will strike most of us as deeply unfair. But just as clearly, the offer is one that benefits *both* parties relative to the status quo ex ante. After all, the victim almost certainly values her continued life more highly than the income she trades for it. If she did not, she presumably would not have agreed to the offer.[8]

This last point suggests another feature of wrongful exploitation—namely, that exploitative transactions can be fully voluntary, at least in the sense of being free from outright coercion, force, or deception. To the extent that exploitative interactions are mutually beneficial, even if unfair, exploited parties will often have good reason to enter into them. Indeed, the more desperate a person's situation, the greater the reason she will

---

[6] I define "wrongful" exploitation in this way because there is a sense of the term "exploitation" that does not connote any wrongdoing on the part of the exploiter, as when a shrewd entrepreneur exploits an opportunity, or when a football coach exploits his opponent's weakness. There is some debate in the literature regarding whether these are two distinct concepts confused by virtue of sharing the same word, or whether it is not the concept of exploitation but its wrongfulness that varies in different contexts. The former view is defended in Wertheimer, *Exploitation*, 6. The latter in Wood, "Exploitation," 137–41. For what it is worth, I find Wertheimer's view more persuasive, but think that little of practical or theoretical significance depends on the issue as a general matter, and certainly not in the debate that follows. Unless otherwise noted, all instances of the term "exploitation" in this article will refer to exploitation that is wrongful.

[7] See Wertheimer, *Exploitation:* 17–18.

[8] This claim is a bit glib. It is possible that the victim was so overwhelmed by panic that she would have agreed to *any* offer that would have gotten her out of her immediate danger, regardless of its long-term effects on her overall well-being. Or, she may be a trained lawyer, familiar with the doctrine of unconscionability, who realized that the rescuer's proposal would never be enforced in a court of law. Revealed preferences are in most cases a good indicator of an agent's interests, but nothing in my argument requires that they be perfect indicators.

have to accept any offer that promises to improve it. To the extent that it is unfair or degrading to take advantage of another person's vulnerability, then, voluntariness and unfairness are not only logically compatible, they often go hand in hand.

So far, my discussion of exploitation has remained deliberately neutral among competing theories. To whatever extent those theories might differ in their finer details, they are all (as far as I am aware) compatible with the broad analysis I have given so far. The most contentious aspect of a theory of exploitation, however, is its specification of precisely which features of a voluntary and mutually beneficial transaction make it wrongfully exploitative. At the beginning of this section, I characterized exploitative transactions as involving taking advantage of another in an "unfair" or "degrading" way. This disjunctive signals two approaches that have been used recently by philosophers to understand the wrongfulness of exploitation—the former focuses on the fairness or unfairness of the transaction, while the latter bases its assessment on a broadly Kantian idea of respect for persons.[9] Both of these approaches, in turn, admit of specification in a broad variety of ways. Unfairness, for instance, can be understood in terms of one party's receiving a disproportionate share of the cooperative surplus, by comparing the gains and losses of each party to that which would emerge in a hypothetical competitive market, or by any number of other measures. Similarly, what constitutes degrading treatment, or a failure of respect, will depend on one's answers to a host of other moral questions, such as whether it is inherently disrespectful to purchase from another—even at a fair market price—services such as their sexual or reproductive labor.[10]

For the most part, I hope to avoid these controversies in this essay. I certainly will not be attempting to put forward any comprehensive theory of what makes exploitation wrong, nor will I assess the theories that others have put forth qua comprehensive theories. My aim in this essay is more limited. It is to explore the relationship between exploitation and background injustice. To the extent that it is possible, I aim to conduct this investigation in a way that is neutral between competing accounts of exploitation's wrongfulness. My hope is that it will be possible to shed light on this particular issue in a way that makes as few controversial assumptions as possible about the overall nature of a theory of exploitation, or the broader moral debates that underlie competing theories.

---

[9] The former approach is defended most notably in Wertheimer, *Exploitation.* Also in Valdman, "A Theory of Wrongful Exploitation." The latter approach has been most influentially defended in Wood, "Exploitation" and Sample, *Exploitation: What it is and Why it's Wrong.*

[10] See, for a discussion, Wertheimer, *Exploitation:* chap. 4; Sample, *Exploitation: What it is and Why it's Wrong,* 154–59.

III. From Transactional to Structural Exploitation

Much contemporary philosophic thought has focused on discrete trans-actions as the locus of exploitation. For instance, Alan Wertheimer's 1996 book, *Exploitation*, which has structured and inspired much of the ensuing literature on the topic, contains chapters on unconscionable contracts, the exploitation of student athletes, commercial surrogacy, unconstitutional conditions, and sexual exploitation in psychotherapy.[11] And each of these topics is analyzed almost exclusively by focusing on some offer that *A* makes to *B*, and asking whether the terms of the offer are sufficiently unfair, or the process by which the offer was made and accepted suffi-ciently defective, to render the interaction wrongfully exploitative. There is little exploration of the sense in which *relationships*, rather than discrete interactions, can be exploitative. And there is little discussion of the way in which exploitation might be a feature of broader, structural features of the economy or the social context in which the interactions he analyzes take place.

Things were not always this way. Prior to Wertheimer's paradigm-shifting book, almost all philosophical discussion of exploitation focused on a Marxist or quasi-Marxist understanding of that concept. And for Marx, exploitation was more a feature of capitalism as such than it was a feature of any particular interaction between a capitalist and a worker. By putting exclusive control of the means of production in private hands, capitalism forces workers to choose between working for the owners of capital and starving to death. Capitalists, in turn, are able to take advan-tage of the existence of a large reserve army of the unemployed to pay workers just as much as is necessary to keep them alive to work another day, but not as much as the value of what their labor produces. In a way, then, capitalists are guilty of exploitation defined as the extraction of surplus value from the workers. But in a more important way, it is cap-italism, and not particular capitalists, that deserves our blame. For the ruthless competitiveness of a capitalist system forces the hand of capital-ists just as much as it does that of workers. Capitalists have no real choice but to attempt to extract as much value from workers as possible, lest their businesses be undercut by a competitor with fewer moral scruples.

Tied as it was, however, to a deeply implausible labor theory of value, to the idea that exploitation must entail forced (and not voluntary) trans-fers, and to a host of other problematic commitments, the Marxist account of exploitation fell almost entirely out of favor among philosophers.[12] This is not to say that philosophers rejected Marx's claim that capitalism and wage labor were inherently exploitative. But his analysis of what

---

[11] Wertheimer, *Exploitation*.

[12] See, for a helpful overview of Marx's theory of exploitation and its challenges, Will Kymlicka, *Contemporary Political Philosophy: An Introduction*, 2d ed. (Oxford: Oxford University Press, 2002), 177–87.

precisely that exploitation consisted in was found to be untenable, and so sympathetic philosophers set about reconstructing the Marxist critique of capitalism in a way that would stand up to more rigorous philosophic scrutiny.[13] By and large, this reconceptualization has been fruitful. Understanding exploitation in terms of unfair or degrading use rather than in terms of the forced extraction of surplus labor allows us to apply the idea of exploitation in contexts other than the economic relationships on which Marx focused, such as relationships between intimates.[14] And it has allowed philosophers to examine the possible injustice involved in capitalist relationships without attempting to fit their inquiry into the awkward Marxist analytic framework. Still, these advances did not come without a cost. For along with those elements of the Marxist analysis that almost certainly deserved to be discarded, much contemporary analysis of exploitation has also neglected Marx's insights into the role of social and economic structures in understanding that concept. And this, many have argued, has been a tremendous mistake.

There has thus arisen a growing consensus that consideration of the ways in which discrete transactions can be exploitative must be supplemented with an analysis of the way in which exploitation is related to structural injustice. Or, as one commentator has recently put it, that we require an account of exploitation that takes into consideration issues of fairness at the "macro" level as well as at the "micro" level.[15] Beyond the agreement *that* structural issues matter, however, there has been little agreement regarding *how* it matters. At least three distinct claims seem to have emerged in the literature.

The first is that the identification of structural injustice is necessary in order to determine which particular interactions are to count as instances of exploitation. This view has been defended most recently by Ruth Sample, who claims as an advantage of her view its recognition that "exploitation is not simply a feature of a particular transaction but derives its badness from preexisting social institutions that underwrite and encourage the transaction."[16] Background injustices, especially those of a structural or institutional sort, establish inequalities between persons that can facilitate the exploitation of some by others. When we gain advantage by interacting with a victim of such injustice, she holds, "and that advantage

---

[13] See, for instance, G. A. Cohen, "The Labor Theory of Value and the Concept of Exploitation," *Philosophy and Public Affairs* 8, no. 4 (1979): chap. 4; Richard Arneson, "What's Wrong with Exploitation?," *Ethics* 91, no. 2 (1981); John E. Roemer, "Should Marxists Be Interested in Exploitation?" *Philosophy and Public Affairs* 14, no. 1 (1985); Jeffrey Reiman, "Exploitation, Force, and the Moral Assessment of Capitalism: Thoughts on Roemer and Cohen," *Philosophy and Public Affairs* 16, no. 1 (1987); John E. Roemer, "What is Exploitation? Reply to Jeffrey Reiman," *Philosophy and Public Affairs* 18, no. 1 (1989). Again, for a helpful overview see Kymlicka, *Contemporary Political Philosophy: An Introduction*: 177–87.
[14] See, for instance, Sample, *Exploitation: What it is and Why it's Wrong*, chap. 4.
[15] Snyder, "Exploitation and Sweatshop Labor: Perspectives and Issues," 191.
[16] Sample, *Exploitation: What it is and Why it's Wrong*, 97–98.

is due in part to an injustice he has suffered, we have failed to give him appropriate respect."[17] On Sample's account, failures of respect of this sort are a form of exploitation. Taking advantage of structural injustice is thus, for Sample, a sufficient condition of exploitation, and hence an identification of macro level or structural injustice is necessary to correctly identify at least certain kinds of micro level or transactional exploitation.

The second claim is that the identification of structural injustice is necessary, not so much in order to classify particular interactions as exploitative or not, but in order to think correctly about blameworthiness and responsibility for actions and situations of injustice. Iris Marion Young's recent essay on global justice, though not specifically focused on the concept of exploitation, makes essentially this point. In attempting to locate responsibility for global injustice, she argues, we too often rely exclusively on a liability model of responsibility that determines faulty conduct as that which deviates from a baseline of a normal, morally acceptable, background situation. A gunman's proposal of "your money or your life," for instance, is judged coercive against what we deem to be the morally acceptable background situation in which I am entitled to both my money *and* my life. But in cases of global injustice, we cannot make this assumption. "When we judge that structural injustice exists, we mean that at least some of the normal and accepted background conditions of action are not morally acceptable. Most of us contribute to a greater or lesser degree to the production and reproduction of structural injustice precisely because we follow the accepted and expected rules and conventions of the communities and institutions in which we act."[18] Young's account of the relevance of background injustices thus differs from Sample's. Unlike Sample, Young does not believe that reflection on structural injustice should lead us to identify as coercive or exploitative actions that, in the absence of that injustice, would have been regarded as morally innocent. Young does not recommend that we reject the liability model as a way of assigning responsibility to individuals. Instead, she argues that the liability model of responsibility must be supplemented by a *different kind* of responsibility—one that is political, rather than individualistic, in nature, and that draws our attention to ways in which collective action can be mobilized to correct injustice in the future, rather than to whom should be blamed for actions that have occurred in the past.[19]

Finally, some have argued that a focus on structural injustice is necessary in order to identify political and economic institutions themselves as exploitative, and not merely as a means to identifying micro level transactions as exploitative. While it is not focused specifically on the concept

[17] Ibid., 74.
[18] Young, "Responsibility and Global Justice: A Social Connection Model," 120.
[19] Ibid., 119–25.

of exploitation, Onora O'Neill's discussion of coercion and consent makes essentially this point. According to O'Neill, a focus on discrete transactions can lead us to lose sight of the real source of moral concern in situations of systematic injustice. Take, for instance, a capitalist's offer of low-wage labor to a worker. Such an offer appears, on its face, to be paradigmatically noncoercive, and the maxim on which the employer acts in making it seems perfectly universalizable and innocent. But, she notes, if we turn from the principles on which the employer herself acts and instead focus on "the principles which guide the institution of employment in a capitalist system," we may find that "the underlying principle of capitalist employment, whatever that may be, may perhaps use some as means or fail to treat them as persons, even where individuals' intentions fail in neither way."[20] On this line of reasoning, the critics of capitalism might be right in finding exploitation in the capitalist system, but it is the system as a whole, and not the discrete actions of individuals within it, that is wrongfully exploitative.

IV. THE SWEATSHOP DEBATE

Before proceeding to evaluate these three claims, a brief detour is warranted in order to review the debate over the moral status of international sweatshops. This debate, which has received a tremendous amount of attention both from philosophers interested in the subject of exploitation and from social scientists interested in the empirical issues surrounding sweatshop wages and working conditions, can provide a useful case study through which the theoretical claims above can be better understood and assessed. This section will provide a brief background on the sweatshop debate, discuss some of the relevant empirical issues, and present the state of the moral debate regarding sweatshops and exploitation.

A. Background

There is no generally agreed-upon definition of the term "sweatshop," but its connotation is clearly pejorative. The U.S. General Accounting Office defines a sweatshop as "an employer that violates more than one federal or state law governing minimum wage and overtime, child labor, industrial homework, occupational safety and health, workers compensation, or industry regulation."[21] For the legal purpose of identifying and regulating industries within the United States, such a definition might be good enough. For the purpose of general moral analysis,

---

[20] Onora O'Neill, "Between Consenting Adults," in *Constructions of Reason* (New York: Cambridge University Press, 1989), 273–4.

[21] Human Resources Division U.S. General Accounting Office, "Sweatshops in the U.S.: Opinions on Their Extent and Possible Enforcement Options," (Washington, D.C., 1988).

however, it is clearly too narrow. Presumably, the kinds of activities in which sweatshops engage are wrong, if they are wrong at all, because they are unfair or disrespectful of persons, and not merely because they are prohibited by law. To avoid this problem, then, we might define a sweatshop as a place of employment in which worker compensation or safety is compromised, child labor is employed, and/or local labor regulations are routinely disregarded in a way that is prima facie morally objectionable. This definition captures the role that the term "sweatshop" plays as a signal of moral disapprobation, while leaving open as a conceptual matter the possibility that sweatshop practices might, on closer examination, be morally justifiable.

Sweatshops, so defined, exist throughout the world, including within the United States. For the most part, however, the moral debate over sweatshops has focused exclusively on sweatshops in the developing world. These sweatshops are typically independent firms that produce goods on a contractual basis for export to MNEs. The outsourcing of production to such sweatshops began in the 1970s when the technological and legal changes associated with globalization began to accelerate, and has been especially common in the apparel industry where the demand for low-skilled labor is high and the ability to avoid the risks associated with developing and stocking products is financially advantageous.[22]

B. Empirical issues

Three kinds of empirical issues regularly come up in debates regarding the moral status of sweatshops. The first involves sweatshop wages; the second has to do with working conditions and safety in sweatshop labor; and the third has to do with the extent of labor law violations by sweatshops.

Perhaps the most widely-repeated claim about sweatshops, at least among nonacademic critics, is that the wages they pay are objectionably low. Ironically, this is also the claim that is the least supported by empirical evidence, of which there exists an abundance. A 1996 study, for instance, found that wages paid by MNEs in the developing world were generally significantly higher than wages paid by domestic firms in the same countries.[23] Because most sweatshops are not owned by MNEs, however, but are instead independent firms that work with MNEs on a contractual basis, it was initially thought that this study might not have much rele-

[22] A brief, helpful overview of the history of sweatshops and recent developments can be found in Denis Arnold and Laura Hartman, "Moral Imagination and the Future of Sweatshops," *Business and Society Review* 108, no. 4 (2003).
[23] Brian Aitken, Ann Harrison, and Robert Lipsey, "Wages and Foreign Ownership: A Comparative Study of Mexico, Venezuela, and the United States," *Journal of International Economics* 40 (1996).

vance for the debate over sweatshops. However, a 2006 study by Benjamin Powell and David Skarbek found that sweatshop wages are higher
than wages elsewhere in the economy regardless of whether they are paid
directly by MNEs or by domestic subcontractors—three to seven times as
high, for example, in the Dominican Republic, Haiti, Honduras, and Nicaragua.[24] This is compatible, of course, with the (obviously true) claim that
sweatshop wages are significantly lower than wages paid for comparable
work in the United States. And it is also compatible with the claim that
sweatshop wages might still be insufficient to allow workers to achieve a
certain standard of living. This means that sweatshops might still be
failing to meet Denis Arnold's often-repeated standard that they "ensure
that employees do not live in conditions of overall poverty by providing
adequate wages for a 48 hour work week to satisfy both basic food needs
and basic non-food needs."[25] But it does demonstrate that sweatshop
wages, even if they are not high enough to lift workers entirely out of
poverty, are generally significantly higher than wages available to workers elsewhere in their economy.

Worker safety is another main complaint of anti-sweatshop activists.
And while comprehensive data on this topic is more difficult to collect,
the literature is replete with shocking anecdotes.[26] Workers are pressured
by employers to remain on the job in spite of serious and pressing injury,
are exposed to dangerous chemicals and airborne pollutants, and often
work on poorly maintained machinery with inadequate training or safety
measures.[27] In some ways, concern over safe working conditions is distinct from concern over wages. The steps needed to correct issues of
workplace safety will be different—perhaps easier, perhaps more difficult—
than those needed to increase wages. And morally, one might hold that
unsafe working conditions violate workers' rights in a way that low
wages do not. In many ways, however, the issues are inexorably linked.
Both increases in wages and improvements in working conditions, for

[24] Powell and Skarbek, "Sweatshops and Third World Living Standards: Are the Jobs
Worth the Sweat?" The "sweatshops" examined in this study were those that were identified
as sweatshops by anti-sweatshop activists quoted in the popular press. See p. 267.
[25] Arnold and Bowie, "Sweatshops and Respect for Persons," 234. See also Arnold and
Hartman, "Moral Imagination and the Future of Sweatshops," 453, n. 1; and "Beyond
Sweatshops: Positive Deviancy and Global Labour Practices," Business Ethics: A European
Review 14, no. 3 (2005): 207; and "Worker Rights and Low Wage Industrialization: How to
Avoid Sweatshops," Human Rights Quarterly 28, no. 3 (2006): 677, n. 1; Denis Arnold, "Work-
ing Conditions: Safety and Sweatshops," in George Brenkert and Tom Beauchamp, ed., The
Oxford Handbook of Business Ethics (New York: Oxford University Press, 2010), 645.
[26] Though, to be fair, the anecdotes regarding the likely alternatives to sweatshop labor
for workers in the developing world are no less shocking. See, for instance, Nicholas'
Kristof's account of children scavenging in the garbage dumps of Phnom Penh in Nicholas
D. Kristof, "Where Sweatshops are a Dream," New York Times (January 14, 2009).
[27] See, for discussion, the essays in Pamela Varley, The Sweatshop Quandary: Corporate
Responsibility on the Global Frontier (Washington, DC: Investor Responsibility Research Cen-
ter, 1998). A discussion of some of the more shocking accounts can be found in Arnold and
Bowie, "Sweatshops and Respect for Persons," 228–33.

instance, cost employers money and resources.[28] From the perspective of the employer, both kinds of cost can be considered as part of workers' overall package of compensation. And while profit-maximizing employers are indifferent to the mix of goods that goes into an employee's compensation package, they are extremely sensitive to the overall cost of that package. Increases in worker safety, therefore, will very often come at the expense of other forms of compensation.[29] Moreover, there is some reason to believe that workers themselves would be unwilling to make this tradeoff. A 2010 survey of Guatemalan sweatshop workers found that few of them are willing to sacrifice any wages in order to receive more health and safety benefits.[30] Employees were asked about ten improvements in working conditions and if they would be willing to accept lower wages to improve any of these conditions. On eight of the questions more than 90 percent of the workers answered "No." Paid vacation was the most popular improvement but even here more than 81 percent of the workers answered that they would not sacrifice any amount of wages for it. Nearly 65 percent of workers surveyed answered that they were unwilling to sacrifice any wages for each of the ten improvements.

A final empirical issue relevant to the debate over sweatshops and exploitation involves sweatshops' violation of labor laws. According to Denis Arnold and Norman Bowie, such violations are widespread and often perpetrated with the implicit or explicit cooperation of state institutions.[31] Employers force workers to work overtime, suppress workers' right to unionize, engage in the illegal pregnancy screening of female potential employees, and fail to pay workers wages on time and in the correct amount. Internal investigations by the clothing company Gap revealed that "between 25 and 50 percent of its contract factories lacked full compliance with local labor laws in North Asia, Southeast Asia, the Indian subcontinent, sub-Saharan Africa, Mexico, Central America, and the Caribbean, and South America. In China, more than 50 percent of its contract factories lacked full compliance

[28] The argument that follows is made at greater length by Benjamin Powell in Benjamin Powell, "In Reply to Sweatshop Sophistries," *Human Rights Quarterly* 28, no. 4 (2006).
[29] Like all economic generalizations, this is a rule of thumb and not a necessary law. Denis Arnold and Laura Hartman have often stressed that the exercise of "moral imagination" by managers is capable of yielding solutions that improve working conditions without raising costs to employers, and document a number of cases where such improvements have been made. See Denis Arnold, Laura Hartman, and Richard E. Wokutch, *Rising Above Sweatshops: Innovative Approaches to Global Labor Challenges* (Westport, Connecticut: Praeger, 2003); Arnold and Hartman, "Beyond Sweatshops: Positive Deviancy and Global Labour Practices."; and "Moral Imagination and the Future of Sweatshops."
[30] Ben Powell and J. Clark, "Guatemala Sweatshops: Employee Evidence on Working Conditions," Department of Economics (Boston, MA: Suffolk University, 2010). The survey was conducted on employees of Nicotex and Sam Bridge, chosen because those firms were identified as sweatshops and protested by the National Labor Committee.
[31] Arnold and Bowie, "Sweatshops and Respect for Persons," 227–28. See also Arnold and Hartman, "Worker Rights and Low Wage Industrialization: How to Avoid Sweatshops," 686–90.

with local labor laws."[32] And this was the situation in a company that was making an active effort to ensure compliance.

There are probably a variety of relatively benign reasons for such noncompliance including ignorance of the law, lack of clarity in the law, and ignorance of implementation mechanisms.[33] But a significant part of the reason for both the lack of enforcement on the part of the state and the lack of compliance on the part of the sweatshop is almost certainly financial. Sweatshops do not want to comply with laws that raise their costs and decrease profitability. Governments, in turn, face cost-pressures of two different sorts. First, there is the expense associated with enforcement itself. Given the strained budgets within which many developing countries operate, this can be a significant constraint. Second, there is the possible cost associated with lost tax revenue should overly-vigorous enforcement lead the sweatshop to shut down, or its affiliated MNE to search elsewhere for a less burdensome regulatory environment. Sweatshops' willingness to violate labor law in the face of weak enforcement is thus another possible source of worker exploitation.[34]

C. Moral issues

How, then, do these empirical issues bear on the question of the moral status of sweatshops, especially the question of whether sweatshops are guilty of exploiting their workers? On an account of exploitation that is focused on transactional fairness alone, the case against sweatshops appears thin. Alan Wertheimer's account, arguably the most influential fairness-based account of exploitation, is founded on the idea that for at least a broad range of cases, the fairness of a transaction between A and B can be analyzed in terms of the agreement that would be reached between them in a hypothetical competitive market.[35] A motorist who comes across a driver stranded in a snowstorm and takes advantage of his monopoly

[32] Arnold, "Working Conditions: Safety and Sweatshops," 638.
[33] Arnold and Hartman, "Worker Rights and Low Wage Industrialization: How to Avoid Sweatshops," 688–89.
[34] Little has been written in the extant literature on the moral issues surrounding labor law violations. I address the issue in a preliminary way in a paper written with Benjamin Powell. See Matt Zwolinski and Ben Powell, "The Ethical and Economic Case for Sweatshop Labor: A Critical Assessment," (San Diego: University of San Diego, 2011).
[35] Wertheimer, *Exploitation:* 230. I should stress, however, that Wertheimer puts forward the model of a hypothetical competitive market only as a *model* of fairness and only as one that is plausible in "a certain range of cases." There has been an unfortunate tendency in the literature, I think, to single out this idea as the core of a general theory of fairness and of exploitation. Construed as such, as numerous commentators have pointed out, it is barely plausible. But Wertheimer's book, as I read it, does not attempt to set out any *general* theory of the unfairness that lies at the heart of exploitation. Commentators who focus too narrowly on the model of competitive markets are thus likely to miss the rich and context-sensitive analysis that pervades the remainder of the book, where Wertheimer reaches penetrating insights about fairness without attempting to squeeze them into an overarching theory.

position by charging the driver an exorbitant sum to be rescued acts exploitatively on this account, because the price he charges is higher than the price that would be charged were multiple rescuers to compete for the driver's "business."[36] But there is little reason to suppose that sweatshops and the multinational companies are operating in a noncompetitive environment.[37] The compensation sweatshop workers receive for their labor is generally no higher than the amount they contribute to the firm (their marginal revenue product), and no lower than the value they place on their next best alternative employment.[38] Their compensation is low because the values of these upper and lower constraints are low, and not because of any failure of competitiveness in the labor market. This is why even Denis Arnold, himself one of the most persistent philosophical critics of sweatshops, thinks that on a transactional account of exploitation of the sort Wertheimer defends, the claim that sweatshop workers are exploited is implausible.[39]

Arnold seems to believe that a Kantian account of transactional exploitation of the sort defended by Allen Wood will be more successful in substantiating the charge of sweatshop exploitation. But it is not clear why this should be so. Demonstrating that the compensation sweatshop workers receive is disrespectful is hardly a simple matter, especially if one has already conceded that the compensation is not unfair. Arnold insists that any wage below a "living wage" is inherently disrespectful and fails to treat workers as beings with dignity and autonomy who are ends in themselves.[40] But it is not at all clear how he would respond to the claim, raised for instance by Sollars and Englander, that the requirement to treat others as ends in themselves generates a duty of beneficence that is imperfect in form, and cannot ground a perfect obligation on the part of employers to pay a specified wage rate.[41]

[36] Ibid., 4–5, 216–23.
[37] Denis Arnold has asserted that sweatshop employers often have monopsony power over workers, but offers no evidence in support of his claim. See Arnold, "Working Conditions: Safety and Sweatshops," 651, n. 63. It is, of course, true that sweatshops do not operate in an environment of *perfect* competition, but although he is somewhat imprecise with his terminology, this could hardly have been what Wertheimer had in mind in setting forth a hypothetical competitive market as a model of fairness. After all, in perfectly competitive markets prices are equal to the marginal cost of production and thus profits are zero. But it would be grossly implausible to say that profit *as such* constitutes sufficient evidence of exploitation. For a more extended discussion of the irrelevance of models of perfect competition to charges of exploitation, see Matt Zwolinski, "Price Gouging and Market Failure," in Gerald Gaus, Julian Lamont, and Christi Favor, ed., *Essays on Philosophy, Politics & Economics: Integration and Common Research Projects* (Stanford: Stanford University Press, 2010).
[38] Powell, "In Reply to Sweatshop Sophistries," 1032–33.
[39] See Arnold, "Exploitation and the Sweatshop Quandry," 252–53; Arnold, "Working Conditions: Safety and Sweatshops," 643.
[40] Arnold and Bowie, "Sweatshops and Respect for Persons," 234.
[41] See Gordon G. Sollars and Fred Englander, "Sweatshops: Kant and Consequences," *Business Ethics Quarterly* 17, no. 1 (2007): 118–20. Actually, Denis Arnold and Norman Bowie did write an article in response to Sollars and Englander, but had nothing more to say about

Jeremy Snyder puts forward a more promising argument, holding that while Kantian ethics grounds only an imperfect duty of beneficence in the abstract, this duty can come to be "specified" by the particular relationships we enter into with others, thereby taking on a "perfect, strict form."[42] In the abstract, we must use our own practical reason to determine who to help, on what occasions, with what kind of and how much assistance, on what conditions, and so on. But when we enter into "relationships of use" with certain, particular others, our wide and imperfect duties become more narrowly specified. In this way "employers do not simply have an imperfect duty to help some of their employees to achieve a decent minimum some of the time; rather, employers are required to cede as much of their benefit from the interaction to their employees as is reasonably possible toward the end of the employees achieving a decent minimum standard of living."[43]

Snyder's account thus has the potential to do what Arnold and Bowie's account could not—ground a perfect obligation on the part of sweatshops to pay a living wage.[44] But Snyder's argument faces difficulties of its own. The most significant of these, I think, is not unique to Snyder's account but is characteristic of almost all accounts that condemn transactions that are mutually beneficial but in some way unfair.[45] There is a certain incoherence, I think, between our intuitions regarding exploitation and our intuitions regarding duties of aid. This incoherence manifests itself when we condemn sweatshops and the MNEs with which they contract for exploiting workers in the developing world, but do not condemn businesses that refrain from outsourcing production at all. If the empirical data we have surveyed about sweatshop wages are correct, sweatshops are providing significant benefits to their workers, while firms that do not outsource are (as far as we know) doing *nothing* to benefit them. How, then, can it be permissible to *neglect* workers in the developing world, but impermissible to *exploit* them, when exploitation is better for both parties (including workers who are in desperate need of better-

the present question than that they felt that Sollars and Englander had ignored some of the claims they had made in defense of their position and had hence failed to engage their argument "in a substantive manner" Denis G. Arnold and Norman E. Bowie, "Respect for Workers in Global Supply Chains: Advancing the Debate Over Sweatshops," *Business Ethics Quarterly* 17, no. 1 (2007): 136–37. Having read the passages to which Arnold and Bowie refer in their response, however, it is not at all clear to me what substantive argument or claim they believe Sollars and Englander have ignored.

[42] Snyder, "Needs Exploitation," 390.

[43] Ibid., 396.

[44] It should be noted, however, that Snyder himself qualifies this obligation in a number of ways, most notably by allowing that competitive pressures may make it impossible for firms to pay as much as they should under more ideal conditions. See ibid., 401.

[45] I have discussed this problem before in Zwolinski, "Sweatshops, Choice, and Exploitation," 707–10; and, "The Ethics of Price Gouging," *Business Ethics Quarterly* 18, no. 3 (2008): 356–60, and in greater detail in "Exploitation and Neglect," (San Diego: University of San Diego).

ment)?[46] Consistency seems to require that we revise our moral beliefs: either by holding that neglect is worse than we previously thought, or by holding that exploitation is less bad than we previously thought. Either way of resolving the inconsistency, however, leads us to abandon the belief that sweatshops who exploit their workers are doing anything *especially* wrong.

Snyder is aware of this objection to his position, and has responded to it by arguing that the idea that special relationships create special moral obligations is one that is supported by both moral theory and intuition.[47] Persons can choose not to enter into relationships with individuals who stand in positions of vulnerability but, Snyder contends, "should they choose to enter these relationships, this choice helps to specify a general duty of beneficence" in a way that prohibits exploitatively low wages.[48] But this is still puzzling. For, suppose we agreed with Snyder that a company's entering into an employment relationship with a needy individual was sufficient to generate a strict, perfect duty of beneficence on the part of the company toward that employee.[49] Compliance with such a duty, let us stipulate, would require the company to provide a benefit to its employee of amount Y. But let us suppose that the employer is only willing to provide its employees with a benefit of amount X, where $X < Y$. Would it be permissible, on Snyder's account, for the employer to make its offer of employment contingent upon its workers' willingness to waive their right to benefits of amount Y? Prior to entering into a relationship with employees, the employer has only an imperfect duty of beneficence. No prospective employee has any valid moral claim upon its assistance. Thus, the company would not be acting wrongly if it refused to hire or assist the prospective employee at all. But if it is permissible for the employer not to hire prospective workers, and if hiring prospective workers at benefit level X is better for both the employer and the worker than not hiring the prospective workers at all, then how could doing so be wrong? If employees' claim to benefits at level Y is one that they may waive when it is in their interest to do so, then employers are not necessarily acting wrongly in providing their employees with benefits at level X. If, on the other hand, employees' claim to benefits at level Y is not waiv-

---

[46] The original statement of this concern comes from Alan Wertheimer in Wertheimer, *Exploitation:* 289-93.

[47] See Jeremy C. Snyder, "Efficiency, Equality, and Price Gouging: A Response to Zwolinski," *Business Ethics Quarterly* 19, no. 2 (2009): 305-06. This piece was published in response to my own Matt Zwolinski, "Price Gouging, Non-Worseness, and Distributive Justice," *Business Ethics Quarterly* 19, no. 2 (2009).

[48] Snyder, "Efficiency, Equality, and Price Gouging: A Response to Zwolinski," 306. Snyder is actually discussing exploitation as it pertains to price gouging in the quoted material, but I believe, given what he has written about the topic elsewhere, that he would support the extension of his claim to sweatshop labor as well.

[49] Actually, Snyder does not quite hold that it is "sufficient." Several other conditions must be met for the employer to have this duty, but as they do not affect the present argument these need not concern us here.

able, then Snyder's account is committed to holding that employers are forbidden from entering into agreements with employees to hire them at wage level X, but permitted to refrain from hiring them at all, even if hiring them at level X is better for both workers and employers than not hiring them at all, and even if both workers and employers would prefer to enter into an employment relationship at wage level X than to not enter into any wage relationship at all. This is deeply counterintuitive.

To be clear, I am not making the strong claim that any agreement that is voluntary and mutually beneficial is thereby nonexploitative and morally permissible. I agree, for instance, with Chris Meyers that someone who offers to rescue another person from the desert only if the other consents to an act of sodomy, or to handing over their entire net worth, is acting in a way that is repugnant, exploitative, and morally wrong.[50] My claim is that the kinds of considerations we have surveyed in the section tend to undermine the claim that MNEs and the sweatshops with which they contract are treating workers unfairly and hence exploitatively. These considerations include the empirical facts about the benefits sweatshops provide to their workers, as well as the fact that MNEs are under no moral or legal obligation to provide any benefits at all to workers in the developing world. It is also worth bearing in mind that the only motivation MNEs have for providing any benefit is the increased profit they hope to gain from the exchange, and that their *capacity* to provide benefit to workers is a function of this motivation. In this way, MNEs are less like the kind of adventitious rescuer described by Meyers and more like a "professional salvor whose rescue capacity results from a planned investment."[51] Admiralty law has long recognized that the awards that may legitimately be claimed by the latter are, while not unlimited, nevertheless significantly higher than those to which the former has good claim.

V. Does Structural Injustice Matter?

Still, even if sweatshops cannot be said to be acting exploitatively on a transactional account of exploitation, perhaps a structural account could do better? After all, most sweatshops operate within a social context that is plagued by longstanding, deep, and massively destructive injustice. For example:

- **Suppression of Unions**—Governments in the countries in which sweatshops operate routinely suppress workers' ability to organize and bargain collectively. The suppression is sometimes vio-

---

[50] Chris Meyers, "Wrongful Beneficence: Exploitation and Third World Sweatshops," *Journal of Social Philosophy* 35, no. 3 (2004): 324–25.
[51] Melvin Eisenberg, "The Principle of Unconscionability," in *Law and Economics Workshop* (Berkeley, CA: Berkeley Law School, 2009), 15–16.

lent, and is sometimes executed at the request of MNEs and/or the sweatshops with which they contract.[52]

- **Seizure of Land and Natural Resources**—Land in developing countries, like land elsewhere in the world, generally did not come into the hands of its current owners by a process of peaceful Lockean labor mixing and voluntary exchange. Violence and theft are as much responsible for current holdings as investment and labor. And Western governments' deference to rulers' alleged property rights in trade and lending reinforces this injustice.[53]

- **Protectionism**—Powerful Western governments, through their influence in international organizations such as the World Trade Organization, compel developing countries to open their markets while at the same time protecting their own markets with "tariffs, quotas, anti-dumping duties, export credits, and huge subsidies to domestic producers," thus crippling developing economies' ability to compete in those areas where they may have a genuine comparative advantage.[54]

This list could be extended indefinitely to include not just Western countries' massive imposition of externalities such as CO_2 on the developing world but, depending on one's theory of justice, their ruthless enforcement of intellectual property rights or perhaps even the system of global capitalism itself. MNEs and the sweatshops with which they contract might provide workers with significant benefits, and the jobs they offer might be better than any of the other options available to workers, but if a large part of the *reason* that workers' options are so limited is the corporatist-capitalist structure of which MNEs are a significant part, then it is not at all obvious that the benefit they provide should be sufficient to get sweatshops off the moral hook.[55]

Earlier, I discussed three ways in which considerations of structural injustice might be relevant to a correct understanding of exploitation.[56] In the remainder of this section, I will critically assess each of those suggestions with specific reference to the moral debate over sweatshop exploi-

---

[52] See, for an extended discussion, Gary Chartier, "Sweatshops, Labor Rights, and Comparative Advantage," *Oregon Review of International Law* 10, no. 1 (2008).

[53] Thomas W. Pogge, "World Poverty and Human Rights," *Ethics and International Affairs* 19, no. 1 (2005): 7.

[54] Ibid., 6.

[55] Careful consideration of this point is necessary in order to avoid the fallacy that Kevin Carson has described as "vulgar libertarianism," in which one appeals to the virtues of free markets in order to justify some aspect of the existing social order, thereby failing to recognize or appreciate the extent to which the existing social order is not an ideally free market but a corporatist system in which the powers of government are all-too-frequently used to enhance the power of land and business interests at the expense of the poor and working classes. See, for a discussion, Kevin A. Carson, "Studies in Mutualist Political Economy," (2007), http://www.mutualist.org/id47.html., chap. 4.

[56] See above, Section III.

tation. I will consider, first, whether identifying structural injustice might be necessary or sufficient in order to determine which particular interactions are to count as instances of exploitation (I argue that it is not); second, whether identifying structural injustice is necessary to think correctly about blameworthiness and responsibility for actions and situations of injustice (I argue that it is, but not in a way that is helpful for thinking about the special obligations of MNEs and sweatshops); and finally, whether identifying structural injustice is necessary in order to identify political and economic institutions themselves as exploitative, and not merely as a means to identifying microlevel transactions as exploitative (I argue that it is).

A. *Structural injustice and transactional exploitation*

Injustice at the structural level is not necessary for particular transactions to be exploitative. Nor is it sufficient. In this, I agree with Alan Wertheimer and Mikhail Vladman, and disagree with Ruth Sample and John Roemer.[57] Injustice at the structural level is not necessary because, as Wertheimer notes, "even in a reasonably just society, people will find themselves in situations in which they can strike an agreement that will produce mutual gain, and some of these cases will give rise to allegations of exploitation."[58] Indeed, the canonical examples of exploitation of the sort offered by Meyers involve no obvious background or structural injustice.[59] Offering to rescue an individual who became stranded in the desert because of her own poor planning in exchange for her entire net worth is wrongfully exploitative because of the unfairness of the terms of the transaction, not because of the history or institutional background to that transaction. Thus it is not the case, as Roemer claims, that "we view exploitation as a bad thing only when it is the consequence of an unjust unequal distribution of the means of production."[60] Nor is it the case that, as Sample claims, "if we gain advantage from an interaction with another, and that advantage is due in part to an *injustice* he has suffered, we have failed to give him appropriate respect" and hence exploited him.[61] Someone who takes pleasure in helping victims of injustice, and performs helpful acts solely in order to receive this pleasure, probably does not act wrongly at all and certainly does not wrong

---

[57] See Wertheimer, *Exploitation:* 9–10; Mikhail Valdman, "Exploitation and Injustice," *Social Theory and Practice: An International and Interdisciplinary Journal of Social Philosophy* 34, no. 4 (2008); Sample, *Exploitation: What it is and Why it's Wrong*, 74; John E. Roemer, *Free to Lose* (Cambridge: Harvard University Press, 1988), 130.
[58] Wertheimer, *Exploitation*, 9.
[59] Meyers, "Wrongful Beneficence: Exploitation and Third World Sweatshops," 324–25.
[60] Roemer, *Free to Lose*, 130.
[61] Sample, *Exploitation: What it is and Why it's Wrong*, 74.

the person whom she helps.[62] Likewise, someone who performs a useful service at a fair price for victims of injustice does not wrongfully exploit them. A contractor who rebuilds a home that was destroyed by arson, but charges only the normal market price, is not taking unfair advantage of the owner. Perhaps a more morally virtuous contractor would rebuild the home at a discount, or for free. But a failure to exhibit supererogatory kindness does not render one's actions exploitative, and at any rate our judgment that it would be nice to give a break to someone whose home was destroyed seems independent of the *cause* of the destruction—cutting a break to someone whose home was destroyed by lightning-induced wildfire seems no more and no less virtuous. The identification of structural or background injustice, then, is not sufficient for identifying particular transactions as exploitative.

That background injustices are neither necessary nor sufficient to the identification of particular transactions as wrongfully exploitative should not be too surprising. To say this, after all, is not to say that background injustices do not matter. It is simply to say that not everything that matters, morally speaking, falls under the category of exploitation. We need not view every issue of moral concern as a nail to be hammered with the concept of exploitation. Political philosophy has other tools.

B. *Structural injustice and moral responsibility*

If considerations of structural injustice are not necessary or sufficient in order to determine the status of a particular transaction as wrongfully exploitative, perhaps they are nevertheless important in some way for thinking about the moral responsibility and/or blameworthiness of agents. For Iris Marion Young, as we have seen, sweatshops are a prime example of structural injustice. Structural injustice "exists when social processes put large categories of persons under a systematic threat of domination or deprivation of the means to develop and exercise their capacities, at the same time as these processes enable others to dominate or have a wide range of opportunities for developing and exercising their capacities."[63] Individuals who contribute to these unjust social processes bear a kind of moral responsibility for them and for the results they produce,[64] though Young notes that it is a different *kind* of responsibility than that with which moral and legal philosophers are most familiar. It is a form of *political* responsibility, which, among other things, is a kind of responsibility that is forward-looking and discharged through collective action, rather than backward-looking and individualistic.[65] For Jeremy Snyder,

---

[62] This point is argued at greater length by Vladman in Valdman, "Exploitation and Injustice," 558–65.
[63] Young, "Responsibility and global justice: A social connection model," 114.
[64] Ibid., 119.
[65] Ibid., 121–23.

this model of responsibility has direct implications for the moral responsibility of sweatshop managers and MNEs, since "even if unjust structures limit the degree of choice that employers have over the wage levels that they may offer while remaining competitive, they may yet have a [political responsibility] to change these structures. If so, the employer's [political responsibility] must be discharged if the employer is to avoid exploiting her workers."[66]

But is it fair to hold MNEs and sweatshops responsible for the unjust background conditions in which they operate?[67] Certainly in some cases it is. Consider those cases in which the MNE is causally responsible for the unjust background conditions in a fairly direct way. Some such cases will involve a form of collusion between the MNE and the host country government. The MNE agrees to contract with firms in the government's jurisdiction and thereby provide the government with tax revenues and other economic benefits, but only in exchange for the government's promise to forcibly suppress labor unions. In cases like this, where the MNE is part of the cause of the background injustice, it is certainly appropriate to say that they hold partial moral responsibility for it.[68] Other cases will be more difficult to analyze. What are we to say about a case in which the structural injustice is perpetrated by the government only because it anticipates that some MNE will show up to take advantage of it? The government suppresses workers' unions, for instance, just because it believes that in doing so it will create a more attractive environment for MNEs, which will then be more likely to do business in the government's jurisdiction and generate various economic benefits of which the government can take advantage. These cases are like those in which a pimp coerces a woman into serving as a prostitute in anticipation of the revenue that will be generated by the customers who will take advantage of her services.[69] To what extent does the person who hires the prostitute bear moral responsibility for the injustice of her situation? To what extent is he blameworthy?

The analysis of such cases is difficult.[70] They are not, however, the kind of cases that Young's account is designed to deal with.[71] For the entire

---

[66] Snyder, "Exploitation and Sweatshop Labor: Perspectives and Issues," 195.

[67] A more general form of the question I ask here is posed (and answered in the negative) by Wertheimer in Wertheimer, *Exploitation*, 234.

[68] Whether they are blameworthy is a more complicated matter. It is, after all, possible that a deal struck between an MNE and the host country government will produce a situation that is on the whole beneficial to workers. Such cases would then seem to involve a conflict between respect for workers' rights and concern for their welfare, in addition to troublesome issues of distributive justice.

[69] I owe this analogy to Alan Wertheimer, in personal conversation.

[70] On the one hand, the prostitute would not be subject to coercion if the pimp did not expect people to hire her. Therefore, if everybody refused to hire prostitutes, she would probably not be coerced. Someone who does hire her thus acts as a defector in a kind of collective action problem, and is partially responsible for her plight. On the other hand, the unjust coercion has already taken place. And given that it has taken place, it might very well be the case that the prostitute really does want people to hire her—if they do not, we might

point of Young's account was to provide a supplement to the standard liability model of responsibility, one that is applicable even to agents who are not "guilty or at fault for having caused a harm without valid excuses."[72] It is an account designed to apply to those who are "connected to but removed from" the harms produced by structural injustice, but not to establish the *blameworthiness* of such agents.[73] Rather, its point is to show that such agents have a forward-looking political responsibility to take part in remedying injustice.

But it is not clear that Young's account can accomplish even this much. Or, rather, it is not clear that it can show that sweatshops or MNEs have any *special* responsibility to remedy injustice, merely by virtue of their "social connection." Young argues, seemingly innocently, that special responsibilities to correct for injustice arise from social connection. And, rather less innocently, that simply pointing out that the persons suffering from injustice are human is "not enough" to ground the claim that we have obligations of justice toward them.[74] But the special status of social connections is never defended in an entirely clear way. Young states that the kind of social connection that generates political responsibility is "participation in the diverse institutional processes that produce structural injustice."[75] And this might make sense if we thought that agents who participated in such structures were wrongly benefiting from them at the expense of victims of injustice. But this cannot be what Young is saying. For, if what grounds responsibility is not participation in unjust structures as such but *wrongful* participation in unjust structures, then Young's account would seem to collapse into a standard liability model of responsibility. One might think instead that participation matters because it provides one with opportunities to fight the injustice. But there is no reason to think that all who participate in unjust structures will have such opportunities, nor that all nonparticipants will lack them.[76] It is hard to see, then, how "social connection" could be specified in any way that would nonarbitrarily assign any kind of special responsibility to sweatshops or MNEs for remedying structural injustice.[77] Those who own or operate

---

suppose, her pimp will make things even worse for her. Failing to hire her is therefore likely only to worsen her situation in the short term, and possibly the long term as well.

[71] The discussion which follows benefited tremendously from discussion with Daniel Silvermint, who discusses them in Daniel Silvermint, "Oppression and Victim Agency," Philosophy (Tucson: University of Arizona, 2011).

[72] Young, "Responsibility and Global Justice: A Social Connection Model," 119.

[73] Ibid., 118.

[74] Ibid., 105.

[75] Ibid., 119.

[76] Menial clerks in the office of a MNE might be participating in an unjust structure without the power to change it. Wealthy or politically powerful individuals in developed countries might be able to change unjust structures elsewhere despite not being participants in them.

[77] Again for a helpful discussion of these issues, see Silvermint, "Oppression and Victim Agency."

sweatshops or MNEs might have the power or opportunity to work to remedy certain kinds of structural injustice, but if this power and opportunity is neither universally nor uniquely present among them, it will not generate any universal or unique obligation on their part.

C. Structural injustice and structural exploitation

Perhaps we have been looking in the wrong place. Instead of taking structural injustice to be evidence that particular interactions within the context of those structures are exploitative, or that parties to those transactions are morally responsible or blameworthy for the results of the injustice, perhaps structural injustice should lead us to conclude that the legal and economic institutions that gave rise to them are themselves exploitive.

This, I think, is the most promising approach for linking structural injustice to a theory of exploitation. And its absence from the contemporary philosophical literature on exploitation should be nothing sort of shocking. The modern centralized state bears significant responsibility in structuring almost every interaction that persons enter into, commercial, professional, legal, social, and otherwise. And yet, when contemporary theorists discuss exploitation, it is almost always exploitation that occurs *within* that structure, between various participants who are subject to the state's rules. To the extent that the state itself is brought up, it is as a kind of *deux ex machina* the powers of which can be brought to bear to correct exploitation in the market, the family, and elsewhere. The notion that the state itself can be a significant source and tool of exploitation is almost never mentioned.[78]

This is not the place to develop a full theory of state exploitation. But we might perhaps make some preliminary points toward the end of developing such a theory. We can note, first, that any theory of state exploitation will need to develop or rely on some theory of collective actions and/or intentions, and to be careful to distinguish those actions that are properly attributable to the collective entity we call "the state" and those that ought to be ascribed to specific individuals. Onora O'Neill's discussion of state coercion illustrates the difficulties inherent in such an approach. For determining whether capitalism is coercive, she notes,

---

[78] This was not always the case. The idea of state exploitation has a rich history among both classical liberal and socialist thinkers that contemporary philosophy appears to have largely lost sight of. Helpful overviews, however, can be found in Leonard Liggio, "Charles Dunoyer and French Classical Liberalism," *Journal of Libertarian Studies* 1, no. 3 (1977); Ralph Raico, "Classical Liberal Exploitation Theory: A Comment on Professor Liggio's Paper," *Journal of Libertarian Studies* 1, no. 3 (1977); Roderick Long, "Toward a Libertarian Theory of Class," *Social Philosophy and Policy* 15, no. 2 (1998); Ralph Raico, "Liberalism, Marxism, and the State," *Cato Journal* 11, no. 3 (1992); and "Classical Liberal Roots of the Marxist Doctrine of Classes," in Ralph Raico, ed., *Classical Liberalism and the Austrian School* (Auburn, Alabama: Ludwig von Mises Institute, 2010).

requires determining "the principles that guide the institution of employment in a capitalist system."[79] But whatever might those principles be?
How are we to ascribe maxims to institutions which may have evolved as
"the product of human action but not of human design"? Similar problems will no doubt plague a theory of state exploitation.

Second, it will be important to distinguish between some of the different forms that state exploitation can take. At least two distinct types
are readily apparent. In one, the powers of the state can be used to
unfairly benefit the state itself, or the persons who constitute it in their
capacity as agents of the state.[80] Suppose, for instance, that an agent of
the state, acting in her official capacity, threatened unfairly to block a
company's access to a particular market unless that company paid a
special tax, the proceeds of which would be used to fund the activities
of the state. To the extent that such a demand is illegitimate, we could
say that it constitutes a kind of state exploitation—an unfair use of
state power to take advantage of the (relatively) vulnerable business. A
second form state exploitation might take, however, involves the use of
state power to benefit persons outside the institution of the state, or
agents of the state in their capacity as private persons. This phenomenon has been exhaustively catalogued and analyzed by public choice
economists under the label of "rent seeking," but to the extent that we
find the activity unfair or otherwise morally illegitimate, it could very
well be described as a kind of wrongful exploitation.[81] A MNE that
makes its entrance into a developing country (and payment of taxes to

---

[79] O'Neill, "Between Consenting Adults," 123.

[80] Even Marx recognized the potential for this form of exploitation. Witness his discussion
of Napoleon's 1851 *coup* in his pamphlet, *The Eighteenth Brumaire of Louis Bonaparte:* "This
executive power, with its enormous bureaucracy and military organization, with its inge-
nious state machinery, embracing wide strata, with a host of officials numbering half a
million, besides an army of another half million, this appalling parasitic body, which enmeshes
the body of French society like a net and chokes all its pores, sprang up in the days of the
absolute monarchy. The Legitimist monarchy and the July monarchy added nothing but a
greater division of labor, growing in the same measure—as the division of labor within
bourgeois society created new groups of interests, and therefore new material for slate
administration. Every *common* interest was straightway severed from society, counterposed
to it as a higher *general* interest, snatched from the activity of society's members themselves
and made an object of government activity, from a bridge, a schoolhouse and the communal
property of a village community to the railways, the national wealth and the national
university of France. . . . All revolutions perfected this machine instead of smashing it. The
parties that contended in turn for domination regarded the possession of this huge state
edifice as the principal spoils of the victor . . . under the second Bonaparte [Napoleon III] . . .
the state [seems] to have made itself completely independent. As against civil society, the
state machine has consolidated its position . . . thoroughly." Cited in Raico, "Classical Liberal Exploitation Theory: A Comment on Professor Liggio's Paper," 179–80.

[81] The *locus classicus* of this analysis is James Buchanan and Gordon Tullock, *The Calculus
of Consent* (Ann Arbor: University of Michigan Press, 1962). More recent explorations can be
found in James Buchanan, R. D. Tollison, and Gordon Tullock, *Toward a Theory of the Rent-
Seeking Society* (Texas A & M University, College Station, 1980); Gordon Tullock, R. D.
Tollison, and C. K. Rowley, "The Political Economy of Rent Seeking," (Boston: Kluwer,
1988).

that country's government) contingent upon the state's illegitimate restriction of potential competition can be said to be using the state as a tool of exploitation in this sense. Perhaps we might also distinguish between two more specific forms this scenario might take: one in which the state agent is neither morally nor legally authorized to restrict competition, and one in which she is legally but not morally authorized to restrict it. In the first, the agent of the state is acting as a kind of rogue—abusing the powers of her office in order to benefit privately. In this case, both the MNE and the state agent are *using* the state as a tool of exploitation. In the second case, only the MNE can be said to use the state in an exploitative way. The agent's action is probably best regarded as an action *of* the state and so, if anything, is an instance of the first type of state exploitation described in this paragraph.

Finally, a full theory of state exploitation will need some way to distinguish between the kinds of legitimate exchanges that occur between private persons, and the exploitative deals that occur between, say, state agents and rent seekers. Nineteenth-century classical liberals tended to make this distinction in a rhetorically powerful but philosophically clumsy way, distinguishing, as in the case of Jean-Baptiste Say, between "productive" exchanges on the market and the "unproductive" activities of government.[82] But the activity of rent seeking can be productive both in the sense of creating actual goods or services, and in the sense of producing an overall increase in utility (obviously for the parties to the exchange but also, perhaps in cases where rent seeking is employed to spur the provision of a genuine public good, for society as a whole). What makes rent seeking exploitative is not its being unproductive, but its being unfair. But what exactly this means in the context of political institutions is something that requires much further exploration.

Before bringing this section to a close, it is worth reminding ourselves that not all forms of structural injustice will be instances of state exploitation. Injustice can take many forms, and exploitation is only one of them. States can oppress their populations as well, in which case the injustice they do may neither yield nor be intended to yield any benefits of the sort at which exploitation characteristically aims.[83] And coercion can be unjust without necessarily being exploitative.[84] State exploitation, then, although it is an unduly neglected form of state injustice, is only one form among many.

[82] See, for a discussion, Patricia J. Euzent and Thomas L. Martin, "Classical Roots of the Emerging Theory of Rent Seeking: The Contribution of Jean-Baptiste Say," *History of Political Economy* 16, no. 2 (1984).
[83] Ann Cudd, *Analyzing Oppression* (New York: Oxford University Press, 2006).
[84] Coercion that is employed for paternalistic purposes, for instance, might be unjust but is not exploitative insofar as it does not involve an unfair or degrading advantage-taking. See, for a discussion, Alan Wertheimer, *Coercion*, Studies in Moral, Political and Legal Philosophy (Princeton: Princeton University Press, 1987).

VI. Conclusion

This essay began with a debate over the moral status of sweatshops. On one side of that debate are economists and others who hold that the benefits sweatshops provide to their workers renders their conduct and the conduct of the MNEs with which they contract not wrongfully exploitative, or at least not seriously so. On the other side are those who hold that the true exploitative nature of sweatshops only becomes apparent once we shift our focus from the particular details of the exchange between sweatshop and worker, and look instead at the deep injustices in the background of that exchange.

This essay has sought to explore the moral debates over sweatshops, and to examine the way in which considerations of structural injustice might or might not be relevant to the charge of sweatshop exploitation. And the result of our inquiry has been a modest vindication of the economists' defense of sweatshops. We have seen that the existence of background injustices does not render an otherwise fair exchange wrongfully exploitative. And we have seen that while sweatshops and the MNEs with which they contract have a moral responsibility to fight unjust institutions, this is an obligation they share with everyone who is able to do so, and so cannot ground any special fault on their part.

Nevertheless, it is important not to overestimate the reach of my argument here. I have not attempted to offer an impossibility proof. It is not only possible, but it is virtually certain that some sweatshops do wrongfully exploit their workers. Those that actively cooperate with government to suppress their workers or their competitors, for instance, are guilty of not only *benefiting* from structural injustice but also *perpetuating* it for their own gain. This is wrongful exploitation of the clearest sort. And even without government intervention, it is possible for sweatshops to wrongfully exploit their workers. The fact that sweatshop workers are willing to accept a certain package of wages and benefits from sweatshops is not enough to show that package to be fair.

Drawing the line between fair and unfair offers—like many cases of conceptual line-drawing—is of course a difficult business. The unfairness that constitutes exploitation, on my view, is not the sort of thing that can be assessed by means of any precise formula. Determining the fairness or unfairness of conduct is largely a matter of balancing the reasons weighing for and against that conduct, and thus often reduces to an exercise of judgment about which reasonable people can disagree. I have argued that canonical conditions of sweatshop labor—low wages, long hours, and unsafe conditions, for instance—do not suffice to render sweatshop labor wrongfully exploitative, once the broader range of empirical and moral features of sweatshop labor are taken into account. But when, for instance, some sweatshops use their employee's fear of termination to perpetrate physical and sexual abuse, then to my thinking at least the balance of reasons tips decidedly toward a judgment of unfairness.

Structural injustice, then, does not render sweatshop labor wrongfully exploitative. But I sincerely hope that readers will not take away from this paper the message that structural injustice does not matter, or is of small importance. The unjust seizure of land and other natural resources by governments and plutocratic interests, the suppression of alternative opportunities for workers through restrictive intellectual property laws and trade barriers, the failure to uphold the right of workers to freely organize into labor unions, and so on are all significant injustices that affect the lives of workers in the developing world for the worse. And they may, indeed, be injustices without which sweatshops as we know them would cease to exist. To the extent that it is in our power to do so, we should work to stop and rectify them.

My concern in this essay has been to explore the moral responsibility of sweatshops, not of humanity in general. And to explore in particular their responsibility for one specific kind of wrongdoing—exploitation. There is a danger, however, in the analytic philosopher's tendency to brush aside as irrelevant those issues that do not fit neatly within the concept he is exploring. Structural injustice may not have much to do with transactional exploitation, but it has a tremendous amount to do with people's ability to live peaceful and fulfilling lives. It is thus an issue of the utmost concern for us not only as philosophers (in other papers, at other times), but as human beings.

Philosophy, University of San Diego

RESCUING JUSTICE FROM EQUALITY*

By Steven Wall

This essay discusses Rawlsian justice in general and the difference principle[1] in particular. It does so in the light of G. A. Cohen's masterful critique of Rawls in *Rescuing Justice and Equality*,[2] a work that not only inspires the present paper, but also serves as a point of contrast for much within it.[3] Like Cohen, I argue that the difference principle and the justifications given for it pull us in opposing directions. Specifically, I argue that Rawlsian arguments for the difference principle present a puzzle and that to respond adequately to the puzzle we must engage in rational reconstruction. To respond to the puzzle we must go beyond asking whether or not a proposed interpretation is one that Rawls himself would have endorsed, and start asking whether it is one that puts Rawlsian justice in its best light.[4]

This much, I believe, is common ground between Cohen and myself. However, in stark contrast to Cohen, I present an interpretation—a rational reconstruction—of Rawlsian justice that shows it to be less intolerant

* Earlier versions of this essay were presented to audiences at a number of venues: the philosophy department at the University of Connecticut, the first annual NOISE conference in New Orleans, the political philosophy colloquium series at Brown University, and the philosophy department at the University of Arizona. Thanks to all participants at these events for their comments and criticisms. Special thanks go to Jeff Moriarity, who served as a discussant for the paper at the NOISE conference. I am grateful to my fellow conference participants for their responses to the essay, and I am especially grateful to Ellen Frankel Paul for her expert editorial interventions. Finally, while it no doubt falls short of his high standards, this essay is a tribute to G. A. Cohen, who sadly is no longer with us. Jerry was one of my teachers in graduate school. He not only helped me to come to a better understanding of Rawlsian justice, but also renewed my excitement and interest in the kind of political philosophy at which he excelled.

[1] The difference principle, in its simple form, holds that social and economic inequalities are to be arranged so that they are to the greatest benefit of the representative man of the least advantaged class in society. This simple statement of the principle leaves many issues open. A full understanding of the difference principle requires close attention to these issues.

[2] G. A. Cohen, *Rescuing Justice and Equality* (Cambridge, MA: Harvard University Press, 2008).

[3] Cohen's penetrating critique of Rawls is wide ranging and multifaceted. Its general thrust is that Rawlsian justice is underlaid with strong egalitarian commitments and that Rawls's own defense of economic inequalities betrays these commitments.

[4] To be sure, any proposed interpretation of Rawlsian justice must be one that fits what Rawls wrote to a sufficient extent to count as an interpretation of his account of justice. But a good account of Rawlsian justice will need to play up some elements in his work and downplay others.

doi:10.1017/S0265052511000136

of economic inequality than it is commonly taken to be. My aim, in short, is to rescue Rawlsian justice from its commitment to equality.[5] A key motivation behind this reconstructive effort is the following simple thought. A signal attraction of the difference principle—understood as a principle of justice and not as a mere guideline for sensible policy in this or that circumstance—is that it saved, or at least seemed to save, broadly egalitarian justice[6] from the so-called "leveling down objection." This objection is that insisting on simple equality as a matter of justice is perverse, for there can be cases in which doing so means insisting on making everyone worse-off. Or, less perverse, but still problematic, it can mean insisting on making some individual worse-off without thereby making anyone else better-off. As students of Rawls standardly have been taught, the difference principle, and in particular a staggered version[7] of it, avoid this problem. That is what I mean when I say that the difference principle saves broadly egalitarian justice from the leveling down objection. A good interpretation of the difference principle must stay true to this underlying motivation.

The argument of the essay unfolds as follows. Section I warns against two distractions. Section II introduces and explains the puzzle. With the puzzle in clear focus, Section III then considers and rejects a number of responses to it. As will emerge, the puzzle invites rational reconstruction, for no response to it captures all of Rawls's commitments. My reconstruction of Rawlsian justice begins in Section IV, where I present the case for viewing the difference principle as a maximizing prioritarian[8] principle of justice, one that contains no trace of commitment to equality as a distributive norm. The final two sections, V and VI, bring out some of the implications of viewing Rawlsian justice in this light.

[5] By equality I mean equality in the distribution of socioeconomic goods. I do not mean equality in a deeper, and less contentful, sense, such as the sense of equality in play when, for example, it is claimed that all persons are equal from the moral point of view.

[6] "Broadly egalitarian justice" is a term of art. It refers to views of distributive justice commonly characterized as egalitarian. Prioritarian views of distributive justice—views that do not assign intrinsic value to how well off people are relative to others—are often characterized as broadly egalitarian.

[7] A staggered version of the difference principle is what Rawls terms a "lexical" version of the principle. It directs a society first to maximize the position of the representative man of the worst-off group. Then, subject to that constraint, it directs a society to maximize the position of the representative man of the next worst-off group, and so on, until it has maximized the position of the representative man of the best-off group. See John Rawls, *A Theory of Justice* (Cambridge, MA: Harvard University Press, 1971), 83. Rev. ed., 72. [Page numbers refer first to the 1971 edition and second to the 1999 edition.]

[8] Prioritarianism refers to a family of maximizing principles that give priority to those who are worse off. Different prioritarian principles assign different weights to this priority. Common to all prioritarian views is the rejection of the view that inequality, as such, is unjust. Prioritarians reject the claim, advanced by strict egalitarians, that it is unjust if some are worse off than others through no fault or choice of their own. For the classic discussion of prioritarianism see Derek Parfit, "Equality or Priority?" Lindley Lecture, 1991, Dept. of Philosophy, University of Kansas, reprinted in Matthew Clayton and Andrew Williams, eds., *The Ideal of Equality* (London: Macmillan, 2000), 81–125.

I. Two Distractions

As I noted, the difference principle and the justifications offered for it present a puzzle that resists easy resolution. I will explain exactly what I mean by this shortly. First, I want to mention, and then put to one side, two potential distractions. In this essay, I propose to take the difference principle seriously as a principle of distributive justice. I am aware that the difference principle is just one component of Rawlsian justice. It is lexically subordinate to both the principle of equal liberty (and its attendant fair value guarantee of the political liberties) and to the principle of fair equality of opportunity. This has led some commentators to claim that the difference principle is not all that important to Rawlsian justice. Not much economic inequality can pass through these lexically prior filters. For this reason, the difference principle has a quite limited scope of application.[9]

I think this claim is incorrect; and I think Rawls also thought it was incorrect. Rawls certainly wrote as if it were, in principle, possible for the difference principle to justify very substantial economic inequality. That is why he thought it necessary to consider the possibility of "excusable envy." Excusable envy would be present if the economic inequality justified by the difference principle were so great that it understandably damaged the self-respect of those on the bottom. If this were to occur, then, Rawls claims, we might need to rethink the permissibility of the inequality justified by the difference principle.[10] All of this assumes that such inequality would not be ruled out by the lexically prior principles. To be sure, this is not decisive. Perhaps Rawls misapplied his own principles. But I will assume here that he did not. I acknowledge that a full rational reconstruction of Rawlsian justice would need to address these principles as well as the difference principle.[11]

That was the first potential distraction. The second one concerns the goods to which the difference principle applies. Following Rawls, I will

---

[9] See, for example, the discussion of David Brink's view from private correspondence in Cohen, *Rescuing Justice and Equality*, 381–87.

[10] Rawls, *A Theory of Justice*, 534–41. Rev. ed. 468–74.

[11] There is a strong case for thinking that the parties in the original position would *not* choose to constrain the difference principle by the fair equality of opportunity principle. See the discussion in Thomas Pogge, *John Rawls: His Life and Theory of Justice* (Oxford: Oxford University Press, 2007), 126–33 and Richard Arneson, "Against Fair Equality of Opportunity," *Philosophical Studies* 93 (1999): 77–112. Perhaps moved by considerations of this kind Rawls himself came to have doubts about the lexical priority assigned to the fair equality of opportunity principle. See *Justice as Fairness: A Restatement* (Cambridge, MA: Harvard University Press, 2001), 163 n. 44. As for the fair value guarantee of the political liberties, this can be achieved not by sharply restricting the scope of the difference principle, but rather by insulating the political process from economic interests. On this point see Rawls's discussion of the American Supreme Court case *Buckley v. Valeo* in *Political Liberalism* (New York: Columbia University Press, 1993), 359–63. The plausibility of the fair value guarantee of the political liberties itself also can be challenged. I do so in my "Rawls and the Status of Political Liberty," *Pacific Philosophical Quarterly* 87, no. 2 (2006): 245–70.

assume that, by and large, the difference principle regulates the distribution of income and wealth—money, for short. In a more complete statement of the principle, however, we would need to consider adding other goods to the mix. Several goods, in particular, warrant mention. These are the goods of leisure time, the goods associated with the powers and prerogatives of office, and the good picked out by the Rawlsian phrase "the social bases of self-respect." Including these latter goods in the bundle of goods to which the difference principle applies will complicate the story I want to tell, but it will not fundamentally change it. So, with this qualification noted, I will assume that the difference principle is a principle that regulates the distribution of income and wealth in a society. And I will discuss leisure time, the powers and prerogatives of office, and the social bases of self-respect only when doing so may reasonably be thought to bear on the claims that I am advancing.

II. The Puzzle Expounded

The puzzle I want to discuss concerns whether "justice as fairness" in general, and the difference principle in particular, require the economic arrangements of a modern democratic society to satisfy a minimal standard of economic efficiency—the standard of Pareto-efficiency. (The Pareto standard requires that, of two distributions D^1 and D^2, if some are better off and none are worse off in D^2 when compared to D^1, then D^2 must be ranked above D^1.) By economic arrangements, I will mean both regime-types—such as welfare-state capitalism or property-owning democracy—and political initiatives that can be pursued within these regimes-types—such as pro-growth or no-growth economic policies.

To introduce the puzzle, I call attention to an important ambiguity in Rawls's statement of the difference principle. To my knowledge, the ambiguity was first detected by Nozick, but it has been noted by a number of commentators on Rawls's work.[12] Here is what Nozick observed.

[T]he difference principle is inefficient in that it sometimes will favor a status quo against a Pareto-better but more equal distribution. The inefficiency could be removed by shifting from the simple difference principle to a staggered difference principle, which recommends the maximization of the position of the least well-off group, and *subject to that constraint* the maximization of the position of the next least well-off group. . . . But such a staggered principle does not embody a presumption in favor of equality of the sort used by Rawls.[13]

---

[12] See, for example, Derek Parfit, "Equality or Priority?" 116-21; Philippe Van Parijs, "Difference Principles," in Samuel Freeman, ed., *The Cambridge Companion to Rawls* (Cambridge: Cambridge University Press, 2003), 200-40 and G. A. Cohen, *Rescuing Justice and Equality*, 157-59.

[13] Robert Nozick, *Anarchy, State and Utopia* (New York: Basic Books, 1974), 229-30.

STEVEN WALL

TABLE 1. *The Difference Principle and Pareto Efficiency*

	State 1	State 2
Better-Off	100	120
Worse-Off	60	60

What Nozick calls the "simple difference principle" is the principle that economic inequality is unjust unless it benefits the worst-off group; and what he terms the "staggered difference principle" is the principle that economic inequality is unjust only if it comes at the expense of the worst-off group *and* economic equality that comes at the expense of better-off groups, without thereby benefiting worst-off groups, is also unjust. The two principles thus exhibit a different commitment to equality. The simple principle mandates Pareto-inefficient equality promoting policies that the staggered principle condemns. Table 1 illustrates the situation.

The extra inequality generated by a transition from State 1 to State 2 does not benefit the worse-off group. It therefore is unjust if it is true that, as the simple difference principle states, inequalities are unjust unless they improve the prospects of the worse-off group. But a transition from State 2 to State 1 worsens the position of the better-off group without thereby improving the position of the worse-off group. It therefore is unjust if is true that, as the staggered difference principle states, economic equality is unjust if it comes at the expense of the better-off group without thereby benefiting the worse-off group.

So the question is, does Rawlsian justice favor the simple or the staggered difference principle? Some may respond by saying that we do not need to answer this question. Table 1 illustrates a situation in which what Rawls terms "close-knitness" does not obtain, but this situation is not appropriately realistic.[14] The difference principle was not meant to apply to "abstract possibilities," but rather to the functioning of a realistic modern economy of a modern society, an economy for which "close-knitness" obtains. But this response is not satisfying, for we want to know the content of the difference principle, and to determine its content we will need to consider unrealistic as well as realistic situations. Rawls must have thought as much himself, since he does contemplate the possibility

---

[14] Rawls uses contribution curves to illustrate the difference principle. Close-knitness obtains when the contribution curves of the representative men from each group from the least advantaged to the most advantaged contain no flat stretches. (See John Rawls, *A Theory of Justice*, 81–82/71–72.) More colloquially put, close-knitness rules out situations in which gains to one group, such as the most advantaged, do not impact the position of the other groups in any way.

that close-knitness will not obtain and he does affirm the staggered difference principle in that contemplated possibility.[15]

Many may think that it is obvious that State 2 is preferable to State 1. What possible considerations, they will ask, would favor opting for the Pareto-inefficient state? But considerations of this kind can be identified. One of them is what I shall term "reciprocity." This value or ideal can be characterized in different ways, but in one form or another it is undeniably an element of Rawlsian justice. Rawls sometimes identifies reciprocity with the good of fraternity:

> The family, in its ideal conception and often in practice, is one place where the principle of maximizing the sum of advantages is rejected. Members of a family commonly do not wish to gain unless they can do so in ways that further the interests of the rest. Now wanting to act on the difference principle has precisely this consequence.[16]

Notice that, if the difference principle is a principle of reciprocity, and if reciprocity is understood in terms of fraternity, then the difference principle will favor State 1 over State 2 in our example.[17] The simple difference principle expresses reciprocity (understood in terms of the good of fraternity) whereas the staggered difference principle repudiates reciprocity (so understood) and endorses Pareto-efficient maximizing transitions. Table 1 thus illustrates a pivotal choice between two rival interpretations of the difference principle.

Next, consider a second case. This case concerns the choice between two possible regime-types for a given modern democratic society. Call them R^1 and R^2.[18] Assume that the efficient operation of each regime-type for the society in question secures a reasonably high social minimum and yields the distributions depicted in Table 2.[19] Assume further that the individual members of the better-off and worse-off classes remain the same under both R^1 and R^2.[20]

---

[15] Rawls calls the staggered difference principle "the lexical difference principle." See his brief discussion of it in *A Theory of Justice*, 82–83/72.

[16] Rawls, *A Theory of Justice*, 105/90.

[17] For perceptive discussion of this point see Cohen, *Rescuing Justice and Equality*, 76–80.

[18] For the purposes of the example, I assume that these two regime-types are the only feasible options for the society in question.

[19] To simplify the discussion, I assume that there are only two socioeconomic classes. I also assume that the increased inequality in R^2 is not so great so as to threaten the stability of the regime by engendering "excusable envy." Finally, I assume that both R^1 and R^2 can be justified in a manner that does not violate the full publicity condition.

[20] This further assumption is necessary to ensure that the Pareto-standard strictly applies in the present case. By contrast, if the individual members of the better-off and worse-off groups switched places in R^1 and R^2, then the Pareto-standard would favor a transition from R^1 to R^2 only when it was supplemented with additional conditions. For discussion of this point see Pogge, *John Rawls: His Life and Theory of Justice*, 48–53.

TABLE 2. *The Difference Principle and Regime Choice*

	R^1	R^2
Better-Off	100	125
Worse-Off	70	75

Does the difference principle, in accord with the Pareto-standard, require the society to adopt R^2 over R^1, or does it permit the society to choose either regime-type?[21] Rawls does not speak unequivocally on this matter. He claims that the difference principle is consistent with the Pareto principle of efficiency and he often asserts that the difference principle "is, strictly speaking, a maximizing principle."[22] These claims imply that the difference principle not only favors economic arrangements that engender only inequalities that raise (or at least do not lower) the economic prospects of the worse-off, but also that it favors the economic arrangements that maximize the economic prospects of the worse-off compared with all feasible alternatives. R^1 satisfies the first, but not the second, of these conditions, whereas R^2 satisfies them both.[23] So the difference principle—on what I shall term its *maximizing interpretation*—requires the society in Table 2 to adopt R^2.

It is possible that the difference principle does not require the society to adopt R^2, however. The maximin feature of the difference principle may apply only within regime-types, but not across them. The difference principle, Rawls writes, "presupposes a rough continuum of practicable basic structures." The difference principle selects the system of social cooperation that, in relation to all "reasonably close and available alternatives," maximizes the position of the worse-off, whomever they may be.[24] The maximin feature of the difference principle thus appears to be indexed to systems of social cooperation that are reasonably close to one another. So, if R^1 and R^2 are not reasonably close alternatives, then the difference principle may not favor R^2 over R^1. It may permit the society to adopt either regime.[25]

[21] A third possibility is that the difference principle requires the society to adopt R^1. Such a view would hold that the difference principle favors the most egalitarian regime among the regimes that permit inequalities that benefit the worse-off.

[22] Rawls, *A Theory of Justice*, 79/69.

[23] In the terminology used in *A Theory of Justice*, R^1 is "just throughout, but not the best just arrangement." R^2, by contrast, is "a perfectly just" arrangement. (See 78–79/68).

[24] Rawls, *Justice as Fairness: A Restatement*, 70.

[25] Commenting on the choice between a capitalist and a socialist regime, Thomas Pogge suggests that this is a decision that each political society is free to make in light of its circumstances and traditions. The decision should be treated as a matter of pure procedural justice. See Thomas Pogge, *Realizing Rawls* (Ithaca: Cornell University Press, 1989), 202–203.

There are, in fact, considerations that support this latitudinarian read-ing of the difference principle. The difference principle can be construed as a principle that articulates a general condition for justified inequality. As such, it does not require maximizing the economic prospects of the worse-off group. It requires only that inequality benefit, or at least not come at the expense of, the worse-off group. This requirement itself can be under-stood as a requirement of reciprocity. Let us distinguish strong from weak reciprocity. Strong reciprocity is the sense of reciprocity mentioned earlier, a sense of reciprocity that expresses the good of fraternity. By contrast, weak reciprocity is consistent with economic inequalities that do not benefit the worse-off group so long as these inequalities do not come at their expense. One who affirms weak over strong reciprocity can favor State 2 over State 1 in Table 1, while also holding that the society in Table 2 can opt for either regime, since both regimes (we are assuming) satisfy weak reciprocity.

Is it possible that the difference principle really is a principle of weak reciprocity and not a maximin principle? In an intriguing passage in *A Theory of Justice*, Rawls distinguishes an economic arrangement that is "perfectly just" from one that is merely "just throughout." The former maximizes the economic position of the worse-off, whereas the latter merely satisfies the condition that the better off do not gain at the expense of the worse-off. An arrangement that is just throughout is one that sat-isfies weak reciprocity. It is not the "best" just arrangement since it fails to maximize the position of the worst-off group. In discussing this dis-tinction, Rawls insists that the difference principle favors the "perfectly just" arrangement. This is exactly what one would expect him to say if he were committed to the maximizing interpretation of the difference prin-ciple. The problem is that a proponent of the difference principle, on the maximizing interpretation, should hold that an arrangement that is not perfectly just, such as the one that Rawls refers to as merely "just through-out," is not, in reality, *just throughout*, since it falls short of what the difference principle prescribes and the difference principle articulates the content of distributive justice.[26]

One way to make sense of what Rawls is claiming in this passage is that the difference principle expresses two fundamental ideas. It expresses an ideal of reciprocity between citizens (namely, that the better-off are not to gain unless doing so either improves the position of the worse-off or at least does not come at the expense of the worse-off) and it expresses a maximizing injunction (namely, the position of the worse-off is to be maximized in comparison with other possible alternative arrangements). Injustice is present when the ideal of reciprocity is violated. But, even when neither of two arrangements violates the ideal of reciprocity, one

---

[26] Bear in mind that we are assuming that the other, lexically prior, principles of justice have been satisfied. Given this assumption, the difference principle articulates the content of (Rawlsian) distributive justice.

arrangement can be judged to be better than the other with respect to distributive justice if it, but not the other, satisfies the maximizing injunction.

The notion that the difference principle gives voice to an ideal of reciprocity is one that Rawls came to emphasize in his late work.[27] Somewhat surprisingly, he stressed that the argument for the difference principle does not, in general, rest on the maximin decision rule. And, he claimed, that the failure to make this point clear was "a serious fault" of *A Theory of Justice.*[28] Instead, the difference principle "is essentially a principle of reciprocity." What it requires is that, "however great the general level of wealth—whether high or low—the existing inequalities are to fulfill the condition of benefiting others as well as ourselves."[29] Call this the "reciprocity-centered" interpretation of the difference principle.

Return now to the choice presented in Table 2. The maximizing injunction clearly favors R^2 over R^1. But if the difference principle is understood as a principle of reciprocity, then it may not require a society to select the regime-type that maximizes the position of the worse-off. On its reciprocity-centered interpretation, the difference principle does not favor either regime-type in Table 1. It is silent on the issue, leaving the matter to be determined by the political process of a democratic society.[30]

Rawls's explicit remarks do not settle the issue of whether the difference principle requires a society to adopt a regime that maximizes the economic position of the worse-off. There is a case both for construing the difference principle on its maximizing interpretation and for construing it on its reciprocity-centered interpretation. And, depending on which interpretation is favored, the difference principle supports different judgments in cases of the sort presented by Table 2. It is natural to suspect, however, that the issue can be resolved by considering it from the standpoint of the parties in the original position. As Rawls characterizes them, the parties are motivated to secure the highest index of social primary goods for those they represent. Limiting the focus to income and wealth, the parties aim to secure the maximum level for those they represent. This yields a powerful and straightforward argument for the view that the parties in the original position would select R^2 over R^1. Yet, as I hinted at a moment ago, Rawls came to reject the notion that the difference principle rests on the maximin decision rule. The parties in the original position, he stresses, do not, at least not in general, appeal to it in justifying the difference principle over alternative principles. This point emerges most clearly in Rawls's discussion of the case for the difference principle over the principle of restricted utility. The principle of restricted utility directs citizens to design a basic structure that maximizes average utility (or average

---

[27] See especially the discussion in Rawls, *Justice as Fairness: A Restatement*, 76–77.
[28] Rawls, *Justice as Fairness: A Restatement*, 95.
[29] Ibid., 64.
[30] See, for example, Pogge, *Realizing Rawls*, 202–204. But compare these claims with the more recent discussion in Pogge, *John Rawls: His Life and Theory of Justice*, 114–115.

TABLE 3. *The Difference Principle and Restricted Utilitarianism*

	Option 1 (O^1)	Option 2 (O^2)
Better-off	90	105
Worse-off	60	55
Suitable Social Minimum	50	50

shares of income/wealth) subject to the constraint that a suitable social minimum is guaranteed for all.[31] Table 3 illustrates the difference between the two principles.

Assuming that the number of people in both the better-off and worse-off classes remains the same under both options, then the difference principle favors O^1 and the principle of restricted utility favors O^2. But Rawls's argument for why the parties in the original position would select O^1 over O^2 does not appeal to the maximin decision rule. The fact that the worse-off fare better under O^1 compared to O^2 does not provide the reason for favoring it. This is the case since both basic structures secure a suitably high social minimum, thereby undercutting one of the conditions that make it rational to be guided by the maximin decision rule.[32]

What considerations then favor the adoption of O^1? The main reason that Rawls offers for why the parties in the original position would favor it over O^2 is that O^2 yields a distribution that violates the ideal of reciprocity expressed by the difference principle.[33] As we have seen, the ideal of reciprocity is subject to competing interpretations; but, at a minimum, it holds that the better-off should not gain at the expense of the worse-off. And this is precisely what is permitted by the principle of restricted utility and what is forbidden by the difference principle.[34]

---

[31] Rawls, *Justice as Fairness: A Restatement*, 120.

[32] As Rawls explains, one of the conditions for the application of the maximin decision rule is that "the worse outcomes of all the other alternatives are significantly below the guaranteeable level." (*Justice as Fairness: A Restatement*, 98) This condition does not obtain in the present case. Nor does it obtain in the comparison case of R^1 and R^2 depicted in Table 1.

[33] Rawls also mentions that the principle of restricted utility is subject to indeterminacy, given the difficulties of making public interpersonal comparisons of utility. But this is not a central problem, since the principle could be construed to require that the share of income and wealth be maximized rather than some utility function. See *Justice as Fairness: A Restatement*, 126–27.

[34] Presumably, the parties in the original position will not appeal to the value of reciprocity. They are motivated to look out for the good of those they represent, not the good of those they represent relative to the good of others. But Rawls stresses that the parties must take an interest in whether "those they represent can reasonably be expected to honor the principles agreed to in the manner required by the idea of an agreement." (*Justice as Fairness: A Restatement*, 103) And he claims further that if the ideal of reciprocity is flouted, then the worst-off may not be disposed to honor the agreement. Thus, or so it appears, from the standpoint of the original position, stability considerations favor selecting a principle of justice that realizes the ideal of reciprocity. (*Justice as Fairness: A Restatement*, 127).

TABLE 4. *The Difference Principle and Economic Growth*

	T^1	T^2
P^1	(100, 80)	(100, 80)
P^2	(100, 80)	(120, 90)

Notice, however, that if the case for the difference principle rests on an ideal of reciprocity rather than on the maximin decision rule, then it will not help to resolve the issue raised by Table 2. Assuming that both regimes provide a suitably high social minimum, the difference principle will not tell us whether a society must adopt R^2 over R^1. For suppose a society with R^2 decided to undertake a transition to R^1. The transition would not violate the ideal of reciprocity expressed by the difference principle, even though it would result in a state of affairs under which the worse-off's economic prospects declined. This view of the difference principle, accordingly, supports the judgment that the principle does not rule out Pareto-inefficient distributive outcomes—at least under conditions depicted in Table 2.

The difference principle is presented as a maximizing principle. Yet when it is viewed from the standpoint of the original position, it is not supported by the maximin rule. (As we have seen, the maximin rule does not apply in comparison cases of the sort depicted in Tables 2 and 3.) This makes it mysterious why the difference principle is characterized by Rawls as a maximizing principle. For if it is truly a maximizing principle, then its maximizing feature is inadequately grounded by the ideal of reciprocity that the principle purportedly expresses.

The puzzle in Rawlsian justice that I have been exposing can be expressed in terms of permissions and requirements. The difference principle, on the maximizing interpretation, requires Pareto-efficient transitions that are merely permissible on its reciprocity-centered interpretation. That it is an inconsistency, since if something is required, then it is not permissible to not do it.

The same inconsistency is manifest in another example, one that Rawls himself did speak to directly. It concerns a choice between policies that can be pursued within the same regime-type. Consider Table 4. P^1 and P^2 refer respectively to no-growth and pro-growth economic policies. Differences in time are represented by T^1 and T^2 and the economic positions of the better-off and worse-off are represented in the parentheses.[35]

---

[35] All the same stipulations remain in place; e.g., both policies secure a suitably high social minimum, neither policy conflicts with other requirements of Rawlsian justice, etc.

Does Rawlsian justice require the society in this example to adopt P^2 over P^1? Rawls's discussion of the just savings principle suggests that societies have some leeway in deciding how much to save for future generations. But he stresses that justice does not require continual economic growth across time. The difference principle, Rawls insists, does not rule out a society in which real capital accumulation reduces to zero, even if conditions were such that continued economic growth remained a possibility.[36] If this is right, however, then it is natural to wonder why the difference principle requires that the economic prospects of the worse-off be maximized over *each* interval of time to which it applies.

Let me now stipulate that the distributive profiles represented in Table 4 do not represent intergenerational distributions. That is, the time interval between T^1 and T^2 is not so great as to shift the case from one of intragenerational to intergenerational justice. (Assume, if you like, that it is less than a twenty-year time interval.) The example Table 4 depicts, we now assume, is not that one that implicates the just savings principle.

The same reasoning rehearsed above now applies to this case. The difference principle, on its maximizing interpretation, supports the judgment that justice requires the society to enact P^2. (Over every 20 year period the society should pursue pro-growth policies.) But the claim that the difference principle does not require economic growth across time, as well as the claim that the maximin decision rule does not apply once a suitably high social minimum has been attained, tell against this judgment. These claims support the conclusion that Rawlsian justice permits the society in Table 4 to enact P^1—the more egalitarian, but Pareto-inefficient policy. This, in turn, makes sense on the reciprocity-centered, but not on the maximizing, interpretation of the difference principle.

So the puzzle manifests itself both with respect to choices between regime-types and to policy choices that can be made within regime-types. Indeed, since the cases illustrated in Tables 2 and 4 exhibit a similar structure, they mutually illuminate each other. For if one holds that Rawlsian justice permits the choice of P^1 in Table 4, then, other things being equal, one should be inclined to allow that Rawlsian justice permits the choice of R^1 in Table 2. By contrast, if one holds that Rawlsian justice requires the maximizing option in Table 2, then, other things being equal, one should be inclined to hold that Rawlsian justice requires selecting P^2 in Table 4. I now offer a diagnosis of the puzzle. Rawls was committed (simultaneously) to two rival understandings of the difference principle and these rival understandings pull in different directions in the cases that we have been considering.

[36] Rawls, *Justice as Fairness: A Restatement*, 64.

III. Responses to the Puzzle

If I am right in my diagnosis of the puzzle, then to make good sense of Rawlsian justice, we will need to engage in some reconstructive surgery. Specifically, we will need to choose between the maximizing and the reciprocity-centered interpretation of the difference principle; and we will need, as a consequence, to discount some Rawlsian claims and play up others. However, before turning to this constructive task, I want to consider some promising, but ultimately unsuccessful, attempts to resolve the puzzle. While not conclusive, the failure of these attempts will strengthen the overall case for thinking that the puzzle is genuine and deep—one that merits the reconstructive efforts that will ensue.

A. Cohen's critique

The first attempt at resolution that I shall consider is suggested by G. A. Cohen's penetrating critique of Rawls. The proposed resolution that I have in mind is not one advanced by Cohen himself, since he did not consider the puzzle I have been expounding. Still, more than any other recent commentator, Cohen exposed tensions in Rawlsian justice. And his critical analysis may point the way toward a solution to our puzzle. Specifically, Cohen maintains that Rawlsian justice, under proper interrogation, is revealed to be not committed to the difference principle, but rather to a more egalitarian principle of distributive justice. If this conclusion were correct, then we would have an explanation of sorts for the puzzle I have been discussing. The explanation is that Rawls failed to identify his most fundamental normative commitments and that the inconsistency expressed by the puzzle is merely a consequence of this failure.

In pressing his case, Cohen seizes on Rawls's statement that the difference principle "relies on the idea that in a competitive economy (with or without private ownership) with an open class system excessive inequalities will not be the rule." Cohen then infers from this statement that Rawls must be committed to "an unarticulated background principle of equality;" for otherwise, Cohen asks, how could Rawls condemn the envisioned inequalities as excessive? In short, as Cohen sees it, "in a more perspicuous presentation of what Rawls really thinks" the injunction to advance the position of the worse-off must be balanced against the injunction to promote equality. The resulting standard of justice is perforce more egalitarian than Rawls's official statement of the difference principle. Put in terms of the distinction I have introduced, a person—who was sympathetic to Cohen's reading of Rawls—could claim that the maximizing interpretation of the difference principle expresses the first of these injunctions whereas the

TABLE 5.

Row (1):	O	N
Row (2):	1/N	1

reciprocity-centered interpretation expresses the second. The difference principle, in turn, represents a balancing of the two demands. The puzzle I have been highlighting, then, is a manifestation of the fact that the difference principle is a compromise between competing injunctions. The statement that Cohen seizes on, however, reveals only one side of what Rawls is trying to say. The statement is part, but only part, of Rawls's response to a general objection that can be pressed against the difference principle. "The objection is," in Rawls's words, "that since we are to maximize (subject to the usual constraints) the long-term prospects of the least advantaged, it seems that the justice of large increases or decreases in the expectations of the more advantaged may depend upon small changes in the prospects of those worst off."[37] Rawls illustrates the objection with the following table of gains and losses, where N refers to a natural number. The maximin rule directs us to always select row (2), since maximizing the minimum requires one to opt for 1/N over 0. But, as Rawls points out, even "if for some smallish number it is reasonable to select the second row, surely there is another point in the sequence when it is irrational not to choose the first row contrary to the [maximin] rule."[38] Notice here that the envisioned irrational choice (if we assume that the columns represent the gains and losses of two different individuals, for example) is not one of excessive inequality, *but rather one that irrationally favors the more egalitarian option.* The objection to the maximin rule, and by extension to the difference principle, is that it makes the justice of very large gains to the better-off turn on very small changes to the position of the worst-off. This objection can come both from the lips of the egalitarian who worries that the difference principle will justify excessive inequality and from the lips of the anti-egalitarian who worries that the difference principle will rule out too much inequality. Put differently, instances of the objection can take the form either of examples that suggest that the difference principle is insufficiently egalitarian or of examples that suggest that it is excessively egalitarian.[39] The statement that Cohen makes much of is an instance of the former, but since there are also instances of

[37] Rawls, *A Theory of Justice*, 157/135–36.
[38] Ibid., 157/136.
[39] The point I am pressing here is confirmed in Rawls's later discussion of the same objection in *Justice as Fairness: A Restatement* (see 66–68). Here Rawls explicitly allows that the difference principle, with respect to some possible counterexamples, can look to be unjust to the more advantaged.

194 STEVEN WALL

the latter, we should not infer, as Cohen invites us to do, that Rawls is really committed to a deeper, unarticulated and more egalitarian principle of justice. For, with equal warrant, we could infer from other instances of the objection that Rawls is really committed to a deeper, unarticulated and less egalitarian principle of justice.[40]

Now, it is true that Cohen also contends that Rawls's arguments to the effect that the generators or sources of inequality are arbitrary from a moral point of view commit Rawls to a standard of justice that is more egalitarian than the difference principle. This is an important line of critique, one that I shall respond to toward the end of this paper. For now, it is important to note that if Cohen were right in his contention, then Rawlsian justice is, as Cohen himself urges, not committed to the difference principle, but rather to the principle of distributive equality. And this result, striking as it may be, does nothing to explain the puzzle that I have been discussing in this paper. Even if one were tempted to follow Cohen (as I am not) in downgrading the difference principle from a principle of justice to a rule of social regulation, one would still not have an explanation for why the principle so understood both seems to require Pareto-efficient transitions and to permit Pareto-inefficient transitions. This line of argument, in short, merely relocates the puzzle. The puzzle is no longer a puzzle about Rawlsian justice, but rather a puzzle about what sound Rawlsian economic policy requires.

One might propose, as Cohen himself intriguingly contemplates at one point, that Rawlsian justice reflects or gives expression to two separable aspects of justice, one comparative and the other noncomparative. The comparative aspect is egalitarian, whereas the noncomparative aspect is Pareto-maximizing.[41] And one might then add that these two aspects of justice are not rationally comparable under a wide range of circumstances. Reason allows different outcomes when the two aspects pull in opposed directions. Construing the difference principle in these terms would show it to be a permissive or latitudinarian principle. Such a construal would explain why a society would have the option to choose either way in the cases we considered in the previous section. But this is a reading of the difference principle that straightforwardly contradicts its maximizing interpretation. For this reason, one

[40] Rawls's own response to the envisioned counterexamples is to argue that they are mere "abstract possibilities" and, as such, that they do not qualify as genuine counterexamples to the difference principle. (See A Theory of Justice, 157–58/136 and Justice as Fairness: A Restatement, 68–71) For forceful criticism of this response see Cohen, Rescuing Justice and Equality, 263–68. With Cohen, and against Rawls, I think consideration of unrealistic examples can be important in helping one identify the content of one's normative commitments. A full consideration of this issue, however, cannot be pursued here. (I return to this point at the end of this essay.)
[41] See Rescuing Justice and Equality, 315–23, especially 322–23.

who was inclined to press for it would need to engage in the same exercise of rational reconstruction that I shall be pursuing.

B. Index good trade-offs

Consider next a second effort to resolve the puzzle, one that invites us to revisit one of the distractions that I noted at the beginning of the paper. The index of goods to which the difference principle applies may include more than income and wealth. It may include leisure time, the power and prerogatives of office, and other determinants of the social bases of self-respect. Rawls is not at all clear on how these different goods are to be weighed against each other in determining how well off citizens are for the purposes of distributive justice; but if trade-offs between goods are brought into the picture, then the cases I have reviewed may mislead.

Let me use the good of leisure time to illustrate the point. Suppose the pro-growth policies envisioned in Table 4 come at the expense of leisure time. They require an extension of the working day, for example. On this supposition, the position of the worst-off group may not be improved by the adoption of these policies, for the loss in leisure time may not offset the gain in income and wealth. The difference principle, on its maximizing interpretation, would then require the society to adopt the no-growth policies. But now suppose, as seems reasonable, that there is no rationally mandated method for combining income/wealth and leisure time into a single precise index of economic goods. Here we could allow that each society is free from the standpoint of justice to balance these different goods in different ways. This allowance would explain Rawls's insistence that justice does not require continual economic growth across time. It permits policies that do not raise the economic position of those at the bottom so long as these policies provide them with a sufficiently large gain in leisure time. This permissive stance on economic growth, moreover, would not be inconsistent with the difference principle on its maximizing interpretation; for the worst-off's index of economic goods, depending on the specification of that index, could be maximized with or without economic growth. A similar story could be told about the choice between regime-types in Table 2.

There is some textual evidence in Rawls's works for this proposed resolution. In response to an objection first pressed by Richard Musgrave, Rawls allowed that it might be necessary to add leisure time to the index of economic goods regulated by the difference principle. Musgrave had pointed out that individuals often substitute leisure time for economic goods. This means that the difference principle, if restricted to regulating the distribution of income and wealth, will arbitrarily favor those with a high preference for leisure.

[The difference principle] is to the advantage of recluses, saints, and (nonconsulting) scholars who earn little and hence will not have to contribute greatly to redistribution.[42]

In a similar fashion, the difference principle so restricted, will arbitrarily favor those members of the worse-off group who choose not to work so that they can enjoy more leisure. They get a full share of economic goods without the burden of work. Rawls replied:

Those who were unwilling to work under conditions where there is much work that needs to be done (I assume that positions and jobs are not scarce or rationed) would have extra leisure stipulated as equal to the index of the least advantaged. So those who surf all day off Malibu must find a way to support themselves and would not be entitled to public funds.[43]

Rawls also called attention to the fact that the general level of wealth in a society depends on the labor decisions of its members.

The general level of wealth in a society, including the well-being of the least advantaged, depends on people's decisions as to how to lead their lives. The priority of liberty means that we cannot be forced to engage in work that is highly productive in terms of material goods. What kind of work people do, and how hard they do it, is up to them to decide in light of the various incentives society offers.[44]

The proposal before us, then, is that a society in a Table 4 case could favor no-growth economic policies over pro-growth economic policies because it valued leisure time over material goods. This would not be inconsistent with maximin policy, so long as leisure time is given its proper due in determining the economic prospects of the worst-off. (For parallel reasons, a society in a Table 2 case could favor a less economically productive regime that was more leisure friendly over a more productive regime that was less leisure friendly.)

The proposal brings out the difficulty of measuring economic productivity. A simple measure is in terms of the aggregate production of material goods, but this simple measure is plainly *too* simple. Suppose two (otherwise similar) societies produce the same level of material goods, but that one does so with one-fourth less labor time than the other. The two

[42] Richard Musgrave, "Maximin, Uncertainty, and Leisure Trade-off," *Quarterly Journal of Economics* 88 (1974): 625–32, at 632.
[43] Rawls, *Political Liberalism*, 182 n. 9.
[44] Rawls, *Justice as Fairness: A Restatement*, 64.

societies are not equally economically productive. The point expressed by this example, albeit overly simplified, is this: increases in the economic productive power of a society can be used either to increase the aggregate level of material goods or to maintain the level of these goods while cutting back on the time the society spends on working to produce them.[45] Suppose now that the difference principle takes this point into account. It then would require a society, other things being equal, to pursue policies that maximize its economic productivity. Pro-growth policies, so understood, would be policies that promote economic productivity, rather than simply policies that do best in terms of increasing the aggregate level of material goods.

An appeal to the good of leisure time, in this way, could reconcile what Rawls says about the case illustrated by Table 4 with the maximizing interpretation of the difference principle. However, it remains unclear, to say the least, whether Rawls himself would have accepted this proposal. Doing so would imply that Rawlsian justice, other things being equal, does require a society to maximize economic productivity across time. And this requirement does not sit well with a Millian steady-state economy in which real capital accumulation reduces to zero.[46]

A similar account could be given of the good associated with the powers and prerogatives of office. Here is a suggestion from one commentator on Rawls.

A market economy with worker-owned firms may conceivably outperform conventional capitalism in terms of the powers and prerogatives associated with the worst position while doing worse income-wise for everyone.[47]

For the sake of argument, suppose that this were true. With this supposition in place, we can reconsider a Table 2 case. Does Rawlsian justice permit a society collectively to decide on an income and wealth versus powers and prerogatives trade-off? If so, then a society could opt for a less productive, but more prerogatives friendly, economic regime. R^1 in

---

[45] For a good discussion of this point see G. A. Cohen, *Karl Marx's Theory of History: A Defence* (Oxford: Oxford University Press, 1978), 302–21.

[46] Mill discusses the steady state or stationary condition of economic productivity in his *Principles of Political Economy* (Oxford: Oxford University Press, 1994). The stationary state occurs when real capital accumulation falls to zero and economic growth stops. This could occur because economic growth is no longer possible. As Mill observes, political economists have seen that "the increase in wealth is not boundless: that at the end of what they term the progressive state lies the stationary state, that all progress in wealth is but a postponement of this." (124) But the stationary state also could occur because economic growth is no longer pursued. Mill argues, for example, that there are circumstances in which the quality of human life would be improved if economic growth were not pursued (128–130). When Rawls claims that justice as fairness does not rule out the steady-state economy, he must have this latter understanding in mind.

[47] Van Parijs, "Difference Principles," 212.

Table 2 could then be construed to be a regime that sacrifices wealth for better powers and prerogatives in comparison to R^2. A choice for R^1 would not then contradict the maximizing interpretation of the difference principle. But, we need to ask, is it legitimate for a Rawlsian society to make this kind of collective decision? Should it attempt to prescribe index good trade-offs for all its members? We need an answer to this question if we are to know whether the resolution proposed here can really help us to resolve the puzzle we have been investigating.

C. Perfectionism

This brings us to a third response. Start by noting that in all of the cases that we have considered it was stipulated that the social minimum guaranteed under the different options is suitably high. Perhaps, then, when this condition is not met, the difference principle requires a society to maximize the position of the worst-off class. In this respect, the difference principle is a maximizing principle. However, when the condition is met, the difference principle may cease to be a maximizing principle. Here, or so it may be said, it permits a society to adopt economic arrangements and enact policies that are not designed to maximize the economic prospects of the worst-off class. In this domain, the difference principle rules out inequalities that do not benefit the worst-off class, thereby expressing reciprocity; but it does not mandate continued improvements in the position of the worst-off class.

This understanding of the difference principle appears to resolve the puzzle, but it does so only if we have an adequate account for why the difference principle ceases to be a maximizing principle once the guaranteed social minimum is sufficiently high. We need to know why at this point the least advantaged cannot object (with force) that their position is worse off than anyone's position need be under alternative feasible economic arrangements. Intriguingly, Rawls provides an explanation of just this sort in *A Theory of Justice*. A high level of wealth, he suggests, is not important to leading a good human life.

> What men want is meaningful work in free association with others, these associations regulating their relations to one another within a framework of just basic institutions. To achieve this state of things great wealth is not necessary. In fact, beyond some point it is more likely to be a positive hindrance, a meaningless distraction at best if not a temptation to indulgence and emptiness.[48]

If these claims were correct (and if they were known to be correct in the original position), then the parties in the original position presumably

---

[48] Rawls, *A Theory of Justice*, 290/257–58.

would not, in general, strive to maximize the income and wealth of those that they represent. They would do so only up to the point where an adequately high material standard of life was available for all. Beyond that point, the continued pursuit of higher wealth would not help, and might hinder, the pursuit of rational plans of life.[49]

This argumentative maneuver neatly addresses the puzzle, and it may capture what Rawls himself had in mind; but it does so by appealing to a contentious premise; namely, it appeals to the claim that a good human life, or perhaps what men conceive to be a good human life, does not require a great deal of wealth and that the pursuit of further wealth beyond a suitable minimum level is an error—"a meaningless distraction at best."[50] Note that the premise is ambiguous between two readings. It expresses either a psychological generalization or a perfectionist claim. If it expresses a psychological generalization, then it certainly looks to be false. Different people with different conceptions of the good, in all likelihood, value additional increments of wealth differently.[51] But if it is understood to express a perfectionist claim, then, while it might be true, it is not a premise that Rawlsians, or so I now claim, are entitled to invoke. For it is a central feature of Rawls's account of justice that there should be no political evaluations of conceptions of the good life.[52] As long as citizens comply with the requirements of justice, they should be free to pursue plans of life of their own choosing, however meaningless these plans may appear to others. And, in formulating principles of justice, we—as citizens—must not presume that some conceptions of the good life are more meaningful or valuable than others.

It might be objected that proponents of Rawlsian justice do not need to appeal to a perfectionist reading of the premise to make the point that

---

[49] These claims also provide an explanation of sorts for why the parties in the original position, as stipulated by Rawls, do not care much about gains above the minimum that is secured by the difference principle.

[50] But can the argumentative maneuver account for the permissive character of the difference principle in Table 2 and 4 cases? If additional wealth is indeed a distraction, then would not the parties in the original position be *required* to select the less productive option, at least in some variants of the cases? Call the point at which additional wealth becomes a burden rather than a benefit the satiation point. We can imagine that societies have some leeway, from the standpoint of justice, in determining where this point lies. The permissive character of the difference principle reflects the fact that the satiation point is not sharp, but (within a certain range) vague or indeterminate.

[51] Perhaps at some extraordinarily high level of wealth everyone would cease to value more of it. But, if so, then, once this level was reached, people would not make conflicting claims on additional wealth. Here the circumstances of justice would not apply. For further criticism of Rawls on this point see Brian Barry, *The Liberal Theory of Justice* (Oxford: Oxford University Press, 1972), 97–99.

[52] Compare the present claim with R. Arneson's critical remarks on Rawls's subordination of the difference principle to the principle of fair equality of opportunity ("Within Rawls' theory, which eschews any social evaluation of people's conceptions of the good, there does not seem to be a basis for affirming that the goods of job satisfaction and meaningful work trump the goods that money and other resources distributed by the Difference Principle can obtain.") "Against Rawlsian Equality of Opportunity," *Philosophical Studies*, 98.

they wish to make here. They can say—consistent with the justificatory strictures imposed by anti-perfectionism—that great wealth is not necessary for the adequate development and the full and informed exercise of the two moral powers of free and equal persons. These two moral powers ground two higher-order interests, one associated with the capacity to form, pursue and revise a conception of the good, the other associated with the capacity to understand and act from a sense of justice. Compactly expressed, the present objection holds that (i) the two moral powers and the higher-order interests associated with them are not perfectionist, but rather key components of the political conception of the person; (ii) that the social and economic conditions necessary for the adequate development and exercise of the two moral powers does not require great wealth; and (iii) the content of justice as fairness is to be identified by reference to the social and economic conditions that are necessary for the full and adequate development of these moral powers and the adequate satisfaction of the associated higher-order interests.

The objection is interesting; but, whatever the truth of (i) and (ii) may be, it cannot rescue the contemplated resolution to the puzzle from the critique pressed above. It cannot do so since (iii) cannot be correct. As Rawls stressed, citizens not only have an interest in the full development and exercise of the two moral powers, but also they have a third higher-order interest in the successful pursuit of a determinate conception of the good. This is "a conception specified by certain definite final ends, attachments, and loyalties to particular persons and institutions, and interpreted in the light of some comprehensive religious, philosophical, or moral doctrine."[53] Primary social goods, such as income and wealth, are not valuable merely because they are related to the development of the two moral powers, but also because they are all-purpose means for the pursuit and advancement of determinate conceptions of the good. That is why the parties in the original position seek to secure the highest index of primary social goods for those they represent rather than some basic minimum necessary for the full and adequate development and exercise of the two moral powers. Thus, to explain why the difference principle ceases to be a maximizing principle once an adequately high minimum has been secured for all, we must do more than point to the fact that great wealth is not necessary to satisfy the higher-order interests of citizens that are associated with the two moral powers. We must hold, in addition, that great wealth is not necessary for the successful pursuit of a rewarding or worthwhile determinate conception of the good. But this claim just is the perfectionist premise that runs afoul of the justificatory strictures imposed by Rawlsian justice.

So much the worse for Rawlsian anti-perfectionism, one might respond. If one rejects the strong resistance to perfectionism, then one can help

---

[53] Rawls, *Political Liberalism*, 74.

oneself to this resolution of the puzzle. Since I myself shall be recommending rational reconstruction in response to the puzzle, I would not
want to rule this gambit out of court. But there is good reason to think
that this is not an especially promising route to take; for the perfectionist
claim in question is not very plausible as a perfectionist claim. At least, it
is not very plausible if one assumes the truth of modest value pluralism—
roughly, the claim that there is a wide range of different ways of leading
a good human life. For, if modest value pluralism is correct, then it is
reasonable to think that different people will not unreasonably value
additional increments of wealth differently. The gambit in question thus
conflicts not only with anti-perfectionism, but also with a modest form of
value pluralism.

This same point explains why a Rawlsian society should not prescribe
a leisure/wealth trade-off or a prerogatives/wealth trade-off for its members. It should not opt for less productive, but leisure-friendly, regimes on
the grounds that additional leisure is more valuable than additional wealth.
Likewise, it should not opt for less productive, but prerogatives-enhancing
regimes, on the grounds that exercising the prerogatives of office is more
valuable than the goods that come with additional wealth. Instead, it
should leave its members free to make these trade-offs in ways that fit
their own conception of the good.[54] Thus, the very reasons that support
a rejection of the perfectionist response to the puzzle also explain why the
index good trade-off response (considered in the previous subsection)
will not work. With no promising resolution in sight, our puzzle persists.
Rawlsian justice both requires Pareto-efficient improvements that redound
to the economic benefit of the worst-off and permits economic arrangements and policies that fail to maximize the material prospects of the
worst-off.

IV. RECIPROCITY AND THE LEVELING DOWN OBJECTION

If the foregoing discussion is on the right track, then there is a serious
tension in Rawlsian justice. The tension is expressed by the puzzle and
the puzzle is illustrated by the examples I have presented. I now want to
suggest that the tension has its source in a more fundamental divide in
egalitarian political thought. This is the divide, very nicely introduced by

---

[54] A Rawlsian society should favor an index of goods that is more rather than less
fungible. (This may explain why Rawls put the emphasis on income and wealth when
discussing the difference principle.) In other words, a Rawlsian society should allow its
members to make their own trade-offs between leisure, wealth and the goods that come
with the prerogatives of office. To facilitate this, we might imagine a Rawlsian society that
regulates the conditions of work so that workers have sufficient options to make these
trade-offs. Such regulations might be inconsistent with a maximally economically productive regime, but they would capture the spirit of the point pressed here. In any event, it
should be plain that, for Rawlsians, index good trade-offs should not be collectively prescribed for all by appealing to perfectionist considerations about "what men really want."

Derek Parfit, between prioritarianism and egalitarianism.[55] Does egalitarian concern mandate that we give priority to the worse-off, or does it require that we value equal distributions intrinsically?

My view is that the difference principle should be understood to be a prioritarian principle. As such, it is a maximizing principle; and it will mandate Pareto-efficient transitions. But I also think—and my examples have illustrated—that Rawls often makes claims about the difference principle that only make sense if we view the principle as expressing reciprocity. And reciprocity is an egalitarian value.

A rational reconstruction of Rawlsian justice, then, must decide which competing elements to emphasize and which to downplay. As the title of this paper indicates, my view is that we should downplay the egalitarian elements. We need to rescue Rawlsian justice *from* equality.

But why should we go down this path? Why not aim instead to rescue Rawlsian justice from its maximizing feature? To answer this question, we will need to address a number of considerations that bear on the relationship between reciprocity and justice. I shall begin by calling attention to a common worry about egalitarian justice; namely that it is rooted in, and gives expression to, the vice of envy. Rawls himself was keenly aware of this worry. Many conceptions of equality, he acknowledged, may spring from this tendency; but the equality recommended by justice as fairness, he insisted, does not. For to show that a conception of equality is rooted in envy one must show that it is "unjust and bound in the end to make everyone including the less advantaged worse off."[56] Let us call this the envy-test. The maximizing feature of the difference principle guarantees that it will pass the envy-test. It is the feature that ensures that the difference principle will not countenance any transition that makes all parties worse off for the sake of greater equality. The same cannot be said of the difference principle on its reciprocity-centered interpretation. For, as we have seen, on this interpretation the difference principle permits, even if it does not mandate, transitions that worsen the prospects of both the best-off and worst-off groups. By so doing, it becomes vulnerable to a version of the leveling down objection.

Strict egalitarians, of course, hold that justice requires leveling down. Such a view, Rawls claims, would be favored in the original position only if the parties were sufficiently envious.[57] But the value of reciprocity can require leveling down as well; for if the staggered difference principle flouts strong reciprocity (as Nozick and Cohen insist), then strong reciprocity favors leveling down in circumstances in which close-knitness does not obtain. For this reason, the staggered difference principle would be rejected in the original position only if the parties were sufficiently

[55] Parfit, "Equality or Priority?"
[56] Rawls, *A Theory of Justice*, 538/471.
[57] Ibid., 538–39/472.

envious. Likewise, while weak reciprocity does not require leveling down, it permits it in a range of circumstances, such as those illustrated in Tables 2 and 4. Only by appealing to the maximizing feature of the difference principle can the leveling down objection be avoided and with it the suspicion that the difference principle expresses the vice of envy.

Now it is true that, in response to the leveling down objection, some writers do not blink. They say that justice requires leveling down because justice requires strict equality, but they then go on to say that other moral considerations can trump the claims of justice. Once one accepts value pluralism, they argue, one need not fear the leveling down objection.[58] This is a fair point. But it is not a point that is available to Rawlsians. Rawlsians hold that justice is the first virtue of social institutions, not merely one virtue among many. The defender of the reciprocity-centered interpretation of the difference principle, if he invoked this line of response to the leveling down worry, would need to reject the idea that the difference principle is a principle of justice. That is a high price to pay; and it is one that should be paid only if there is no other way to make good sense of Rawlsian justice.[59]

A different response to the leveling down objection may seem to be close at hand. There is a sense in which Rawlsian justice requires leveling down. Leveling down is justified when doing so is necessary to avoid social conditions that predictably will generate excusable envy.

A person's lesser position as measured by the index of objective primary goods may be so great as to wound his self-respect; and given his situation, we may sympathize with his sense of loss . . . For those suffering this hurt, envious feelings are not irrational; the satisfaction of their rancor would make them better off.[60]

As the last sentence of this passage makes plain, the leveling down contemplated here is not genuine leveling down. The reduction of inequality in income and wealth *benefits* the worse-off by increasing their self-respect. The response to the leveling down objection, at least when it is directed at the reciprocity-centered difference principle, is that it misdescribes the situation. Leveling down is objectionable only when all factors have been taken into account.

---

[58] See, for example, L. Temkin, "Equality, Priority, and the Leveling Down Objection," in M. Clayton and A. Williams, eds., *The Ideal of Equality*, 126–61.

[59] Cohen can be understood to be arguing that this price must be paid. Only by downgrading the difference principle from a principle of justice to a rule of regulation can we make good sense of Rawls's moral commitments. The present reconstruction of Rawlsian justice seeks to vindicate the difference principle's claim to be a principle of justice.

[60] Rawls, *A Theory of Justice*, 534/468. Assume here that the person's lesser position in this passage refers to the position of the worst-off under the difference principle on its maximizing interpretation.

As I noted at the beginning of this paper, the difference principle reg-ulates the distribution of income and wealth. But it must do so in a way that is sensitive to the good of self-respect, since this is, as Rawls main-tains, a central social primary good. One is tempted to reply, then, that the good of self-respect already has been taken into account in the examples we have discussed (Tables 2 and 4). These examples included all relevant information; and so the response to the leveling down objection that we are now considering is no response at all. But this reply, tempting as it may be, is too quick. It is too quick since the value of reciprocity may be the very consideration that explains the importance that Rawls attributes to the good of self-respect.

I have been construing reciprocity as if it were a distributive norm, or at least a consideration that informs a distributive norm, but reciprocity also can be viewed as a general ideal of human relationships. On this view, its value lies in the kind of political and social relationships it makes possible. Rather than being committed to either some form of prioritarian or some form of egalitarian distributive justice, Rawlsian justice can be viewed as an ideal of reciprocity in this ideal human-relations sense. Here is how one commentator on Rawls expresses the thought.

> For Rawls, people are conceived of as free and equal citizens, and the aim is to determine which principles of distributive justice are most appropriate for a modern democratic society whose members are so understood. . . . Equality is understood as a social and political ideal that governs the relations in which people stand to one another. The core of the value of equality does not, according to this understand-ing, consist in the idea that there is something that must be distrib-uted or allocated equally, and so the interpretation of the value does not consist primarily in seeking to ascertain what that *something* is. Instead, the core of the value is a normative conception of human relations, and the relevant question, when interpreting the value, is what social, political, and economic arrangements are compatible with that conception.[61]

With this understanding of Rawlsian justice in mind, imagine now a situation in which the difference principle justifies economic inequality that is inconsistent with the specified ideal of human relations. This inequal-ity could then be judged to be "excessive" and it could be viewed as unjust at the bar of Rawlsian justice. Nor would taking this line leave Rawlsian justice vulnerable to the leveling down objection; for, or so it might be argued, damage to the ideal of human relations that Rawlsian justice makes possible, sets back the interests of all citizens.

---

[61] S. Scheffler, "What is Egalitarianism," *Philosophy and Public Affairs* 31 (2003): 5–39, at 31. (italics in original)

Now, for present purposes, it is not necessary to examine this interpretation of Rawlsian justice in detail. The ideal of human relations envisioned does not specify economic distributions. It merely rules out
distributions that are inconsistent with its realization. There is no reason
to suppose, however, that the cases we have been considering in this
essay fall under its purview. The inequalities depicted in Tables 1–4 need
not be such that they run afoul of the ideal of human relations specified
by Rawlsian justice. So the appeal to reciprocity (in the ideal human-
relations sense) does not help us think about our puzzle. Moreover, it also
does not explain either of the rival interpretations of the difference principle that we have been considering. It does not explain the reciprocity-
centered interpretation of the difference principle; for, as we have seen,
this view of the difference principle includes a commitment to equality as
a distributive norm; and this understanding of reciprocity is precisely
what is rejected by the view we are now considering.[62] And it does not
explain the maximizing interpretation of the difference principle, since it
is very hard to see why an ideal of human relations would require maximization of income and wealth.

The problem here no doubt lies, in part, in the vagueness of the
ideal of human relations being considered. Even if one holds that reciprocity (in the ideal human-relations sense) gives us "compelling reasons to avoid excessive variations in people's share of income and
wealth,"[63] one still needs an account of what does and does not count
as "excessive variations," and it is natural to view the difference principle as providing us with that account. But if we say this, then we
must acknowledge that the difference principle informs the ideal of
reciprocity rather than being derived from it. And we will then need to
ask all the questions about the difference principle that I have been
raising in this essay.

V. Further Issues

Proponents of the view that Rawlsian justice expresses reciprocity (in
the ideal human-relations sense) often contrast their view with the so-called
luck egalitarian[64] reading of Rawlsian justice.[65] They do so for good
reason. To the extent that Rawlsian justice expresses luck egalitarian intuitions, the idea that Rawlsian justice is fundamentally a matter of securing

[62] Cohen presses this point against Scheffler's reading of Rawls. See *Rescuing Justice and Equality*, 166–68.
[63] S. Scheffler, "What is Egalitarianism?" 23.
[64] There are different versions of luck egalitiarianism. The core idea behind the view is
that "inequalities in the advantages that people enjoy are acceptable if they derive from the
choices that people have voluntarily made, but that inequalities deriving from unchosen
features of people's circumstances are unjust." Ibid., 5.
[65] See Scheffler, "What is Egalitarianism?" and Elizabeth Anderson, "What is the Point of
Equality?" *Ethics* 109 (1999): 287–337.

an ideal of human relations will look less compelling. Having just cast some doubt on this reading of Rawlsian justice myself, I now want to consider briefly the case for viewing Rawlsian justice in terms of luck egalitarian moral commitments. Doing so is important for my argumentative purposes, since luck egalitarianism clearly speaks against the maximizing interpretation of the difference principle.

There is some textual support for luck egalitarianism in Rawls's presentation of his theory. Rawls distinguishes a democratic from a liberal conception of the two principles of justice. The liberal conception combines fair equality of opportunity with a commitment to the principle of efficiency, whereas the democratic conception combines fair equality of opportunity with a commitment to the difference principle.[66] Discussing the superiority of the democratic over the liberal conception, Rawls writes:

> While the liberal conception seems clearly preferable to the system of natural liberty, intuitively it still appears defective. For one thing, even if it works to perfection in eliminating the influence of social contingencies, it still permits the distribution of wealth and income to be determined by the natural distribution of abilities and talents.[67]

Cohen cites this very passage. He then comments: "This implies that the income distribution should *not* be determined by the talent distribution. . . ."[68] Cohen is right, as far as it goes. The question is how seriously we should take these remarks from Rawls.

Luck egalitarian commitments favor the democratic over the liberal interpretation of the two principles of justice, but they also favor the principle of redress over the difference principle. The principle of redress holds that "undeserved inequalities call for redress; and since inequalities of birth and natural endowment are undeserved, these inequalities are to be somehow compensated for." Consider now the following construction, which parallels the remarks quoted above.

> While the difference principle seems clearly preferable to the system of natural liberty, intuitively it still appears defective. For one thing, even if it works to perfection in eliminating the influence of social contingencies, it still permits the distribution of wealth and income to be determined by the natural distribution of abilities and talents.

---

[66] The contrast between these rival interpretations of the two principles of justice is discussed more fully in *A Theory of Justice*, 65–75/57–65.

[67] Ibid., 73–74/63–64.

[68] G. A. Cohen, *Rescuing Justice and Equality*, 166. (italics added) See also Nozick's discussion in *Anarchy, State and Utopia*, 216–19, esp. 219.

These claims naturally come off the lips of the luck egalitarian, for the difference principle permits, and indeed it may require, the talented to benefit from their talents, even though they cannot claim to deserve their talents. This will look objectionable if one is committed to luck egalitarianism.

Since Rawls affirms the difference principle and rejects the principle of redress, it may seem clear as day that he is not a proponent of luck egalitarianism. But matters are not this straightforward. Rawls goes on to say that the principle of redress may "represent one of the elements in our conception of justice,"[69] to be weighted against others. This claim can provide support for the reciprocity-centered interpretation of the difference principle, and it can help make sense of some of the anti-maximizing claims about the difference principle reviewed in our discussion of the cases in Section II. We do well then to consider whether the principle of redress is indeed an element of a sound understanding of Rawlsian justice.

I believe that it is not. The principle of redress is well supported by luck egalitarian intuitions, but I believe that luck egalitarianism is a false view. This is not something that I shall try to demonstrate here.[70] Instead, I will argue that the primary Rawlsian appeal to the moral arbitrariness of the distribution, natural or otherwise, of talents and abilities does not support the principle of redress. Since Rawls's claim that the distribution of talents and abilities is morally arbitrary is the key claim that has led many to view him as a luck egalitarian, its failure to support the principle of redress will remove the grounds for viewing Rawlsian justice as giving voice, even partial voice, to luck egalitarian commitments.

The claim that the distribution of talent is morally arbitrary, on its face, does nothing to justify equality. As a number of commentators have pointed out, the claim (if true) just defeats a reason for objecting to an economic distribution favored by the difference prinicple.[71] It shows that one cannot object to a difference principle distribution on the grounds that it does not give the talented what they deserve as a result of their talents. But it can be said, in reply, that the claim functions as a key premise in the Rawlsian argument for the difference principle. It does so if one begins by attributing to Rawls a strong presumption in favor of equality. The argument then maintains that inequality is unjust unless there is a compelling reason to depart from equality. A compelling reason, in turn, cannot appeal to a morally arbitrary factor. And, given the strength of the initial presumption in favor of equality, the only reason of sufficient strength that could overturn the presumption is the fact that an inequality would benefit the worst-off group.

---

[69] Rawls, *A Theory of Justice*, 101/86.
[70] Perhaps it is not something that can be demonstrated. Luck egalitarian commitments may be bedrock normative commitments.
[71] See, for example, S. Scheffler, "What is Egalitarianism?" 25–26.

Let us call this "Barry's Argument" for the difference principle, since it was first advanced by Brian Barry.[72] It was later endorsed by Parfit and Cohen. The proponents of the argument concede that it does not fit with much of what Rawls claims. The official Rawlsian argument for the difference principle from the original position not only does not mention a strong presumption in favor of equality, but it is inconsistent with it. As Rawls himself explained,

> It has been taken for granted that if the [difference] principle is satisfied, everyone is benefited. One obvious sense in which this is so is that each man's position is improved with respect to the initial agreement of equality. But it is clear that nothing depends upon being able to identify this initial arrangement; how well off men are in this situation plays no essential role in applying the difference principle.[73]

The official argument for the difference principle supports the staggered version of the principle and the staggered difference principle is inconsistent with the strong presumption in favor of equality assumed by the argument. Be this as it may, Barry's Argument is consistent with the simple difference principle.[74] This principle disallows all inequalities except those that redound to the benefit of the worst-off group. By so doing, it permits, and indeed requires, leveling down policies. Thus, to the extent that there is textual evidence for Barry's Argument, it provides support for the reciprocity-centered interpretation of the difference principle.

I have been arguing that there is indeed textual support for both the reciprocity-centered and the maximizing interpretations of the difference principle. That is why a good account of Rawlsian justice must engage in rational reconstruction. For this reason, we need to consider Barry's Argument on its merits. Rawlsian exegesis aside, is the argument any good? I think not. As we have seen, the argument simply assumes the strong presumption in favor of equality. If it is directed against those who are not already convinced egalitarians, then it is a toothless argument. However, it does not fare much better when it is directed against those who are already convinced egalitarians. For, as Barry himself worried, if the initial

---

[72] This is B. Barry's interpretation of (what he takes to be) the best Rawlsian argument for the difference principle. See B. Barry, *Theories of Justice* (Berkeley: University of California Press, 1989), 226–34. It is taken over by Cohen in *Rescuing Justice and Equality*, 166–68.

[73] Rawls, *A Theory of Justice*, 80/69.

[74] Rawls's diagrams illustrating the difference principle may encourage the thought that the difference principle is premised on a strong presumption in favor of equality. For the diagrams depict an original point in which all social primary goods are equally distributed. See, for example, *Justice as Fairness: A Restatement*, 62. But the diagrams illustrate the simple difference principle. They do not depict the staggered version of the principle, which, as both Nozick and Cohen correctly pointed out, is inconsistent with a strong presumption in favor of equality.

moral case for equality is very strong, then difference principle departures from it start to look like compromises with justice rather than realizations of it. Barry's worry is powerfully exploited by Cohen in his critique of the difference principle, and Barry's own response to the worry is not convincing.[75]

Seen with clear vision, Barry's Argument should appeal to neither egalitarians nor anti-egalitarians. But it might be thought that it captures an insight that I have so far overlooked. I have been writing as if Barry's Argument simply assumes a strong case for equality and then appeals to claims about morally arbitrary factors to block proposed departures from equality. Against this, it might be said that the need to insulate distributions from morally arbitrary factors is what grounds the presumption in favor of equality in the first place. This response makes Barry's Argument look more interesting, but it rests on a mistake. There is no reason to think that equal distributions are morally nonarbitrary. From the fact that an unequal distribution would be influenced by morally arbitrary factors one cannot infer that an equal distribution would not be. That fallacious inference stands behind the effort to make Barry's Argument look better than it is. In reality, the appeal to moral arbitrariness establishes neither a presumption in favor of equality nor against it. The presumption in favor of equality must be grounded in some other way.[76]

To be sure, proponents of equality may want to reject the suggestion that the presumption in favor of equality needs deeper justification. They can say that equality should be viewed as a bedrock normative commitment. If it is viewed in these terms, then it will be difficult to show that it is mistaken. But egalitarian commitment opens the door to leveling down policies; and, as I have been arguing, a signal attraction of the difference principle is that, at least on its maximizing interpretation, it saves Rawlsian justice from that objection.[77]

---

[75] See Barry, *Theories of Justice*, 393–400. For the reasons why this response is inept see Cohen, *Rescuing Justice and Equality*, 113–114.

[76] The points in this paragraph owe much to the discussion in S. Hurley, *Justice, Luck and Knowledge* (Cambridge, MA: Harvard University Press, 2003), 146–80. See also Richard Arneson, "Justice is Not Equality," *Ratio* 21 no. 4 (2008): 385–91.

[77] Two points about the leveling down objection can be registered here. First, it is true that one can acknowledge that Rawlsian justice requires leveling down, but insist that sensible all things considered policy does not. Such a response has the upshot that the difference principle does not express justice, but compromises it. This is Cohen's considered view. Second, the leveling down objection can be challenged by attacking an assumption behind it; namely, that a distribution cannot be worse than another distribution if it is not worse for anyone. This assumption looks suspect when we consider cases of moral desert. If in one distribution the sinners fare better than the saints, then is not a distribution in which the sinners fare a little less well and the saints remain the same a little better? This challenge is pressed by Temkin. My sense is that if the challenge succeeds, then it shows that moral desert, not equality, has intrinsic moral value. This is not the place to consider these issues fully, however. Suffice it to say that, in my view, a successful interpretation of the difference principle will show it be a principle of justice, and not merely good policy in this or that circumstance, and a principle that is desert-insensitive. It may be true that desert is more

VI. BEYOND THE DIFFERENCE PRINCIPLE

Rawls's writings contain a battery of arguments for the difference principle. Some of these arguments support the maximizing interpretation of the principle, others support the reciprocity-centered interpretation. Taken together, the lines of argument that support the two rival interpretations of the difference principle generate the puzzle introduced in Section II. To overcome the puzzle, Rawlsian justice must be reconstructed. I have argued that the best reconstruction downplays the egalitarian elements that support the reciprocity-centered interpretation of the difference principle. The difference principle is best viewed as a maximizing prioritarian principle of distributive justice. As such, it avoids the leveling down objection, but it remains an egalitarian principle in one sense—the priority it assigns to the worst-off group is absolute. The issue we must now confront is whether this residual egalitarianism is defensible.

The difference principle is an extreme member of the family of prioritarian principles. And, on inspection, it looks to be too extreme. Recall Table 5, the table of gains and losses Rawls provided. As I pointed out in Section III(a), Rawls allows that even "if for some smallish number it is reasonable to select the second row, surely there is another point in the sequence when it is irrational not to choose the first row contrary to the [maximin] rule."[78] This is Rawls's own concession that the absolute priority that the difference principle assigns to the worst-off group is too extreme.

Rawls does not step back from his endorsement of the difference principle, however. This requires explanation. Parfit asks, "if we are not concerned with relative levels, why should the smallest benefit to the representative worst-off person count for infinitely more than much greater benefits to other representative people?"[79] He answers that the absolute priority assigned to benefiting the worst-off only makes sense if we bring the value of equality back into the picture. On this reading, Rawls's difference principle reflects both prioritarian and egalitarian commitment. However, on the understanding of the difference principle that I am proposing, egalitarian reciprocity has been purged from its content.

Does this mean that the difference principle, on the rational reconstruction of it defended here, must be abandoned in favor of a less extreme, and perhaps much less determinate, prioritarian principle of justice? My own view is "yes." The maximizing interpretation of the difference principle ultimately pulls us beyond the difference principle. But following Rawls's own lead, another response is available. The difference principle

---

relevant to justice than Rawlsian justice allows, but there are limits to rational reconstruction. Desert-sensitivity is too alien to the spirit of Rawlsian justice to be included within it.
[78] Rawls, A Theory of Justice, 157/136.
[79] Parfit, "Equality or Priority?" 121.

does not apply in situations in which we confront a choice between benefiting the worst-off group by a very small amount or benefiting better-off groups by a very large amount. The difference principle is not meant to apply to such abstract possibilities. In the situations in which it is meant to apply, the absolute priority assigned to the worst-off group is not intuitively unreasonable, even on the maximizing interpretation of the principle.

Building on this response, it can be said that the difference principle is a domain-specific principle that instantiates a more general prioritarian principle of justice—one that, outside of that domain, may permit (or require) economic distributions in which the better-off gain at the expense of the worse-off.[80] That more general prioritarian principle of justice is free of all egalitarian commitment. On the present rational reconstruction of Rawlsian justice, it represents the truth about justice that the difference principle expresses in the limited domain in which it applies.

With Cohen, some will protest that the difference principle, so construed, is not really a principle of justice. They will say that to identify the content of justice we must be prepared to consider the full array of abstract, counterfactual, possibilities. And, when we do so, we will see that the difference principle is excessively egalitarian. But this Cohen-inspired objection is not one we need to assess here.[81] If Rawls is right that in thinking about distributive justice we must hold certain facts fixed, then the difference principle escapes the objection. If Rawls is wrong about this, then the difference principle may not be a fundamental principle of justice, but it may still be a principle that realizes justice in the domain in which it was intended to apply.

VII. CONCLUSION

Cohen was right. Justice, or Rawlsian justice at least, needs to be rescued. But he was wrong to think that the rescue effort must pull Rawlsians toward strict equality. The puzzle expounded in this essay exposes a fault line in Rawlsian justice. The difference principle both requires Pareto-efficient improvements that redound to the economic benefit of the worst-off and permits economic arrangements and policies that fail to maximize the material prospects of the worst-off. Appreciating the puzzle thus forces a choice between two rival conceptions of the difference principle, one that sacrifices efficiency for egalitarian reciprocity and one that stays faithful to the maximin demand commonly associated with the principle.

---

[80] Such a view also coheres well with Rawls's discussion of the relationship between the difference principle and the just savings principle. See my "Just Savings and the Difference Principle," *Philosophical Studies* 116 (2003): 79–102.

[81] In calling this a Cohen-inspired objection, I mean to say that its form is inspired by Cohen's critique of Rawls. Its substance is plainly alien to Cohen's strongly egalitarian sympathies.

In response to the puzzle, Rawlsians can embrace strong equality or maximizing prioritarianism. I have made the case for the latter option. The difference principle is best viewed as a maximizing principle, one that assigns strong priority to the worst-off group. The maximizing injunction behind the difference principle, however, does not sit well with a number of Rawls's egalitarian commitments and claims. Purifying Rawlsian justice of these egalitarian commitments puts it in a better light by allowing it to retain its integrity as an account of justice (and not a mere compromise with justice) and by safeguarding it from the leveling down objection.

Philosophy, University of Arizona

REINTERPRETING RAWLS'S *THE LAW OF PEOPLES**

By Christopher Heath Wellman

No political theorist of the twentieth century has been more celebrated than John Rawls, and none has been more frequently misinterpreted. *A Theory of Justice (TJ)* was routinely misunderstood because readers were unprepared for the breathtakingly original types of arguments therein.[1] *Political Liberalism (PL)* was systematically misjudged because many of us did not understand that it was concerned principally with legitimacy rather than justice.[2] In this essay, I suggest that many commentators may have also misinterpreted John Rawls's project in *The Law of Peoples (LP)*.[3] In particular, I raise the possibility that many of the standard criticisms of this work miss their mark by presuming that Rawls sought to offer a comprehensive theory of global justice, when he meant more minimally to respond to a specific, practical problem: "How can we eliminate the great evils of human history?"

I divide this essay into three sections. First, I offer a very brief summary of *The Law of Peoples*. In the second section, I survey a number of criticisms that have been raised against Rawls's arguments and the conclusions he draws from them. Finally, I suggest an alternative interpretation of *LP*, one that both squares with Rawls's own description of his project and enables the rebuttal of the standard objections to this work.

I. The Law of Peoples

In *LP*, Rawls argues on behalf of the following eight principles:

1. Peoples are free and independent, and their freedom and independence are to be respected by other peoples.

* I am grateful to Andrew Altman, Thomas Pogge, Carl Wellman and especially Leif Wenar for generously commenting on an earlier version of this paper. I am also indebted to the other contributors to this volume, and to Ellen Paul for her many helpful suggestions for revision.
[1] John Rawls, *A Theory of Justice (TJ)* (Cambridge, MA: Harvard University Press, 1971). One of the most common early mistakes was the failure to appreciate that Rawls's analysis was institutional, rather than interactional. In particular, not everyone understood that the difference principle is meant to shape the basic structure of society, not each of our individual interactions therein.
[2] John Rawls, *Political Liberalism (PL)* (rev. ed.; Cambridge, MA: Harvard University Press, 1999). On this interpretation, see David Estlund, "The Survival of Egalitarian Justice in John Rawls' *Political Liberalism*," *The Journal of Political Philosophy* 4, no. 1 (1996): 68–78.
[3] John Rawls, *The Law of Peoples (LP)* (Cambridge, MA: Harvard University Press, 1999).

doi:10.1017/S0265052511000148
© 2012 Social Philosophy & Policy Foundation. Printed in the USA.

2. Peoples are to observe treaties and undertakings.
3. Peoples are equal and are parties to the agreements that bind them.
4. Peoples are to observe a duty of non-intervention.
5. Peoples have a right of self-defense but no right to instigate war for reasons other than self-defense.
6. Peoples are to honor human rights.
7. Peoples are to observe certain specified restrictions in the conduct of war.
8. Peoples have a duty to assist other peoples living under unfavorable conditions that prevent their having a just or decent political and social regime. (*LP*, p. 37)

Rawls's defense of these eight principles is reminiscent of the argument offered on behalf of his two principles of domestic justice in *A Theory of Justice*: he suggests that they would be affirmed by parties in a duly modified version of the original position. The most significant (and controversial) change in the hypothetical contract situation is that the parties choosing the principles to govern international matters represent "peoples" rather than individual persons, where a "people" is a specific type of group with its own state.[4] Rawls writes: "The term 'peoples,' then, is meant to emphasize these singular features of peoples as distinct from states, as traditionally conceived, and to highlight their moral character and the reasonably just, or decent, nature of their regimes." (*LP*, p. 27)

Rawls's distinction here between "just" and "decent" is crucial because he maintains that, while only liberal democratic societies are ideally just, a people need be neither fully liberal nor fully democratic in order to be decent or reasonable. More specifically, Rawls suggests that a nonliberal, nondemocratic hierarchical society might qualify as decent as long as it secures basic human rights, takes all of its citizens' interests into account, and is not aggressive against other peoples. Thus, while Rawls never retracts his preference for liberal democracy, he leaves open the possibility that two types of groups might be considered what he calls "well-ordered societies": liberal democratic and decent hierarchical peoples.[5] This is pivotal because the core of Rawls's argument is that parties representing all well-ordered societies would affirm the eight principles enumerated above. In other words, neither representatives of liberal democratic

---

[4] In my view, the best way to think of Rawls's use of the term "people" is to understand a people as occupying the same relationship to a state as an individual with the two moral powers occupies in relationship to a person in Rawls's work on domestic justice and legitimacy. (An individual possesses the two moral powers if she has "a capacity for a sense of justice and for a conception of the good" [*PL*, p. 19]). I should acknowledge, though, that this reading is in tension with his note 45 on page 38 of *LP*, where Rawls apparently considers blacks in the Antebellum South to be a people, despite the fact that they lacked their own state.

[5] Rawls uses the example of a decent hierarchical society, but presumably there could be decent nonhierarchical societies that nonetheless were illiberal and/or undemocratic.

peoples nor representatives of decent hierarchical peoples would hesitate to commit to the Law of Peoples. Thus, both because the principles are plausible in their own right and because they would emerge from a duly modified version of the original position, we can endorse the Law of Peoples as those principles that should govern international affairs. I will not develop this extremely brief summary any further at this stage because I want to remain neutral on the question of interpretation explored in this essay. Hopefully, this skeletal account is at least substantial enough to help the reader appreciate the objections surveyed below.

II. THE CRITICAL RESPONSE

The Law of Peoples is not without its defenders, but the general reaction to it has been tepid at best. Without attempting to supply an exhaustive recapitulation of the various complaints that have been lodged against *LP*, I will list what I consider to be eight representative concerns about Rawls's arguments and conclusions: (I) Rawls wrongly focuses on "peoples" rather than individual persons; (II) Rawls is either wrong to include representatives of decent hierarchical peoples or wrong to exclude representatives from nondecent, unreasonable groups from the original position; (III) Rawls fails to offer any competing sets of principles among which the parties might choose; (IV) Rawls's list of basic human rights wrongly omits core rights, including those to democracy, freedom of expression, and equality; (V) Rawls justifies human rights in the wrong way; (VI) Rawls's duty of assistance is far too weak and inegalitarian; (VII) Rawls fails to focus on the global basic structure; and (VIII) Rawls's eight principles say nothing about intrastate conflict.[6]

(I) Why should the parties in the original position represent peoples rather than individual persons, and why do Rawls's eight principles concern exclusively the rights and duties of peoples, as opposed to what might be owed by or to individual persons? Given that individual persons are of fundamental moral importance and groups are valuable only insofar as they contribute to the well-being of individuals, it seems wrongheaded for Rawls to concentrate on peoples as groups. A more natural way to extend the original position to international matters, it might be thought, would be to have the parties

---

[6] My list of objections draws heavily upon the following articles: Charles Beitz, "Rawls's Law of Peoples," *Ethics* 110, no. 4 (2000): 669–96; Allen Buchanan, "Rawls's Law of Peoples: Rules for a Vanished Westphalian World," *Ethics* 110, no. 4 (2000): 697–721; Simon Caney, "Cosmopolitanism and the Law of Peoples," *Journal of Political Philosophy* 10, no. 1 (2002): 95–123; Andrew Kuper, "Rawlsian Global Justice: Beyond the Law of Peoples to a Cosmopolitan Law of Persons," *Political Theory* 28, no. 5 (2000): 640–75; Darrel Moellendorf, "Constructing the Law of Peoples," *Pacific Philosophical Quarterly* 77 (1996): 132–54; Thomas Pogge, "An Egalitarian Law of Peoples," *Philosophy and Public Affairs* 23, no. 3 (1994): 195–224; Kok-Chor Tan, "Liberal Toleration in Rawls's Law of Peoples," *Ethics* 108, no. 2 (1998): 276–95; and Fernando R. Tesón, "The Rawlsian Theory of International Law" in his book *A Philosophy of International Law* (Boulder, CO: Westview, 1998).

in the original position continue to represent individual persons, and to stipulate that the (duly modified) veil of ignorance precludes them from knowing various features of the society in which they live.

Indeed, one might suggest that the primacy of the individual is a core, nonnegotiable element of liberal political thought, and thus any approach focusing so steadfastly on the group as a whole would fail to qualify as liberal. Finally, it is especially surprising that Rawls would turn his gaze from the individual as he does in *LP*, because his other work has championed this understanding of liberalism. As he says in *A Theory of Justice*:

> The essential idea is that we want to account for the social values, for the intrinsic good of institutional, community, and associative activities, by a conception of justice that in its theoretical basis is individualistic. For reasons of clarity among others, we do not want to rely on an undefined concept of community, or to suppose that society is an organic whole with a life of its own distinct from and superior to that of all its members in their relations with one another. (*TJ*, p. 264)

It is no surprise, then, that Thomas Pogge objects to Rawls's focus on groups as follows: "The danger here is not merely moral implausibility, but also philosophical incoherence between Rawls's conceptions of domestic and of global justice. According to the latter, a just domestic regime is an end in itself. According to the former, however, it is not an end in itself, but rather something we ought to realize for the sake of individual human persons, who are the ultimate units of moral concern."[7] In short, by having the parties in the choice situation represent peoples rather than persons, it is as if Rawls forgot the very liberal lessons that he taught the rest of us.

(*II*) *If the parties are to represent peoples, then it seems as though they should represent all groups, not just the well-ordered societies.* Rawls suggests that both liberal and nonliberal decent peoples would affirm the eight principles, but he never argues that all societies would commit to these eight principles. Denying nondecent groups any representation in the original position is worrisome, though, given that the principles putatively affirmed there would profoundly affect them. Since Rawls's principles allow for intervention in cases where basic rights are not being respected, for instance, it seems important to justify these principles to outlaw states who would be vulnerable to military invasion. Without giving these groups representation, Rawls could not establish that they would be unreasonable to reject these principles. And, if this could not be established, then Rawls would not have demonstrated that the coercion licensed by his favored principles could not be reasonably rejected by those liable to this coercion.

---

[7] Thomas Pogge, "An Egalitarian Law of Peoples," 210.

Of course, Rawls might respond that outlaw states need not be represented because, insofar as they are unreasonable, their affirmation is irrelevant and they could not possibly reasonably reject the principles. While his response might justify excluding nondecent societies, it raises another awkward question for Rawls: If we may exclude nondecent groups on principled grounds, then why are nonliberal but so-called decent peoples allowed representation in the hypothetical choice situation? Although it is true that not all hierarchical societies are equally tyrannical, it certainly seems as though any society that failed to secure democratic rights, freedom of expression, and equality of all its citizens should not be called reasonable. Again, one can imagine some denying the importance of freedom, equality or democratic governance, but it is hard to imagine a liberal theorist like Rawls doing so. Kok-Chor Tan complains of this tension within Rawls's theory:

> . . . certain views not permitted in domestic liberal society are deemed permissible if expressed in foreign societies. It seems that while Rawls would say that a liberal state should criticize a domestic comprehensive view which forbids its members from exercising their public rights (like the right to vote in public elections), this same state should not criticize a WHS [well ordered society] which denies some of its citizens this same right. This seems blatantly inconsistent to me.[8]

To put it bluntly, if one is in no way being unreasonable in denying these core liberal democratic values, then what was all the fuss about in *A Theory of Justice* and *Political Liberalism?*

(III) *It seems objectionable that Rawls does not give the parties in the original position any choice among competing sets of principles; only the eight he favors are given.* Critics of *A Theory of Justice* have objected to the lack of options Rawls introduced there (it was common to protest that while the representatives in the original position might admittedly prefer Rawls's two principles over utilitarianism, they would not have favored them over utilitarianism with a guaranteed decent minimum, for instance), but at least there were options. Rawls suggests that the parties would affirm the Law of Peoples, but unless we are given evidence that these principles *would be chosen over all the alternatives*, we have no reason to believe they are the best proposal for international law. In short, because Rawls does not even introduce alternative sets of principles (let alone argue that they

---

[8] Kok-Chor Tan, "Liberal Toleration in Rawls's Law of Peoples," 283. Simon Caney shares Tan's worry: "Rawls's argument presupposes an unsustainable contrast between domestic and global contexts. His defence of neutral principles of justice in *Political Liberalism* (and his requirement that these be applied to non-liberal peoples) clashes with his defence of the Law of Peoples (and his refusal to apply the very same liberal values to the very same non-liberal peoples)" in his article, "Cosmopolitanism and the Law of Peoples," 107.

would be dispreferred by those in the relevant choice situation), it is unclear to what extent his arguments support the Law of Peoples.

(IV) Rawls's list of basic human rights is objectionably anemic. Put plainly, it is striking that Rawls would advance a list of rights so truncated as to exclude those to democracy, freedom of expression, and equality. As Fernando Tesón puts it:

> But it should certainly count against a liberal theory that in the tension between human rights and states' rights, between freedom and nationalism, between collective forms of oppression and the quest for human progress, between the individual and the government, the theory sides with rulers (provided that they are not 'demonic' tyrants) and not with the people. It is as if Rawls believed that the human rights movement had gone too far in recognizing rights such as freedom of expression; those rights are, in some sense, too liberal.[9]

(V) Rawls grounds basic human rights in an objectionable manner. He writes:

> It may be asked by what right well-ordered liberal and decent peoples are justified in interfering with an outlaw state on the grounds that this state has violated human rights. . . . Liberal and decent peoples have extremely good reasons for their attitude. Outlaw states are aggressive and dangerous; all peoples are safer and more secure if such states change, or are forced to change, their ways. Otherwise, they deeply affect the international climate of power and violence. (*LP,* p. 81)

Rawls's explanation as to why decent peoples might permissibly interfere in cases of grave rights abuses is stunning. Presumably what is most objectionable about outlaw states disregarding the basic rights of their constituents is the grave harm thereby done to these political subjects, not the potential disruption of international relations. As Charles Beitz puts it:

> . . . whatever might be said about intervention, it is clear that the strategic interest in international stability does not bear on the moral status of human rights. For example, the reason why people have human rights not to be tortured does not seem to be that regimes that torture are dangerous to other regimes: although the latter fact (if it is a fact) might justify intervention, it does not imply anything about the moral situation of the tortured.[10]

---

[9] Fernando R. Tesón, "The Rawlsian Theory of International Law," 121.
[10] Charles Beitz, "Rawls's Law of Peoples," 685.

Thus, even if Rawls is correct about the broader dangers posed by outlaw states, this observation clearly seems secondary; concern for those individual persons whose rights are being violated presumably must constitute the core of any justification for interfering with outlaw states.

(VI) The so-called duty of assistance is doubly inadequate: Not only does Rawls wrongly conceive of this duty as obtaining among societies rather than individual persons, he demands too little redistribution from the "haves" to the "have-nots." First, conceiving of the duty of assistance as obtaining among peoples is problematic because it renders one incapable of ensuring that each individual receives what justice requires. This is because, even if the "haves" as a people give all that can legitimately be asked of them to the "have-nots" as a society, there is no guarantee that the "have-nots" will distribute it so as to ensure that all among them have enough to satisfy even their most basic needs. Second, even if Rawls were right to insist that international redistribution should occur between groups, it is not clear why he believes that the wealthy must give burdened societies only as much as they need to become minimally well-ordered. Put another way, why think that no inequality can be objectionable as long as no people is so poor as to be what Rawls calls a "burdened" society? It seems at least curious that the same reasons Rawls invokes in defense of the difference principle at the domestic level would not apply, mutatis mutandis, with equal force to international inequalities.

(VII) Rawls inexplicably fails to focus on the global basic structure, a structure that is a paradigmatic subject of justice. In *A Theory of Justice*, Rawls writes: "The basic structure is the primary subject of justice because its effects are so profound and present from the start. The intuitive notion here is that this structure contains various social positions and that men born into different positions have different expectations of life determined, in part, by the political system as well as by economic and social circumstances. In this way the institutions of society favor certain starting places over others. These are especially deep inequalities." *(TJ*, p. 7) *LP* appears seriously flawed, then, because Rawls commits either the empirical error of failing to recognize that a global basic structure exists or the normative mistake of thinking that the international basic structure is not as morally significant as its domestic counterpart. Either way, this oversight is thought to be enormously important because if there is a morally significant global basic structure, it would have profound implications for whatever duties of assistance one should posit. Not only would the "haves" be required to give the "have-nots" much more than Rawls currently suggests, these transfers would be under the title of distribution, not *re*distribution. As Thomas Pogge explains:

> ... the tenor of his remarks throughout is that a global difference principle is too strong for the international case, that it demands too much from hierarchical societies. ... This suggests a view of the

difference principle as a principle of *re*distribution, which takes from some to give to others: The more it redistributes, the more demanding is the principle. But this view of the difference principle loses an insight that is crucial to understanding Rawls's own, domestic difference principle: There is no prior distribution, no natural baseline or neutral way of arranging the economy, relative to which the difference principle could be seen to make *re*distributive modifications. Rather, there are countless ways of designing economic institutions, none initially privileged, of which one and only one will be implemented. The difference principle selects the scheme that ought to be chosen. The selected economic ground rules, whatever their content, do not *re*distribute, but rather govern how economic benefits and burdens get distributed in the first place.[11]

In sum, Rawls's failure to attend to the global basic structure leads him to mistakenly advance an overly cautious principle of *re*distribution instead of an appropriately ambitious theory of international distribution.

(VIII) *Finally, it is problematic that none of Rawls's eight principles provides guidance for how we should adjudicate intrastate conflicts.* Critics object that not only has Rawls failed to supply this important element, his argument renders him necessarily unable to do so. In particular, by stipulating that the parties in the original position represent not only peoples but *unified peoples with their own states*, Rawls leaves no room for international law to address matters of intrastate conflict. As Allen Buchanan notes:

> The question of whether, and if so how, international legal institutions should respond to intrastate conflicts cannot even be raised within Rawls's framework because the parties who choose the Law of Peoples are understood to be representatives of "peoples," groups characterized by deep political unity and already possessing their own states. Rawls's political homogeneity assumption is not a mere detail; it shapes his understanding of what international law is for, by eliminating from the Law of Peoples principles designed to cope with important conflicts that arise within states.[12]

This point is particularly worrisome not only because virtually every existing state contains a variety of distinct groups, but also because the divisions between these groups all too often give rise to precisely the types of violence and unrest that Rawls hopes for his Law of Peoples to contain. Indeed, in the real world as it is currently configured, human

---

[11] Thomas Pogge, "An Egalitarian Law of Peoples," 212.
[12] Allen Buchanan, "Rawls's Law of Peoples: Rules for a Vanished Westphalian World," 716.

rights and geopolitical stability seem more acutely threatened by *intra*- than *inter*state conflict.[13]

Having enumerated these eight distinct objections, it is worth reflecting on the tone of the critical reaction taken as a whole. Whether or not any of these criticisms is apt, it is striking how lopsided the reception has been. Notice that, by requiring societies to protect human rights, allowing for humanitarian intervention when these rights are not protected, and requiring peoples to provide assistance to burdened societies, the Law of Peoples is in some respects quite revisionist. (Imagine how different our world would be if wealthy societies continued transferring funds until no society remained burdened, or if all states that failed to respect Rawls's list of basic human rights were generally regarded as morally liable to intervention, for instance.[14]) Despite advocating these modestly progressive principles, however, Rawls has been consistently criticized for how *little* he demands, not how much. And interestingly, it is the Rawlsians who seem most vociferously to criticize *LP*. Time and again, critics do not merely respectfully point out what strike them as errors, they appear to lament in particular that *Rawls*, of all people, would write such a conservative text.[15] Just as Marx reflected that many were "plus Marxiste que moi," Rawlsians now protest that Rawls's *LP* is not Rawlsian enough.

For decades, liberal, democratic egalitarians have hailed Rawls's account of justice as fairness as the most compelling theory of domestic justice, and more than a few have suggested how this account can and should be extended to matters of global justice. The disappointment was palpable, then, when Rawls finally turned his attention to the international arena, and his conclusions proved to be considerably less ambitious and egalitarian than anyone could have imagined. Many appeared not merely disappointed, but almost betrayed that the greatest political theorist of the century would so dramatically turn his back on the very same liberal, democratic, egalitarian values that he taught us to understand and admire. Tesón puts the point plainly:

> There are two John Rawlses. The first John Rawls is, I believe, the greatest political philosopher of this century. *A Theory of Justice* is a work that not only set the agenda for political philosophy but, as important, served as inspiration for many who were resisting oppres-

---

[13] Witness the atrocities that tragically occurred during the violent disintegration of the former Yugoslavia, for instance.

[14] It should be noted that not everyone is sanguine about either of these proposals. For a discussion of the potentially negative consequences of relaxing the international legal restrictions on armed intervention, for instance, see my article (coauthored with Andrew Altman), "From Humanitarian Intervention to Assassination: Human Rights and Political Violence," *Ethics* 118, no. 2 (2008): 228–57.

[15] In calling Rawls's views in *LP* surprisingly "conservative," I mean to emphasize that they are both less ambitious and less egalitarian than students of his earlier work would have predicted.

CHRISTOPHER HEATH WELLMAN

sion in many parts of the world. The second John Rawls moved toward a more relativistic, context-based conception of justice and political morality, where rights and liberties no longer have a foundation in higher principles or liberal views of human nature but are merely the result of the peculiar history and traditions of the West.[16]

Such a dramatic retreat demands an explanation, and two candidates immediately present themselves. The most straightforward explanation is simply that Rawls lost confidence in his earlier views. Philosophers constantly modify their positions, so why is it inconceivable that Rawls would not also have evolved? Indeed, it is hard to think of a contemporary philosopher who has endured more criticism for his views than Rawls did for espousing the difference principle, so I suppose it is not altogether unbelievable that he would ultimately shy away from it. Moreover, Rawls seemed gradually but decidedly to grow ever more circumspect about the metaphysical reach of his arguments, so such a shift in values would seem to be merely one component of a more general, wide-ranging conservatism.

A second possible explanation for the disconnect between Rawls's boldly liberal egalitarian domestic theory and his relatively modest international principles is that, while he did not retreat from the core values that led him to embrace justice as fairness, his limited understanding of contemporary international relations interfered with his seeing the implications that these values should have in the international context. The idea here is that perhaps Rawls did not recognize the global basic structure because it is in many ways different from its domestic counterpart, and, as a result, he did not appreciate the implications that his own theory should have globally.

While I cannot rule out either of these explanations, I find neither entirely satisfying. As a consequence, I think it is at least worth exploring alternative interpretations of *LP*, ones that do not require us to posit the existence of two John Rawlses. Toward this end, in the next section I will propose that perhaps the eight objections to Rawls's theory of global justice miss their mark because Rawls never sought to provide a theory of global justice in *LP*.

III. An Alternative Reading

I believe that Rawls never intended to supply a full-blown, comprehensive theory of global justice in *LP*. As he says: "This monograph on the Law of Peoples is neither a treatise nor a textbook on international law. Rather, it is a work that focuses strictly on certain questions connected

---

[16] Fernando R. Tesón, "The Rawlsian Theory of International Law," 121. In quoting Tesón in this context, I do not intend to portray him as a liberal egalitarian.

with whether a realistic utopia is possible, and the conditions under which it might obtain." (*LP*, pp. 5–6) But if Rawls understood his project to be more limited than many of his critics conceive of it, this raises the question of what in particular Rawls sought to accomplish in *LP*.

Here I think we must be less confident and more speculative. One possibility is that Rawls did not believe that it is the job of political philosophy to supply a complete theory of global justice because such an account is more properly the product of morally legitimate international politics. On this view, Rawls sought only to specify the framework within which a morally legitimate international politics can take place.[17] A second interpretation regards *LP* as particularly Kantian in spirit. Recall Kant's understanding of the three questions of philosophy: What can I know? What ought I to do? What can I hope for? On this interpretation, Rawls is not offering a theory of international justice because he is addressing Kant's third question about what we can hope for, not his second question about what we ought to do. In particular, just as Kant reflected that "If justice perishes, then it is no longer worthwhile for men to live upon the earth," (quoted in *LP*, p. 128) Rawls wonders why we should not despair if a reasonably just Society of Peoples is not possible. Thus, this proposal suggests that Rawls hoped to show merely that we need not despair, if only because we can in our mind's eye picture what he calls a "realistic utopia."[18] A third option maintains that *LP* could not provide a theory of global justice because it is an extension of *Political Liberalism*, not *A Theory of Justice*. The central idea here is that because *Political Liberalism* is concerned principally with legitimacy rather than justice, *The Law of Peoples* is about what principles it would be morally permissible to impose internationally. The reason for the much less ambitious set of principles, according to this interpretation, stems from Rawls's view that it is illegitimate to force others to comply with principles that they could reasonably reject. The Law of Peoples is by comparison conservative, then, because constituents of nonliberal societies do not necessarily endorse the liberal understanding of society as a fair system of cooperation among free and equal persons. As a result, it would be illegitimate to impose a full-blown liberal theory of justice globally, as this would involve coercing people according to principles that they could reasonably reject.[19] I think all three of these interpretations are extremely interesting and deserve further exploration. I will not do so here, however. Instead, I introduce a fourth, less orthodox possibility that I believe also merits consideration.

---

[17] David A. Reidy defends this proposal in "Rawls on International Justice: A Defense," *Political Theory*, vol. 32, no. 3 (June, 2004): 291–319.

[18] Thomas E. Hill, Jr. suggested this possibility to me in conversation. I do not know that he would describe it precisely as I do here.

[19] Although Kok-Chor Tan speaks (on page 279) of Rawls arriving at "the global principles of justice," I understand Tan to interpret *LP* this way in his article, "Liberal Toleration in Rawls's Law of Peoples." Leif Wenar also affirms this general approach in his excellent essay, "The Unity of Rawls's Work," *The Journal of Moral Philosophy* 1, no. 3 (2004): 265–75.

My reading of *LP* is shaped first and foremost by Rawls's stated motivation for undertaking this project. He writes:

> Two main ideas motivate the Law of Peoples. One is that the great evils of human history—unjust war and oppression, religious persecution and the denial of liberty of conscience, starvation and poverty, not to mention genocide and mass murder—follow from political injustice, with its own cruelties and callousness. . . . The other main idea, obviously connected with the first, is that, once the gravest forms of political injustice are eliminated by following just (or at least decent) social policies and establishing just (or at least decent) basic institutions, these great evils will eventually disappear." (*LP*, pp. 6–7)

My suggestion is that we take Rawls here at his word. Let us understand *LP* not as "A Theory of International Justice," but rather as a blueprint for solving a limited practical problem: "How can we eliminate the great evils of human history?" [20]

Before defending this interpretation, let me say a little bit about how I understand this "limited practical problem." First, to see why I call it a *practical* problem, imagine that Rawls sought not to eliminate history's great evils, but to duplicate history's great achievements. For instance, suppose he asked: "How can we build a pyramid?" As strange at it might initially sound, I think that this is essentially what Rawls sought to do in *LP*; he hoped to answer a limited practical question that is importantly analogous to how we can duplicate one of human history's great accomplishments, the building of a pyramid.

I appreciate that this reading of the *LP* might seem wildly implausible both because (1) it would be curious (to put it mildly) for a great political philosopher to be so concerned with an essentially practical problem and because (2) *LP* is filled with unmistakable moral analysis. Let me address these points in turn. First, while it might be odd for a moral philosopher to be so concerned with a practical problem that involves a merely aes-

---

[20] I cannot claim that Leif Wenar would embrace the details of the following account, but it should be noted that he highlights the importance of the "great evils" quote in his entry on Rawls for the *Stanford Encyclopedia of Philosophy*, available at http://plato.stanford.edu/entries/rawls. Of those accounts in the literature with which I am familiar, my emphasis on the limits of Rawls's ambitions in *LP* is most reminiscent of Samuel Freeman's insistence that "The Law of Peoples is not a general theory of global justice that is designed to address all of the problems that arise in the contemporary world. Rather, it is set forth as part of political liberalism, to provide principles of foreign policy for a well-ordered society." ("The Law of Peoples, Social Cooperation, Human Rights and Distributive Justice," in Ellen Frankel Paul, Fred D. Miller, Jr., and Jeffrey Paul, eds., *Justice and Global Politics* [Cambridge: Cambridge University Press, 2006], 29–68, at 33.) Still, there are elements of Freeman's account about which I am skeptical (e.g., the emphasis he places on the fact that Rawls is doing ideal theory and the importance of the putative qualitative difference between a society's basic structure and the global basic structure), and there is ample reason to think that Freeman would distance himself from much of what I say here.

thetic achievement like building a pyramid, it is perfectly understandable that Rawls would care so deeply about a practical problem like eliminating the greatest evils of human history because the consequences of doing so are not merely aesthetic, they are of supreme moral importance.

Second, *LP* undeniably contains much by way of moral justification, but this makes perfect sense once one recalls that the "we" in "How can we eliminate the great evils of human history?" refers to liberal democratic societies. Just as a liberal society could never regard "with masses of slave labor" as an acceptable proposal for how to build a pyramid, it would not consider something like "by ruthlessly dominating all illiberal, undemocratic groups" an acceptable means to eliminating the great evils of human history. And because Rawls thinks both that (1) a core liberal tenet is that coercion is legitimate only when it cannot be reasonably rejected by those coerced and that (2) an appropriately designed original position can be a reliable heuristic device for discerning what parties would reasonably accept, it is no surprise that Rawls should invoke original position reasoning *en route* to establishing that liberals need have no worries about imposing upon others their means of eliminating the great evils of human history.[21] Thus, neither the prima facie implausibility of supposing that Rawls would concern himself with a "mere" practical problem nor the fact that he unquestionably engages in moral analysis ultimately dissuades me from pursuing this admittedly unorthodox reading of *The Law of Peoples*.

According to my interpretation, then, the reasoning in *LP* is something like the following:

(1) Rawls cared deeply about the human suffering caused by the great evils of history—war, oppression, religious persecution, the denial of liberty of conscience, starvation, poverty, genocide, and mass murder.

(2) Much of this suffering could be avoided if we were to eliminate political incompetence and oppression.

(3) History confirms that instituting the eight principles is an effective way to eliminate political incompetence and oppression.

(4) Original position reasoning demonstrates that no one could reasonably reject these eight principles.

(5) Therefore, liberal societies may permissibly impose the Law of Peoples upon the world in order to eliminate political incompetence and oppression, thereby eliminating the horrible suffering that has historically attended our greatest evils.

---

[21] On (1), which Rawls labels the "liberal principle of legitimacy," Rawls writes: "Our exercise of political power is fully proper only when it is exercised in accordance with a constitution the essentials of which all citizens as free and equal may reasonably be expected to endorse in the light of principles and ideals acceptable to their common human reason." (*PL*, 137)

Having explained this alternative interpretation, let us revisit the eight criticisms of *LP* to see how Rawls might respond if he did in fact conceive of the Laws of Peoples in the manner I suggest.

(I) Rawls wrongly focuses on peoples rather than individual persons. The worry here is twofold: Not only does his argument rely upon the parties in the original position representing groups; his eight principles ignore individuals to concentrate almost exclusively on the rights and responsibilities of peoples. If Rawls's aim is only to suggest a way to eliminate the greatest evils of human history, however, then there is nothing suspicious about focusing on groups with states because (i) politically organized groups have historically been the agents responsible for these great evils (i.e., "unjust war and oppression, religious persecution and the denial of conscience, starvation and poverty, not to mention genocide and mass murder"), (ii) politically empowered groups stand the best chance of imposing the reforms necessary to eliminate these evils, and (iii) international law has traditionally been the law of nations, created by and applied primarily to nation states. Rawls need not be understood as suggesting that individuals do not matter morally or that individuals should be indifferent to these issues (indeed, he would not have cared about these features of human history if they did not lead to individuals suffering, and he would not have penned *LP* if he were convinced that he, qua individual, was utterly insignificant or impotent). Rather, Rawls focuses on groups here simply because the most realistic way to eliminate the great evils of human history is to have relatively enlightened states both police the abusive states ("rogue" states) unwilling to protect those within their borders and help support those burdened societies ("failed" states) unable to eliminate suffering within their borders. Most importantly, notice that such an *empirical* assertion about the most effective way to address this practical problem says nothing about whether or not individual human beings are the fundamental units of *moral* significance, and thus it in no way conflicts with the moral primacy of individuals Rawls endorses elsewhere.

(II) It seems objectionable that Rawls would either leave nondecent societies unrepresented in the original position or give nonliberal but so-called decent hierarchical peoples such representation. The idea here is that either it must be shown that no society affected by the Law of Peoples could reasonably reject the principles or, if only the acceptance of just societies is required, then only liberal peoples should be represented, and there would be no need to represent any nonliberal, nondemocratic, or nonegalitarian society in the original position.

The standard defense against this objection is that a society need not be fully just in order to be reasonable, and thus, establishing that decent hierarchical societies would accept the eight principles is important because such societies are akin to reasonable moral agents. Excluding outlaw states and burdened societies (i.e., those societies with social and economic conditions that undermine their capacity to sustain liberal or decent institutions) is nonetheless appropriate, though, because the former are unreasonable, nonmoral agents and the latter are not agents at all.[22] If so, then an outlaw state's rejection of the Law of Peoples would not be reasonable and a burdened society could neither accept nor reject the eight principles.

Without commenting on the adequacy of this response, it is worth noting that Rawls has a second rejoinder open to him if his goal in *LP* is limited in the ways I have suggested. Specifically, while the differences between liberal and decent hierarchical societies might be germane to anyone designing a comprehensive theory of international justice (or legitimacy, for that matter), these differences are not important to the task at hand. Given that his aim is limited to eliminating history's great evils, societies can be sorted into two main groups depending upon whether they are part of the solution or part of the problem. Because decent hierarchical peoples, *by definition*, do not cause unjust wars, oppression, religious persecution, the denial of liberty of conscience, starvation, poverty, genocide and mass murder, they clearly are not part of the problem. Moreover, insofar as they are able and willing to help assist burdened societies and intervene against outlaw states, they can be part of the solution in eradicating these great evils.

What I am suggesting is that just as a war against a sufficiently evil empire would incline two otherwise unfriendly countries to unite against a common enemy (as the United States and the Soviet Union did to fight Nazi Germany in World War II, for instance), Rawls rightly marshals all well-ordered societies in the effort to eliminate the great evils of human history. Crucially, though, there is nothing about this limited merger that implies that Rawls has abandoned his preference for liberalism, democracy, or egalitarianism. In other words, Rawls might well favor a fully liberal, democratic and egalitarian set of principles if he were crafting an ideal and comprehensive code of international law, but it would be premature to theorize such a code when these great evils still exist. His present, more pressing chore is to offer a more limited set of principles that might effectively eliminate the worst causes of human suffering. Only once this is accomplished can we turn our attention to a more robust theory of global justice, and no one would be surprised if at that point the differences among the well-ordered societies would be paramount (just as the divisions between the United States and the Soviet Union loomed larger after World War II).

(III) Rawls never allows the representatives in the original position to consider alternatives to the eight principles. He suggests that the parties would affirm the Law of Peoples, but, without an argument that they would prefer this set of principles over all competitors, it is not clear how his argument

---

[22] Reidy develops this response in "Rawls on International Justice: A Defense."

supports these principles over possible alternatives. If I am right that
Rawls means for *LP* to provide a solution to a practical problem, however,
then it makes perfect sense that he would feel no need to consider alternatives in the original position because the original position, in this case,
would not be needed to determine what is morally best; it is invoked
merely to confirm that the practical solution is not morally illegitimate.
Given that Rawls advances the eight principles as an effective means to
eliminating the great evils of human history, the way in which they would
need to be compared to competitors is in terms of their effectiveness. In
other words, the key comparative question is not whether *moral analysis*
recommends a competing set of principles as more *ideal*, it is whether
historical evidence indicates that another set could more *fully and effectively*
eliminate the political oppression and such. Once Rawls concludes that
the evidence suggests that the Law of Peoples provides the most effective
way to eliminate the relevant evils, he needs to utilize the original position device only to establish that there is nothing objectionable (from a
liberal's perspective) about imposing these principles internationally—
that is, that no party could reasonably object to their imposition. In sum,
it may be neither a coincidence nor an oversight that Rawls does not
weigh his favored principles against competitors in the original position.
If he seeks a set of principles as a solution to a practical task rather than
as a moral ideal, moral comparisons are beside the point.

(IV) *Rawls advances a list of basic rights that excludes rights to democracy,
freedom of expression, and equality.* Why in the world would a liberal theorist omit these paradigmatically liberal rights from the list? If Rawls is
concerned to provide a practical means to eliminating particularly great
evils rather than to supply a comprehensive theory of global justice, then
it is no mystery why he would omit some of these rights. The point is not
that rights to freedom of expression, democracy, and equality are in general unimportant, it is merely that their protection is irrelevant to the
question at hand. The more restricted list of rights *is* relevant to eliminating the evils in question, however, because Rawls postulates that states
which fail to respect these basic rights are the ones responsible for the
political injustices (both at home and in war) that cause the profound
suffering he seeks to eliminate. Thus, without in any way retracting his
support for the more expansive list of rights that he has defended elsewhere, Rawls can exclude those rights to freedom of expression, democracy, and equality in this context simply because their protection is not
necessary to eliminate the severe political oppression upon which this
project focuses.

(V) *Rawls offers an appalling explanation for why we should care about
human rights violations.* By citing the aggressiveness of outlaw states rather
than the well-being and autonomy of individual human beings, Rawls
seems to badly miss the core justification of these rights. If Rawls's project
is the practical one of eliminating the suffering that flows from political

injustice, however, then it is entirely understandable that he might focus on the tendency of rights-violating societies to wage unjust wars. Certainly the bellicosity of outlaw states is beside the point for anyone defending human rights, but it is perfectly on topic for someone concerned with the causes of history's great evils. With this in mind, consider again Rawls's statement that has been so widely regarded as both curious and offensive:

> "It may be asked by what right well-ordered liberal and decent peoples are justified in interfering with an outlaw state on the grounds that this state has violated human rights. . . . Liberal and decent peoples have extremely good reasons for their attitude. Outlaw states are aggressive and dangerous; all peoples are safer and more secure if such states change, or are forced to change, their ways. Otherwise, they deeply affect the international climate of power and violence." (*LP*, p. 81)

In short, my interpretation of *LP* puts this discussion of rights in a light that shows it to be neither curious nor offensive.

(VI) The duty of assistance is inadequate insofar as it both demands too little redistribution and is wrongly said to obtain between societies rather than individuals. Neither prong of this objection is compelling, though, if Rawls sought to determine, not what each individual in the world is owed as a matter of justice, but what type of distribution would be required to effectively address certain grave evils, chiefly starvation and poverty. Of course, some starvation and poverty exists within outlaw states which abuse their constituents, but Rawls covers these cases by understanding the right to sovereignty and the corresponding duty against intervention to include an exemption in cases of sufficiently malicious governments. The duty of assistance, however, is designed to help burdened groups who, despite being well-intentioned, lack the resources necessary to avoid these sources of suffering. It remains an open question whether these groups as a whole (or the individuals within them) deserve a more equal share of the world's wealth, but Rawls need not speak to what each person is owed as a matter of moral right, if he seeks to say only what the well-ordered societies must do in order to address the great evils of starvation and poverty.

(VII) Rawls scarcely acknowledges the existence of the global basic structure.[23] This international basic structure is thought to be important because, if

---

[23] While Rawls by no means fastens upon the importance of the global basic structure, he certainly seems to acknowledge it. As Leif Wenar has emphasized in personal correspondence, Rawls repeatedly refers to the global basic structure in *LP* on pages 33, 62, 114, 115, 122, and 123. For an interesting interpretation of Rawls's take on the existence (but relative insignificance) of the global basic structure, see Samuel Freeman, "The Law of Peoples, Social Cooperation, Human Rights, and Distributive Justice, especially pages 39–41.

Rawls were to remain consistent with his arguments in *TJ*, international transfers would be a matter of just distribution, not *re*distribution. As things stand, however, Rawls conceives of *TJ*'s difference principle as a matter of distribution and *LP*'s duty of assistance as a matter of *re*distribution. However, Rawls must bear the burden of consistency between *TJ* and *LP* only if he were engaged in the same type of project in both instances. But if I am right that he sought to answer a moral question in *TJ* and a practical question in *LP*, then there would be nothing objectionable about attending to different matters in these two books. Thus, it is open for Rawls to concede that while the global basic structure is undeniably important for anyone developing a comprehensive theory of international justice, he need not focus on it in *LP*, where he sought merely to design a practical solution to eliminate some of the chief sources of human suffering.

(VIII) None of his eight principles offers instructions for handling intrastate conflicts. What is worse, Rawls appears *unable* to address this lacuna since he assumes throughout that the parties in the original position represent unified peoples, societies with no cleavages within them. Finally, it would be no good for Rawls to respond that he seeks only to eliminate the world's great evils because, in the contemporary world at least, intrastate conflicts are a lamentably frequent and explosive source of some of humanity's greatest tragedies. Here Rawls could respond by noting that, although none of his eight principles explicitly deals with intrastate conflict, they nonetheless provide guidance for those violent divisions that cause the types of suffering he sought to avoid. In particular, Rawls's interpretation of the duty of nonintervention allows for well-ordered societies to intervene in outlaw states when one group is systematically violating the basic rights of another. To this an objector might respond that, because Rawls's list of human rights is so short and includes no distinct rights for minority groups, the Law of Peoples remains lamentably mute on many of the divisions within states like that between the minority Quebecois and the majority Anglo-phonic Canadians or the Scottish within the United Kingdom.

Here I think Rawls could acknowledge that his eight principles provide no instruction but insist that this is unproblematic since he is concerned only with the great evils of human history, and the relatively tame conflicts like those within Canada and the United Kingdom do not give rise to such extreme evils. In short, Rawls could respond to this objection with the following disjunctive answer: An intrastate conflict either involves the violations of basic human rights or it does not. If it does (as in the case of the former Yugoslavia), then the eight principles clearly speak to the issue. If not (as in the case of Canada), then the Law of Peoples does not offer guidance, but this is not worrisome because the principles are recommended not as a complete theory of international law but more minimally as an effective means to eliminate the worst sources of human suffering.

In light of how this construal of Rawls's project supplies compelling answers to the standard objections, we can now see that there is a strong case in favor of what initially appeared to be a quite implausible interpretation of *The Law of Peoples*. Let me be clear: I do not claim that my reading is entirely straightforward and uniformly supported by all aspects of the text. On the contrary, there are numerous passages (particularly his accounts of why liberal toleration of other societies requires positing a restricted list of human rights and a severely limited duty of assistance) where Rawls plainly seems to argue for more ambitious conclusions than are consistent with my interpretation. It would be wrong to reject my proposal on this score alone, however, because *LP* is a rich, complex work which does not univocally recommend any single interpretation. Thus, without pretending that Rawls speaks throughout in one voice that uniquely confirms my interpretation, we can nonetheless see several compelling reasons to regard Rawls's project in *LP* as offering neither an ideal theory of global justice nor a comprehensive theory of international law, but as more modestly reflecting on how liberal democratic societies might justifiably go about the important practical project of eliminating the world's great evils.

First and most obviously, my interpretation squares with Rawls's own description of the project in two crucial respects: when he insists that his work is "neither a treatise nor a textbook on international law" and when he explicitly describes his main motivation as eliminating "the great evils of human history." Second, it strikes me as a decided advantage of my view that it is in keeping with Rawls's more gradual and general retreat from metaphysics, whereas the traditional interpretation of *LP* requires its advocates to construe Rawls as abruptly abandoning (or misinterpreting) his own celebrated values and methods of argumentation. Third and perhaps most important, my reading of *LP* provides straightforward and plausible responses to the standard criticisms. If Rawls is interpreted as supplying a grand theory of international justice, however, then the commonly-voiced objections seem quite damning; they reveal Rawls's theory to be woefully inadequate and, what is worse, fundamentally inconsistent with what he has argued elsewhere. In other words, charity would seem to recommend my reading of *LP* because, while the principle of charity often suggests interpreting an author as giving the most defensible answers, in this case it favors understanding the author to be asking a question that best matches his answers.[24] For all of these reasons, then, I think it is worth considering whether Rawls's project in *LP* is not to provide a full-scale normative theory of global justice but is more modestly to suggest only how liberal societies could effectively work to elim-

[24] As Thomas Pogge has pointed out to me, there is a sense in which this interpretation is decidedly *un*charitable to Rawls, because if Rawls's project in *LP* is really as I speculate here, then it seems uncharitable to think that he could not have articulated this more clearly than he did.

inate the profound human suffering caused by the worst cases of political malice and incompetence.

IV. CONCLUSION

Many of the eight objections canvassed in the second section would be compelling if Rawls sought for *The Law of Peoples* to supply a theory of global justice, but I think we should doubt that he meant to do so. I recommend that we take him at his word when he claims to have a more modest project. What precisely this project involves is more difficult to say with any real confidence, but here I have suggested that perhaps he meant only to answer a relatively limited practical question: How can we eliminate the great evils of human history? I confess that there is much in *The Law of Peoples* that seems to conflict with this interpretation, but given that there is no clear, straightforward and unproblematic interpretation of this important text, the principle of charity recommends that we take seriously the idea that Rawls's aspirations for this book were far less normatively ambitious than most critics have assumed.

Philosophy, Washington University and Centre for Applied Philosophy and Public Ethics, Charles Sturt University

RESPONSIBLE CHOICES, DESERT-BASED LEGAL INSTITUTIONS, AND THE CHALLENGES OF CONTEMPORARY NEUROSCIENCE*

By Michael S. Moore

I. Subjective Selves, Moral Agents, and Legal Subjects

Both law and the moral/political philosophy on which it is built presuppose certain views in psychology. These are fundamental views about who we are as persons, as moral agents, and as legal subjects. Much of our political philosophy and our legal institutions depend on these views being true of us; indeed much that we value in ourselves seems indefensible without these views being true. Yet the rise of cognitive science in general, and neuroscience in particular, is commonly taken to undermine these views. We thus need to assess whether this is true, either now given the present state of neuroscience, or in the future given what foreseeably may be developed by that science. The aim of this paper is to lay the groundwork for such an assessment by isolating as clearly as possible both what in our legal/political institutions is challenged by neuroscience, and what in neuroscience is doing the challenging. In particular I shall seek to clarify the different challenges that arise from work in neuroscience, for only when such challenges are distinguished, one from the other, can one begin to assess whether they are true.

I shall begin by spelling out more completely the legal, moral, and psychological suppositions about persons that seem to be challenged by recent advances in the brain sciences. Then in the next section I shall lay out the challenges to this view presented by current neuroscience.

* In the researching and writing of this essay I have benefitted from the generous support, both financial and otherwise, of the MacArthur Foundation's Project in Law and Neuroscience 2007-2010. The paper is a (considerably) expanded version of the Responsibility Group Working Paper on the Challenges of Neuroscience, presented by me to the winter 2010 Santa Monica meeting of the Criminal Responsibility and Prediction Research Network of the MacArthur Foundation's Law and Neuroscience Project. My thanks go to my colleagues in the Network for their suggestions and comments. The essay has since been presented to the Workshop in Law and Philosophy, University of Texas, Austin and to the Conference on Law and the Science of Moral Judgment, Centre for the Study of Mind in Nature, University of Oslo, Norway. My thanks go to the participants at these two presentations for their helpful comments as well as to the other contributors to this volume. My particular thanks go to Robert Kane, who was my commentator at the University of Texas, and to Michael Gazzaniga and Stephen Morse, each of whom read and commented separately on this paper.

doi:10.1017/S0265052511000082
233

A. Legal institutions and political philosophies challenged by neuroscience

The most common legal institution and concommitant political philosophy thought to be challenged by contemporary neuroscience is that
of retributive punishment in the criminal law.[1] The defining mark of
retributivism as a political philosophy is its insistence that moral desert is
by itself a sufficient justification for inflicting punishment.[2] As Kant said
clearly long ago, even if a society were disbanding so that no incapacita-
tive, educative, expressive, or other reason existed to punish an offender,
still, that he deserves to be punished is sufficient warrant to give him
what he deserves.[3] Retributive justice demands punishment in such cases,
even if no other good is achieved by such punishment.

A retributive theory of criminal law and of punishment of course requires
some ideas of when someone *deserves* to be punished. For this we have to
look to moral theory. On the moral theory I think to be most plausible,
moral desert is built on two moral properties, wrongdoing and culpabil-
ity.[4] One who unjustifiably kills an innocent does *wrong;* one who does so
inexcusably intending to kill that innocent, does that wrong *culpably.*
Culpable wrongdoing is the touchstone of moral desert. Yet each of these
two moral properties can exist only for creatures who can act, will, reason, and intend, in the manner that I shall shortly explore. Culpable
wrongdoing requires that a certain psychology, and not others, be true of
us.[5] This psychology is what contemporary neuroscience appears to
challenge.

A popular way to sidestep this challenge is one that I shall eschew; but
to be clear-headed about what *is* at stake here, one has to see this finessing
strategy for what it is. I call this strategy "cheap compatibilism," or sometimes, "compatibilism-on-the-cheap." The basic move is to regard the
retributivist political philosophy sketched above as but a disguised form
of utilitarianism. Harvard's well known psychologist Steven Pinker has
recently rediscovered this old move: "punishment even in the pure sense

---

[1] Those guilty of this sin (and no doubt deserving of serious punishment) include Robert
Sapolsky, "The Frontal Cortex and the Criminal Justice System" *Philosophical Transactions of
the Royal Society of London* vol. 359 (2004): 1787–96; Josh Greene and Jonathan Cohen, "For
the Law, Neuroscience Changes Nothing and Everything," *Philosophical Transactions of the
Royal Society of London* vol. 359 (2004): 1775–85; Richard Dawkins, "Let's All Stop Beating
Basil's Car," posted 2006 at http://www.edge.org/q2006/q06_9.html; William Banks, "Does
Consciousness Cause Misbehavior?" in S. Pockett, W. Banks, and S. Gallagher, eds., *Does
Consciousness Cause Behavior?* (Cambridge, MA: MIT Press, 2006), 253; Thomas W. Clark,
"Fear of Mechanism: A Compatibilist Critique of 'The Volitional Brain,'" *Journal for Con-
sciousness Studies* vol. 6 (1999): 279–93.
[2] Michael Moore, *Placing Blame: A General Theory of the Criminal Law* (Oxford: Clarendon
Press, 1997), 87–92.
[3] Immanuel Kant, *The Metaphysical Elements of Justice,* J. Ladd, trans. (Indianapolis: Bobbs-
Merrill, 1965), 102.
[4] Moore, *Placing Blame,* 45–60, 191–193, 403–404.
[5] Explored at length by me in Michael Moore, *Law and Psychiatry: Rethinking the Relationship* (Cambridge: Cambridge University Press, 1984), 67–84, 100–112.

of just deserts is *ultimately* a policy for deterrence."[6] Pinker's is a familiar form of indirect utilitarianism:[7] the idea is that we should develop retributive urges to punish because a society with such urges makes for the most effective deterrent in the long run. *Then*, the next move (for those like Pinker) is to observe that much in contemporary neuroscience that *seems* to challenge punishment practices—such as, the claim that there is no free will—in fact does not challenge deterrence-based justifications of punishment. After all, deterrence requires causal *determination* of human behavior (by legal sanctions) and so, on its face, is fully compatible (indeed, requires) that some kind of causal determination of choice be possible.[8]

One wants to resurrect French Statesman Georges Clemenceau here:[9] cheap compatibilism stands to real compatibilism as military music stands to real music. Pinker's kind of move "saves" institutions of retributive punishment only by destroying them first. It is like saving your house from an approaching fire by burning it down first yourself. Retributive punishment cannot be reduced to an indirect utilitarian strategy and remain retributive punishment. On retributive views punishing just deserts is not a proxy for deterrent policy; it is, as any retributivist will say, a freestanding, intrinsic good that those who deserve punishment receive it, even when no other good (such as deterrence) is thereby achieved.[10]

Not only would no retributivist accept Pinker's kind of "retributivism," no clear thinking utilitarian would accept the categorical injunction Pinker's indirect utilitarianism recommends, "punish the deserving even if no social good is achieved thereby." For a utilitarian this would be irrational.[11] Pinker tries to motivate such irrationality by suggesting that threatened/promised punishments just have to be delivered: "The only

[6] Steven Pinker, "The Fear of Determinism," in J. Baer, J. Kaufman, and R. Baumeister, eds., *Are We Free? Psychology and Free Will* (Oxford: Oxford University Press, 2008), 317.

[7] On "indirect," or "two-step," utilitarianisms generally, see Larry Alexander, "Pursuing the Good—Indirectly," *Ethics* vol. 95 (1985), 315–32. Pinker's is a trait or motive kind of indirect utilitarianism. So-called "trait" or "motive" utilitarianism (according to which we should adopt those traits that in the long run will maximize utility), is usually associated with Richard Brandt, "Towards a Credible Form of Utilitarianism," in B. Brody, ed., *Moral Rules and Particular Circumstances* (Englewood Cliffs, NJ.: Prentice-Hall, 1970).

[8] As many besides Pinker have noticed. See, e.g., Greene and Cohen, "Neuroscience Changes Nothing"; see also Daniel Dennett, *Elbow Room: The Varieties of Free Will Worth Wanting* (Cambridge, MA: MIT Press, 1984), where in the last chapter Dennett unwittingly adds cheap compatibilism to the more genuine form of compatibilism expressed in the earlier chapters of his well-known compatibilist tract.

[9] Clemenceau's celebrated simile was that military justice stands to justice as military music stands to music.

[10] Moore, *Placing Blame*, 155–58, 160–63.

[11] As Jack Smart, a trenchant but clear-headed act-utilitarian once put it, following a practice when it does not maximize utility to do so, is "blind rule-worship." J. J .C. Smart, "Utilitarianism: For," in J. J. C. Smart and Bernard Williams, *Utilitarianism: For and Against* (Cambridge: Cambridge University Press, 1973). David Lyons has classically shown that indirect utilitarianisms like Pinker's collapse either into such blind rule-worship or into a direct (or "act") utilitarianism. David Lyons, *Forms and Limits of Utilitarianism* (Oxford: Oxford University Press, 1965).

solution is to adopt a resolute policy of punishing wrongdoers *regardless* of the immediate effects,"[12] and (quoting Justice Holmes) "the law must keep its promises."[13] Surely not. A clear-headed utilitarian about punishment will see that the threat value of punishment does not demand such exceptionless carrying out of the threat of punishment—after all, a mere *appearance* of such inexorability of punishment would suffice for deterrent purposes.[14]

I conclude that no "cheap compatibilism" can save retributive punishment schemes from having to confront the challenges of neuroscience that this paper is about. Less often noticed is that what are standardly called mixed punishment schemes[15] also must face these challenges. A widely accepted mixed punishment scheme[16] is one whereby punishment is justified by the conjunction of *two* intrinsic goods: punishment is justified, on this view, only if both just deserts and reduction of crime is achieved by such punishment. The widely perceived advantage of mixed schemes over retributivist ones is the ability of the former to avoid punishing when no reason based on crime prevention is present. The widely perceived advantage of mixed schemes over utilitarian ones is the ability of the former to supply the categorical ban on punishing the innocent that clear-headed utilitarians about punishment know they cannot justify. To gain this latter advantage, mixed punishment theories must use just deserts as a categorical limit on punishment. While only the retributivist asserts that desert is a *sufficient* condition of justified punishment, the retributivist is joined by the mixed theorist in asserting that desert is a *necessary* condition of such punishment. Desert, therefore, enters even non-retributive, mixed schemes as a categorical limit (or "side-constraint") on when criminal punishment may be used to achieve social benefits like prevention of crime. Desert—culpable wrongdoing—has to exist to perform this limiting function no less than to perform the more ambitious function assigned to it by retributivism. Such moral desert can exist only if the natural properties on which it supervenes (such as voluntariness of action, intentionality, etc.) are not illusory. Mixed punishment schemes are thus as much challenged by contemporary neuroscience as are retributivist schemes.

The vulnerability to the challenges of neuroscience of mixed punishment schemes is shared by all desert-based schemes for areas of law other than the law of crimes. Corrective justice theories of tort, promissory theories of contract, and natural rights theories of property, all ground

[12] Pinker, "Fear of Determinism," 318.
[13] Ibid.
[14] Moore, *Placing Blame*, 101.
[15] Mixed schemes are discussed ibid., 92–94.
[16] H. L. A. Hart, *Punishment and Responsibility* (Oxford: Oxford University Press, 1968).

legal rights and liabilities on notions of moral desert.[17] By way of illustration, consider the natural rights theory of property adumbrated by
John Locke[18] and contemporary Lockeans, such as Robert Nozick.[19] On
this view legal property rights should be assigned to those who possess
moral (or "natural") rights with respect to the exclusive use, consumption
and disposition of a thing. Such moral rights with respect to a thing are
acquired originally by those who "mix their labor" with that thing, i.e.,
they intentionally improve that thing in a way that others are also free to
do if they had the competence and desire to do so. Such moral rights can
also be acquired derivatively by transfer from one who did such laboring
as to acquire original title. Such transfers creating derivative title, too, are
matters of intentions and voluntary actions by both those who transfer
and those who receive the transfers. Both original and derivative modes
of creation of such moral and, thus, legal property rights presuppose a
psychology similar to that presupposed by retributivist and mixed punishment schemes in the criminal law, and is thus subject to the same
challenges to that psychology.

B. *The folk psychology presupposed by legal institutions and political
philosophies*

It is time we describe just what that psychology is that is presupposed
by all desert-based political philosophies, be they retributivist, natural
right, corrective justice, promissory, or whatever. This is a pre-scientific,
commonsense psychology that is often called (non-pejoratively) "folk psychology." This psychology is best described in terms of ten properties
arguably essential to the psychology of persons.

1. *Intentionality.* "Intentionality" is the label coined by the Scholastics
in the Middle Ages to describe a basic feature of our psychology, which
is that we act and believe guided by our representations of the world.[20]
Many but not all of our mental states are representational states in that
they take "objects," have "content," are "directed upon propositions,"
and so on. One does not just hope, fear, intend, desire, simpliciter; rather
one hopes that tomorrow will be better than today, fears that it will not be,
wants it to be so, or intends to make it the case that it will be so. What

---

[17] I chart the place of moral desert in all of these schemes in Michael Moore, "Four
Reflections on Law and Morality," *William and Mary Law Review* vol. 48 (2007), 1523–69, at
1553–68.
[18] John Locke, *The Second Treatise of Government* 25–31 (J. W. Gough, ed., Barnes and
Noble, 1966) (originally published 1690).
[19] Robert Nozick, *Anarchy, State, and Utopia* (New York: Oxford University Press, 1974).
[20] Roderick Chisholm reintroduced the term (which is conventionally capitalized to avoid
confusing it with the less technical idea of intentional action) into modern discussions. See
his *Perceiving: A Philosophical Study* (Ithaca, N.Y.: Cornell University Press, 1957), 120–70. For
an update, see John Perry, "Intentionality (II)," in S. Guttenplan, ed., *Blackwell's Companion
to the Philosophy of Mind* (Oxford: Blackwell, 1994), 386–94.

follows the "that" in such constructions is said to be the content of an Intentional state.

Intentionality is basic for creatures who would understand and manipulate their environment. For it is our capacity to represent (as the objects of our beliefs) the world as it is that gives us theoretical understanding, and it is our capacity to represent the world as the objects of our desires and intentions that gives us some measure of control over that world.

Despite its familiarity, and despite its rock-bottom status within folk psychology, Intentionality is a surprisingly complicated affair. For it is notoriously difficult to fix the sense and the reference of words used to describe the content of Intentional states.[21] This has led some to the far-fetched schemes of a kind of dualism about the mind, such as Franz Brentano's idea that the objects of Intentional states exist in a special way he termed, "Intentional Inexistence." [22] This difficulty about the content of Intentional states has led others to a skepticism about their existence on grounds antedating and existing independently of the discoveries of neuroscience.[23] At present, it is something of an article of faith that the best cognitive science will find a place for the Intentional states of folk psychology. Nonetheless that is a faith to which common sense, morality, and the law wholeheartedly subscribe.[24]

2. *Three parts to the soul.* Plato famously divided the soul into appetitive, rational, and executory "parts." [25] Despite its ancient lineage, this is still a fairly good functional division among the Intentional states that guide our actions and that, thus, constitute our agency.[26] Such states are

---

[21] See, e.g., James Cornman, "Intentionality and Intensionality," *Philosophical Quarterly* vol. 12 (1962), 44–52; Moore, *Placing Blame*, 372–84.

[22] Franz Brentano, *Psychologie vom Empirischen Standpunkt* (Leipzig, 1874), a selection translated in R. Chisholm, ed., *Realism and the Background of Phenomenology* (Glencoe, Ill.: Free Press, 1960): "Every mental phenomenon is characterized by what the scholastics of the Middle Ages called Intentional Inexistence of an object . . ."

[23] The basic motive for this "eliminativist-materialism" skepticism (based in philosophy rather than in scientific psychology) lies in the difficulty of individuating mental states with Intentional content in a way that any physical system could realize. See, e.g., Richard Rorty, "The Brain as Hardware, Culture as Software," *Inquiry* vol. 47 (2004): 231: "Beliefs cannot be individuated in such a way as to correlate with neural states." The idea is that *propositional* content (if that is what it is) takes into account features of the world in such individuation, and such features "can't be in the head." See generally John Greenwood, ed., *The Future of Folk Psychology* (Cambridge: Cambridge University Press, 1991).

[24] "[I]f commonsense intentional psychology were really to collapse, that would be, beyond comparison, the greatest intellectual catastrophe in the history of our species. . ." Jerry Fodor, *Psychosemantics: The Problem of Meaning in the Philosophy of Mind* (Cambridge, MA: MIT Press, 1987), xii.

[25] Plato, *The Republic*, Book IV (R. E. Allen, trans., New Haven: Yale University Press, 2006).

[26] Whether there are two or three distinct states involved in practical rationality has been the subject of contemporary debate. Compare Donald Davidson, "Intention," in his *Essays on Actions and Events* (Oxford: Oxford University Press, 1980), with Michael Bratman, *Intention, Plans, and Practical Reason* (Cambridge, MA: Harvard University Press, 1987). For reasons explored in Michael Moore, *Act and Crime: The Implications of the Philosophy of Action for the Criminal Law* (Oxford: Clarendon Press, 1993), chap. 6, I favor Bratman's triad of distinct intentional states to Davidson's two.

motivational, cognitive, or conative: we represent the world as we *desire* it to be, as we *believe* that it is, and as we *intend* to make it into. Beliefs, desires, and intentions are the three modalities of representional states most constitutive of us as agents who act.

3. *Practical rationality.* The three representational states of desire, belief, and intention come in ordered triads within our psychology. Although often explicit reference is made to just one state in the explanation of human action, such seemingly sole references are elliptical for a triad of such states. Moreover, there is an order to this triad in the form Aristotle called a practical syllogism.[27] Suppose I am headed toward an umbrella store and that this action requires explanation. A full, reason-giving explanation would consist of three "premises":

a. I desire not to get wet.
b. (Believing as I do that it will soon be raining, nonetheless): if I buy an umbrella, I will not get wet.
c. I intend to buy an umbrella soon.

Notice that the content of my intention matches the antecedent clause of my means/end belief, and that the content of my desire matches the consequent clause of that belief. Notice also that I have not yet fully explained my walking toward the umbrella store. To complete the rational reconstruction of my reasoning process I must add another means/ end belief and a volition:

d. I believe that if I move my feet thus and so, I will get to the store and buy an umbrella.
e. I will my feet to move thus and so.

These relationships are so definitive of our understanding of each other as rational actors that we readily ascribe the full set to an actor even if only one of them is explicitly mentioned. For example, idiomatic answers to the question, "Why are you headed toward the umbrella store," could easily be: "because I do not want to get wet;" or, "because I believe it is going to rain soon." These highly elliptical answers are fully intelligible to us because we are so familiar with the form of a full practical syllogism.

4. *Emotionality and the rationality of emotion.* Both psychopathic personality types and some silicon-based intelligence systems imagined in science fiction remind us that an absence of emotions marks a being as less

[27] A good explication of Aristotle's practical syllogisms in light of the contemporary philosophy of action is Martha Nussbaum's dissertation, done under David Cooper's supervision and published as *Aristotle's De Moto Animalum* (Princeton, N.J.: Princeton University Press, 1977). See also Moore, *Placing Blame,* 604–5.

than fully human.[28] An older view regards the necessary emotionality as a regrettable aspect of human nature; this, on the picture that emotions distract us from the rational and the moral.[29] Yet a better view sees rational functions for the emotions: they can be the harbingers of moral insight (their epistemic role),[30] and they can create value for projects that morality makes discretionary (their constitutive role). There is also an intelligence to the emotions that fits them for these roles, an intelligence cashed out in terms of the virtue/vice of holding certain emotions on certain occasions, of the norms of appropriateness of kinds of emotions in relation to their objects, and of the norms of proportionality in the intensity of emotion measured against its causes.[31] A recognizably human person is one who is passionate about certain projects, hates injustice, and grieves over objects whose loss is worth grieving about.

5. *Character structure at a time and over time.* Everybody has many beliefs, desires, intentions, and emotions. To be recognizably human requires more order to them beyond their being grouped into the forms of valid practical or theoretical inference. In addition, the entire constellation of an individual's Intentional states must instantiate an intelligible character structure.[32] This must be true at a given time; but it also must be true to some extent over time as well. Acts out of (one's present) character are possible; and changes of character over time are even more familiar. But fractured personalities, and temporally disjointed chameleons, are not the kind of beings we each take ourselves to be.

6. *Autonomy.* It is the basic sense of "autonomy" that I intend here (there are other senses of the word). Namely, folk psychology supposes that our belief/desire/intention ("BDI") sets *cause* our voluntary actions.[33] That is *not* a "free will" postulate, at least not in the sense of "free will" that demands the will to be uncaused. Rather, the supposition is that the will causes the behaviors that are represented in its objects.[34] When I intend to kill a man by moving my finger (on the trigger of a gun), both

---

[28] On psychopaths, see Stephen Morse, "Psychopathy and Criminal Responsibility," *Neuroethics* 1 (2008), 205–12.

[29] Explored briefly by me in Moore, *Law and Psychiatry*, 108.

[30] Moore, *Placing Blame*, 127–38.

[31] David Sachs nicely charted how Freud's theory of defense mechanisms presupposed hidden norms of proportionality of emotional response. David Sachs, "On Freud's Doctrine of the Emotions," in R. Wollheim, ed., *Freud: A Collection of Critical Essays* (Garden City, N.Y.: Doubleday, 1974).

[32] Moore, *Law and Psychiatry*, 390–91; Moore, *Placing Blame*, 615–16.

[33] Usually termed the "causal theory of action," a basic tenet of folk psychology. See Moore, *Act and Crime;* Moore, "Renewed Questions About the Causal Theory of Action," in J. Aguilar and A. Buckareff, eds., *Causing Human Action: New Perspectives on the Causal Theory of Action* (Cambridge, MA: MIT Press, 2010). Jerry Fodor regards this as basic to the folk psychology: "If it isn't literally true that my wanting is causally responsible for my reaching . . . then practically everything that I believe about anything is false and it is the end of the world." Jerry Fodor, *A Theory of Content and Other Essays* (Cambridge, MA: MIT Press, 1990), 196.

[34] Moore, *Placing Blame*, 610–14.

my finger moving and his death are the causal products of my intent to kill and my intent (or volition, willing) to move my finger.

7. $Consciousness_1$: *phenomenal experience.* The other deeply mysterious feature of our mind (along with Intentionality) is that we have conscious experience. This is how we are supposed to differ from "mindless" robots and, perhaps, from other animals. It once was thought that the Intentional states of belief, desire, intention, and emotion only existed as different forms of conscious experience. As an early philosophical critic of Freud once put this idea, "when I reflect on what I mean by a wish or an emotion or a feeling, I can only find that I know and think of them simply as different forms of consciousness."[35] But this is plainly too circumscribed a view of when those Intentional states exist. Conscious experience is crucial to us being who we are, but it is not *that* crucial. We have many beliefs, desires, intentions, and emotions that are not conscious in this sense. Long before Freud became popular, William James noted that many of the mental states that guide skilled or habitual behavior do so without being the subject of conscious attention.[36]

Still, if none of such states were the subject of conscious experience, we would be very different creatures than in fact we are. There is a centrality to *conscious* deliberations in terms of desires, beliefs, intentions, and emotions such that the nonconscious versions of these are nonetheless tied in one way or another to the conscious versions. As even Freud acknowledged, "the property of being conscious or not is in the last resort our one beacon-light in the darkness of depth-psychology."[37]

This is because there is a core identification of self with our conscious experience. Each of us experiences himself or herself as a unified self because we experience a continuity between our conscious experiences, both at a time and over time through memory, as Locke famously noted.[38] We identify mental states as part of ourselves through their accessibility via our conscious experience of them. And we sense that we are in control of our bodies and, through our bodies, the larger environment, by virtue of our conscious willings issuing causally in our voluntary actions.[39]

---

[35] G. C. Field, "Is the Conception of the Unconscious of Value in Psychology?," *Mind*, 31 (1922): 413–23, at 413–14.

[36] William James, *The Principles of Psychology* (Cambridge, MA: Harvard University Press, 1890), Vol. 2, p. 496.

[37] Sigmund Freud, *The Ego and the Id*, in Vol. 19 of *The Standard Edition of the Complete Psychological Works of Sigmund Freud*, James Strachey, ed. (London: Hogarth Press 1953–1975), 18.

[38] Locke's doctrine of the continuity of consciousness is explored in David Wiggins, "Locke, Butler, and the Stream of Consciousness: And Men as a Natural Kind," in A. Rorty, ed., *The Identities of Persons* (Berkeley: University of California Press, 1976).

[39] Ownership of actions through conscious experience of agency is explored in Suparna Choudhury and Sarah-Jayne Blakemore, "Intentions, Actions, and the Self," in S. Pockett, W. Banks, and S. Gallagher, eds., *Does Consciousness Cause Behavior?* (Cambridge, MA: MIT Press 2006).

8. Consciousness₂: privileged access. Paradoxically, we can be conscious of a mental state without having any datable experience in consciousness of that state. James's examples of skilled or habitual behavior serves to illustrate this. We can guide our automobile through complicated maneuvers on a curvy mountain road "with our mind on something else."[40] In such cases we are conscious of our behaviors and the mental states that guide them, in a nonexperiential sense of "conscious." What we mean in such cases is dispositional: we can become aware experientially if the need arises, and we can state what we are doing and why if the need arises; this is because we have the same noninferential way of knowing these items as we do for consciously experienced states. Such immediate, noninferential, nonobservational knowledge of the contents of our mind is usually termed a kind of "privileged access."

This attribute of our minds—our epistemic advantage in the way we each know our own mind—is often confused with two stronger claims.[41] These are the claims of incorrigibility and of transparency. We would be *incorrigible* in our beliefs about the contents of our own minds if we could not be wrong about them, so that, for example, if I believe I intend to help another, then necessarily I do indeed intend to help another. Transparency is the converse of the incorribility claim. Our mental states would be *transparent* to us if their existence necessarily generated a belief in their existence by us, so that, for example, if I intend to help another, then necessarily I know that I intend to help another.

In their criticism of folk psychology cognitive scientists and neuroscientists often attribute to folk psychology these much stronger theses. But in this they are unjustified. The folk psychology on which law and morality are built only supposes a privileged access in its weakest sense (of noninferential way of knowing).[42] It is not committed to the kind of omniscience about our own minds that would be true if the incorrigibility and transparency theses were true.

These eight characteristics I take to be the fundamental features of ourselves constituting us as commonsense selves, persons, moral agents, and legal subjects. Often in the scientific literature critical of folk psychology, a number of other characteristics are assigned to it, unsurprisingly making it more vulnerable to criticism. Two such characteristics are particularly salient.

9. Free will. Many cognitive scientists, joined by not a few lawyers, assume that desert-based political theories such as retributivism are hos-

[40] Dan Dennett's James-inspired example in *Contents and Consciousness* (London: Routledge and Kegan Paul, 1969).

[41] I separate the three claims in Moore, *Law and Psychiatry*, 254–65.

[42] For a discussion, see Richard Rorty, "Incorrigibility as the Mark of the Mental," *Journal of Philosophy*, 67 (1970): 399–424.

tage to the supposition that our wills are free in the sense of uncaused. The idea is that only if we are free in this sense do we have any real options, any real choice. Often this idea is conjoined with the autonomy claim (number 6 above) by saying that we need not only to be uncaused, but uncaused *causers*. Aquinas's *prima causa* is the idea. But it is important to separate these two claims. That our choices cause voluntary actions is one claim (the autonomy claim); that such choices themselves are uncaused is another, quite distinct claim.

Stephen Morse has shown quite persuasively that nothing in the criminal law as stated by its doctrines requires a finding that the accused had free will.[43] If a rational agent performs a voluntary act that in fact and proximately causes a legally prohibited result, and if he does so intending, foreseeing, or unreasonably risking that result in circumstances where he had adequate capacity and opportunity not to do so, then he is responsible and punishable under the general doctrines of Anglo-American criminal law.[44] Morse is right that formally nothing here is said about free will.

Yet those who think that free will is a supposition of both moral responsibility and of desert-based legal institutions would locate that supposition beneath and behind such legal doctrines, not in them. The idea is that no act can truly be *voluntary*, no *intention* or *belief* can cause such acts, no acts can be those of a *rational agent*, no *capacity* or *opportunity* to do otherwise can exist, unless the actor possesses free will. The supposition, in other words, is thought to be a hidden, metaphysical supposition required by morality, not an on-the-surface requirement of explicit legal doctrine. As Josh Greene and Gerald Cohen see it:

current legal doctrine, although officially compatibilist, is ultimately grounded in intuitions that are . . . libertarian . . . the law *says* that it presupposes nothing more than a metaphysically modest notion of free will that is perfectly compatible with determinism. However, we argue that the law's intuitive support is ultimately grounded in a metaphysically overambitious, libertarian notion of free will that is threatened by determinism and, more pointedly, by forthcoming cognitive neuroscience.[45]

---

[43] Stephen J. Morse, "New Neuroscience, Old Problems," in B. Garland, ed., *Neuroscience and the Law: Brain, Mind, and the Scale of Justice* (New York: Dana Press, 2004), 157–98.

[44] Moore, *Placing Blame*, 43–64.

[45] Greene and Cohen, "Neuroscience Changes Nothing," 1776. It is a bit disingenuous of Greene and Cohen to interpret Morse as dealing *only* at the level of legal doctrine. One of Professor Morse's lifetime projects has been to show that there is no presupposition of free will in the morals and metaphysics that make sense of the legal doctrines we have. See, for example, most recently, Morse, "Determinism and the Death of Folk Psychology: Two Challenges to Responsibility From Neuroscience," *Minnesota Journal of Law, Science, and Technology*, 9 (2008): 1–35.

10. Cartesian dualism. The free will supposition tends to require an even more extraordinary supposition,[46] which is that our mental states exist in an entirely different plane of existence than that in which physical states (including brain states) exist. This is the supposition of metaphysical dualism. Because Descartes proposed the best known form of this doctrine, the supposition most commonly is that of a Cartesian kind of metaphysical dualism.[47]

It is not difficult to see from where the dualist temptation arises. Supposing our wills to be free from causation requires some account of how that is possible. Cartesian dualism supplies such an account: mental states, existing in time but not in space, and having no mass and no energy, are not subject to the causal influences of items (like brain states) that are located in space as well as in time and do possess both mass and energy.

This of course is to leave the frying pan for the fire, in light of the stunning implausibility of all forms of Cartesian dualism.[48] A long tradition in philosophy has argued that one can avoid both the fire and the frying pan by not supposing that we have free will.[49] But again, my point here is more preliminary: it is to see that folk psychology is often stuck with a separate presupposition about who we are that, if made, would make that psychology (and anything built upon it) very vulnerable to criticism indeed.

We now need to turn to the challenges offered up by contemporary neuroscience to this view of who we are. As we shall see, neuroscientists tend to reject Cartesian dualism (point 10), free will (point 9), and all forms of privileged access (point 8). Some neuroscientists also reject the autonomy thesis (point 6) and that part of the consciousness thesis (point 7) that ascribes causal efficacy to our willings or to our consciousness of those willings. In addition, there is a sprinkling of criticisms in cognitive science that deny the Intentionality thesis and the thesis of the tripartite soul (points 1 and 2), the coherence over time of character (point 5),[50] and various other aspects of folk psychology. What we now need to see is how all such challenges are mounted.

---

[46] The drive to Cartesian dualism from concerns about free will was classically charted in Gilbert Ryle, *The Concept of Mind* (London: Hutcheson, 1949). Not all libertarians take refuge in dualism. See Robert Kane, *The Significance of Free Will* (Oxford: Oxford University Press, 1996); Kane, "Responsibility, Luck, and Chance," *Journal of Philosophy,* 96 (1999): 217–40.

[47] Descartes, *The Passions of the Soul* (New York: Hackett Publishing, 1989) (originally published 1649).

[48] If the different plane of existence insulates mind from causal influences, that seemingly is purchased by a like inability of mind to do any causing.

[49] My own compatibilist views may be found in Moore, *Placing Blame,* chap. 12.

[50] See, e.g., Gilbert Harman, "Moral Philosophy Meets Social Psychology," *Proceedings of the Aristotelian Society* 99 (1999): 315–31. A recent summary of the "situationism versus character" debate is Hagop Sarkissian, "Minor Tweaks, Major Payoffs: The Problems and Promise of Situationism in Moral Philosophy," *Philosophers Imprint,* 10 (2010): 1–15.

II. The Challenges of Modern Cognitive Science

I shall proceed as follows. I shall first discuss the three sorts of data from which the challenges of modern cognitive science are mounted. I will then provisionally extract six distinct challenges mounted from such data. In the conclusion I shall reorganize these challenges along the lines suggested in the discussion in the body of the paper. My intent in proceeding in this "bottom up" (or inductive) way, is to let neuroscientists make their case in their own terms, as much as possible.

A. The challenging data of neuroscience

It is common to group the neuroscientific challenges to folk psychology as stemming from two sorts of data:[51] that associated with the name of the late Benjamin Libet, and that associated with the name of Daniel Wegner. While I shall shortly summarize each of these challenging sets of data, there is another set of data that is much more diffuse, much more a product of a century of research rather than any particular experimental program, and much more still a promise of future success than a matter of already established fact. I shall start with this last data.

1. Reductionism. The greatest challenge(s) presented by neuroscience seems (judging at least from the popular literature) to stem from the anticipated reduction of mental states, and the actions they produce, to physical states of the human body. That each mental state of belief, desire, intention, and emotion is in fact a brain state, and that each voluntary human action is at base no more than a bodily movement caused in a certain way by these mechanistic brain states, seems to challenge many people's conception of themselves as responsible agents.

Why such data seems challenging I will describe in subpart B below. But here I shall describe more of what the data is that seems to ground such challenges. Let me start with the idea of reductionism itself: Reductionism comes in different flavors. An older form of reductionism was to conceive of the reducibility of one discourse to another in terms of the *synonymy* of the terms used in each of the two (putatively) different discourses. Thus, talk about bachelors can be reduced to talk about unmarried male persons because "bachelor" and "unmarried male person" mean the same thing. Let us call this *analytical* reductionism, because the connecting statement ("All bachelors are unmarried male persons") is thought to be an analytic truth, namely, true by virtue of the meaning of the words alone.[52]

---

[51] Susan Pockett, William Banks, and Shaun Gallagher, "Introduction," in Pockett, Banks, and Gallagher, eds., *Does Consciousness Cause Behavior?* (Cambridge, MA: MIT Press, 2006), 1–4.

[52] I discuss analytical reductionism (in ethics particularly, where it is associated with G. E. Moore), in Michael Moore, "Legal Realty: A Naturalist Approach to Legal Ontology," *Law*

Less ambitious than analytic reductionism is metaphysical (or "onto-logical") reductionism.[53] The crucial relation here is (numerical) identity, not synonymy. Even if "Evening Star," "Morning Star," and "Venus" do not *mean* the same thing (in some sense of meaning), still one can be reduced to the other in the sense that these are all but different ways of referring to the same thing (namely, the planet Venus). Likewise, even if "water" and "H_2O" do not mean the same thing, each can be reduced to the other in that these two expressions refer to the same natural kind of thing.

Analytical and metaphysical reductions permit some form of substitution of one term for another. In the case of analytic reductions the substitution of one term for another with which it is synonymous cannot change the *meaning* of the sentences in which such terms appear. In the case of metaphysical reductions, the substitution of one term for another cannot change the *truth value* of the sentence in which such terms appear.

Thirdly, there are what are usually called *nomological* reductions.[54] Here the key relationship is neither synonymy between words nor identity between the things referred to by such words; rather, it is the extensional equivalence between statements using the different words. Thus, if "x is M if and only if x is P" is true, then the extensions (the class of things of which a predicate is true) of M and P are the same. This can be true even if the properties, M, P, are not identical, and even if the words, "M" and "P" are not synonymous. Still, such extensional equivalences allow one to substitute "P" for "M," and vice-versa, and still preserve truth. Laws in terms of M predicates, thus, may be replaced with laws in terms of P predicates. Thus the name: *nomological* reductionism.

Usually those who have talked of the "reduction of mind to brain" have meant a metaphysical reduction: mental states just are brain states. Such reductionists may or may not expect or hope for a nomological reduction as well—that depends on one's view of the independence of laws when the identity of mind to brain is of the "multiple realizability" kind. Some versions of this last view hold that the best laws (and thus the best explanations in terms of such laws) may be framed in mental state terms, even if mental states are "nothing but" (a complex disjunction of) brain states.[55]

On the merits, there are two identities we should consider. The first is the identity of actions with the movements of the human machine. It is a long-held thesis (originating in the philosophy of action rather than neuro-science, but no matter)[56] that all the diverse kinds of actions we do—such

---

and Philosophy, 21 (2002): 619–705, at 665–69, reprinted in Michael Moore, *Objectivity in Ethics and Law* (Aldershot, UK: Ashgate, 2004), 365–69.

[53] Ibid., 369–70.
[54] Ibid., 370–71.
[55] Ibid., 372–93.
[56] See Moore, *Act and Crime;* Moore, "Renewed Questions."

as signaling our allies, deceiving a friend, checkmating an opponent in chess, etc.—are no more than movements of the human body. The thesis is that each particular action that we do ("act-token") is identical or partially identical to some discrete bodily movement. Such movements become instances of types of actions ("act-types") like signaling, deceiving, and checkmating, when those movements take place in certain circumstances and/or produce certain consequences in the external world.

Actions are thus at base physical things, specifically movements of the human body. To understand the nature of such movements is thus to understand human actions. Cognitive science for the past century has contributed much to our understanding of the mechanics of such movements. An organized sketch of such an understanding should start with the muscles and work upwards to higher functions.[57] The immediate cause of voluntary movement lies in the muscles themselves. On the limbs these are arranged in flexor/extensor pairs, the flexor muscles bringing limbs closer to the body and the extensor muscles drawing limbs away. Early on the well-known psysiologist Sir Charles Sherrington charted how these pairs are subject to the principle of reciprocal innervation.[58] This means that as a flexor muscle contracts its paired extensor muscle is inhibited from contracting, and vice versa. Such coordination prevents deadlock and allows movement to take place.

The muscles themselves are stimulated or inhibited by pairs of efferent neurons ending in the motor end plates attached to the muscles. These efferent neurons are matched by pairs of afferent neurons that transmit from muscle back to brain (rather than from brain to muscle, the direction of the efferent neurons). These afferent neurons are the feedback communication channels giving the brain information about how the muscles are performing.

What happens above the efferent neurons attached to the motor end plates depends on what kind of bodily movement is involved. The shortest story is that about the spinal reflexes, so called because the origin of these movements never gets higher than the spine itself. Some spinal reflex circuits, like the monosynaptic stretch reflex exemplified by the knee jerk (patellar) reflex, contain but a single synapse, which connects directly onto the efferent neurons that stimulate/inhibit the relevant muscle pairs. This is what makes such reactions so quick (about fifty milliseconds). Other reflexes, like the pain withdrawal reflex, use a reflex arc

[57] I am indebted to my MacArthur Foundation Law and Neuroscience Project Decisions and Intentions Working Group co-chair John Cacioppo of the University of Chicago for much of the information that immediately follows. See Cacioppo and Moore, "Decisions and Intentions Working Group," Working Paper of the MacArthur Foundation Law and Neuroscience Project, Normal Decision-Making Research Network, January, 2008. See also Susan Pockett, "The Neuroscience of Movement," in Pockett, Banks, and Gallagher, Does Consciousness Cause Behavior? (Cambridge, MA: MIT Press, 2006), 9–24.
[58] Sherrington's work is summarized briefly in M. R. Bennett and P. M. S. Hacker, Philosophical Foundations of Neuroscience (Oxford: Blackwell, 2003), 41–42.

248   MICHAEL S. MOORE

passing through multiple synapses. Even so, such reflexes also do not leave the spinal cord, processing afferent signals and sending out efferent signals to the flexor muscles without going higher.

The spinal cord and the reflexes working through it are part of the lower (or "common," or "final") motor pathway. All human movement is generated by signals in this pathway, consisting anatomically of the spinal cord, brain stem, pons, and the axon fibrils extending to motor end plates on muscle fibers. Aside from the reflexes, efferent signals in the lower motor pathway are caused by signals from one of the two upper motor pathways. It has long been known that these two upper motor pathways are functionally as well as structurally differentiated. The phylogenetically oldest of these upper motor pathways, the extrapyramidal, handles motor reactions that are spontaneous, unplanned, or reactive to cues; such as laughing at a joke, reacting to a paper bag popped behind one's head, or smiling spontaneously at a pleasant face. These reactions are not spinal reflexes, because areas of the brain above the brain stem and the pons are involved. Structurally, most of the extra-pyramidal system is located in the basal ganglia.

It is the pyramidal upper motor pathway that handles most of what we think of as voluntary motor movement. This is the system used when we execute more general intentions after planning and deliberation about them. Structurally it consists of the motor strip of the primary motor cortex, which is functionally divided between the different body parts being controlled. Thus, there is an area of the strip to control the movement of thumbs, fingers, elbows, wrists, neck, brow, eyelids, lips, tongue, toes, ankles, knees, etc.

Above the primary motor cortex things get sketchier because they are less well-known. It seems well established that the supplementary motor area (SMA) and pre-supplementary motor area (pre-SMA) are activated in voluntary movement,[59] and that this takes place before activation of the primary motor cortex.[60] SMA activation is not a perfect indicator of voluntariness of motor movement, however. Such activation takes place for stray, unconscious finger movements,[61] and for movements engaged in due to hypnosis.[62] It also occurs when transcranial magnetic stimula-

[59] John C. Eccles, "The Initiation of Voluntary Movements by the Supplementary Motor Area," *Achieves of Psychiatry and Neurological Sciences*, 231 (1982): 423–39; Gary Goldberg, "Supplementary Motor Area Structure and Function: Review and Hypotheses," *Behavioral and Brain Sciences*, 8 (1985): 567–88; R. E. Passingham, *The Frontal Lobes and Voluntary Action* (Oxford: Oxford University Press 1998).

[60] Richard Passingham and Hakwan Lau, "Free Choice and the Human Brain," in Pockett, Banks, and Gallagher, eds., *Does Consciousness Cause Behavior?* (Cambridge, MA: MIT Press, 2006), 53–72.

[61] A. I. Keller and H. Heckhausen, "Readiness Potentials Preceding Spontaneous Motor Acts: Voluntary vs. Involuntary Control," *Electroencephalography and Clinical Neurophysiology,* 76 (1990): 351–61.

[62] Patrick Haggard, Peter Cartledge, Meilyr Dafydd, and David Oakley, "Anomalous Control: When 'Free-Will' Is Not Conscious," *Consciousness and Cognition,* 13 (2004): 646–54.

tion artificially causes movement through the pyramidal upper motor pathway.[63]

Things are much more speculative for the reasoning, goals, and general or distal intentions that in commonsense psychology cause volitionally caused bodily movement. Areas within the parietal cortex and the frontopolar cortex have been provisionally linked to these higher functions.[64] The picture of human action that emerges from all of this is a picture of a complicated well-organized machine, the human body. The neuroscientific picture of the mental states of more general intention, belief, desire, and emotion that cause human action, is similarly mechanical and machine-like. This is the second identity we need to consider, that of mental states like intentions being identical with certain brain events. Locating the areas of the brain that oxygenated blood flows reveal to be activated when we form a certain intention is a start in identifying such intentions with some brain states.[65] But it is only a start, and a modest one at that. For left untouched by such area mappings is the basic question of what the mechanisms are by which such areas of the brain produce such mental states. How does a decision (choice, intention) about what to eat for lunch arise out of the mechanical equipment that is the brain—a complicated set of two-valued switches going off? How does the pattern of firing of such two-valued switches in the brain give rise to mental phenomenon, with its Intentionality,[66] its privileged access, and its subjective experience?[67]

Contemporary neuroscience cannot answer such questions at present. But there is nothing that suggests that, in principle, it will not be able to

[63] I. Fried, A. Katz, G. McCarthy, K. J. Sass, P. Williamson, S. S. Spencer, and D. D. Spencer, "Functional Organization of Human Supplementary Motor Cortex studied by Electrical Stimulation," *Journal of Neuroscience*, 11 (1991): 3656–66.

[64] John-Dylan Haynes, Katsuyuki Sakai, Geraint Rees, Sam Gilbert, Chris Frith, and Richard Passingham, "Reading Hidden Intentions in the Brain," *Current Biology*, 17 (2007): 323–28; Chun Siong Soon, Marcel Brass, Hans-Jochen Heinze, and John-Dylan Haynes, "Unconscious Determinants of Free Decisions in the Human Brain," *Nature Neuroscience*, 11 (2008): 543–45.

[65] R. A. Anderson and C. A. Buneo, "Intentional Maps in Posterior Parietal Cortex," *Annual Review of Neuroscience*, 25 (2002): 189–220; Michael Desmurget, Karen Reilly, Nathalie Richard, Alexandru Szathmari, Carmine Mottolese, and Angela Sirigu, "Movement Intention After Parietal Cortex Stimulations in Humans," *Science*, 324 (2009): 811–13.

[66] Patrick Haggard, "Conscious Intention and Motor Cognition," *TRENDS in Cognitive Science*, 9 (2005): 290–95; at 295:

> "The phenomenology of intention is poorly understood . . . the phenomenal content of intentions has hardly been studied experimentally. Reliable psychophysical procedures for investigating when and how the effects of an action are represented during preparation and intention would represent a major advance."

[67] Michael Gazzaniga quotes Roger Sperry thusly:

> "the centermost processes of the brain with which consciousness is presumably associated are simply not understood. They are so far beyond our comprehension that no one I know of has been able to imagine their nature."

do so in the not so distant future. Indeed, my colleague Mike Gazzaniga guesses that 98 to 99 percent of neuroscientists believe that this possibility will become a reality.[68] I thus attribute to neuroscience reductionist "data" that is at present only a speculative possibility.[69] I do this because it is this possibility that gives rise to the broader challenges that many people feel neuroscience presents to our conception of ourselves. This possibility is nicely illustrated by this imagined bit of neuroscience by Greene and Cohen:

> At some time in the future we may have extremely high-resolution scanners that can simultaneously track the neural activity and connectivity of every neuron in a human brain, along with computers and software that can analyse and organize these data. Imagine, for example, watching a film of your brain choosing between soup and salad. The analysis software highlights the neurons pushing for soup in red and the neurons pushing for salad in blue. You zoom in and slow down the film, allowing yourself to trace the cause-and-effect relationship between individual neurons—the mind's clockwork revealed in arbitrary detail. You find the tipping-point moment at which the blue neurons in your prefrontal cortex out-fire the red neurons, seizing control of your pre-motor cortex and causing you to say, 'I will have the salad, please'.[70]

Greene and Cohen hypothesize that many people would find such a reduction of decisions to a mechanical process of neuronal firings (the content of the decision being dictated by sheer numbers of firings of one kind of neuron over another) to challenge their sense of themselves as responsible agents. In this bit of speculative sociology about popular belief, I think they are right, for reasons I shall explore in subpart 2 below.

Gazzaniga, *Human: The Science Behind What Makes Us Unique* (New York: Harper Collins, 2008), 246.

[68] Gazzaniga, quoted in Richard Monastersky, "Religion on the Brain," *Chronicle of Higher Education*, May 26, 2006, A–15. Gazzaniga can't claim 100 percent adherence to reductionism because of outliers within neuroscience like Sir John Eccles. See Eccles, "The Initiation of Voluntary Movements;" Eccles and Popper, *How the Self Controls Its Brain* (Berlin: Springer-Verlag, 1994).

[69] Consider, for example, the large promissory notes issued in this reductionist view of intentions:

> "Intentions . . . are patterns of neural activity; or perhaps patterns of synaptic strength which are eventually played out into patterns of neural activity. Either kind of pattern clearly has both temporal and spatial extension, which means it must be located somewhere."

Susan Pockett, "The Neuroscience of Movement," 22 n. 1.

[70] Greene and Cohen, "Neuroscience Changes Nothing," 1781.

2. The Data of the Libet and Libet-Inspired Experiments. If we leave the globally reductionist ambitions of neuroscience for more concrete data actually collected, there are two sets of data that seem particularly challenging to folk psychology and to the moral and legal institutions built on that psychology.[71] The first of these stems from the experimental work of Benjamin Libet.[72] Libet's initial paper has been touted as "one of the most philosophically challenging papers in modern scientific psychology."[73] That paper, we are also told, reported a "groundbreaking experiment" that "forced upon the scientific and philosophical community" fundamental questions of free will, conscious efficacy, and the like.[74]

Libet built on work by two German neuroscientists in the early to mid-60's, who discovered that there was a slow negative shift in electrical potential in the brain of subjects who performed spontaneous (unplanned and not externally stimulated) voluntary movements of their fingers.[75] Using the technology of the day, electroencephalograms (EEG), Kornhuber and Deecke discovered that approximately one second before such movements took place this slow negative shift began, a shift they termed the "Bereitschaftspotential," and that has since been called in English the "Readiness Potential" (RP). The RP was detected by electrodes attached at the vertex of the scalp, and it evidences events taking place in the Supplementary Motor Area of the brain. Such SMA activity involved in voluntary motor movement has been shown by subsequent functional magnetic resonance imaging ("fMRI") and other techniques to precede the activation of the primary motor cortex (as well as the activation of motor pathways, motor plates, and muscles).[76]

Libet's innovation was to conjoin his longstanding interest in consciousness to this data about the brain area involved in voluntary motor movement. In Libet's best known experiments his subjects were told to flex their right wrists or the fingers of their right hands whenever they wished. EEG readings were taken from the subject's scalps over the relevant portions of their brain, the SMA. Such readings detected the negative shift, or RP, beginning about 550 milliseconds prior to the time at which their

[71] Susan Pockett, "Introduction," 1–4.
[72] B. Libet, C. A. Gleason, E. W. Wright, and D. K. Pearl, "Time of Conscious Intention to Act in Relation to Onset of Cerebral Activities (Readiness Potential); The Unconscious Initiation of a Freely Voluntary Act," *Brain*, 106 (1983): 623–42. These findings are restated in Libet, "Unconscious Cerebral Initiative and the Role of Conscious Will in Voluntary Action," *Behavioral and Brain Sciences*, 8 (1985): 529–39.
[73] Patrick Haggard, Chris Newman, and Elena Magno, "On The Perceived Time of Voluntary Actions," *British Journal of Psychology*, 90 (1999): 291–303, at 291.
[74] William Banks, "Does Consciousness Cause Misbehavior?," in Pockett, Banks, and Gallagher, eds., *Does Consciousness Cause Behavior?* (Cambridge: MA: MIT Press, 2006), 235–56.
[75] H. H. Kornhuber and L. Deecke, Hirnpotentialanderungen bei willkurbewegungen und passiven bewewungen des Menschen: beireitschaftspotential und reafferente potentiale," *Pflügers Archiv*, 284 (1965): 1–17.
[76] Passingham and Lau, "Free Choice and the Human Brain."

muscles began to move so as to flex their wrists or move their fingers. These subjects were also told to watch a spot revolving on a spatial clock and to register when their initial awareness of intending to move their wrist/fingers began. They reported the beginnings of awareness of their decision to move their finger or wrist on average 350 milliseconds after the shift in readiness potential began. Such beginning of awareness preceded the beginning of actual movement by 200 milliseconds.

We can represent these results along a simple schema that I will use throughout the remainder of this article. Let "t_1" be the time of the onset of the shift in readiness potential; "t_2," the time of initial awareness of an intention to move, and "t_3," the time of the beginning of the bodily movement in question. The basic schema is represented below:

t_1	t_2	t_3
(onset of RP)	(onset of awareness of intention to move)	(onset of bodily movement)

The total time from t_1 to t_3 is 550 milliseconds, t_2 being located 350 milliseconds after t_1 and 200 milliseconds before t_3. Libet added two more times of some interest here. One is Libet's corrected time of the onset of awareness; finding from other studies an error of about 50 milliseconds in subjects' estimation of the onset of awareness of sensations generally, Libet corrected the temporal location of t_2 to be 50 milliseconds closer to t_3, and 50 milliseconds further from t_1, than the subjects reported. Secondly, Libet notes that (what I shall call) the "Rubicon Point"—the point beyond which the subject cannot stop the movement already decided upon—occurs 50 milliseconds prior to actual muscle movement initiation (t_3) and 100 milliseconds after the corrected time for onset of awareness of the decision to move (t_2).

The values above for t_1, t_2, and t_3 are given for what Libet called "Type II RP's." These are readiness potentials and awareness onsets measured when subjects both were instructed to move whenever they wished and when they reported (in post movement debriefings) no experience of any advanced pre-planning to move. Shifts in readiness potential measured when there was such experience of pre-planning, or where subjects were not free to move spontaneously (i.e., where they moved in response to a pre-set signal), Libet termed "Type I RP's." Type I RP's had considerably earlier onsets than did Type II RP's (about 1050 milliseconds prior to movement).

In what follows I shall focus on Type II RP's, as did Libet. For Libet thought "that the RP component that starts at about—550 milliseconds, the one that predominates in Type II RP's, . . . is the one uniquely associated with an exclusively endogenous volitional process."[77] It is this

---

[77] Libet, "Unconscious Cerebral Initiative," at 532.

data that thus forms the core of the neuroscientific challenge(s) to the presuppositions about intentions made by the law and morality in their responsibility assessments.

Libet's results have been replicated in subsequent experiments.[78] Considerable critical commentary and research attention have been focused on the accuracy of persons' perceptions of when awareness of their decision to move begins.[79] But however one construes the degree of inaccuracy here, or their skewing effects by various influences, Libet's main result seems secure: brain processes initiating voluntary motor movement began before reported awareness of any decision to move.

Libet's result has been extended to a variety of other circumstances. Haggard and Elm found the RP pattern to exist when subjects were given the freedom to use either their left or their right hand, thus involving more choice than simply whether to move a given finger or a given wrist.[80] In such cases a lateralized RP ("LRP") was discovered later than the onset of RP, indicating when one hand's movement rather than another has been specifically selected. Movements taking place when greater freedom of movement is open to subjects have also shown the RP pattern, as have experiments giving greater freedom as to *when* a movement takes place.[81] Movements done under hypnosis[82] and movements induced by transcranial magnetic stimulation,[83] have also been studied, showing activation of the same brain areas.

The time before awareness of decision by the subject has also been considerably extended. Lau has found distinctively movement-initiating brain activity (in the pre-SMA) two to three seconds prior to motor movement, much earlier that the .5 to 1.5 seconds typical for the RP pattern in the SMA.[84] John-Dylan Hayne's even more recent study[85] isolated activity in areas of the frontopolar cortex and the parietal cortex, which activities were predictive of which finger the subject would move, left or right

---

[78] Passingham and Lau, "Free Choice and the Human Brain," 55.

[79] Much of the peer commentary in the 1985 symposium in *Behavioral and Brain Sciences* was on this topic. See, e.g., Richard Latte, "Consciousness as an Experimental Variable: Problems of Definition, Practice, and Interpretation," *Behavioral and Brain Sciences*, 8 (1985): 545–46; James Ringo, "Timing Volition: Questions of What and When About W," ibid., 550–51. See also Patrick Haggard, Sam Clark, and Jeri Kalogeras, "Voluntary Action and Conscious Awareness," *Nature Neuroscience*, 5 (2002): 382–85; Patrick Haggard and Sam Clark, "Intentional Action: Conscious Experience and Neural Prediction," *Consciousness and Cognition*, 12 (2003): 695–707. And the debate continues. William Banks and Eve Isham, "We Infer Rather Than Perceive the Moment We Decided to Act," *Psychological Science*, 20 (2009): 17–21.

[80] Patrick Haggard and Martin Elmer, "On the Relation Between Brain Potentials and the Awareness of Voluntary Movements," *Experimental Brain Research*, 126 (1999): 128–33.

[81] Passingham and Lau, "Free Choice and the Human Brain," 55–56.

[82] Haggard, Cartledge, Dafydd, and Oakley, "Anomalous Control."

[83] Fried, Katz, et al., "Functional Organization."

[84] This was when subjects were told to attend to their intention to move. H. C. Lau, R. D. Rogers, P. Haggard, and R. E. Passingham, "Attention to Intention," *Science*, 303 (2004): 1208–10.

[85] Haynes, et al., "Reading Hidden Intentions in the Brain."

index finger, up to seven to ten seconds prior to movement (and up to six to nine seconds prior to awareness of the decision to move one finger or the other). One of Haynes's other studies found a similar pattern of brain activity when the choice was about adding or subtracting—a purely mental operation involving no motor movement by the subject.[86] This suggests his measurements are of a more distal intention or decision, as opposed to the motor-related and immediate "act now" decision studied by Libet.

3. *The data of the Wegner and Wegner—Inspired Experiments.* The third major type of specific psychological literature taken to be challenging of our actions of responsible agency is that associated with the work of Daniel Wegner. Wegner's work should be seen as part of a larger set of data dealing with the degree to which we are accurate in judging the causes of our own behavior. Nisbett and Wilson much earlier explored a fact widely recognized by good novelists long before Freud, namely, that even our most sincere judgments of what *moves* us to action (that is, our motives) are often mistaken.[87] John Bargh's more recent work has shown in convincing detail how many unconscious influences there are on what we (consciously) decide and do,[88] influences of which we are not aware (and which we disavow when others bring them to our attention). For example, in reaction time experiments, subjects are found to make faster approach movements of their arm (such as pulling a lever toward oneself) if they have, however unconsciously, positively evaluated the object named on the screen, and they are found to make faster avoidance movements (such as pushing the lever away) if they have, however unconsciously, negatively evaluated the object on the screen.[89] Bargh extends this to explain everyday behavior. He explains some of voting behavior, for example, in terms of immediate visceral reactions to one second showings of the facial appearance of candidates for election.[90]

Despite these antecedents, the best known of this literature is Daniel Wegner's misleadingly titled book, *The Illusion of Conscious Will.*[91] This sounds like a book producing evidence that the will is caused by unwilled brain events, and/or that the will does not in fact cause the bodily move-

---

[86] Haynes, et al., "Unconsciousness Determinants of Free Decision."

[87] R. E. Nisbett and T. D. Wilson, "Telling More Than We Can Know: Verbal Reports on Mental Processes," *Psychological Review*, 84 (1977): 231–59.

[88] Bargh helpfully summarizes into ten categories a lifetime of his research on what he has called "the automaticity of everyday life," (Bargh, "The Automaticity of Everyday Life," in R. S. Wyer, ed., *Advances in Social Cognition*, 10 (1997): 1–61), in his "Free Will Is Un-natural," in J. Baer, J. Kaufman, and R. Baumeister, eds., *Are We Free?: Psychology and Free Will* (Oxford: Oxford University Press, 2008), 128–54, esp. at 136–49. These include evidence of "unconscious goal pursuit over time," "the absence of ability to accurately report on one's intentions," "the scarcity of conscious self-regulatory capacity," "the unconscious mimicry of others' behavior," and other items. Ibid., 148.

[89] Ibid., 138.

[90] Ibid.

[91] Daniel Wegner, *The Illusion of Conscious Will* (Cambridge, MA: MIT Press, 2002).

ments it seems to cause. Yet the data produced are not of this sort and in fact support quite different theses.[92] The book's theses are epistemic: we do not have direct access to the causing of bodily movements by our consciously willing them, and as a result, we are (perhaps sometimes, often, or always) wrong in our judgments of whether our willings have caused the bodily movements they seem to cause. As Wegner puts his thesis, "The illusion of conscious will is the belief that we are intrinsically informed of how our minds cause our actions by the fact that we have an experience of causation that occurs in our minds."[93] Or more crisply: "The experience of conscious will . . . is not direct evidence of a causal relation between thought and action."[94] Rather than our knowledge of our own minds being a direct, non-inferential privileged access, Wegner holds that "conscious will is an experience that arises from the interpretation of cues to cognitive causality" and that this is "an interpretive process that is fundamentally separate from the mechanistic process of real mental causation."[95]

One implication of the fact that our knowledge is inferential and "not a direct readout of some psychological force that causes action from inside the head,"[96] is that we are fallible knowers of when we acted. Wegner assembles experiments and historical anecdotes both ways: both where we think we have not acted but in reality we have; and where we think we have acted but in reality we have not. He, thus, denies the transparency and incorrigibility claims of strong privileged access.

Wegner calls instances of the first kind "automatisms." These include: the alien hand syndrome (think Dr. Strangelove), where "a person experiences one hand as operating with a mind of its own";[97] movements during hypnosis, where sometimes subjects report that "they felt no sense of moving their arm voluntarily but rather experienced the downward movement as something happening to them";[98] the table turning done in nineteenth-century séances where a group sitting at a table for an extended period experiences the table as rotating on its own when, in fact, by minute movements people in the group are collectively moving it;[99] the modern descendant of this, the Ouija Board, where a group may produce an intelligible message with each member of the group experiencing a "sense of involuntariness" that can be "quite stunning";[100] automatic

---

[92] In his reply to the open peer commentary on his book, Wegner acknowledges that "people often read much more into *ICW* than is there," and that part of the fault for that lies with Wegner's choice of a "fighting" title. Wegner, "Author's Response," *Behavioral and Brain Sciences* 27 (2004): 679-88, at 679, 682.
[93] Ibid., 682.
[94] Ibid., 679.
[95] Wegner, *The Illusion of Conscious Will*, 96.
[96] Ibid., 65
[97] Ibid., 4.
[98] Ibid., 6.
[99] Ibid., 7-8, 100–102.
[100] Ibid., 110.

writing, which despite a lack of consciousness about the content being produced or despite a lack of experience of willing the movements involved, can produce intelligent prose;[101] the Chevreul pendulum which moves when the subject wishes not to move it and which can even move in directions the subject wants not to move it;[102] movements of dowsing rods, which can be experienced as involuntary even though clearly responsive to knowledge of the moving subject.[103]

Wegner also spends considerable time detailing the old (William James, e.g.) and new (John Bargh, e.g.) experiments on ideomotor actions. These are movements guided by thoughts without any apparent mediation by will between thought and action. Absent-minded munching during social conversations, tilting in response to imagining falling over, unconscious mimicry of others' acts, are examples.[104] Wegner's conclusion about all such behaviors is that "thinking about acting can produce movement quite without the feeling of doing," [105] and that "these actions seem to roll off in a way that skips intention." [106]

In a way, Wegner's focus on automatisms is curious. If one wanted to show that sometimes we act voluntarily without knowing that we do so, these would not be the sort of examples that would come to mind. For although Wegner dubs them "unconscious actions," [107] few of them would be considered the kind of voluntary movements with which we identify human action. Freud's older examples of unconscious actions—certain dreams, parapraxes, and neurotic symptoms—seem to make the point better, because Freud's distinctive claim here was that the subject could recapture (in principle, at least) the act-ish phenomenal feel that was lacking when the actor acted.[108]

Yet Wegner's target here is not so much the transparency thesis—if we are acting, we know that we are. Rather, what he wants to infer from examples of automatism is that there is no causal connection between what really causes our behavior, on the one hand, and our experience of causing our behavior, on the other. As Wegner puts it, "automatism and ideomotor action may be windows on true mental causation as it occurs without apparent mental causation." [109] The suggestion is not like Freud's; Wegner is not out to expand the category of behaviors we should consider actions, as was Freud. Rather, he is out to establish that we in general have no privileged access to the real workings that produce our voluntary

---

[101] Ibid., 103–108.

[102] Ibid., 113–16.

[103] Ibid., 116–20.

[104] Ibid., 120–30.

[105] Ibid., 125.

[106] Ibid., 130.

[107] Ibid., 100

[108] On Freudian examples and analysis of unconscious actions, see Moore, *Law and Psychiatry*, 311–22.

[109] Wegner, *The Illusion of Conscious Will*, 130.

behavior, because the source of that access—our experience of will—has no connection to those real workings.

The trick for Wegner is moving from the somewhat recherché phenomena of automatisms to his desired truth of general psychology. The move for him is from the observed fact that in the automatisms, thought controls action without the mediation of will or intention. The general truth which he wishes to infer from this is that this is no less true for ordinary voluntary actions.[110] These too, he urges, are produced by the "empirical will" unmediated by the workings of the conscious will that we experience, no matter how much our experience of that conscious will inclines us to believe otherwise.

The other kind of phenomena that are the focus of Wegner's attentions are those where there is an experience of willing the behavior but that behavior does not in fact occur. Wegner calls these cases of the "illusion of control."[111] Examples from everyday life include "body English" executed on erring golf shots, the sense in gambling that we had some control of dice, coins, or roulette balls,[112] perceived "sports jinxes" where one thinks one's mere presence at a sporting event affects the outcome of that event, and the like.[113] More persuasive, perhaps, are the data of more scientific studies and experiments. One of these is Wegner's own, the "I spy" study. Here the subject infers that *she* has selected items on a screen showing a group of items taken from the familiar child's game, "I Spy"; in reality, a confederate moved the cursor. The illusion of control in the subject was created by priming the thought of the item selected just before the item was selected on the screen. The illusion was measured by the subject's self-report of intending and allowing the movements.[114]

Other "illusion of control" cases include dramatic instances of confabulation, where the subject makes up intentions he could not possibly have had. These occur in both split-brain patients and in those making movements in response to post-hypnotic suggestions. "Split-brain" subjects are those whose connecting tissue between the two hemispheres of their brain has been severed or damaged. In experimental conditions with such persons in which the input and output functions of each hemisphere are separated (so the left hand literally does not know what the right hand is doing), subjects nonetheless confabulate intentions to explain behavior to which really they must be clueless.[115] Similar confabulation has long been studied by subjects who move their limbs in response to post-hypnotic suggestions: people invent inten-

[110] Ibid., 143–44.
[111] Ibid., 8.
[112] Ibid., 80.
[113] Ibid., 10.
[114] Ibid., 74–78.
[115] Ibid., 181–84.

tions they couldn't possibly have had in order to explain why they did what they did.[116]

About all such cases of the "illusion of control," Wegner concludes that "we are not infallible sources of knowledge about our own actions and can be duped into thinking we did things when events conspire to make us feel responsible."[117]

B. The challenges presented by the data of neuroscience

I think that many people find these three sorts of data unsettling of their sense of self, their sense of moral agency, and their sense that we can fairly be blamed and punished for our misdeeds. Yet just why this data seems threatening of basic aspects of our self-understanding may be unclear. This is because several different and distinct challenges to our self-understanding are raised by this data, and these separate points are often merged together as if they were one. This is done both by those raising these challenges and by those who would rebut them. It would help in the assessment of the merits of these challenges if we first get clear just what they are. That is the main task of the present paper.

1. *The eliminativist challenge.* Start with the (at present largely imagined) data of reductionism. One challenge directly spawned by this "data" is what I shall call the eliminativist challenge. This challenge is so named because the reduction of minds to brains, and of actions to physical movements, is taken by some to eliminate the self (or the "I") of conscious experience and agency. Consider this lament by Francis Crick:

"You, your joys and your sorrows, your memories and your ambitions, your sense of personal identity and free will are in fact no more than the behavior of a vast assembly of nerve cells and their associated molecules. Who you are is nothing but a pack of neurons."[118]

The challenge of reductionism is that we are said to lose our mental life and our agency—indeed, our very *selves*—if we are "nothing but" machines. Holding us responsible, or attributing to us subjective experience, would make no more sense than it would to do so for other, more obvious machines, namely, robots, automobiles, or lunar landers. As Richard Dawkins once said, punishing us (if reductionism is true) would make as much sense as John Cleese's famous scene in *Faulty Towers*, where Cleese

---

[116] Ibid., 149–51.
[117] Ibid., 10–11.
[118] Francis Crick, *The Astonishing Hypothesis* (New York: Scribrer's, 1994), 3.

punishes his automobile for its poor performance by beating it with a sledge hammer.[119]

Despite its popularity, inferring this challenge from the reductionist ambitions of neuroscience is puzzling. One can grasp just how puzzling this is by comparing the present eliminativist challenge to the metaphysical position known as "eliminative materialism" in philosophy.[120] The eliminative materialist also believes that we should jettison talk of minds, selves, agency, and all that is built upon these (such as moral blameworthiness); yet she derives this skeptical conclusion from a *non*reductionist premise. It is precisely because we *cannot* reduce intentions to brain states, minds to brains, that we should dispense with these ghosts. It is because mental states (given their Intentionality) cannot be reduced to brain states that they can have no place in (what will turn out to be) the best explanation of human behavior, an explanation, in terms of brain states. In Greene and Cohen's imagined string of neural firings determining a decision of salad over soup for lunch, for example, there is no room for persons, selves, or moral agents, on nonreductionist premises. We—our agency—would have to be something extra, a ghostly commander leading the blue neurons (for salad with blue cheese dressing?) to victory over their red (for tomato soup?) competitors. And this is silly—it would make the soup versus salad decision at the neural level like the battle scenes in Kurosawa's film, Kagemusha, with all the roles in the scenes filled before selves enter the stage.

If, however, we reject the premise of philosophy's eliminative materialism—if in other words we embrace reductionism—this will have the potential to get us on the stage. Then, we, our intentions, agency, and the like, will be identical to some swatch of what is happening on that stage at the neural level; so if *it* is on stage, then so are "we."

Thus the puzzle: why is reductionism a challenge to all we value? How can it threaten us with loss of our selves and our responsibility when it is *non*reductionism that seems to threaten us with that kind of loss? We have faced this kind of puzzle before. Recall that a generation or more ago, Fred Skinner propounded two bases for moving "beyond freedom and dignity," beyond the "autonomous man," beyond the inner life of the mind.[121] One came to be called logical behaviorism, and it was reductionist: mental states like intentions just were logical constructs out of behavior, not inner causes of that behavior. The other came to be called

---

[119] Richard Dawkins, "Let's All Stop Beating Basil's Car." Dan Dennett recounts how Dawkins later came to regret his inference that retributivism and moral responsibility disappear with the reduction of us to machines. Dennett, "Some Observations on the Psychology of Thinking About Free Will," in J. Baer, J. Kaufman, and R. Baumeister, *Are We Free? Psychology and Free Will* (Oxford: Oxford University Press, 2008), 253.

[120] Alluded to briefly above, text at nn. 22–24, supra. Patricia Churchland is a standard example of an eliminative materialist in philosophy. See her *Neurophilosophy: Toward a Unified Science of the Mind/Brain* (Cambridge, MA: MIT Press, 1986).

[121] Discussed in Moore, *Law and Psychiatry*, 36–37.

methodological behaviorism, and it was nonreductionist: since mental states were not publicly observable in replicable experiments as was behavior itself, there was no place for these distinctively non-behavioristic, inner, private episodes in a properly scientific psychology.

A younger Dan Dennett once excoriated Skinner, declaring it "unfathomable" how Skinner could be so sloppy as to vacillate on such a watershed issue.[122] Yet if we look carefully at the kind of reduction Skinner's logical behaviorism was proposing, perhaps we can see how his reductionist logical behaviorism was as skeptical about mental states as was his nonreductionist, methodological behaviorism. This will not mean that one would not have to choose between these two kinds of skepticism—after all, the admission ticket to rational discussion of anything is not knowingly embracing a contradiction (like affirming and denying reductionism). Yet perhaps we can see how both rejection and acceptance of reductionism has (inconsistently, to be sure) made some people skeptical about minds, selves, and responsibility.

The skepticism of methodological behaviorism was easy to see. Explanations framed in terms of those methodologically inferior, private, nonobservable, nonreplicable things Skinner thought mental states to be, would inevitably lose out to explanations framed in terms of scientifically respectable entities like environmental stimuli and behavioral responses. Today's eliminative materialism is the direct descendent of methodological behaviorism, except that what makes mental state explanations inferior now includes Intentionality and what is better is brain state (rather than behaviorist) explanations. The skepticism of both is easily intelligible, however, and is of the same kind: physicalist explanations of behavior (of either kind) will be complete, with no need or room for mental state explanations; the latter explanations will lose out in any explanatory competition; and the entities and qualities such mental state explanations posit will disappear from our commitments "when our thoughts turn seriously ontological."[123]

The skepticism of logical behaviorism is more difficult to see. Logical behaviorism is an instance of what I call a skeptical reduction.[124] Saul Kripke's example of this is Hume on causation.[125] Hume famously identified the causal relation with the regular concurrence of events. For this reduction Humeans are rightly regarded as skeptics about causation,

---

[122] Daniel Dennett, *Brainstorms* (Montgomery, Vt.: Bradford Books, 1978), 63.

[123] W. W. O. Quine, *Ontological Relativity and Other Essays* (New York: Columbia University Press, 1969), 100 ("many of our causal remarks in the 'there are' form would want dusting up when our thoughts turn seriously ontological").

[124] Michael Moore, "Legal Reality: A Naturalist Approach to Legal Ontology," *Law and Philosophy*, 21 (2002): 619–705, at 649–53, reprinted in *Objectivity in Ethics and Law: Essays in Moral and Legal Ontology* (Aldershot, U.K.: Ashgate, 2004, 349–53).

[125] Saul Kripke, *Wittgenstein on Rules and Private Language* (Cambridge, MA: Harvard University Press, 1982), 66–68.

because that reduction leaves out what many thought distinctive of that relation, what Hume called the "cement" of the universe.

Logical behaviorism was a skeptical reduction in the same way, and so, for many people, is the neuroscientific reduction of mental states to brain states. For seemingly left behind by both is all that we prize in the life of the mind, all that (we thought) makes us different than robots and other "mere machines." Such reductions, whether behaviorist or neuroscientific, make many people skeptical because such reductions classify us differently than we previously thought. We thought we were special, and reductionism seemingly shows that we are not. We too are just machines.

2. *The lack-of-free-will challenges.* Apart from the threatened dissolution of self, a second and distinct challenge arises from reductionism, albeit as an indirect inference. This is the familiar challenge that we lack free will. This challenge, of course, has been with us for a very long time, well antedating the rise of neuroscience. In religious form the challenge was presented to Calvinists by their own doctrine of "predestination." According to this doctrine, God had already picked those who would enjoy the Christian Heaven before they were born—in which case, the challenge was, why make the effort to do good works? It was the rise of materialism with Hobbes that gave this challenge its distinctively modern form, a form in which mechanical processes replaced God as the cause of all we do.

Despite the fact that this challenge has been with us for a very long time, reductionist neuroscience presents the lack of free will challenge to responsible agency in a particularly dramatic and hard-to-ignore way. This is partly due to the immediacy of the causes presented by neuroscience: unlike genetic and environmental influences, brain states are much closer (spatiotemporally) to the behaviors they cause. Hence, it looks like there is less room for extraneous factors, or even chance, to intervene. "Brain states don't influence behavior; they fully cause it," is the inference sometimes drawn from this spatiotemporal closeness. This sense of *sufficient* causation is enhanced by another feature of neuroscientific explanations. This is that they are *complete*. All environmental and generic influences have to do their causal work *through* the human brain (the behaviorists' mistake was to think otherwise); Greene and Cohen nicely call this the "bottleneck" nature of neuroscientific explanations.[126] The result is, again, an enhanced sense of inevitability, here arising from neuroscientific explanations that by their nature are sufficient (during their "bottleneck" time-slice) to produce behavior.

The enhanced challenge presented by neuroscience is also partly due to the greater knowledge we are coming to possess about the causes of behavior that neuroscience posits. It is one thing to speculate in the abstract about there being causes of human choice; it is another to be told that

---

[126] Greene and Cohen, "Neuroscience Changes Nothing," 1781.

262   MICHAEL S. MOORE

certain patterns of firing by certain neurons in certain areas of the brain fully determine your choice for salad at lunch.

The concreteness of the causes that are the subject of neuroscientific explanation joins the immediacy, the completeness, and the better-known nature of such causes, in explaining why neuroscientific causation seems more challenging to responsible agency than is determinism generally. For neuroscience is not committed to a general determinism, one that denies that there are *any* uncaused causers in the universe; it can be agnostic about whether God, the Big Bang, energy level shifts by electrons, or some other form of Aquinas's *prima causa*, has ever existed. More importantly, neuroscience can be indifferent regarding whether determinism in general is true, either at the micro level of modern physics or at the macro level of everyday life. For the challenge presented *by brain-state* causation is independent of whether *universal* causation (determinism) is true. Even if the micro level (of energy shifts in electrons, e.g.) is irreducibly probabilistic, making the macro level the same but with much higher probabilities, that won't blunt the challenge to responsible agency presented by brain state explanations.

To see that this is so, let us isolate that challenge. There are, in fact, two versions of this lack-of-free-will challenge to responsible agency which need to be dealt with separately. The first, more radical version denies that choice is even possible if choice is caused by factors themselves unchosen. To show that "choice" is caused, on this version, is to show that choice does not exist. I call this the analytical version of the lack of free will challenge. For the plausibility of the challenge seemingly presupposes that it is analytic of the word, "choice," that the referent of the word be uncaused. Choices on this view differ markedly from most natural phenomena with which we are familiar. Take lakes for example. Imagine a claim that something could be a lake only if it was uncaused (no glaciation could explain Lake Michigan, for example). Since this is wildly implausible about lakes, choices must be very different from lakes in order for the analytic version of the lack of free will challenge to be very plausible.

The second, more moderate version, admits that there can be choices even if they are caused by factors themselves unchosen. Yet, this version asserts, there cannot be *responsible* choices in such a case. Being morally responsible and legally punishable for our choices is incompatible with causation of choice, even if choice itself is not. The nerve of this second thought is that if choice is caused by factors themselves unchosen, then we have no (real) choice, no (real) options to choose between, because in such a case we could not have acted other than we did. While our choices can still cause the behaviors chosen, the choices themselves constitute no (real) control over those behaviors because there is no control over the unchosen factors causing choice.

Neither of these challenges depend on determinism being true. Even if there were an irreducible randomness in the determination of human choice (because there were such randomness in the micro-physical processes constituting such choice), that would hardly give us more *control*, more *options*, more real *choice*. Such randomness is not more subject to our control than is a full causal determination. The probabilities of us choosing tomato soup for lunch would be completely fixed by factors over which we have no control, even if actually choosing tomato soup would not be completely fixed. Such randomness gives us no window of opportunity in which to effect our control. It is as dumb, as impervious to our efforts, as is full causal determination. Such randomness cannot frame a choice set giving us real options to choose between. It is nothing like the framing of real options done, for example, by the existence of both salad and soup for lunch.[127]

The upshot is that we can put the grand issues connected to the truth (or even the meaning) of determinism to the side. Neuroscience's concrete version of the lack of free will challenge(s) should be put as: *in whatever sense and to whatever extent macro-sized natural events and natural processes are caused*, so too are both human actions, and the choices that cause them, caused by brain states.

It remains to say how this challenge, like the eliminativist challenge, arises from the reductionist nature of neuroscience. How is it that for many neuroscientists, "if the self reduces to the brain . . . then the individual doesn't have real contra-causal free will . . . ?"[128] The answer lies in a straightforward inference. According to reductionism, mental states like intention are identical to certain brain states, and human actions are identical to those motions of the human body that are caused in the right way by such intentions/brain states. There is nothing in such identity claims mandating that intentions themselves be caused; in principle they could be uncaused-causers even though they are brain states. Yet if intentions are themselves brain states that cause other physical states, it is a reasonable (if separate) thesis that they must themselves be caused by earlier brain states. Only if intentions were not brain states but existed in some non-physical way would it be plausible to think that they could be uncaused. Getting rid of Cartesian dualism, as almost all neuroscientists do, forecloses this possibility. For a respectable neuroscience there can be no ghost in the machine that is the brain, no more than there can be such ghosts in robots, automobiles, or lunar landers.

---

[127] Notice that the text phrases the matter comparatively, that is, that indeterministic chance gives us *no more* control, etc., than does deterministic causation, It may well be that one can imagine an indeterminism that is compatible with there being choice, effort, control, and therefore responsibility. See Robert Kane, *The Significance of Free Will* (Oxford: Oxford University Press, 1998), chap. 8. But such compatibility will have no leg up on a like compatibility of deterministic causation with that same choice, effort, control, and therefore responsibility.

[128] Thomas Clark, "Fear of Mechanism," *Journal of Consciousness Studies*, 6 (1999): 279–93, reprinted in B. Libet, A. Freeman, and K. Sutherland, eds., *The Volitional Brain: Towards a Neuroscience of Free Will* (Exeter, U.K.: Imprint Academic, 2004), 279–93, at 281.

It would be a mistake to think that the lack of free will challenge stems only from the global (and still speculative) data of reductionism. For some neuroscientists believe that such lack has been experimentally demonstrated by the second set of data I described above, that developed in the Libet and post-Libet experiments. Susan Pockett, for example, prefaces her volume collecting recent literature on this issue by urging that "one of the philosophical outcomes of Libet's experiments is that they might be taken as suggesting we do not have conscious free will." [129] The well known London psychologist, Patrick Haggard, for one, so takes the Libet experiments:

> An influential series of experiments by Libet has suggested that conscious intentions arise as a result of brain activity. This contrasts with traditional concepts of free will, in which the mind controls the body ... Libet was the first to attempt a scientific psycho-physiology of free will. His experiment brought scientific method to a question that had previously been purely philosophical. Using this method, he produced data that ... deeply undermine the concept of conscious free will: preparatory brain activity causes our conscious intentions ... if the moment of conscious intention followed the onset of the readiness potential, then conscious free will cannot exist ...[130]

The idea is that the readiness potential evidences certain brain states (mostly in the supplementary motor area), and that these SMA states cause intentions (choice, willings) to occur. The question of whether there is a global determinism can be put aside, for here, it is thought, we can *see* that the will is caused by factors themselves unwilled, and is thus not free. It is for this reason that for many neuroscientists, "Libet's experiments have stood the test of time and become the scientific spine of the anti-free will movement." [131]

Libet shares with much of popular literature the thought that having (contra-causally) free will is essential to being morally responsible and blameworthy. Libet's thought is that if brain states precede and cause one's choices, then such choices cannot ground a true responsibility. In order for choice to give one *control* (and, thus, responsibility), it would have to be undetermined by any brain events that are outside the control of the chooser. If there are such unchosen brain events causing us to will what we do, "the individual would not consciously control his actions; he would only become aware of an unconsciously initiated

[129] Pockett, "Introduction," 5.
[130] Patrick Haggard and Benjamin Libet, "Conscious Intention and Brain Activity," *Journal of Consciousness Studies*, 8 (2001): 47–63, at 47–48.
[131] Azim Shariff, Jonathan Schooler, and Kathleen Vohs, "The Hazards of Claiming to Have Solved the Hard Problem of Free Will," in J. Baer, J. Kaufman, and R. Baumeister, eds., *Are We Free?: Psychology and Free Will* (Oxford: Oxford University Press, 2008), 186.

choice. He would have no direct conscious control over the nature of any preceding unconscious processes. . . . We do not hold people responsible for actions performed unconsciously, without the possibility of conscious control." [132]

True enough, Libet himself drew back from consigning our blaming practices to the dust-heap. Yet he did this only by positing a veto function that the will can possess.[133] According to Libet, the will does not initiate actions, but is the mere puppet of the brain events that cause it; yet the will has about a 100 millisecond window (the difference between corrected awareness time and the Rubicon Point) in which to exercise a veto over the movement already initiated by the SMA. By exercising such a veto, the will can prevent a movement already initiated. Remarkably, Libet held that such preventative choices are uncaused.[134] Unlike the *initiation* of movements, *blocking* the movements is an effort of pure will. Here, Libet thought, is where free will resides (or as some wags put it, where "free won't" resides). Needless to say, many neuroscientists who otherwise admire Libet's work do not follow him here.[135] For them, the exercise or nonexercise of a veto function is as caused by earlier brain events that precede awareness as is the exercise of the function that initiates motor movements. For them, thus, the implication of Libet's experiments is that there is no free will, full stop, with no caveats for last minute, "free" vetos. For them, thus, the Libet experiment shows that there is no responsibility or blameworthiness.

3. *The challenge of a merely epiphenomenal will.* It is common to elide the challenge of there being no free will with a quite distinct challenge, one that regards the will as epiphenomenal with behavior rather than being the cause of that behavior. These are in fact quite distinct challenges. The first is based on the will being caused; the second is based on the will doing no causing but is silent about whether the will is itself caused.

One can picture the difference in the two skeptical claims this way. The free will skeptic pictures the relation between brain states, willings, and bodily movements (on which he bases his skepticism) as a simple causal chain:

[132] Benjamin Libet, "Do We Have Free Will?," *Journal of Consciousness Studies*, 6 (1999): pp. 47–57, reprinted in Benjamin Libet, Anthony Freeman, and Keith Sutherland, eds., *The Volitional Brain: Towards a Neuroscience of Free Will* (UK: Imprint Academic, 2004), 52.
[133] Libet, "Unconscious Cerebral Initiative," 536–38.
[134] Libet, "Do We Have Free Will?," 52–53.
[135] E.g., Marcel Brass and Patrick Haggard, "To Do or Not to Do: The Neural Signature of Self-Control," *Journal of Neuroscience*, 27 (2007): 9141–9145, at 9144:

"Our data identify a clear neural basis for inhibiting intentions and thus identify the neural correlate of the veto process. The hypothesis of a special, non-neural veto process could therefore become unnecessary."

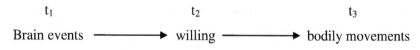

FIGURE 1. Willings as Caused Causes of Bodily Movements

On this picture, willings do cause the bodily movements that are their objects. But the willings are themselves caused by certain brain events, and it is this aetiological feature that the free will skeptic says robs willings of the freedom allegedly needed for responsibility. Contrast this with a second picture:

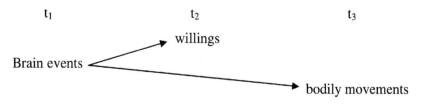

FIGURE 2. Willings as Epiphenomenal with Bodily Movements (simple version)

Willings are caused on this picture too, but what here grounds the skepticism about responsibility is not the existence of this causal relation but rather, the non-existence of a causal connection between willings and bodily movements. Willings and bodily movements are conceived here as being epiphenomenal of each other, co-effects of a common cause, which is why they might look like they are (even though they are not) in a causal relationship with one another.

Despite this plain difference between the two skepticisms, neuroscientists and many others have a tendency to run these claims together. Benjamin Libet, for example, often summed up what he took to be challenging from his findings this way: "If the 'act now' process is initiated unconsciously, then conscious free will is not doing it." [136] Is the challenge being expressed by Libet that the "'act now' process" is being caused so that there is no free will? Or is it that the will is not causing ("doing") either that process or the bodily movement that that process causes? My interpretation is that Libet thought that both of those things were challenging to our folk psychological notions of responsible agency, but that does not make them the same.

---

[136] Benjamin Libet, "Consciousness, Free Action and the Brain," *Journal of Consciousness Studies*, 8 (2001): 59–65, at 61.

Or consider three other psychologists' interpretation of Libet's experimental work:

> What does this tell us about free will? First, these data contradict the naïve view of free will—that conscious intention causes action. Clearly conscious intention cannot cause an action if a neural event that precedes and correlates with the action comes before conscious intention.[137]

Notice the clear equation of free will with the causal efficacy of the will. Notice also how that equation leads its authors to treat evidence that there are causes of conscious intention (and thus no free will) as if it were evidence that conscious intentions do not cause actions.

Or consider this description by Daniel Wegner of what it is that we suppose about ourselves that neuroscience will displace:

> Our actions are an astonishing realm of events that bend to our desires when so much of the world does not. Perhaps this is why each person views self with awe—*The Great Selfini* amazes and delights! We are enchanted by the operation of our minds and bodies into believing that we are "uncaused causers," the origin of our own behavior. Each self is magic in its own mind.[138]

Which is it of which we are to be convinced by neuroscience—that we are not causers, or that we are not uncaused in our causings? Again, Wegner probably thinks both of these challenging truths are delivered up by neuroscience; and again, that is to make two claims, not one.

It is not difficult to see why neuroscientists and others often join these two claims together. The assumption behind the linking of the two claims is that we cannot be agents—choosers, "origins of our own behavior,"—if our choices are caused by factors themselves unchosen. This is the more radical, analytical version of the lack of free will claim mentioned earlier. *Persons* have to be free in order to be causers, even if other items (like stones, stars, lakes, and brains) do not need to be uncaused in order to be causers. If one rejects that claim, as I believe we should, then separation of the epiphenomenal challenge from the lack of free will challenge becomes not only possible but necessary.

The separation of epiphenomenal skepticism from lack-of-free-will skepticism shows that the usual evidence given in support of epiphenomenalism is not sufficient. Just because brain events both cause bodily movements

---

[137] Henry Roediger, Michael Goode, Franklin Zaromb, "Free Will and the Control of Action," in J. Baer, J. Kaufman, and R. Baumeister, eds., *Are We Free?: Psychology and Free Will* (Oxford: Oxford University Press, 2008), 208.
[138] Daniel Wegner, "Self is Magic," in J. Baer, et al., *Are We Free?*, 226.

and precede willings does not count as evidence against the possibility
that such brain events cause bodily movements *through* such willings. The
possibility is that the right picture is that first depicted above in figure 1,
where willings are causative of bodily movements even if themselves
caused by earlier brain events. The epiphenomenal skeptic thus needs to
say more than that the mental events of willing are preceded by brain
events that cause bodily movements. Such a skeptic may have one of two
additional thoughts here.

First, he might think that the brain events at t_1 are the last events
needed for the bodily movements in question. This is the idea that not
only are the brain events sufficient to produce the bodily movements, but
that these early brain events do not operate through any other, subsequent brain events. Once the early brain events have occurred at t_1, in
other words, the bodily movements at t_3 are going to happen without
need of any other events occurring, willings included. (For a complete
causal chain to exist from t_1 to t_3, there must be *states* existing, but these
are not the *changes of state* we think of as events.)[139] This is depicted in
figure 2 above.

Alternatively, he might think that the brain events at t_1 cause the bodily
movements at t_3 via a series of other brain events. For ease of exposition,
assume just one other set of brain events occurring at t_2, call them BE'.
Then the picture is that depicted as:

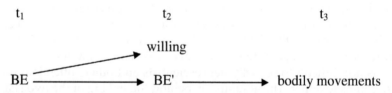

FIGURE 3. Willings as Epiphenomenal with Bodily Movements (complex version)

Willing on this picture is still epiphenomenal because BE' at t_2 is sufficient
for the bodily movements at t_3, and at no point in time is there room or
need for some other event, such as a "willing," to do any causing of
bodily movements.

One's choice between the two pictures depicted in figures 2 and 3 will
not be settled by armchair philosophy. The issue is an empirical one, to be
settled by the best neuroscience available. I nonetheless separate the two
versions of this skepticism because how one answers it depends on which

---

[139] On causal influence going across unchanging states as well as chains of events, see
Michael Moore, "The Nature of Singularist Theories of Causation," *The Monist*, 92 (2009):
3–23, reprinted in Moore, *Causation and Responsibility* (Oxford: Oxford University Press,
2009), 500–501, 510.

of these pictures one takes to be true. Notice that both of these skeptical pictures crucially depend on willing not being necessary for bodily movements to occur because the brain events at t_1, or the brain events at both t_1 and t_2, are *sufficient* by themselves to cause those bodily movements.

There is one construal of either of these versions of the epiphenomenal challenge that needs to be put aside on grounds of redundancy. This is the view that takes "willing" to refer exclusively to some conscious, mental experience and not to any brain state(s). Daniel Wegner for one is guilty of this move insofar as he identifies the will with what he calls the "phenomenal will." But this interpretation is not peculiar to Wegner. It is a hidden assumption by many that makes the epiphenomenal challenge seem all but unanswerable. For if willings are to be thought of in dualistic terms, *of course* they are epiphenomenal to the brain states that cause bodily movements—how could such ghostly willing-experiences cause anything physical like a bodily movement? Such an interpretation of the epiphenomenal challenge makes it redundant to the physicalistic premise of the challenge of eliminativism. That premise says there are no such ghostly willing experiences, so of course they cannot be causes of anything real.

The epiphenomenal challenge only becomes interesting when it is construed to be non-redundant to the rejection of dualism. Assume the experience of willing is identical with some kind of brain state. The interesting, non-redundant epiphenomenal challenge is to assert that this experiential brain state of willing does not cause the bodily movements it seems to cause. That would be challenging indeed.

If our choices, intentions, and willings truly do not cause our voluntary actions, that challenges directly the folk psychology assumption of autonomy. Seemingly what gives us *control* over the world, what makes us *agents* who can be responsible for the results we cause, what makes us at least in part the authors of our own lives, is such autonomy, such ability to bend the world to our will. Moreso even than freedom, this seems a rock-bed requirement for us to be the kind of creatures that can be rewarded or punished by the law according to what we deserve.

4. *The challenge of a merely epiphenomenal consciousness.* For a long time (even antedating Freud) many have thought that one can *unconsciously* intend or will things.[140] If so, then one response to the epiphenomenal skepticism about the will above described is to identify the brain events at t_1 as being nothing other than a willing, albeit an unconscious willing. This move preserves the causal efficacy of willings. It is this possibility that brings into focus an alternative challenge raised by the Libet experiments. That challenge is this: even if willings are the brain events at t_1 that cause bodily movements, still these are not *conscious* willings, and

---

[140] As Freud is reported to have said (at an awards ceremony in 1927 celebrating his "discovery of the unconscious"), "My only claim to discovery is by being ill-read." On Freud's non-psychoanalytic antecedents, see Moore, *Law and Psychiatry*, 126–34, 250–51, 265, 327.

only *conscious* willings make one responsible, is the idea. We can only control that of which we are aware, this thought continues, so that even if the will is both free and causally efficacious, that would be without implications for responsibility because the willings that initiate movements are unconscious.

One should conceive of this as a second kind of epiphenomenal objection, pictured thusly:

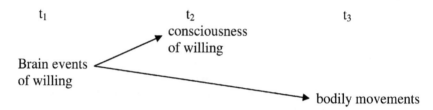

FIGURE 4. Consciousness as Epiphenomenal with Bodily Movements

Consciousness of willing is now pictured in the "dangler" position, an effect of the willing/brain events at t_1 but without effect itself on the movements it doesn't control. This is the third thing that is elided in Libet's statement earlier quoted, to the effect that, "If the 'act now' process is initiated unconsciously, then *conscious free will* isn't doing it." We have seen that this is construable as both a denial that the will is *free* (of being caused), and as a denial that the *will* does any causing; now see that this statement is also construable as the claim denying that *consciousness* of willing does any causing.

It is easy to miss the separation of this skepticism about responsibility from the skepticisms produced by the claimed epiphenomenal status of the will. If one thinks that intentions and willings must be conscious if they are to be intentions or willings at all, then the subject can will or intend the movement of his finger only when he is conscious of that fact, which on Libet's evidence seems to be at t_2; this means that *both* consciousness and intending are necessarily in the same "dangler" position in the epiphenomenal chart, and so this fourth skepticism collapses into the epiphenomenal challenge already considered. For reasons I have gone into elsewhere,[141] I do not share the supposition that willings and intendings must be conscious. There is in that case this separable challenge to be considered.

That this second epiphenomenal thesis is a challenge to our sense of who we are as responsible agents should be clear. What is challenged is the central place occupied by consciousness in our sense of self. If con-

[141] Ibid., 126–42, 249–80, 322–37.

sciousness is just along for the ride, enjoying the show perhaps but unable to do anything about it, that seems to strongly erode our sense of self and agency at the root of responsibility. We would be shown to be (as Freud put it about his own epiphenomenal claims about consciousness) "not even masters in our own house."[142]

It might seem that there is yet one more epiphenomenal challenge to be considered. We can access this last possibility by speculating that consciousness itself is a brain process, just like willing. It is immensely likely that this brain process begins before phenomenal awareness is experienced by the subject—for all brain processes take real time. This requires of us an old Freudian conclusion: what is conscious can be unconscious. More exactly, the thing referred to by consciousness (i.e., the brain process underlying conscious experience) can, in its early phases, be phenomenally unconscious. With this under our belt, then suppose one identified the brain events at t_1 not just to be willings, but also to be the beginnings of consciousness of willings. Then there would be no epiphenomenal objection because consciousness of willing (in this sense) would not be in the dangler position.

This would give rise to yet a third form of the epiphenomenal objection: although conscious willings cause actions, *phenomenal awareness* of those willings does not. Phenomenal awareness is a mere dangler, pictured thusly:

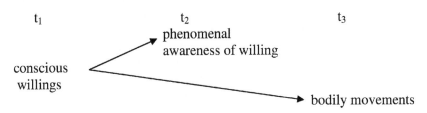

FIGURE 5. Phenomenal Awareness as Epiphenomenal with Bodily Movements

Now the charge would be that phenomenal awareness causing action is what responsibility demands, and neuroscience has shown that it does not do this causal work.

Yet notice that this challenge is illegitimate on the same redundancy ground I used before against a like use of Wegner's "phenomenal willing." If consciousness is conceived of, not as a brain process, but as a thing in some other realm of existence, this is just dualism again. And again, there are conclusive reasons to reject any such dualism. The epi-

[142] Sigmund Freud, *Introductory Lectures on Psycho-Analysis, in the Standard Edition,* Vol. 16, 285.

phenomenal challenge construed in this third way does no more than try to resuscitate this dead horse—at least long enough to then beat it to death again. *Of course* phenomenal awareness—cut off from any realization in the brain—can do no causal work in moving our bodies. Let's move on! We need to chart new challenges arising from neuroscience, not look at old ones in new verbal garb.

5. *The challenge that consciousness is not veridical or privileged in its knowledge of mental states.* Daniel Wegner plainly intends two challenges to arise out of his work. The first is a challenge to our infallibility in knowing the genesis of our voluntary actions. His examples are designed to show that we misjudge the voluntary status of our behaviors both ways: sometimes we misjudge that we did not perform an action when in fact we did; and sometimes we misjudge that we did perform an action when in fact we did not. The challenges here are that we are not *incorrigible* in our beliefs about whether or not we have acted, nor are our actions *transparent* to us. If folk psychology presupposed that we were infallible in either of these directions, this would be a serious challenge.

But it does not. One might read Wegner as strengthening these claims by saying that we are *always* wrong about whether we have exercised voluntary agency in our overt behaviors. This strong a claim would certainly challenge our sense of control, because to be *typically* wrong about what we are doing (or even whether we are doing anything) would leave us completely in the dark about what we are responsible for. Yet (with the caveat mentioned below) this would be too strong a claim. The truly general claim made by Wegner is different. It is that we have no direct access to causings of our bodily movements. This *mode of access* claim is distinct from any *error* claims. Like the proverbial broken clock, we could lack a reliable knowledge-producing mechanism and yet could still be correct in our readings at least some of the time.

Wegner's real challenge is this second one about privileged access. This is indeed (in contrast to Wegner's not-infallible point) a more plausibly general point: none of us, ever, has direct access to the causing of our bodily movements by our wills. Here the peripheral phenomena that he examines—automatisms, and illusion-of-control behaviors—looks more like the tip of the proverbial iceberg Wegner wants them to be. The general challenge is to the privileged access each of us is supposed to have to the contents of his own mind, his willings included. For the non-observational, non-inferential, direct knowledge we are supposed to have here, Wegner substitutes a theory-laden, inferential, interpretive mode of knowing.

This denial of privileged access is more challenging than it might seem at first blush. Such privileged access is arguably a main marker of the boundaries of self and personhood.[143] It is what marks off a process as

---

[143] Moore, *Law and Psychiatry*, 128, 133, 256, 274–75.

something a person feels, thinks, or does, from what Dan Dennett once called the "sub-personal" processes that go on in a person's brain but that are only functionally defined subroutines of various structures within his body.[144] Much of the afferent-conducted feedback on our voluntary actions, for example, is not accessible to consciousness.[145] These feedbacks and adjustments are subroutines a person's body has to do for him to perform well. Anyone who can read and observe can infer by theoretical inference that these subroutines must be going on in him as he stands erect, and so on. But by being unknowable in the mode of experiencing them in consciousness, these subroutines are not actions he performs for reasons. If this line between the actions we do as persons, and the subroutines our bodies do ("without us" so to speak), is eroded, that would be a challenge to our sense of selves.

Wegner's arguments and data are also often taken to suggest many of the four bolder challenges already described. That is, an "illusion of conscious will" could be taken to suggest: the disappearing self (i.e., the self that is reduced to nothing by reductionism); that there is no free will; or either or both of the epiphenomenal challenges earlier described. Indeed, Wegner himself rather flirts with and thus encourages this more challenging reading of his data. Yet the data do not support such larger readings. That the will *sometimes* does not cause what it seems to cause (the illusion of control cases), for example, hardly supports the metaphysical claim that wills *never* cause bodily movements.[146] It only supports the epistemic claim that we can be mistaken in what our wills in fact cause, and (perhaps) the further epistemic claim that we have no privileged way of knowing what our wills have in fact caused.

Of course if we have other grounds to believe that the will, or consciousness of willing, is epiphenomenal, that would support Wegner's

[144] Dennett, *Content and Consciousness*, 90–96. The role of consciousness (in the sense of privileged access) is also emphasized by Suparna Choudhury and Sarah-Jayne Blakemore, "Intentions, Actions, and the Self," in S. Pockett, W. Banks, and S. Gallagher, eds., *Does Consciousness Cause Behavior?* (Cambridge, MA: MIT Press, 2006), 48–49 as crucial to ownership of actions and self-construction:

> "the feeling of agency . . . is a mark of selfhood . . . the conscious awareness of unconsciously monitored actions is the means by which our actions are experienced as subjectively real, willed, and owned. Consciousness is thus embodied: it is through action that we become conscious of ourselves as "distinct selves." (Emphasis in original, citation omitted).

[145] Pockett, "The Neuroscience of Movement," 19–21.

[146] Wegner gets the universal claim only by separating what is referred to by "will" into the phenomenal (or conscious) will, and the empirical will. If the claim is that the conscious will (i.e., phenomenology alone, with no physical realization) never causes movement, all can agree (for this would be a dualism). But Wegner's data on what he calls the illusion of control cases is much more interesting than this; the data suggest that in such cases, willing as such (the deep reference being to its essentially physical nature) does not cause the behavior. The only point in the text is that this more interesting point is also limited to the data explored by Wegner, viz, the illusion of control cases.

epistemic claims.[147] For then, there would be no causing (by wills or by consciousness) for us to perceive via our experience of will, and we could have neither privileged access nor infallibility. But Wegner's epistemic challenges should be seen as resting on their own evidential base, not as some corollaries of the challenges earlier discussed.

6. *The challenge of secondary agency.* A distinct kind of challenge can be seen by anthropomorphizing three of the challenges already considered. Take the second, the lack-of-free-will challenge, for illustration. Suppose what causes the will is not just some dumb, brute physical phenomena; suppose it is "someone else," another person-like entity residing within us but not identical to our own agency. I call these "second agent" conceptualizations. Such second agencies seem to challenge our sense of self and of responsibility more than their non-anthropomorphized counterparts do.

Daniel Wegner documents this effect in our judgments when (literally) other people's agency impinges on our own. As he recounts, "we become ill at ease when we are faced with questions of our own free will not so much because we have some aversion to causal determinism arising within us, but because of the concern that we are being pushed around by others. . . . All it seems to take is another's prior movements, or even the hint of a command, and we relinquish much of our own experience of will and allocate responsibility to the other." [148]

Freud's "metapsychological" theories famously posited other agencies within us that were "not-me,"—the topographic "System Ucs," replaced by Freud in 1923 by the structural "id." Of these second agents, Freud said, "All the acts and manifestations which I notice in myself and do not know how to link up with the rest of my mental life must be judged as if they belonged to someone else and are to be explained by the mental life ascribed to that person." [149] This anthropomorphic feature of Freudian theory made it particularly challenging of our sense of will and responsibility.[150] If physical causes that we can't control are already a challenge to free will, when such causes are conceived of as second agents, that seems to up the ante for many people. Being the puppet of an alien intelligence seems to many people to be more threatening than being the causal product of purely mechanical forces. (If this is right, Predestination must have been more of a challenge for Calvinists than materialism was for Hobbesians.)

When contemporary neuroscientists interpret the Libet-to-Haynes results anthropomorphically, they are inviting the greater challenges of second, "not-me" agencies controlling our decisions. In his 1985 article, Libet

[147] As Wegner notices in his discussion of Libet's findings. Wegner, *Illusion of Conscious Will*, 49–55; Wegner, "Author's Resopnse,"684: "The idea of *ICW* is not dependent on Libet's finding . . . this is because *ICW* . . . is not about whether thought causes action. It is about whether the experience of conscious will reflects such causation."
[148] Wegner, "Self Is Magic," 233.
[149] Sigmund Freud, "The Unconscious," *Collected Papers*, IV, J. Strachey, ed. (New York: Basic Books, 1959), 102.
[150] Moore, *Law and Psychiatry*, 142–52.

interpreted his findings thusly: "the brain 'decides' to initiate or at least to prepare to initiate the act before there is any reportable subjective awareness that such a decision has taken place."[151] John-Dylan Haynes much more recently has also characterized Libet's results in similarly anthropomorphic terms: "it has been argued that the brain has already unconsciously made a decision to move even before the subject became aware of it."[152] Haynes similarly anthropomorphizes his own more recent findings, seemingly attributing decisions to his favored brain areas: "One interpretation of this finding is that the frontopolar cortex was the first cortical stage at which the actual decision was made, whereas precuneous was involved in storage of the decision until it reached awareness."[153]

If you take this anthropomorphic gloss seriously, neuroscientists would be replacing Freud's inner demons with another, equally alien second agent, namely, our brains. For some people this would intensify the challenge presented to free will by the Libet-to-Haynes data. It would similarly magnify the epiphenomenalist challenges earlier described, because now the common cause of (conscious) willing and behavior would not just be some dumb physical events, but "someone else" who competes with us for control of our own bodies.

One might think that the anthropomorphic description of Libet, Haynes, and others is just loose talk, that unlike Freudian theory there is nothing in neuroscience that commits it to such second-agent descriptions. While ultimately I think that this is right, still the immediacy of the causes of movement with which neuroscience deals, and their spatially proximate location (within our own head), peculiarly gives rise to ideas that "brains decide." Suppose Haynes becomes almost as infallible a predictor of human choice as was Hume: suppose Hume's predictive success (about how if a pot of gold is left at Charing Cross station someone will pick it up)[154] is at 98 percent, and Haynes achieves a like accuracy from studying the goings on in the precuneous region of the parietal cortex. Isn't the temptation to say, "the matter has already been decided," much more natural about Hayne's prediction than about Hume's? "The decision was already made" describes Haynes situation more naturally than Hume's (where we might say that the decision had been *predicted* but it hadn't yet been *made*), because Hume's environmental causes are not in the head. In Hayne's cases the conscious subject seemingly has not made the decision until six to nine seconds later; but since (by the above inference) the decision has been made at the earlier time, someone or something must have made it. Who else but the brain? This is undoubtedly better science

[151] Libet, "Unconscious Cerebral Initiative," 536.

[152] Haynes, "Unconscious Determinants of Free Decisions," 543.

[153] Ibid., 545. Bennett and Hacker, *Philosophical Foundations of Neuroscience*, 68–72, collect numerous other examples of neuroscientific animizing of the brain.

[154] David Hume, section 8.20 of *An Enquiry Concerning Human Understanding*, "Liberty and Necessity."

than were Freud's mysterious homunculi, but it challenges our sense that we are in charge as much as Freud ever did.

One can feel this challenge, of course, only if one does not have a reductionist perspective clearly in mind. If all of our mental states are brain states, so that we *are* (identical with) our brains, there could be no second agent challenges. On reductionist assumptions, there is only one agent, and it is our mind/brain. So this challenge can be mounted only by one rejecting reductionism. Although this rejection was true of Libet and other dualists like Eccles, it is not true of Haynes and most neuroscientists. For them this last kind of challenge has bite only in moments of forgetfulness of their true ontological commitments. For lay people it may be that there are many such moments.

III. Conclusion: The Nine Challenges and Two Possible Queries About Them

I would group the challenges from neuroscience that we have explored into the following four pairs:

A. Eliminativist Challenges
   1. *Eliminative materialism:* because mental states like intention *cannot* be reduced to brain states of any kind, such mental states will not feature in the best explanations of human behavior science can produce; those best explanations will refer to brain states alone.
   2. *Eliminative reductionism:* because mental states like intention *can* be reduced to brain states of various kinds, such mental states (and the self or "I" that has them) will disappear from explanations of human behavior.
B. Determinist Challenges
   3. *Analytical hard determinism:* Because "choice" and other mental states terms include as part of their meaning, "uncaused," the causation of such mental states by brain states shows there really is no such thing as choice.
   4. *Non-analytical hard determinism:* because (as a matter of moral fairness) *responsibility* for choice requires that the chooser could have acted and could have chosen other than he in fact did, and because such capacity cannot exist if choices are caused, the causation of choice by brain states implies that no one is responsible or blamable for either his choices or his behavior.
C. Epiphenomenalist Challenges
   5. *Epiphenomenal wills:* because willings are caused by the brain events that also cause voluntary bodily movements, such willings are merely epiphenomenal with such movements and do not cause them to occur.

6. *Epiphenomenal consciousness:* because consciousness of willings is caused by the brain events that also cause voluntary bodily movements, such states of consciousness are merely epiphenomenal with such movements and do not cause them to occur.

D. Fallibilist Challenges

7. *Denial of transparency and incorrigibility:* because mental states are not transparent to their possessors, and because each person's beliefs about his own mental states are not incorrigible, each person is fallible in his beliefs about his own mental states; he is also actually ignorant or mistaken about them much of the time.

8. *Denial of privileged access:* because persons are so fallible and inaccurate in their beliefs about their own mental states, such persons can have no direct, non-inferential, non-interpretive way of knowing their own mental states.

In addition to these eight challenges, I have also separated out an anthropomorphic version of the determinist and the epiphenomenal challenges. I call this the challenge of secondary agency:

9. *Secondary Agency:* We must conceptualizes the causes (or alternatively, competitors) of our choices to be agencies in their own right, serving their own ends; this heightens the determinist and epiphenomenal challenges because we and/or our bodies are in the control of "someone else," as opposed to *something* else.

In assessing each of these challenges on the merits, one should ask two sorts of questions about each of them. These two questions were distinguished by the well-known Cornell philosopher of metaethics, Nicholas Sturgeon who once said that he had discovered that his teaching assistant was dividing the discussion of Sturgeon's lectures into two parts, corresponding to the questions, "Oh yeah?," and, "So what?"[155] I envy Sturgeon his graduate assistant. For these are often the right two questions to ask of any thesis: is the thesis true? And does it matter to anything we care about whether it is true?

So here: there are two questions that might be asked of each of these neuroscience-based challenges to our conceptions of self, agency, and responsibility. The most obvious question is whether the scientific claims on which the challenges are based are true. Are willings identical to certain brain events? Are willings caused by brain events? Are willings merely epiphenomenal of the bodily movements they putatively cause? Is consciousness of willing merely epiphenomenal with those bodily movements that are willed? Is consciousness sometimes (often, always) wrong

---

[155] Nicholas Sturgeon, "What Difference Does It Make Whether Moral Realism Is True?," *Southern Journal of Philosophy*, 24 (1986): Supplement, 115–41, at 136 n.1.

in its beliefs about the contents of our own minds? Do we lack privileged access to those contents? Is the brain really a second agent that determines or competes with our conscious will? These sound like empirical questions for the best science to answer, which ultimately they are. But because the conclusions suggested by such questions require disputable interpretations of the empirical data, resolving such questions also involves a good deal of "philosophizing," that is, conceptual work in the philosophy of mind.

The second question to ask is whether it matters to our basic sense of our selves, our agency, our responsibility and our punishability, whether any of these claims is true. Does self, responsibility, and so on, require that minds not be identical to brains? Does it require freedom of the will? Does it require that willings cause actions? Does it require that consciousness of the willings cause actions? Does it require that consciousness knows itself in a privileged way and to some degree of accuracy? Does it require an absence of competing agency in the brain? These are more obviously philosophical questions, although the relevant branch of philosophy here is moral philosophy rather than the philosophy of mind.

These two questions of truth and relevance have a third person mode of being asked as well as the first person mode just described. That is, rather than asking whether the challenges of neuroscience are *really* true or *really* relevant, we can ask whether many or most people now *believe* them to be true and relevant, or whether many or most people will in the future or would in certain circumstances come to *believe* certain things about such issues. For designers of legal institutions these third person (or sociological) questions cannot be ignored. In a democracy the pure, undiluted philosophical truth will not carry the day and get translated into legal institutions unless it is believed by enough people. There is, thus, a sociological version of our two questions that also demands (and has been receiving) attention. Greene and Cohen in their well known article devote much of their attention to this sociological version of the questions, speculating that even if philosophy can show that responsibility is fully compatible with the challenges of neuroscience, most people will increasingly think that it is not, so that retributive punishment institutions will wither away.[156] This is a testable hypothesis of social science on which all the evidence is hardly in.[157]

My own interests are mainly in getting the philosophy straight, both in the philosophy of mind and in moral philosophy. Selling the product can come later. It is thus the two first person questions just distinguished that primarily interest me. With regard to these two questions of philosophy,

[156] Greene and Cohen, "Neuroscience Changes Nothing."

[157] Felipe De Baigard, Eric Mandelbaum, and David Ripley have a go at testing these sociological speculations of Greene and Cohen. See their "Responsibility and the Brain Sciences," *Ethical Theory and Moral Practice*, Springer Science on-line publishing, 24 December 2008.

the situation is that described by Columbia's philosopher of action, Arthur Danto, when Libet's experimental results were first released: "It is a truth universally acknowledged that a physiologist in possession of a meta-physical prejudice must be in want of philosophical help."[158] Wanted by neuroscientists or not, philosophical help is needed if we are to see clearly the implications of neuroscientific research for our larger conceptions of ourselves as morally responsible and legally punishable agents. This paper has been a modest start in offering such help, seeking to clarify both that which is challenged and that which is doing the challenging here. In a subsequent paper, I shall answer such separated challenges on the merits.[159]

Law and Philosophy, University of Illinois

---

[158] Arthur Danto, "Consciousness and Motor Control," *Behavioral and Brain Sciences*, 8 (1985), 540–41.

[159] The beginnings of my answers to some of these challenges may be found in Moore, "Libet's Challenge(s) to Responsible Agency," in Walter Sinnott-Armstrong and Lynn Nadel, eds., *Conscious Will and Responsibility* (Oxford: Oxford University Press, 2010), 207–34, and in lecture form, at http://www.cas.illinois.edu/Events/ViewPublicEvent.aspx?Guid=8A6A6DD2-699A-478F-8651-C8C2C6D1F389, (Nineteenth Annual Center for Advanced Study Lecture, September, 2009), and http://www/nmc.uni-freiburg.de/video/Video aufzeichnungen/rechtswissenschaften/recht-ws-2009-10, (Lecture to the Institute for Legal Philosophy and Public Affairs, Albert-Ludwigs University, Freiburg-im-Breisgau, Germany, March, 2010). My colleagues Al Mele, Adina Roskies, and Stephen Morse have also done recent work that tracks some of these concerns. See Alfred Mele, *Free Will and Luck* (Oxford: Oxford University Press, 2006); Alfred Mele, *Effective Intentions: The Power of Conscious Will* (Oxford: Oxford University Press, 2009); Adina Roskies, "Neuroscientific Challenges to Free Will and Responsibility," *Trends in Cognitive Science*, vol. 10, no. 9 (2006), www. sciencedirect.com; Stephen Morse, "Determinism and the Death of Folk Psychology: Two Challenges to Responsibility from Neuroscience," *Minnesota Journal of Law, Science, and Technology*, 9 (2008): 1–35.

GENOCIDE AND CRIMES AGAINST HUMANITY: DISPELLING THE CONCEPTUAL FOG

By Andrew Altman

I. Introduction

The unconditional defeat of Nazi Germany, with its egregious doctrine of racial superiority and its unspeakable policies of extermination and enslavement, had a profound influence on postwar law and moral thought. The legal documents through which the Allies sought to articulate the values and to establish the institutions of a new international framework explicitly affirmed the moral principle that all humans possess equal and inherent dignity. Thus, the Charter of the United Nations stated that among the purposes of the organization were "promoting and encouraging respect for human rights and for fundamental freedoms for all without distinction as to race, sex, language, or religion."[1] And the Universal Declaration of Human Rights declared that "recognition of the inherent dignity and of the equal and inalienable rights of all members of the human family is the foundation of freedom, justice and peace in the world."[2]

The principles of human dignity and equality are extremely abstract, and various specifications of them are found in the international human rights agreements that came into force in the decades after the war. But developments in international criminal law also helped to specify and implement the principles by explicitly defining two crimes: genocide and crimes against humanity. Genocide was defined by a postwar international convention in terms of certain acts "committed with intent to destroy, in whole or in part, a national, ethnical, racial or religious group, as such."[3] Crimes against humanity were defined by postwar agreements and enactments in terms of certain "inhumane acts committed against any civilian population ... or persecutions on political, racial or religious grounds ... whether or not in violation of the domestic law of the country where perpetrated."[4] These two categories of crime came to symbolize

---

[1] Charter of the United Nations, Art. 1, Para. 3 (1945), available at http://www.un.org/en/documents/charter/index.shtml.

[2] Universal Declaration of Human Rights, Preamble (1948), available at http://www.un.org/en/documents/udhr/index.shtml.

[3] Convention on the Prevention and Punishment of the Crime of Genocide, (1948), available at http://www.hrweb.org/legal/genocide.html.

[4] "Charter of the International Military Tribunal," in *Trial of the Major War Criminals Before the International Military Tribunal*, vol. 1 (Nuremberg: International Military Tribunal, 1947),

doi:10.1017/S0265052511000033

the Third Reich's most egregious violations of the moral principle affirming the dignity and equality of all humans.

However, there are crucial differences between genocide understood as
a violation of the law, on the one hand, and as an episode of mass violence
directed at the members of a particular social group, on the other.[5] Moreover, the term "crimes against humanity" is also ambiguous between
legal and nonlegal meanings. The legal and philosophical literature has
ignored or glossed over these differences, with the result that a conceptual fog hovers over the discussion of these two categories of crime. The
fog is generated in part by the fact that the term "crime" can mean either
a violation of the criminal law or, in a somewhat metaphorical sense, a
violation of morality—a moral wrong. But the problem is deeper: there is
a pervasive failure to adequately distinguish crucial features of the legal
concepts of genocide and crimes against humanity from features of the
concepts in terms of which we represent moral outrages of historic dimensions such as the Holocaust. Moreover, even if we focus on the legal
concepts alone, international lawyers misconstrue the conceptual relation
between genocide and crimes against humanity.

The paper proceeds as follows. Section II provides a brief account of the
history and current state of the international law of genocide and crimes
against humanity. I argue that, despite a widely held view among scholars, genocide is not, under the law, a type of crime against humanity. In
Section III, I argue that the question "What is genocide?" can be disambiguated into three questions, each corresponding to a distinct concept of
genocide: the existing legal concept, the ideal legal concept, and the moral
concept. I show how the conflation of these three genocide concepts has
led to various confusions in the literature. Section IV distinguishes two
models for understanding genocide, the cultural model and the discrimination model, and argues for the superiority of the latter. In Section V, the
legal concept of crimes against humanity is distinguished from the moral
concept, and, in Section VI, I argue that the conflation of those two concepts is due to the mistake of regarding the Holocaust as a paradigmatic
crime against humanity.

II. International Law

Genocide and crimes against humanity are now among the core crimes
of international law. They are prohibited by customary international law

---

11, available at http://avalon.law.yale.edu/imt/imtconst.asp#art6. Also see Control Council
Law No. 10, Art. 2 (1945), available at http://avalon.law.yale.edu/imt/imt10.asp.
[5] My use of the term "episode" should not be misconstrued as minimizing the moral
horror of the events to which I refer. By "episode" I mean a particular set of related actions,
however numerous, that in their totality constitute mass violence. Accordingly, I write of the
Holocaust as one such episode and the Turkish massacre of Armenians as another, and so
on.

and a number of authoritative legal instruments, including the Charter of
the International Military Tribunal (IMT−1945) before which the major
Nazi war criminals were tried at Nuremberg,[6] the Statute of the International Criminal Court (1998), and the Statutes of the international criminal tribunals for Yugoslavia (1993) and Rwanda (1994). Additionally,
genocide is outlawed by a special international convention.

A. Crimes against humanity

The first legally authoritative document in which the term "crimes
against humanity" appears is the London Charter, establishing the IMT
and spelling out the categories of crime over which the tribunal had
jurisdiction. The Charter was signed by the United States, Great Britain,
France, and the Soviet Union and was subsequently acceded to by an
additional nineteen states.[7] The categories of crime it laid out were crimes
against peace, war crimes, and crimes against humanity. The Charter also
declared that individuals were liable for "participating in . . . a common
plan or conspiracy to commit any of the foregoing crimes."[8]

It remains unclear why the drafters of the Charter decided to use the
exact phrase "crimes against humanity" to refer to its third category of
crime. The suggestion to use the phrase seems to have come from the
prominent scholar of international law, Hersch Lauterpacht, and to have
been advocated by the leading figure in drafting the Charter, U.S. Supreme
Court Justice and lead U.S. prosecutor before the IMT, Robert Jackson.[9]

It is reasonable to think that the phrase "crimes against humanity" was
an allusion to language that was part of previous international documents concerned with crimes committed during wartime. For example,
the phrase "laws of humanity" had appeared in what was called the
"Martens Clause" of the Preamble of the 1899 Hague Convention codifying the rules of land warfare.[10] And the term, "crimes against humanity

---

[6] At the IMT, the acts constituting the Nazi genocide against Jews were treated as war
crimes and crimes against humanity. See text accompanying note 26, below. Genocide did
not become a distinct crime until 1951. See note 27, below.
[7] M. Cherif Bassiouni, *Crimes Against Humanity in International Criminal Law* 2d rev. ed.
(The Hague: Kluwer Law International, 1999), 83.
[8] "Charter of the International Military Tribunal," Art. 6, Sec.(c), in *Trial of the Major War
Criminals*, vol. 1 (Nuremberg: International Military Tribunal, 1947), 11. The first count in the
indictment at Nuremberg charges the defendants with having "participated as leaders,
organizers, instigators, or accomplices in the formulation or execution of a common plan or
conspiracy to commit, or which involved the commission of, Crimes against Peace, War
Crimes, and Crimes against Humanity." *Trial of the Major War Criminals*, vol. 1, 29.
[9] Michael R. Marrus, *The Nuremberg War Crimes Trial, 1945–46.* (Boston: Bedford Books,
1997), 187.
[10] The Martens Clause was named after a Russian delegate to the Hague peace conference
of 1899. It read: "Until a more complete code of the laws of war is issued, the High
Contracting Parties think it right to declare that in cases not included in the Regulations
adopted by them, populations and belligerents remain under the protection and empire of
the principles of international law, as they result from the usages established between

and civilization," had been used during the First World War in a declaration issued by Great Britain, France, and Russia, pledging to prosecute
the Turkish officials responsible for "new crimes" connected to the massacre of the Armenian population.[11] Additionally, an international commission on war crimes established by the Paris Peace Conference found
that Germany, Austria-Hungary, and Turkey had waged war "by barba-
rous or illegitimate methods in violation of . . . the elementary laws of
humanity."[12]

However, Lauterpacht and Jackson would also have been well aware of
the fact that efforts to prosecute Turkish and German officials had largely
come to naught. Only two, local officials were convicted for crimes connected to the Armenian massacres, a special Turkish court-martial having
found them guilty under Islamic jurisprudence for acting "against humanity and civilization."[13] And the trials before national courts in Leipzig of
a few Germans for war crimes resulted in acquittals or very light sentences.[14] So while Lauterpacht and Jackson might have wanted to maintain some continuity with language that international lawyers would
recognize, the two of them also would have wanted to signal that the
Allies would not let the enemy architects of mass atrocities go unprosecuted
and unpunished for a second time in scarcely more than a generation.
Accordingly, the London Charter set out definitions of the crimes for
which leading figures in the Third Reich would be prosecuted, and it
constituted the IMT—a kind of international court-martial—to hear the
charges.

The London Charter defined crimes against humanity as: "murder,
extermination, enslavement, deportation, and other inhumane acts com-

---

civilized nations, from the laws of humanity, and the requirements of the public conscience."
Convention with Respect to the Laws and Customs of War on Land (Hague, II) (1899),
available at http://avalon.law.yale.edu/19th_century/hague02.asp. The clause reappears in
subsequent international conventions and protocols.

[11] Bassiouni, *Crimes Against Humanity in International Criminal Law*, 62.

[12] Commission on the Responsibility of the Authors of the War and on Enforcement of
Penalties, *Violation of the Laws and Customs of War* (Oxford: Clarendon Press, 1919), 19. It is
noteworthy that the U.S. delegation to the Commission wrote a dissenting report in which
it criticized the majority's invocation of the "laws of humanity" and drew a sharp distinction
between the laws of war and the laws of humanity: "the laws and customs of war are a
standard certain, to be found in books of authority and in the practice of nations . . . [but]
the laws and principles of humanity vary with the individual, which, if for no other reason,
should exclude them from consideration in a court of justice, especially one charged with
the administration of criminal law." *Violation of the Laws and Customs of War*, 64. In other
words, the U.S. government insisted on a sharp separation between positive law and morality. In contrast, there was no such insistence by the government during and after World
War II, due in part to the influence of Herbert Pell, U.S. delegate to an Allied commission
on war crimes. Pell argued that "crimes committed against stateless persons or against any
persons because of their race or religion [are] crimes against humanity." Quoted in Marrus,
The Nuremberg War Crimes Trial, 186.

[13] Gary Bass, *Stay the Hand of Vengeance: The Politics of War Crimes Tribunals* (Princeton:
Princeton University Press), 125.

[14] Ibid., 59.

mitted against any civilian population, before or during the war, or persecutions on political, racial or religious grounds in execution of or in
connection with any crime within the jurisdiction of the Tribunal, whether
or not in violation of the domestic law of the country where perpetrated."[15] The proviso, 'in execution of or in connection with any crime
within the jurisdiction of the Tribunal', is sometimes referred to as the
"war-nexus requirement." It meant that an act does not count as a crime
against humanity unless there is some connection between the act and a
crime against peace or a war crime. On the basis of this requirement, the
IMT ruled that it could not "make the general declaration that the [inhu-
mane] acts before [the outbreak of war in] 1939 were crimes against
humanity within the meaning of the Charter."[16]

The war-nexus requirement created a very large overlap between crimes
against humanity and war crimes. The Hague Convention (1907) on land
warfare had provided that in occupied territory "[f]amily honour and
rights, the lives of persons, and private property, as well as religious
convictions and practice, must be respected,"[17] and thus most crimes
against humanity—including the Nazi extermination of nearly three million Polish and over one million Russian Jews—counted as war crimes as
well.[18] Moreover, the IMT did little to separate clearly the two categories.
The most significant respect in which the two categories were distinct
concerned a state's maltreatment of part of its own civilian population;
such maltreatment could count as a crime against humanity but would
not count as a war crime. War crimes involve only cases in which a state
acts against the nationals of an enemy state. Thus, Germany's murder of
170,000 of its 210,000 Jews, who had previously been rendered stateless
by Nazi law, was a crime against humanity but not a war crime.[19]

In the years since the Nuremberg trial, several main developments
have characterized the international law of crimes against humanity. These
developments have come from a combination of sources, including reports
of the International Law Commission, which was given the task by the
United Nations of codifying the legal principles of the London Charter
and the IMT judgments;[20] the statutes establishing international tribunals

---

[15] "Charter of the International Military Tribunal," Art. 6, Para. (c), *Trial of the Major War
Criminals*, vol. 1, 11.

[16] Ibid., 254.

[17] Convention Respecting the Laws and Customs of War on Land (1907), Art. 46, available
at http://avalon.law.yale.edu/20th_century/hague04.asp.

[18] William J. Fenrick, "Should Crimes Against Humanity Replace War Crimes?" *Columbia
Journal of Transnational Law* 37, 3 (1999): 772.

[19] Paul Mendes-Flohr and Jehuda Reinharz, eds. *The Jew in the Modern World: A Docu-
mentary History*, 2d ed. (New York: Oxford University Press, 1995), 696. For accounts of Nazi
mass murders and persecutions of groups other than Jews, see Michael Berenbaum, ed., *A
Mosaic of Victims: Non-Jews Murdered and Persecuted by the Nazis* (New York: New York
University Press, 1990).

[20] International Law Commission, *Principles of International Law Recognized in the Charter
of the Nürnberg Tribunal and in the Judgment of the Tribunal* (1950), available at http://

to prosecute and decide cases arising out of the Rwandan genocide (ICTR) and the breakup of Yugoslavia (ICTY);[21] the case law emerging from those tribunals;[22] and the Rome Statute establishing the International Criminal Court (ICC).[23] For our purposes, the key development is that "all definitions of crimes against humanity adopted since the ICTR Statute (1994) require a nexus between the individual crime and a widespread or systematic attack against a civilian population."[24] In particular, the individual crime must be "part of" such an attack and undertaken with knowledge of the attack.[25] The requirement of a widespread or systematic attack on a civilian population is referred to as the "contextual element" of a crime against humanity, because it demands that a criminal act—such as murder or rape—take place in a certain context constituted by the conduct of third parties in order for that act to count as a crime against humanity. The particular third parties and their specific offending acts are typically too numerous to identify and do not need to be specified or proven by the prosecution in a case of crimes against humanity. It is sufficient that the prosecution prove that there was a widespread or systematic attack and that the defendant intentionally committed the specific acts attributed to him as part of the attack and with knowledge of it.

Although there is general agreement that a contextual element is needed to distinguish a crime against humanity from murder, rape, and other ordinary crimes, the contextual element carries with it questions about how to specify its meaning. Many of those questions have yet to be authoritatively settled, including whether multiple acts are needed for an attack to count as widespread or systematic, whether such an attack need be the product of a policy, whether the acts constituting the attack must be violent, and whether an attack can count as widespread simply in virtue of the number of victims. It is likely that the answers to these questions will remain unsettled for some time, although the emerging

---

untreaty.un.org/ilc/texts/instruments/english/draft%20articles/7_1_1950.pdf, and *Draft Code of Crimes Against the Peace and Security of Mankind* (1996), available at http://untreaty.un.org/ilc/texts/instruments/english/draft%20articles/7_4_1996.pdf.

[21] Statute of the International Criminal Tribunal for Rwanda (2010), available at http://www.unictr.org/Portals/0/English%5CLegal%5CStatute%5C2010.pdf, and Updated Statute of the International Criminal Tribunal for the Former Yugoslavia (2009), available at http://www.icty.org/x/file/Legal%20Library/Statute/statute_sept09_en.pdf.

[22] All ICTR cases are available at http://www.unictr.org/Cases/tabid/204/Default.aspx, and all ICTY cases are available at http://www.icty.org/action/cases/4.

[23] Rome Statute of the International Criminal Court (2002), available at http://untreaty.un.org/cod/icc/statute/english/rome_statute%28e%29.pdf.

[24] Margaret M. deGuzman, "Crimes Against Humanity," in Bartram S. Brown, ed., *Research Handbook on International Criminal Law* (Northampton, MA: Edgar Elgar Publishing, forthcoming, 10; available at http://ssrn.com/abstract=1745183. Other developments include the elimination of the war-nexus requirement and the addition of rape, torture, enforced disappearance and apartheid to the list of underlying criminal acts. Ibid., 9 and 18.

[25] See Rome Statute of the International Criminal Court, Article 7, Para. 1. The knowledge requirement has been variously interpreted by international tribunals. See deGuzman, "Crimes Against Humanity," p. 17.

case law of the International Criminal Court is bound to have considerable influence on the eventual answers.

B. Genocide

None of the defendants before the IMT was indicted under a charge of
genocide, although the war-crimes charge in the indictment did use the
term "genocide" in passing.[26] There was no distinct crime of genocide
until an international convention prohibiting it entered into force in 1951,[27]
several years after the end of the war. The very term, "genocide," had
only appeared in print for the first time in 1944, coined by Raphael Lemkin,
a Polish jurist and a Jew, who had fled to the United States in 1939.[28]
Lemkin subsequently explained that he created the term from the Greek
genos for tribe or race and the Latin *cide* for killing.[29] Elaborating on its
meaning, he wrote that genocide "refers to a coordinated plan aimed at
the destruction of the essential foundations of the life of national groups
so that these groups wither and die.... Genocide is directed against a
national group as an entity and the attack on individuals is only secondary to the annihilation of the national group to which they belong."[30] But
why should the annihilation of a group, over and above the murder of the
individual members, be a crime? Lemkin does not tiptoe around this
question: "By the formulation of genocide as a crime, the principle that
every national, racial and religious group has a natural right of existence
is claimed. Attacks upon such groups are in violation of that right to
exist."[31]

After the war, Lemkin campaigned for a treaty that would make genocide an international crime, and in 1948 the UN General Assembly adopted
the Convention on the Prevention and Punishment of the Crime of Genocide. The Convention defined genocide as:

> any of the following acts committed with intent to destroy, in whole
> or in part, a national, ethnical, racial or religious group, as such: (a)
> Killing members of the group; (b) Causing serious bodily or mental
> harm to members of the group; (c) Deliberately inflicting on the
> group conditions of life calculated to bring about its physical destruc-
> tion in whole or in part; (d) Imposing measures intended to prevent

[26] *Trial of the Major War Criminals*, vol. 1, 43.
[27] The Convention was adopted by the UN General Assembly in 1948 but did not enter
in force until it was ratified by the requisite number of states, which occurred in 1951.
[28] Raphael Lemkin, *Axis Rule in Occupied Europe* (New York: Howard Fertig, 1973), 79.
[29] Raphael Lemkin, "Genocide—A Modern Crime," (1945), 1, available at http://www.
preventgenocide.org/lemkin/freeworld1945.htm.
[30] Ibid., 1–2.
[31] Raphael Lemkin, "Genocide," *American Scholar* 15, no. 5 (1946): 229. I return to Lemkin's
group-based conception of genocide in Section IV, below.

births within the group; (e) Forcibly transferring children of the group to another group.[32]

The Convention deliberately omitted any war-nexus requirement, distinguishing (at the time) genocide from crimes against humanity. Moreover, the Convention did not contain any explicit contextual element in its definition of genocide, creating another key difference between genocide and crimes against humanity. The war-nexus distinction between the two categories of crime has been superceded by developments in the definition of crimes against humanity (see section II, subsection A, above). Nonetheless, there is currently debate over whether the legal definition of genocide contains a contextual element, either as an implicit component of the Convention's definition or as a part of a post-Convention development of international law. In this connection, the establishment of the International Criminal Court has proven crucial.

The state parties to the ICC adopted a document, "Elements of Crimes," intended to guide the Court's interpretation of the definitions of genocide, crimes against humanity, and war crimes contained in the Rome Statute.[33] According to the "Elements," genocide involves "conduct [that] took place in the context of a manifest pattern of similar conduct directed against [the] group or was conduct that could itself effect . . . destruction" of the group in whole or in part.[34] In other words, in order for an isolated act to count as genocide, it must by itself be capable of destroying in whole or part the targeted group; otherwise an act such as murder or rape would amount to genocide only if it occurred "in the context of a manifest pattern of similar conduct." This provision thus seems to add a contextual element to the definition of genocide.

However, some courts and theorists deny that the ICC's "Elements" has authoritatively determined that, under international law, genocide has a contextual element. For example, Florian Jessberger contends that the "Elements" does not concern the definition of genocide under international law but merely declares limits on the jurisdiction of the ICC. He argues that "[g]enocide does not require that the individual act be part of a genocidal campaign or part of a systematic or widespread attack on a protected group" and that, in contrast to a crime against humanity, "an isolated act may suffice" for genocide.[35] The ICTY has taken a similar view, arguing that the "offence of genocide . . . does not require proof that

---

[32] Convention on the Prevention and Punishment of the Crime of Genocide, Art. 2. The term "in part" is interpreted as meaning "in substantial part."

[33] Rome Statute of the International Criminal Court, Art. 9.

[34] "Elements of Crimes," (2002), Art. 6 (a), Element 4, available at http://www.icc-cpi.int/Menus/ICC/Legal+Texts+and+Tools/.

[35] Florian Jessburger, "The Definition and the Elements of the Crime of Genocide," in Paola Gaeta, ed., The UN Genocide Convention: A Commentary (Oxford: Oxford University Press, 2009), 95.

the perpetrator of genocide participated in a widespread or systematic attack."[36] On the other hand, Claus Kress argues that ICC's "Elements" articulates a condition implicit in the part of the legal definition that requires an "intent to destroy" the targeted group. He claims that a genocidal intent must pose "a real danger" for the targeted group.[37] In almost all actual cases, Kress argues, such a danger requires a context in which there is a "manifest pattern of similar conduct" by many others who are also targeting the group. In a similar vein, the ICC has itself ruled that "the contextual element of the crime of genocide is only completed when the relevant conduct presents a concrete threat to the existence of the targeted group, or part thereof."[38]

For current purposes, it is not necessary to explore the question of whether there is some contextual dimension to genocide and, if so, exactly what that dimension is. The main point to keep in mind is that, at this stage in the development of international law, the answer is not well settled among the various legal authorities. This situation does not, by itself, entail that there is no determinate legal answer. Perhaps some of the authorities are correct in what they assert to be the law. But it also seems possible that there is no determinate answer at present and that such an answer will only come to exist when the law becomes more settled than it currently is.[39]

C. Is genocide a crime against humanity?

There is a long train of scholars and international lawyers from the end of World War II to the present who have affirmed that, under international law, genocide is a type of crime against humanity. In 1949, Joseph Dautricourt declared that "genocide is . . . a crime against humanity and the wickedest of all."[40] More recently, Steven Ratner et al. have held that "genocide has typically been regarded as part of the genus crimes against

---

[36] *Prosecutor v. Krstić.* (IT-98-33-A), Appeals Chamber (19 April 2004), Sec. 223, available at http://www.icty.org/x/cases/krstic/acjug/en/krs-aj040419e.pdf.

[37] Claus Kress, "The Crime of Genocide and Contextual Elements," *Journal of International Criminal Justice* 7, vol. 2 (2009): 302.

[38] Decision on the Prosecution's Application for a Warrant of Arrest against Omar Hassan Ahmad Al Bashir (ICC-02/05-01/09), Pre-Trial Chamber I, (4 March 2009), Sec. 124, available at http://www.icc-cpi.int/iccdocs/doc/doc639096.pdf. Kress regards the "concrete threat" requirement laid down by the Court as excessively demanding. See "Crime of Genocide and Contextual Elements," 306.

[39] In the context of domestic law, Ronald Dworkin famously argues that virtually all questions of law have a legally correct answer, even when there is substantial disagreement among the legal authorities on what the answer is. I bracket the question of whether his right-answer thesis plausibly applies to international criminal law. See Ronald Dworkin, *Taking Rights Seriously* (Cambridge: Harvard University Press, 1978).

[40] Joseph Y. Dautricourt, "Crime Against Humanity: European Views on Its Conception and Its Future," *Journal of Criminal Law and Criminology* 40, vol. 2 (1949): 173.

humanity."[41] Gareth Evans tells us that genocide "is the most extreme of all crimes against humanity."[42] William Fenrick writes, "Genocide [is] the supreme crime against humanity."[43] And Ronald Slye maintains that "[t]he crime of genocide falls under the general category of crimes against humanity."[44] The idea behind these statements is that genocide is a particular type of attack on a civilian population—an attack distinguished by its specific intent to destroy (in whole or part) a certain kind of group. As Micaela Frulli explains, "The crime of genocide belongs to the class of crimes against humanity, but may now also be considered as a separate crime—itself constituting a category—because of the specific intent it requires."[45]

Although this view is held by many international lawyers, it is, surprisingly, incorrect. Under the legal definitions, genocide does not count as a type of crime against humanity. One way to see this is by considering a hypothetical case in which a genocide is directed solely against persons who have the status of combatants. Thus, imagine a state in which all soldiers come from a certain religious group, a group different from the religion to which the rest of the population belongs. An enemy state might attack those soldiers, intending to destroy the religious group as such. Under the law, such an attack would be a case of genocide but not a crime against humanity. It would be genocide because the attack was undertaken with the intent to destroy a religious group as such. It would not be a crime against humanity because it was not an attack against a civilian population.[46] Accordingly, genocide and crimes against humanity are not only distinct legal concepts, the former cannot be correctly considered to be a special case of the latter.

One should also note that, if—as some courts and commentators have argued—there is no contextual element for genocide, then genocide cannot be a type of crime against humanity, because crimes of the latter sort require such an element. Accordingly, one cannot consistently maintain that there is no contextual element to genocide and also assert that genocide is a crime against humanity. Moreover, if no determinate answer yet

[41] Steven R. Ratner, Jason S. Abrams, and James L. Bischoff, *Accountability for Human Rights Atrocities in International Law* 3rd ed. (New York: Oxford University Press, 2009), 27.
[42] Gareth Evans, *The Responsibility to Protect* (Washington D.C.: Brookings Institution Press, 2008), 20.
[43] Fenrick, "Should Crimes Against Humanity Replace War Crimes," 780.
[44] Ronald C. Slye, "Apartheid as a Crime Against Humanity," *Michigan Journal of International Law* 20, no. 2 (1999): 297.
[45] Micaela Frulli, "Are Crimes Against Humanity More Serious Than War Crimes," *European Journal of International Law* 12, no. 2 (2001): 332.
[46] It should also be noted that international courts have held that persons can be prosecuted and punished under charges of both genocide and crimes against humanity for the same act. If genocide were, legally speaking, a crime against humanity, a conviction for the more specific criminal violation, in this case, genocide, would cancel any liability for crimes against humanity. See David L. Nersessian, "Comparative Approaches to Punishing Hate: The Intersection of Genocide and Crimes Against Humanity," *Stanford Journal of International Law* 43, no. 2 (2007): 251.

exists to the question of whether there is a contextual element to geno-cide, then genocide cannot be a type of crime against humanity, because there *is* a determinate answer to the question of whether crimes against humanity have a contextual element. In sum, then, it seems that inter-national lawyers are mistaken when they assert that genocide is a type of crime against humanity.

III. THREE CONCEPTS OF GENOCIDE

The question "What is genocide?" can usefully be disambiguated into three distinct questions: 1) What is the legal definition of genocide? 2) What should the legal definition of genocide be? and 3) What concept of genocide should be used in discussing large-scale episodes of wrongful violence against certain populations? The answer to question (1) gives us the existing legal concept of genocide. The answer to question (2) gives us the ideal legal concept, and the answer to (3) gives us the moral concept. One can regard the ideal legal concept as a kind of moral concept as well, because moral considerations will be among those determining the con-tent of the concept, but I think that characterizing it as an ideal legal concept is more informative than calling it a moral concept.

It is clearly possible that the existing legal concept of genocide is not identical to the ideal legal concept. Many scholars have argued, for exam-ple, that the limitation of genocide under current law to acts against four types of groups—national, ethnic, racial, and religious—is arbitrary and should be relaxed.[47] Other scholars have defended the existing definition as better than the proposed alternatives.[48] But my concern here is not with taking sides in this debate or with proposing an answer to the question of what the ideal legal definition would be. Rather, my key point is that, whatever legal definition is ideal, the existing legal concept and the ideal one will be different in crucial ways from a concept of genocide appropriate for use in discussing large-scale episodes of wrongful vio-lence, such as the Holocaust or the Turkish massacres of Armenians. The reason is that the function of criminal law categories is quite different from the function of categories meant to capture and make moral judg-ments about large-scale social phenomena. Criminal law categories are meant to regulate and judge the conduct of individuals under the rule of law and to provide for the punishment of identifiable individuals when they are judged guilty. Accordingly, the categories must be sufficiently

---

[47] Among the critics of the legal definition's limitation of genocide to just four types of groups are Israel W. Charny, "Toward a Generic Definition of Genocide," in George J. Andreopoulos, ed., *Genocide: Conceptual and Historical Dimensions* (Philadelphia: University of Pennsylvania Press, 1994), 64–94, and Martin Shaw, *What Is Genocide?* (Malden, MA: Polity, 2007), 98–99.

[48] William Schabas, *Genocide in International Law* 2nd ed. (Cambridge: Cambridge University Press, 2009), 10.

precise to provide fair warning to persons and to allow for prosecution by procedures that treat defendants fairly. The criminal law should thus operate with a definition of genocide that enables prosecutors and courts to do their jobs consistent with due process of law.

In contrast, the question of whether the Turkish massacres of Armenians during the First World War amounted to genocide is not primarily a question of categorizing the particular acts of individuals for the purpose of regulating conduct through the threat of legal punishment. Rather, it is a question of morally categorizing a historical episode involving wrongful violence on a massive scale. Whether a genocide occurred in Turkey is different from the question of whether acts were perpetrated there that would have counted as genocide under some legal definition.

My claim, then, is that we should distinguish three concepts of genocide: the concept of genocide as an existing legal category defining a particular kind of act; the concept of genocide as an ideal legal category defining a particular kind of act, and the concept of genocide as a moral category defining a particular kind of large-scale episode of violence in the history of a society. The former two concepts function in proscribing a certain precisely defined act and in making judgments about the actual or hypothetical criminal liability of individuals alleged to have performed such acts. The latter concept functions in making moral judgments, not directly about individual persons and their discrete acts, but about episodes of wrongful violence in which the totality of violent acts reaches a certain scale and intensity not commonly found outside of war.[49] One way in which ordinary language marks the difference between the moral concept, on the one side, and the two legal concepts, on the other, is that when we use the term "a genocide" (with the indefinite article), we are invoking the moral concept, referring to a totality of related acts involving wrongful violence against a particular population on a massive scale. The problem is that the term "genocide" (without the indefinite article) can be used to refer to a totality of such acts, on the one hand, or to discrete kinds of acts defined as crimes under existing or ideal law, on the other.

One might claim that there is less to my threefold distinction than meets the eye because "a genocide" as a large-scale episode of wrongful violence simply consists of very many related discrete acts that count as genocide under the existing or some ideal legal definition.[50] Accordingly, it might seem that the only important distinction here is the one between the existing and ideal legal concepts. The distinction between those two

---

[49] I am not suggesting that a war-nexus is essential for a genocide but only that the scale and intensity of the violence is on the order that one *characteristically* finds in war but not outside of it.

[50] Cf. Steven Lee, "The Moral Distinctiveness of Genocide," *Journal of Political Philosophy* 18, no. 3 (2010): 354–55. Lee holds that "a genocide is composed of a large number of genocidal harms" (355).

concepts, on the one hand, and what I have called the moral concept of genocide, on the other, looks to be without much significance.

However, the problem with this plausible objection to the threefold distinction is that it seems possible for the machinery of violence in a genocide (i.e., a large-scale episode) to be such that most of the acts of violence would not count as acts of genocide under the law. To see why this is so, let us assume that something similar to the intent requirement in current law would be included in any viable legal definition.[51] A genocide could be planned and directed by persons with the specific intent or purpose to destroy, for example, a certain religious group as such, and yet the killings might be carried out by persons who do not have that specific intent but rather the intent to obey orders or to curry favor with the powerful or to seize the property of those whom they kill.[52] Amidst the killings and other violence in cases of this kind, there might only be a few acts of genocide as defined by (actual or ideal) law, namely, those acts undertaken by the leaders. Their acts would have the purpose of destroying the group as such, and they would be legally (and morally) responsible for the murders that they ordered. Thus, the leaders would be guilty of criminal acts of genocide. But for the totality of the acts of violence in this case to count as a genocide, it is not necessary that the persons who carried out the orders share in their leaders' purpose. In a typical case of genocide, of course, the leaders' purpose is shared by many of those who carry out the violence with their own hands. But in order for there to be a genocide, it is sufficient that the leaders had a genocidal intent and translated that intent into acts of murder, regardless of the intent of those carrying out the murders.

A genocide, then, requires that there be at least some act of genocide. But under the existing legal definition, the converse does not hold: there can be a criminal act of genocide, under the existing definition, without being accompanied by a totality of acts that amount to a genocide. The reason is that the totality of relevant acts can fail to achieve the scale needed to count as a genocide, even if there are individual criminal acts of genocide within the totality. Put another way, the existing legal definition of genocide does not require criminal acts of genocide to be part of an episode of large-scale violence directed at a certain population. Moreover, there is a strong reason for omitting any such requirement: the scale of violence needed for some totality of acts to count as a genocide cannot be specified with the kind of precision that definitions of crime should

---

[51] The existing intent requirement is widely accepted, but it is problematic, beyond its limitation of genocide-eligible groups to four. The deeper problem is that it bears the marks of Lemkin's group-based model of genocide, a model which I reject in Section IV below. The model that I defend, a "discrimination model," reformulates the intent requirement, but for the time being, I will use the existing formulation. The argument I give here goes through on either formulation.

[52] Cf. Lee, "The Moral Distinctiveness of Genocide," 355.

have. Judging a totality of acts of violence as a genocide inescapably involves relatively vague criteria. The key point here is that the definition of the crime of genocide rightly avoids questions of what makes an episode of violence a genocide and instead sets down precise criteria that provide persons with fair warning but have some appropriate connection to genocide as a large-scale episode of violence. In section IV, I sketch a model for understanding genocide that formulates criteria for genocide as a large-scale episode of violence and delineates the connection between those criteria and a suitable account of the crime of genocide.

The failure to recognize the difference between genocide as an episode of mass violence and genocide as an act contrary to existing (or ideal) law leads to many confusions in discussions and disagreements about genocide. Consider, for example, the U.S. war in Vietnam. In 1966, with the war raging, Bertrand Russell organized a war crimes tribunal in order to address, among other issues, the question of whether there was genocide against the Vietnamese by Americans. In her summary of the evidence and judgments of the tribunal, Arlette El Kaïm-Sartre refers to the "massive bombings" by Americans and other such "infringements on the life and liberty" of the Vietnamese, and she states that the tribunal "wanted to determine if the totality of these acts, committed within a war of aggression, could be classified as genocide." She then explains that "[t]he legal commission of the Tribunal, in order to answer this question, examined the terms of the International Convention . . . on Genocide, which defines this crime."[53]

Kaïm-Sartre (and perhaps the legal commission, as well) has conflated the moral concept of genocide, which categorizes episodes of massive violence, with the legal concept of genocide, which defines a certain criminal act. The Convention on Genocide is of little help in determining whether "the totality of . . . acts" taken by the United States against the Vietnamese can be "classified as genocide." Whether it can be so classified is a matter of the moral concept. It is true that the definition given by the Convention helps to answer the question of whether particular U.S. officials or military officers or personnel perpetrated criminal acts of genocide. As we have seen, one cannot have a genocide without some act of genocide. But the question of whether particular Americans perpetrated criminal acts of genocide is much different from the question of whether the totality of the violence perpetrated by Americans during the war could be "classified as genocide."

The distinction between genocide as an episode of massive violence, on the one hand, and genocide as an act in violation of existing or

---

[53] Arlette El Kaïm-Sartre, "A Summary of the Evidence and the Judgments: An Introduction," in Jean-Paul Sartre, *On Genocide* (Boston: Beacon Press, 1968), 50. In its judgment, "the Tribunal unanimously declared the United States guilty of the crime of genocide" (53). For the tribunal's rationale for its finding, see Jean-Paul Sartre, *On Genocide*, 57–85. Sartre was the executive president of the tribunal.

ideal law, on the other, should make one wary of arguments that move directly from a claim about which historic episodes of violence properly count as genocide to a conclusion about what the legal definition of genocide should contain. For example, Frank Chalk argues that political groups should be added to the list of eligible groups in the legal definition, on the ground that Stalin's mass murders of so-called "class enemies" and "enemies of the people" count as genocide.[54] But this argument conflates a question about the ideal legal definition with a question about which episodes of large-scale killing count as genocides. Moreover, almost all discussions of the legal definition of genocide are guilty of the same conflation, because they fail to distinguish the use of the term 'genocide' to characterize, for example, the Holocaust or the Rwandan killings, on the one hand, and its use to characterize a criminal act, on the other.

One might claim that the contextual element that the ICC has arguably added to the legal definition of genocide undercuts my distinction between genocide as massive violence and genocide as an act that violates existing or ideal law. The argument would be that the contextual element does two things: first, it requires that a criminal act of genocide take place within the context of a genocide, and, second, it provides a standard for determining whether there is a genocide. However, this argument fails because the ICC's contextual element falls well short on both counts.

Recall that the contextual element requires that a criminal act of genocide either a) be accompanied by a "manifest pattern" of similar acts against the members of the targeted group or b) be such that it "could itself effect . . . destruction" of the targeted group in whole or part. Under the second disjunct, it is clear that a genocide is not needed as the context for a criminal act of genocide. For example, under the disjunct, killing just one person on account of his religion in a failed attempt to use deadly biological materials to kill thousands of persons of the same faith could count as a criminal act of genocide.[55] Yet, it is clear there is no mass violence of the kind needed for a genocide to have taken place. The act was one that "could itself effect . . . destruction" of the targeted group, but through the perpetrator's miscalculation or bad luck, the intended destruction failed to materialize.

The first disjunct contains a standard that might look at first glance to provide a criterion that determines when there is a genocide: a "manifest pattern" of acts against members of the targeted group must exist. However, closer inspection shows that the standard is not plausible as such a criterion. A manifest pattern of acts causing serious mental or even phys-

---

[54] Frank Chalk, "Redefining Genocide," in Andreopoulos ed., *Genocide: Conceptual and Historical Dimensions*, 50.

[55] One can suppose that, in the hypothetical case described in the text, the only one harmed by the attack is the one person who was killed.

ical harm to members of a certain religious group does not, by itself, rise to the level of a genocide. For example, the pattern could be part of a national spike in "hate crimes," (i.e., crimes committed from some form of prejudice) but not reaching the scale needed for a genocide.[56] The manifest-pattern standard is meant to exclude from the definition of genocide most isolated acts against the members of a targeted group. (The second disjunct is meant to specify those exceptional isolated acts that would count as genocide). But the exclusion of isolated acts by the manifest-pattern standard does not come close to requiring the scale of violence that is needed for a genocide.

David Nersessian claims that an act of genocide under international law need not involve the infliction of any harm whatsoever. He writes that such an act "becomes an international matter based solely upon the offender's malevolent intent and an underlying act against group members. It can be stopped and punished as soon as it starts; as an inchoate offense, it need not blossom into actual harm."[57] An inchoate offense is one that, as with attempted murder or solicitation to murder, need not involve the realization of an actual harm. Such offenses are often characterized as "incomplete," and a person charged with an incomplete offense (attempted murder of individual A) cannot be simultaneously charged with the completed offense (murder of A). An examination of the acts that can count as genocide under international law lends support for Nersessian's claim. Those acts are: 1) killing, 2) causing serious bodily or mental harm, 3) inflicting on the targeted group conditions of life calculated to bring about its physical destruction, 4) imposing measures intended to prevent births within the group, and 5) forcibly transferring children of the group to another group. The first two types of act, as well as the last, are inherently harmful. But that leaves two other sorts of genocidal act: inflicting conditions calculated to bring about physical destruction and imposing measures intended to prevent births. It is possible that such acts do not cause any harm: conditions calculated to destroy the group might be poorly calculated and fail to harm anyone, and measures intended to prevent births might prove wholly ineffective and harmless. So Nersessian is right to think of genocide as an inchoate crime insofar as two of the five genocidal act-types enumerated in international law do not necessarily involve any harm.

But there is a deeper way in which he is right: genocide is essentially a crime of attempt, even in cases where a harm such as killing or serious injury is achieved by the perpetrators. What is attempted is massive harm against members of a group, and it would be rare that such harm could be accomplished by the hands of a single genocidaire. It typically takes

---

[56] I accept the idea that there is an analogy between hate crimes and crimes of genocide, as my discrimination model of genocide will make clear, but there are also differences that will become clear. Also see Lee, "The Moral Distinctiveness of Genocide," 346.

[57] Nersessian, "Comparative Approaches to Punishing Hate," 263.

many hands working together. It is true that the acts of those many hands can be attributed to the planners and organizers, and so we can say that those individuals are morally responsible for the massive harm that resulted. But if there is to be a crime of genocide that can be used to prosecute, not just the leaders, but the persons who are perpetrating the violence with their own hands, then the crime cannot be conceived as one that completes or realizes the massive harm that is intended by the leaders. Rather, the crime must be conceptualized as a kind of attempt, in which, for example, killing or forcibly sterilizing forty or fifty or one hundred persons is regarded as a step—but only a step—toward the realization of the massive harm. Accordingly, I think that Nersessian is right to characterize genocide as an inchoate crime, even though some of its elements do involve actual harm.

IV. GENOCIDE: THE CULTURAL AND DISCRIMINATION MODELS

When Lemkin coined the term "genocide," he was trying to capture the moral core of such large-scale episodes of violence as the Turkish massacre of Armenians and the Nazi slaughter of Jews. But he was also concerned with crafting a legal definition of genocide that would criminalize acts undertaken in furtherance of such episodes. Crimes have victims, but if the victims of genocide were individuals, then it seemed to Lemkin that there would be no reason to have a new category of crime. The perpetrators of mass violence were guilty of old-fashioned crimes that victimized individuals, crimes such as homicide, albeit homicide on a vast scale. If his new category of crime was to be justified, Lemkin thought, he needed to show that it had a different sort of victim. He regarded his key insight to be that the victims of genocide *qua* genocide were not individuals but groups. Although he did not explicitly draw the distinction between genocide as an episode of large-scale violence and genocide as a criminal act, we can construe his insight as follows: genocide as large-scale violence is the killing of a cultural group, and genocide as a criminal act is, roughly, an act intentionally taken in furtherance of such a killing.

For Lemkin, conceiving of the large-scale phenomenon of genocide solely in terms of the mass murder of individuals had two serious flaws. First, it failed to recognize that cultural groups can be killed by means other than the murder of their members. A cultural group depends on a shared form of life that is transmitted from one generation to the next and so can be destroyed by sterilizing its members, forcibly dispersing its children to other groups, outlawing the group's distinctive language or customs and so on. Second, the idea of "mass murder did not convey the specific losses to civilization in the form of the cultural contributions which can be made only by groups of people united through national, racial or cultural characteristics."[58] Elaborating on the importance of cultural diversity, Lemkin claimed that "[o]ur whole cultural heritage is a product of the contributions of all peoples" and that genocides constituted a loss to "human culture."[59] It was, evidently, this high value that he placed on the cultural diversity of humanity that led Lemkin to claim that groups organized around a distinctive culture have a right to exist.

Ironically, there appears to have been considerable doubt about Lemkin's cultural model of genocide among the parties who adopted the final version of the Convention Against Genocide. An earlier draft of the Convention had contained the category of cultural genocide and defined it as "[d]estroying the specific characteristics of the group."[60] Acts counting as cultural genocide under the draft included: prohibiting the use of the group's national language, systematically destroying the group's religious texts or others books written in its national language, and forcibly transferring its children to other groups. However, the category of cultural genocide was voted out of the final draft, although a remaining residue was the inclusion of the forcible transfer of children in the enumeration of the kinds of acts that can count as genocide.

There is good reason to find the cultural model problematic. For example, it is unclear how the model is consistent with the existence of genocide against racial groups, without the assumption that different racial groups have, by their nature, different cultural forms. Genocidaires might believe in such racial essentialism, but there is no reason for our understanding of genocide to rest on the premise that the mass killing of the members of a certain race amounts to genocide only when the racial group has distinctive cultural forms. It would seem that, whether or not the members of a certain race form a distinct cultural group, it is enough to judge that a genocide has occurred that there were mass killings of persons belonging to the race simply because they belonged to the race. Moreover, in those genocides in which there are not only mass killings but also the destruction of the cultural life of a certain group, such as was the case with the Nazi annihilation of Jewish life in Eastern Europe, the moral horror of the genocide stems mainly from the mass killings.[61] The cultural model thus fails to get to the moral heart of the matter, and Lemkin's rationale for his neologism notwithstanding, a genocide should not be understood as a killing with a cultural group as its victim.

But if Lemkin's model is problematic, what model is better? Unfortunately, the parties who adopted the Convention on Genocide did not

---

[58] Raphael Lemkin, "Genocide as a Crime under International Law," *American Journal of International Law* 41, no. 1 (1947): 147.

[59] Lemkin, "Genocide—A Modern Crime," 9–10.

[60] Convention on the Prevention and Punishment of the Crime of Genocide, Secretariat Draft, Article I, Sec. II, Para. 3. (1947), available at http://www.preventgenocide.org/law/convention/drafts.

[61] Cf. Douglas P. Lackey, "Extraordinary Evil or Common Malevolence? Evaluating the Jewish Holocaust," *Journal of Applied Philosophy* 3, no. 2 (1986): 174.

explain what alternative to the cultural model, if any, they had in mind, and widespread confusion about the different concepts of genocide has obstructed the development of a sound alternative. My suggestion is that the problems confronting Lemkin's model can be avoided by thinking of genocide as an extreme case of discrimination.[62]

Beginning with genocide as a large-scale episode of violence, it should be understood as a totality of violent acts such that the acts are a) organized, b) guided by the intent or purpose of severely harming the members of a certain social group because they are members of the group,[63] c) inflicted on a massive scale, and d) taken to the extremes of killing, torture, beatings, and other grave assaults on the fundamental interests of the members of the group. On this model, there is no assumption that some distinctive cultural group has been destroyed, in whole or in part. Instead, there is the idea that large numbers of individuals have suffered severe and wrongful harm on account of an organized campaign against them for belonging to a certain social group. If a distinctive culture is thereby destroyed, then that fact certainly should be taken into account in discussing the things of value that the genocide has destroyed. But the discrimination model does not take the destruction of a cultural group or shared form of life to be the gravamen of genocide. The essential wrong of a genocide consists in wrongs to individuals, and the moral horror of a genocide lies in the scale and the severity of those wrongs as well as their purposeful and organized character.[64]

If genocide is not understood as the killing of a group, should the forcible transfer of children, then, be deleted from the list of genocidal acts? Not necessarily. Such a transfer is a grievous wrong, harmful in the extreme to the parents and often to the children. So the inclusion of forcible transfer in a conception of genocide as an episode of large-scale

---

[62] Discrimination is sometimes divided into two main forms: direct (intentional) and indirect (structural). It is the direct form that I am using here as the model for understanding genocide. On the difference between direct and indirect discrimination, see Andrew Altman, "Discrimination," The Stanford Encyclopedia of Philosophy (Spring 2011 Edition), Edward N. Zalta (ed.), forthcoming, ⟨http://plato.stanford.edu/archives/spr2011/entries/discrimination/⟩. My discrimination model of genocide shares much with the account offered in Lee, "The Moral Distinctiveness of Genocide." However, I do not accept his explanation of which groups are "genocide-eligible," (336) and I think that his account would be strengthened by including the threefold distinction that I draw among concepts of genocide and by more explicitly taking discrimination as a model for understanding genocide in its legal and moral senses.

[63] For there to be a genocide, someone must have the intent described in (b), and the intent must guide the mass violence referred to in (c) and (d). However, it is not required that each agent of the violence, or even most of them, have this discriminatory intent; only the leaders might have it.

[64] Critics of antidiscrimination law might balk at using the idea of discrimination in an account of genocide. However, most such critics aim at those antidiscrimination laws that apply to private persons and groups, rather than laws prohibiting discrimination by public entities. See, for example, Richard Epstein, Forbidden Grounds (Cambridge: Harvard University Press, 1992).

violence could be justified without invoking the idea that genocide is essentially about cultural group destruction.

Aside from questions about what kinds of acts can count as genocidal, one might ask why there should be a requirement that a genocide be organized. After all, it does seem possible for there to be a situation in which uncoordinated and independent discriminatory acts of violence against the members of a certain group add up to the scale of violence that is needed for a genocide. Why should such a situation not count as a genocide against the members of the group? The answer is that the requirement of organized violence is needed to capture the central cases of genocide. Cases in which an aggregate of uncoordinated and independent discriminatory acts of violence amount to massive and extreme violence against the members of the targeted group are certainly possible. However, such cases are anomalous, because coordination—even if it is only informal—is ordinarily such a powerful multiplier of the effects of human action, including its harmful effects, and independent action is ordinarily quite meager in what it can accomplish.

Still, one might ask what work the moral concept of genocide really does. We already have the concepts of mass murder, mass atrocity, and so forth. What good is yet another moral concept? The answer is that many of the great evils of history are instances of organized, purposeful, massive, and extreme discrimination directed at the members of various social groups. The concept of genocide, understood in terms of a discrimination model, does a better job of capturing and conveying the character of these evils than does the coarser-grained categories of mass murder and mass atrocity.

Turning to genocide as a criminal act, the main difference between the existing definition and what would be suggested by a discrimination model concerns the intent requirement. The existing requirement bears the marks of Lemkin's cultural group model: "intent to destroy, in whole or in part, a national, ethnical, racial or religious group, as such." This way of understanding genocidal intent makes perfect sense, assuming that the gravamen of genocide is, as Lemkin holds, the effort to contribute to the destruction of a group as such. But the discrimination model regards such an effort as adventitious. The essence of the crime should be delineated, not in terms of the intent to contribute to a group's destruction, but rather in terms of the intent to contribute to organized, massive, and extreme discrimination directed against the members of a group. Accordingly, the law should not refer to the intent to destroy a group as such but rather to the discriminatory intent to severely harm members of the group because they are members; more specifically, the law should define genocide in terms of such intent *and* the perpetrators' accompanying knowledge that their acts are part of an organized and massive campaign of extreme discrimination against the group. Moreover, it is the knowledge requirement that distinguishes an act of genocide from a hate crime, because the latter does not necessarily occur as a conscious part of an organized and massive campaign of extreme discrimination.

Nothing in my criticism of the Lemkin model should be taken to deny that the existing legal concept has proven to be of value in the effort to prosecute and punish persons who have perpetrated egregious wrongs. But contrary to Lemkin, this value has not derived from finding a special victim of genocide, "the group," over and above the individual victims. Rather, it has come from the fact that the legal concept solved a practical problem for lawyers: How could the perpetrators of genocidal murders, rapes, and so forth be prosecuted in courts other than the domestic tribunals of the states where those crimes took place? By tradition, murder, rape and other crimes of violence are firmly entrenched within the domestic jurisdiction of states, and even the horrors of World War II could not dislodge those crimes from their domestic homes. But a new crime would not have that jurisdictional limitation if it were declared at the outset to be an international crime within the jurisdiction of international tribunals. It is true that the Convention on Genocide did not go as far as some had hoped in the matter of jurisdiction: it declared that the crime "shall be tried by a competent tribunal of the State in the territory of which the act was committed, or by such international penal tribunal as may have jurisdiction with respect to those Contracting Parties which shall have accepted its jurisdiction."[65] Because no such tribunal was established by the Convention, or by any other treaty until the ICC was created some five decades later, the jurisdictional provision of the Convention was seen as something of a toothless tiger. But the Convention had laid down the important principle that genocide was not an ordinary domestic crime, such a murder or rape, but rather a crime that potentially fell within the jurisdiction of an international criminal tribunal. The step to create the tribunals for Rwanda and Yugoslavia, and later the ICC, was long in coming, but, conceptually, it was a short one from the Convention.

Lemkin's cultural model of genocide tried to solve what was essentially a lawyer's problem of jurisdiction by positing that genocide had a special victim that traditional domestic crimes such as murder lacked, namely, the group. But aside from the problems already enumerated in making the group the victim, it is not necessary to do so in order to meet the jurisdiction problem. If a population within a state is subjected to organized, purposive, massive, and extreme violence, and the state is failing to prosecute the perpetrators (perhaps because its agents are among the perpetrators), then there is no good argument that international courts should be barred from exercising jurisdictional authority in the matter. Thus, the discrimination model can dispense with the group-victim idea and still affirm that international tribunals can legitimately exercise jurisdiction in cases of genocide.

[65] Convention on Genocide, Art. VI.

As with any conception of genocide, the discrimination model faces the difficult question of which types of social groups should count as genocide-eligible. I leave that question open here. My suspicion, though, is that the answer is connected to the answer to the question of which categories are properly protected by antidiscrimination law. Thus, an examination of the various arguments about protected categories in antidiscrimination law might prove helpful in addressing what seem to be parallel questions regarding the law of genocide.

V. Crimes Against Humanity: The Legal and Moral Concepts

I now turn to the legal and the moral concepts of crimes against humanity. My aim is to show that these are two very different concepts that have been conflated with one another due to the powerful moral resonance of the phrase "crimes against humanity."

As we have seen in section II above, the legal concept of crimes against humanity refers to a widespread or systematic attack on a civilian population or the persecution of persons based on political, racial, or religious grounds. Notice that there is nothing in the definition that requires an egregiously high toll in the number of persons killed or otherwise severely harmed. A widespread or systematic attack might aim for an egregiously high death toll, or its perpetrators might only aim to kill a handful of civilians as an object lesson to the rest. Of course, even in the latter case, reasonable fear for their safety will be spread among the entire targeted population. The same goes for persecution, where, for example, a few offenders might be tortured as a lesson to the rest. Those who live in reasonable fear for their safety, as well as those who are killed, tortured or otherwise abused are among the victims of crimes against humanity.

However, the moral concept of crimes against humanity extends the scope of victimhood well beyond those who are directly abused and those who live in reasonable fear for their own safety as a result of the direct abuse of others. The moral concept centers on the idea of a wrongful harm done to humanity or humankind.

Perhaps the first philosophers to discuss the moral concept were Karl Jaspers and Hannah Arendt.[66] Shortly before the trial of Adolf Eichmann (1961), Arendt and Jaspers exchanged letters on the proceedings and on the Holocaust. Jaspers wrote to Arendt, "what was done to the Jews was done not only to the Jews but essentially to humankind. . . . From the very beginning we have been in complete agreement on the main point: the

---

[66] Arendt sometimes gives the credit to Francois de Menthon, French prosecutor at Nuremberg, who spoke at the trial of "crimes against human status (*la condition humaine*)" and their violation of both human dignity and "the permanence of the human being considered within the whole of humanity." *Trial of the Major War Criminals*, vol. V, 406 and 408. However, I find de Menthon's remarks about "the whole of humanity" to be obscure.

302   ANDREW ALTMAN

Eichmann case concerns humankind and should not be reduced to an Israeli issue."[67] Subsequently, Arendt wrote in her account of the Eichmann trial that she and Jaspers agreed that the Nazi genocide was a crime against humanity because "the crime against the Jews was also a crime against mankind."[68]

More recently, many scholars have given voice to the moral concept that Jaspers and Arendt discussed. Thus, Larry May argues that, while domestic crimes harm a particular national community, acts that are punished under the law as crimes against humanity "must be shown to be in some sense assaults against humanity, not merely against the domestic State."[69] Alain Finkielkraut writes of the crimes for which Klaus Barbie was prosecuted that they "attack, as their name indicates, all of humanity."[70] Margaret deGuzman asserts that crimes against humanity "violate not only the individual victim but all of humanity."[71] And former Canadian foreign minister, Lloyd Axelworthy, claims that "some crimes are so horrific, so offensive, that they are perpetrated not only against their victims but against humanity."[72]

Courts have also employed the moral concept of crimes against humanity in their explanation of the legal concept. Thus, the International Criminal Tribunal for Yugoslavia (ICTY) has written that "it is . . . the concept of humanity as victim which essentially characterises crimes against humanity."[73] And in the Klaus Barbie case, the French Court of Cassation has declared that, unlike murder, in a crime against humanity "there is not merely a single victim but humanity."[74]

Additionally, there are many contemporary thinkers who employ the moral concept of crimes against humanity to characterize the crime of genocide. Thus, Raimond Gaitra contends that genocide is a "crime against the constituency of humankind as that is represented in the community of nations."[75] And Adam Jones poses the rhetorical question, ". . . if the

[67] Lotte Kohler and Hans Saner, eds., *Hannah Arendt, Karl Jaspers, Correspondence* (New York: Harcourt Brace Jovanovich, 1992), 420, 424.
[68] Hannah Arendt, *Eichmann in Jerusalem* (New York: Penguin Books, 1994/1963), 269. Also see Karl Jaspers, "Who Should Have Tried Eichmann?" *Journal of International Criminal Justice* 4, no. 4 (2006): 853–58.
[69] Larry May, *Genocide* (Cambridge: Cambridge University Press, 201), 12.
[70] Alain Finkielkraut, *Remembering in Vain* (New York: Columbia University Press, 1982), 9.
[71] Margaret deGuzman, "The Road From Rome: The Developing Law of Crimes Against Humanity," *Human Rights Quarterly* 22, no. 2 (2000): 338.
[72] Lloyd Axelworthy, "Afterword: The Politics of Advancing International Justice," in Stephen Macedo, ed., *Universal Jurisdiction* (Philadelphia: University of Pennsylvania Press, 2004), 260.
[73] *Prosecutor v. Erdemovic* (IT-96-22-T), Trial Chamber (29 November 1996), Sec. 28, available at http://www.icty.org/x/cases/erdemovic/tjug/en/erd-tsj961129e.pdf.
[74] Court of Cassation, Judgment of 20 December 1985, quoted in Frulli, "Are Crimes Against Humanity More Serious Than War Crimes," 347.
[75] Raimond Gaitra, "Refocusing Genocide: A Philosophical Responsibility," in John K. Roth, ed., *Genocide and Human Rights* (New York: Palgrave MacMillan, 2005), 164.

crime [of genocide] is not against human beings on a massive and systematic scale—therefore, in the contemporary understanding, a crime against all humanity—then what is?"[76]

It is not immediately obvious just what is involved in the thought that crimes against humanity (or criminal acts of genocide) victimize humanity or humankind. Perhaps, the idea is that such crimes, as defined by the law, constitute wrongful harms against all or almost all human beings. But little explanation is offered to clarify or make credible the claim that humanity is the victim. If someone were deliberately to start a nuclear war, resulting in high amounts of radiation spreading across the globe and the attendant calamitous consequences for the entire human race, then the idea that such a persons was guilty of a crime that victimized humankind would be reasonable: the crime would result in severe harm for virtually every human being. But no crime against humanity (as defined by the law) that has so far been perpetrated has even remotely approximated such a calamity.

One might argue that the Nazi extermination of Jews, which was tied to the global calamity of World War II, would fit the bill for a crime that victimized humanity. However, the calamitous collapse of the global political and economic structure was the product of German aggression against other states and not the result of the extermination of Jews. This understanding of history is reflected in the fact that the IMT regarded the Third Reich's crimes of peace (i.e., its aggression), and not its crimes against humanity, as the "supreme crime."[77] Moreover, even if the Nazi exterminations were, in their totality, correctly thought of as resulting in a global calamity, few other genocides or crimes against humanity, if any, could be plausibly said to have had harmful effects on the same order of magnitude.

The skeptical assertions of certain scholars reflect the suspicion that no crime against humanity, as the law defines it, actually victimizes humanity. In discussing the sentencing of persons found guilty of crimes against humanity in the former Yugoslavia and Rwanda, Allison Danner criticizes the suggestion that courts should be guided by the idea that the guilty parties have victimized humanity. Danner writes that "it is hyperbolic to assert... that the defendant's act has affected humanity as a whole," and she argues that basing sentences on the exaggeration "that humanity is a victim... weaken[s] international criminal justice."[78] David Nersessian is even more blunt:

---

[76] Adam Jones, *Crimes Against Humanity: A Beginner's Guide* (Oxford: Oneworld, 2008), 19.

[77] Bernard D. Meltzer, "A Note on Some Aspects of the Nuremberg Debate," *University of Chicago Law Review* 14 (1947): 463. "Genocide is now often said to be the most serious crime, the "crime of crimes." See Schabas, *Genocide in International Law*, 11.

[78] Allison Danner, "Constructing a Hierarchy of Crimes in International Criminal Law Sentencing," *Virginia Law Review* 87, no. 3 (2001): 476–77.

The notion of "humanity" as a victim is more rhetorical flourish than legal substance. As horrible as atrocities in Yugoslavia and Rwanda were, it is doubtful that people in Central China or New York (equal members of "humanity") were legitimate "victims" of those tragedies. Exactly the opposite is true. It is demeaning to suggest that a woman who lost her husband and sons in Srebrenica and was herself raped somehow is on equal footing with a London resident who read about Serbian atrocities in the newspaper.[79]

These skeptical remarks of Danner and Nersessian are well taken. I do not mean that the remarks settle the issue, but they do raise doubts about whether there is some plausible account of how humankind or humanity is literally victimized by acts that meet the legal definition of crimes against humanity.[80] Larry May aims to provide such an account, arguing that, "because of the shared interests in peace and basic human rights protection, on the part of all humans in all political communities, there is enough solidarity among humans to speak nonmetaphorically about the human or international community . . . . Even though the community that is humanity is not a political community, it is a community that can be harmed."[81] But even if May is right that humanity is a community that can be wrongfully harmed, it does not follow that a crime against humanity, as defined by law, actually does wrongfully harm humanity.

Arendt once suggested that a crime against humanity is "an attack upon human diversity as such, that is, upon a characteristic of the 'human status' without which the very words 'mankind' or 'humanity' would be devoid of meaning."[82] The meaning of this suggestion is obscure. She might be gesturing at Lemkin's idea that the destruction of a religious or national group deprives the rest of humanity of the distinctive cultural contribution of that group (see section IV, above). But even if Lemkin's idea is true, it would only apply in those few cases in which a group was completely destroyed. Moreover, it would also need to be shown that the rest of humanity has a right to the contribution of the group, not merely that the destruction of the group is against the interests of the rest of humanity. For otherwise, humanity would not be *wrongfully* harmed and so it would be inaccurate to characterize humanity as a victim.

Another effort to explain how crimes against humanity are literally wrongful harms to humankind is provided by Christopher Macleod. He

[79] Nersessian, "Comparative Approaches to Punishing Hate," 259.

[80] In addition to the discussions of crimes against humanity cited above, important contributions to the argument are made by David Luban, "A Theory of Crimes Against Humanity," *Yale Journal of International Law* 29, no. 1 (2004): 82–167, and Richard Vernon, "What is Crime Against Humanity?" *Journal of Political Philosophy* 10, no. 3 (2002): 231–49.

[81] Larry May, "Humanity, International Crime, and the Rights of Defendants," *Ethics and International Affairs* 20, no. 3 (2006): 375–76.

[82] Arendt, *Eichmann in Jerusalem*, 268–69.

begins by distinguishing humankind as the collection of all humans from humankind as a "singular body," or "*grand-etre*," as he calls it (borrowing from Comte).[83] Macleod's argument is intended to make plausible the idea that "[h]umanity, thought of as one entity, can be said to have . . . interests on its own terms." The core of the argument appeals to ordinary ways in which we talk about humanity and humankind, outside of the context of international criminal law. Thus, Macleod writes that "we describe human-kind (*sic*) as having achievements, interests, and goals" when we are not talking about crimes against humanity, and he points out that there is nothing amiss in saying that "human-kind has landed on the moon . . . [,] is trying to create a peaceful and just world . . . , and needs to find a sustainable form of energy." Additionally, "[w]e often treat universities, nations, and clubs as having attitudes and objectives which do not seem in any clear way identical to those of the persons who make them up. Talking of humankind in this way is merely to talk of another group."[84] And just as other groups have interests which can be set back, Macleod asserts that so does humanity as a singular body: "Human-kind . . . can be plausibly said to have interests and to be capable of damage as one agent." Crimes against humanity count as wrongs, according to Macleod, in virtue of the fact that, "[w]hen . . . a state massacres a population, damage is done to the *grand-etre* because its interests are seriously violated."[85]

MacLeod's argument circumvents the problem that virtually no actual crime against humanity seems to harm all or almost all humans. However, it suffers from the problem that humankind—the *grand-etre*—is not plausibly represented as an agent. It is true that the human species has a kind of overall structure, segmented into various political units and legal associations. But the structure is not one that could ground the literal truth of claims to the effect that humanity has performed a certain action or otherwise exercised agency. The United States can act, and NATO can act. But humanity has no institutional structure through which it can act. Even if one day some altered form of the UN could act for humanity, the current UN falls far short on that score, containing as it does many authoritarian states that cannot even be said to be the agents of their own people. And the assertion that humankind has landed on the moon is simply a way of saying that certain members of the human species conceived, organized, and successfully carried out a moon landing. Those members and their associations, not humankind, are the relevant agents. The rest of us humans might stand in the reflected glory, but it *is* reflected glory: we do not merit credit for the impressive achievement of sending some humans to the moon.

[83] Christopher Macleod, "Towards a Philosophical Account of Crimes Against Humanity," *European Journal of International Law* 21, no. 2 (2010): 293.
[84] Ibid., 296.
[85] Ibid., 298.

It might turn out that there is some plausible way to explain how crimes against humanity victimize humanity. However, no actual crime against humanity seems to come close to harming all or most humans, and no actual crime against humanity seems to come close to seriously damaging the global political or economic structure of humanity. At best, a large question mark hangs over the oft repeated claim that crimes against humanity literally have humanity as their victim. Accordingly, it is not clear that the moral concept of crimes against humanity sheds any light on the criminal actions and historical episodes to which it has been applied.

VI. Crimes Against Humanity: Sources of Confusion

The conflation between the legal and moral concepts of crimes against humanity derives from the combination of two ideas. First is the idea that the enormities for which the Nazis were prosecuted at Nuremberg were so great that they wronged humankind. Second is the assumption that those enormities are paradigmatic cases of the legal category of crimes against humanity. Putting these two ideas together, one naturally—but unsoundly—infers the conclusion that crimes against humanity, in the legal sense, are wrongful harms to humankind. Let us examine more closely the two ideas.

It is understandable that many people have sympathy for the idea that the Nazi enormities wrongfully harmed humankind. The scale and horror of those enormities are staggering to anyone with a remotely adequate sense of justice. But we have seen that it is questionable to claim that crimes against humanity (or genocides) literally victimize humanity. My own view is that characterizing Nazi atrocities as crimes that victimize *humankind* is best understood as a metaphor that helps to emphasize how morally outrageous the crimes were.[86] In other words, by so characterizing the atrocities, one is saying that, in their totality, they were so massively wrong that it is as though the Nazis grievously wronged billions of innocent humans. But even if I am mistaken in this view and Nazi atrocities were so vast and egregious that they did wrongfully harm humankind in some literal sense, it would still be a mistake to think that crimes against humanity under the law are crimes that wrong humankind. The reason is that, in virtually every case, crimes against humanity, as defined by the law, are crimes involving wrongful harms that are of a much lower order of magnitude than the crimes perpetrated by the Nazis. Thus, even if the Nazi crimes wronged humankind, the same cannot be plausibly said of most other legal cases of crimes against humanity.

---

[86] Vernon holds that the phrase "crime against humanity" "is a figure of speech." See his "What is Crime Against Humanity?" 232. He does not make it clear, though, exactly how it is a figure of speech or why he thinks that it is a fitting figure of speech.

One might argue that, if it is conceded that Nazi atrocities wrongfully harmed humankind, then the conclusion can be drawn that the typical crime against humanity, in the legal sense, also does wrongful harm to humankind, because the Nazi atrocities are paradigmatic crimes against humanity, in the legal sense. But it is a mistake to take the Nazi crimes as paradigmatic crimes against humanity, i.e., it is incorrect to treat Nazi crimes as a standard case of crimes against humanity. The mistake is understandable in light of the strong psychological association between the term 'crimes against humanity' and the enormities perpetrated by the Third Reich. But it *is* a mistake: although Nazi crimes are incontestable instances of the legal category of crimes against humanity, they are also extreme cases.[87] Extreme cases make bad paradigms because they are idiosyncratic and have morally important features that typical cases lack. Accordingly, one cannot infer that crimes against humanity, in the legal sense, typically do wrongful harm to humanity from the assumption that Nazi crimes against humanity did such harm.[88]

VII. Conclusion

Over the past sixty years, international criminal law has played an increasingly important role in efforts to translate the moral lessons that emerged out of the ruins of the Second World War into the concrete realities of political and social life. That it has not been effective in deterring large-scale atrocities or even ending impunity for such events goes without saying. That greater effectiveness is something for which one should hope would be questioned only by a few. At least in the short term, greater effectiveness does not depend on greater conceptual clarity about the law but rather on better institutions at the national and international levels. Still, over the long run, increased conceptual clarity might play some modest role.

In this paper, I have tried to put two of the core categories of international criminal law—genocide and crimes against humanity—into sharper conceptual focus. I have argued that scholars, lawyers, and judges have widely misunderstood these categories, in large part because they have conflated the legal concepts of genocide and crimes against humanity with the moral concepts. This conflation is not the same kind about

[87] I do not mean to take a stand here on whether or not the legal category of crimes against humanity was retroactively applied to Nazi atrocities. The atrocities fit the legal definition of such crimes, even assuming that the legal category needed to be applied retroactively.

[88] Larry May holds that the Holocaust is a paradigmatic case of the concept of genocide but that understanding the concept requires us to take account of other examples. See his *Genocide*, 80–81. If May means that the Holocaust is an incontestable case of the legal and moral concepts of genocide, then I agree with him. But if he means that the Holocaust is a good model for understanding those two concepts of genocide, then I disagree: it is not a good model for either concept.

which legal positivists complain when they charge that natural law thinkers confuse law and morality, and my concern has not been the positivist one relating to the conditions under which a norm has legal validity. Rather, the concern has been to clarify the concepts that scholars, lawyers, and judges are deploying when they seek both to grasp the moral significance of episodes of large-scale violence and to prosecute and punish persons for their involvement in such violence. A conceptual division of labor is needed for these two jobs—moral concepts for the former task and legal ones for the latter.

The legal concept of crimes against humanity has done valuable work in bringing a small measure of justice to men who organized and participated in some of the worst atrocities of the past century. But I have tried to cast some doubt on the value of the moral concept of crimes against humanity, suggesting that it does not literally apply to the acts and episodes that it is meant to capture. The legal concept of genocide has also done valuable work in bringing some measure of justice to those who richly deserve punishment for their complicity in large-scale violence. And I have argued that the moral concept of genocide, unlike its counterpart for crimes against humanity, does valuable work in capturing a kind of extreme discrimination that humans perpetrate against one another with dismaying regularity.

Philosophy, Georgia State University

HARM AND THE VOLENTI PRINCIPLE

By Gerald Dworkin

This is an essay on the limits of the Criminal Law. In particular, it is about what principles, if any, determine whether it is legitimate for the state to criminalize certain conduct. Joel Feinberg in his great work on the moral limits of the criminal law argues that we need only two principles.[1] One is a principle regulating harm to other people and the other is an offense principle regulating certain kinds of offensive conduct. I examine various aspects of his argument. In particular I concentrate on his use of the Volenti Principle: He who consents cannot be wrongfully harmed by conduct to which he has fully consented. Feinberg uses the principle to argue that certain kinds of consensual conduct cannot be forbidden unless we adopt some kind of legal moralism, that is, unless conduct can be forbidden on the grounds that it is immoral even though the conduct harms no other person. The first section provides an overview of Feinberg's account of the limits of criminalization. The subsequent sections explore the possibility of prohibiting certain kinds of consensual conduct while avoiding legal moralism by limiting the use of the Volenti Principle.

I. FEINBERG ON THE LIMITS OF CRIMINALIZATION

The main issue for Feinberg is whether there are principles which govern the question of what conduct falls within the legitimate powers of a state to regulate by means of the criminal law. Of course, the state may seek to change, alter, and limit the behavior of its citizens by many means other than criminalizing the conduct. It can do so by providing incentives for people to act one way rather than another (e.g., if you have children you get a break on your income taxes). It can do so by making it costly to engage in certain conduct (e.g., if you smoke you will have to pay a very large tax on each pack of cigarettes). It can do so by using the law of torts to make it the case that if you act in certain ways you are open to civil suits which may cost you a lot of money (e.g., you can be held liable for the torts of those to whom you serve alcoholic beverages). It can do so by making it more difficult to enter into contracts, thus limiting the ability to secure goods by mutual agreement (e.g., minors may not be sued for breach of contract, gambling debts are not enforceable). It can do so by

[1] Joel Feinberg, *Harmless Wrongdoing* (New York, NY: Oxford University Press, 2000).
doi:10.1017/S0265052511000057

providing warnings and information about dangerous products (e.g., explosives or toxic substances). It can do so by tying the receipt of federal funds to states' adopting certain laws (e.g., only states that require cyclists to wear helmets may get federal highway funds). Those who think that when the state cannot legitimately criminalize conduct it is helpless to try to change behavior are as mistaken as those who think that if John Stuart Mill's argument is correct that the state should not punish people for self-destructive behavior, we are left without resources of criticism, social pressure, and ostracism to use on those who act foolishly, irrationally, or imprudently.

Nevertheless, there are types of conduct which we believe the state may legitimately seek to forbid or require by means of criminal sanctions, and Feinberg believes there are what he calls "liberty-limiting" principles which distinguish between those acts which the state may legitimately criminalize and those it may not. For Feinberg, these principles are a "harm to others principle" and an "offense principle." The harm principle states that it is always a good reason in support of penal legislation that it would probably be effective in preventing harm to persons other than the one prohibited from acting. The offense principle states that it is always a good reason in support of penal legislation that it would probably prevent serious offense to persons other than the one prohibited from acting. These exhaust the set of liberty-limiting principles. Conduct may not be sanctioned if it merely causes harm to the actor, or (crucially, as we shall see) if the harm it causes to others is consented to by the others.

Conduct may not be sanctioned merely because it is wrongful. It must, in addition, cause harm to others. Even if it is wrongful, and does cause harm to others, it may not be sanctioned unless it wrongs others, i.e., there are specific individuals who have what Feinberg calls a "grievance." We shall see later what that amounts to.

There has been a remarkable consensus that whatever other principles might be required for an adequate theory of criminalization, some form of a harm to others principle is required. Indeed, the only exception I know of is a recent essay by Arthur Ripstein which seeks to defend what he calls the "sovereignty principle."[2]

Most of the debates about the harm to others principle concern how to specify the term "harm": What are the links between our agency and harm, e.g., are we required to prevent harm, or may we also seek to promote benefit? Do only acts cause harm or may we harm by omission? What are the limits of harm, i.e., can we harm the dead, can we harm those whom we bring into existence? How do we delimit the cases of harm that are appropriate for state interference, i.e., does the harm have

---

[2] Arthur Ripstein, "Beyond the Harm Principle," *Philosophy and Public Affairs*, vol. 34, no. 3, (2006): 216–45.

to be a violation of a right, does it have to be wrongful, does it have to harm particular persons? And so on.

In this essay, I am going to look at Feinberg's views about harms and point out some problems and puzzles in his theory. Some of these are ones he himself has recognized and attempted to deal with. Some are ones that he did not recognize or did not deal with adequately.

As is well-known, Feinberg distinguishes between two types of harms. The first involves any setback to interest. The second is a wrong, a violation of persons' rights. It is the latter conception which is regulated by the harm to others principle. Given this conception, there is conceptual space for the idea of "non-harmful wrongs" and "non-wrongful harms." The former are violations of rights that do not set back the wronged party's interests, i.e., they involve harmless wrongdoing. The latter are setbacks to interests but are not violations of the wronged party's rights. The most common examples of the latter are harms to which the harmed party consented.

I shall now discuss some puzzles and problems that arise in Feinberg's treatment of the issues of harm and wrongdoing.

II. Problems with Feinberg's Account

It might be thought that if I poke you in the eye with a sharp stick causing pain but no lasting injury to the eye I have harmed you. But, for Feinberg, this is not the case. He distinguishes between harmful conditions and all "the various unhappy and unwanted physical and mental states that are not states of harm in themselves."[3]

Among the disliked but not harmful states are "hurts." The other two categories are offenses and a residual category which includes things like embarrassment, boredom, etc. For Feinberg, the exact details of classification are not important. What is important is the contrast between harmful conditions and all the undesirable states which are harmful only when their presence is sufficient to impede an interest. A state of extreme and unrelenting pain can interfere with the pursuit of various goals and objectives and is thus a harm as well as hurtful.

It is because of this distinction that Feinberg has to go beyond what might be called "minimal liberalism," the view that only the harm to others principle justifies restrictions on liberty. A "moderate liberalism" upholds an offense principle as well.

The interesting theoretical issue is why Feinberg denies that we have an interest in not being hurt as such. Even on his own view of what are interests he lists a certain amount of "freedom from interference."[4] Since most inflictions of pain do involve interference with someone's body by

---

[3] Feinberg, ibid., 47.
[4] Ibid., 37.

others, it is unclear why we do not have a derived interest in being free
from being hurt by others. One might still think, however, that even if we
include the infliction of pain under the harm to others principle we still
need the offense principle to include as harms things like being exposed
to sounds and sights which are emotionally disturbing. So this issue is not
of great theoretical moment.

A second issue is of more theoretical interest. According to Feinberg,
the fact that a person's character has been worsened, coarsened, corrupted, damaged, etc. does not count as a harm to the person. If a wicked
person has no ulterior interest in having a good character, and if such a
character is not in his other interests, then the depraved character is not
a harm to him, and even if he becomes worse, he does not necessarily
become worse off. This view has important implications for what I call
"moral paternalism." By this I mean interference with a person against his
will to prevent him from becoming (morally) worse off.

If Feinberg's view is correct, then moral paternalism is impossible in
some cases. If a person does not value having a good moral character, or
if having such a character does not have contingent connections with
goods he does value, i.e., if being a better person does not make him
happier, then we cannot improve his (moral) welfare by restricting his
freedom. We can, however, as I have argued elsewhere invoke a different
kind of principle which is intermediate between legal moralism—the
view that it is permissible for the state to interfere simply on the grounds
that the conduct in question is immoral—and moral paternalism. Unlike
the interference prescribed by the former, we do not interfere simply
because the acts interfered with are immoral. Unlike the interference
advocated by the latter, we do not interfere simply to make the person
better off (morally). Rather we interfere to make the person a better person even if he is not better off as a result.

The next oddity to notice in Feinberg's conception of harm is that it
does not include various cases of unfairness, in particular the case of
exploitative injustices. We now begin to approach the area of harmless
wrongdoing since some of these injustices will not cause harm to those
who suffer them. This will be for either of two reasons. First, these injustices might not cause harm because they do not set back the interests of
those who are exploited. Second, they might not cause harm because
those who are exploited may have consented to them freely, i.e., the
Volenti principle is satisfied.[5] Actually it should be noted that this discussion is one of two ways in which Feinberg invokes the Volenti principle. Here he says that the exploitative injustices "may not harm their
victims . . . because the exploitees have freely consented to them." This
seems to interpret the Volenti principle as "to he who has consented no
harm is done." But this contradicts the introduction of the Volenti prin-

[5] Ibid., 13.

ciple in Volume I, *Harm to Others,* where he says that "There is no doubt that a person can be harmed . . . by . . . the conduct of others to which he fully consents." He then goes on to consider "the more interesting question . . . whether a person can ever be wronged by conduct to which he has fully consented." And he introduces the Volenti principle as the principle that "to one who has consented no wrong is done."[6]

Assuming the latter is the view that Feinberg wants to defend, he is faced with the issue of whether it is permissible to criminalize coercive, mutually beneficial exploitation. An example would be a case in which you fall into a river and cannot swim. I come by and offer to pull you out for a very large sum of money. You agree, I rescue you, and you pay me.

Under the harm to others principle, this conduct cannot be criminalized. Far from harming you, I have saved your life. Yet, at the least, we might think that such a contract should not be enforceable—even though one can foresee that fewer people will be rescued under a regime in which such contracts are not enforceable. Feinberg believes that since no one has been harmed, the only principle which might justify criminalizing this conduct is legal moralism. But since, in his view, the Volenti principle operates here, the exploitee has no complaint, and therefore it is illegitimate to interfere. The issue of whether unfairness is a distinct principle or can be encompassed under the harm to others principle is one that Feinberg discusses sensitively in the case of noncoercive exploitation. Sometimes he finds a harm; sometimes he says that although evil, such exploitation cannot be criminalized. The use of the Volenti principle, therefore, requires further examination.

III. Problem Cases for the Volenti Principle

"To one who has consented no wrong has been done." This principle, used in conjunction with the harm to others principle, plays an important role in Feinberg's arguments about harmless wrongdoing. In particular, it plays an important role in attacking legal moralism. The most important use is against the counterexample to his view posed by Irving Kristol's proposal to have gladiatorial contests in Yankee Stadium open to consenting adult audiences.[7] Kristol assumes that our intuitions are that such contests should not be allowed. If the only legitimate liberty-limiting principles, however, are the harm to others and offense principles, then how can such contests be restricted? The only people present who could complain about being offended are there voluntarily and freely, so the

---

[6] Joel Feinberg, *Harm to Others* (New York, NY: Oxford University Press, 1984).

[7] Irving Kristol, "Pornography, Obscenity, and the Case for Censorship," *New York Times Magazine* March 28, 1971. Reprinted in Gerald Dworkin, *Morality, Harm, and the Law,* (Boulder: Westview Press, 1994) 46–49.

offense principle does not apply. But what about the harm to others principle? Are not the gladiators who lose the contest, and their lives, seriously harmed? Are they not the victims of assault and murder?

Feinberg thinks not. "The primary evil relied upon by the legal moralist is not that anyone was harmed (i.e., injured *and* wronged) for no one was, and not that anyone was injured even without being wronged, since that "otherwise evil" is nullified by consent, and there would be an even greater evil, indeed a wrong, if consent were overruled."[8]

Note that although Feinberg is attributing this view to the legal moralist, he is actually doing so because he (Feinberg) believes it to be the correct view.

Now there are a number of distinct notions being employed here. I will break them down so they can be examined separately.

(1) A moralized notion of "harm" which is an amalgam of injury plus wrong. One does not count as being "harmed" in this sense, either because one is not injured or because one is not wronged.

(2) A notion of injury distinct from being wronged which can be nullified by consent.

So, one can be injured but not harmed (no wrong). One can be wronged but not harmed (no injury). Consent can nullify injury. Consent can nullify being wronged.

From this follows the idea of harmless wrongdoing. To be harmed one must both have one's interests set back and be wronged. If one's interests are not set back one is not harmed even if one has been wronged. This is one example of harmless wrongdoing. Even if one's interests are set back and there has been wrongdoing one may not have been wronged. This is another example of harmless wrongdoing. It is the latter kind of harmless wrongdoing that I am mainly concerned with in this paper.

Now let us return to the gladiatorial contest example. Here is an outline of the argumentative strategy used by Feinberg.

There is a strong inclination (shared by Feinberg) to think it legitimate to criminalize the conduct in gladiatorial contests.

The only liberty limiting principles are the harm to others principle and the offense principle.

The conduct in gladiatorial contests falls under the harm to others principle. The spectators are being morally corrupted with respect to dispositions about the suffering of other people. Therefore, the interests of others become vulnerable.

---

[8] Feinberg, *Harmless Wrongdoing*, 130.

This argument may fail because people may be able to compartmentalize their attitudes so that they distinguish between killing volunteers for profit and other kinds of nonconsensual killings.

There are sufficient doubts about the voluntariness of the gladiators' actions such that we are justified in criminalizing these contests (bold liberalism).

An evil such as this is a relevant reason for coercion but the reason, in fact, will never be weighty enough to outweigh the case for liberty (moderate liberalism).

Now, in fact, there is an alternative strategy to hold on to bold liberalism. One could give up the Volenti principle. In the gladiator case, this would involve bringing the relevant conduct under the purview of the harm to others principle by denying that the mere fact that one has consented to some harm, i.e., the risk of death, makes it a case of harmless wrongdoing. If, as some have contended, there are certain rights which cannot be alienated, then one retains the right not to be harmed (even if one has consented to the harm). So the issue becomes one of relative costs to the theory. Does Feinberg lose more than he gains by abandoning the Volenti principle?

The first thing to note is that it would surely be a mistake to abandon the Volenti principle in general. It is clear that consent is a moral power to alter the normative status of various acts. What would otherwise be theft is a gift if I consent to your possession of a good of mine. What would otherwise be rape is merely sex if mutual consent is present. What would otherwise be battery is simply surgery if I consent to its performance on me. Feinberg is surely right to argue that often the issue of whether someone has been wronged depends on whether, and how freely, she has consented to what is done to her.

The Volenti principle is an essential part of his arguments against paternalism as well. Otherwise, the manufacturer and distributor of cigarettes to willing purchasers is on a par with the person who puts poison in your food.

The essential question, therefore, is not whether the Volenti principle is ever valid but whether it has limits. Are there kinds of acts which are still wrongs even if they have been (freely) consented to? Are there limits to what a person may (permissibly) consent to?

We should recall that even Mill, that stalwart opponent of paternalism, made an exception in the case of voluntary slavery. His argument is in effect that the decision to become a slave represents not simply a decision to abandon autonomy temporarily (retaining the possibility of regaining it) but to enter a situation in which one cannot rethink the decision and decide to regain one's autonomy. Given Mill's theory of value according to which the development of autonomous individuals is required for utility, a utilitarian theory cannot accept such a permanent abandonment of future autonomy. Whatever the nature of the argument, it is clearly an instance in which Mill abandons the Volenti principle. Consent in *this* type of case cannot perform its normal task of immunizing what is done against legal sanction.[9]

It is true that Mill's argument in this case does not concern the use of criminal law in order to threaten, but rather the use of civil law to deny enforcement of a contract. But I see no reason to suppose that Mill could not support the former as an additional tool to prevent voluntary slavery.

Arthur Ripstein in a recent article on the harm to others principle argues for a limitation on the Volenti principle in terms of sovereignty.[10] Ripstein means by sovereignty, roughly, that every person is entitled to use her powers as she sees fit provided that others may do the same. Here is his argument:

> The sovereignty principle provides a different account, one that takes off from the respects in which the familiar exceptions to the consent principle are distinctive. Because it regards independence as relational, the sovereignty principle must also regard consent as a relationship between persons, rather than as a sort of blanket abandonment of rights. If you court danger by walking alone through a dangerous neighborhood after dark, you don't thereby give anyone who attacks you the right to do so; if you consent to my napping in your bed, you don't thereby consent to anyone else doing so, even if I invite them to. The sovereignty principle dictates that consent be understood as a transfer of rights between two persons, and any such transfer is something the two of them do together. The idea of independent people doing something together precludes two people from jointly terminating the independence of one of them. The sovereignty principle has no resources to prohibit suicide, since it doesn't involve domination. But it doesn't need to prohibit suicide in order to deny that consent is a defense to murder. The problem is with one person giving another the power of life and death over them, not with the fact that the victim chooses to die.[11]

The problem with this argument is that it seems too strong. For it rules out cases of physician-assisted suicide and euthanasia which I believe can be legitimate in certain circumstances. Ripstein seeks to avoid this difficulty by making a distinction between physician-assisted suicide and euthanasia.

> It seems to me not to be a problem to say that a person can enlist the support of others in taking his or her own life—getting them to

[9] John Stuart Mill, *On Liberty* (Oxford: Clarendon Press, 1980) chap. 7, Part 3.
[10] Ripstein, ibid.
[11] Ibid., 223.

purchase a gun or the poison, for example. And assuming, of course, that all of this is done with appropriate safeguards regarding the person being of sound mind and so on. Now I realize that this way of describing the situation might seem excessively narrow. Nonetheless, it seems to me to be the right way to frame the issue: helping someone to do something is not the same as doing it to them with their consent. Assuming that suicide is not a legitimate object of criminal prohibition, then being an accessory before the fact of suicide cannot be criminalized either.[12]

My objection to this is that it gives moral weight to the issue of who performs the last causal act in somebody's death, and this does not seem correct. For instance, Doctor Jack Kevorkian had a machine hooked up to the patients whose suicide he assisted, and asked them to press the button to release the lethal medication. But it has always seemed to me that there cannot be a moral difference between those cases and the case in which, say because the patient is paralyzed, Kevorkian has to push the button. If we hold everything else constant, i.e., continued life is not a benefit to the patient, she freely consents to what is being done, she has the right to change her mind at the last moment, and so on, then the difference in who takes the last causal step to securing her death cannot make a moral difference.

I want to present two more cases before turning to argument.

(1) Dwarf-tossing. This is a "bar sport" in which dwarfs are fitted out with padding and a helmet, and have a handle attached to their backs. The contest is to see who can throw them the farthest.
(2) German cannibal case. A German man advertised for someone willing to be killed and consumed. A person answered the advertisement. He was killed—after some preliminaries which are too grisly to relate—hung on a meat hook, and consumed over a period of ten months.

The issue for me becomes whether one can find limits to the Volenti principle which enable us to reconcile the following views:

A. It is legitimate to forbid slavery contracts and gladiatorial contests, and perhaps cases like the German cannibal case and dwarf-tossing.
B. It is legitimate, in some circumstances, legally to permit physician-assisted suicide and euthanasia.
C. The Volenti principle is valid for many cases of harm to which people consent.

---

[12] Ripstein, personal communication.

Why is the Volenti principle valid at all? Why does it seem plausible in many cases? The obvious explanation is that consent is a moral power to change the moral status of acts. But it is not clear exactly what the explanation of that power is? There are alternative models.

On one model, by consenting I give up something and transfer it to you. I had the right to use this hat. I had the sole power to determine how it would be used. By giving you the hat, by consenting to your possession of it, I give up my right to determine use and transfer it to you. It is a corollary of this transfer that I no longer have a right to complain when you destroy the hat or wear it in a way that I do not approve.

On another model, that of Kant, consent involves two people "uniting their wills." It is not a matter of my giving up something. So when I consent to your doing something to me, when you perform the action it is as if we are acting jointly. I have the same responsibility for what you do, as if I were doing it to myself.

On a third model, consenting just *is* giving up one's right to complain about the crossing of a moral boundary.

These models can have various moral implications. For example, on the third model it does not follow from the fact that *you* have waived the right to complain that others may not have the right to complain on your behalf. The fact that you are willing to undergo debasing and humiliating conduct (e.g., dwarf-tossing) does not settle the issue of whether we can criticize you and the others for such an agreement. Whether we can, in addition, make it legally difficult for the consensual action to take place will depend on whether some principle such as moral paternalism or legal moralism can be justified. Recall that the former is the view that it is permissible for the state to interfere with consensual acts in order to make the parties morally better off. The latter is the view that it is permissible for the state to interfere simply on the grounds that the conduct in question is immoral.

Suppose we accept the view that the source of the change of moral status is the waiving of one's right to complain about what is done to one. This has a weaker and a stronger version. The weaker is just that one no longer has the status to complain, but it may still be that one's rights have been violated. The stronger is that one no longer has the status to complain because one's rights cannot be violated if one waives them. The Volenti principle seems better explained by the latter reading. It is clearly the one that Feinberg uses in his arguments. The law is limited to the protection of people's rights. Only if there is someone who has been wronged may the state intervene; mere wrongdoing is not enough. What the law may enforce is grievance morality. Satisfaction of the Volenti principle removes the case from the purview of grievance morality.

If we accept Feinberg's premises, then to make them compatible with interference with gladiators and dwarfs we must interpret the Volenti principle in such a way that it is not satisfied in these cases. This means that there are some acts, fully consensual, which leave rights intact (although it may be the case that the person has forfeited her right to complain about the violation). This, of course, is just the doctrine of inalienable rights.

Now "inalienability" comes in weaker and stronger versions as well. The weaker version is that one cannot abandon one's rights permanently, i.e., effect a general abandonment of one's rights. The stronger version is that one cannot abandon them even on a single occasion. Note that the gladiator case differs from the dwarf case just in the fact that the former involves permanent abandonment (at least it risks that) whereas the latter might only involve abandoning one's rights to dignity on a single occasion.

Another ambiguity is between rights which can neither be forfeited nor waived, and those which can be forfeited but not waived. Thus, one might have a right to life which could be forfeited by one's attempting to take the life of another, but not waived, e.g., by consenting to be killed by another.

Finally we must distinguish between waiving the exercise of a right one continues to possess, and waiving the right itself. If I ask your assistance in committing suicide I do not wave my right to life; I relinquish the exercise of that right.

What kind of theory could explain the judgments in the four cases— gladiatorial contest, voluntary slavery, dwarf-tossing, and justified euthanasia?

First, no inalienable rights theory will do. If the right to life is inalienable, then both the gladiator and the euthanasia cases must be classified as violations of the individual's right to life. For similar reasons, a theory such as Ripstein's according to which assigning a right to kill one to another person is incoherent because it is inconsistent with the idea that the individual must retain the legal personality that is a requirement of his "uniting his will" with the other party. If the judgment about euthanasia is correct then rational persons must, in certain circumstances, be entitled to lift the moral barrier against being killed by others.

Second, it does not look plausible that a single theory explains both the slavery and dwarf-tossing cases. The intuition behind not allowing people to enter into slavery contracts is that it is wrong for people to renounce their autonomy on a permanent and irrevocable basis. The intuition behind the dwarf-tossing case is that it is wrong for people to allow themselves to be degraded in certain ways. Of course, if one is prepared to allow as a single theory a view which says that we must weigh the reasons for and against in each case and judge which reasons are weightier, then there could be a single theory. But it would not be informative.

If we accept Feinberg's view that what is done by others to you, with your consent, negates any rights violations (owed to you) then if one is seeking to justify the target cases one must argue against what I shall call the "Feinberg premise":

(FP) The only wrongs it is legitimate to criminalize are those which violate the rights of some particular victim.

As we have seen, when he talks about "harmless wrongdoing" he really means to cover "harmful wrongdoings which do not wrong any person."

What is Feinberg's argument for the Feinberg premise? Here are the relevant texts that I could find.

> "The free-floating evils do not hurt anybody . . . To prevent them with the iron fist of legal coercion would be to impose suffering and injury for the sake of no one else's good at all." [13]
>
> "[the weight of non-grievance evils] is insufficient to counterbalance the case for liberty, since it is impossible to name anyone who can demand "protection" from the evils in question." [14]
>
> When a person has been harmed in one of his vital interests . . . a *wrong* has been done to him: he is *entitled to complain; he has a* grievance *to voice; he is the victim of an* injustice; he can demand *protection* against recurrences; he may deserve *compensation* for *his* losses.[15]

The argument of the first quote assumes that the only reason for using coercion is to produce a good for someone. But this begs the question.

The argument of the second assumes that the only reason for using coercion is to protect someone against harm. But this begs the question.

The argument of the third quote simply repeats in different ways what a grievance morality consists of. It provides no additional argument why only grievance morality can justify coercion. In addition, it equates things which should be kept distinct. Whether or not one is entitled to complain about something depends on many different considerations. The person who launches a deadly attack on you is not entitled to complain if you oppose him with deadly force. Nevertheless, if he is a so-called innocent threat, it is at least arguable that you have no right to use such force. Someone might not be entitled to complain about some treatment because he himself advocates and defends such treatment. But that does not show we are wrong to treat him in that way.

In truth, unlike Feinberg's argument against paternalism, which involves a fair bit of theory about the nature of personal sovereignty, and the way drawing the boundaries as the paternalist suggests is in conflict with a conception (an ideal!) of the autonomous person, his argument here consists largely of making various illuminating distinctions about kinds of evils, and then simply asserting that some of them are not serious enough to warrant preventing by coercion.

[13] Feinberg, *Harmless Wrongdoing*, 80.
[14] Ibid., 174.
[15] Ibid., 67.

The general form of his argument is that, given the importance of personal liberty, if we cannot justify a restriction of liberty by pointing to someone who can complain, then we cannot restrict liberty. But there are various ideals that are at least as important to us as some of our minor grievances. If it is wrong to show contempt for dwarfs by using them like inanimate objects because it is always wrong to be contemptuous of persons on the grounds of their physical characteristics, and if the fact that the dwarfs freely consent does not make the exhibition any less contemptuous, then why is there not as good a reason for criminalizing the conduct as some violation of someone's rights? This, of course, is not an argument but a rhetorical question. In the absence of some argument against it, however, it is entitled to prevail until defeated.

IV. Conclusion

Although this essay is substantive and not methodological in nature, looking back we can see that it illustrates what a normative argument of any complexity looks like. There is first the use of considered judgments about particular moral issues, e.g., that the state is within its rights (or not) to ban consensual gladiatorial contests, and physician-assisted suicide is (sometimes) legitimate. So we need a theory that can accommodate both judgments.

But it is not simply a matter of developing a theory to accommodate such judgments; there may be more than one theory that does so. In our case there are competing ways of coming to the conclusion that we are entitled to interfere with the willing gladiators. We can hold fast to the Volenti Principle and then seek to show that there are harms to non-consenting parties, e.g., those who do not attend the event but are subsequently harmed by those who do. Thus, we bring the harm to others principle to bear.

Or we can abandon the Volenti Principle in this case and insist that there is a wrongful harm to the willing participants. In either case there are difficulties, new problems that are raised, and further cases to judge. Ultimately, we have to make some global assessment of which theory has independent plausibility, which theory seems less ad hoc, and so forth. Perhaps neither is satisfactory and we must invoke some kind of legal moralism or moral paternalism. But this then will create new difficulties, e.g., where we draw the line. Why dwarf-tossing and not reality television?

As Wilfred Sellars once observed, philosophy is about how things, in the broadest sense of the term, hang together, in the broadest sense of the term.

Philosophy, University of California, Davis

EDUCATION AND THE MODERN STATE

By Anthony O'Hear

I. Introduction: Listening to the Dead

One of the most extraordinary passages in modern literature is that presented to us by Ezra Pound as his *First Canto*.[1] Indeed, as the start of what eventually became the very backbone of twentieth-century poetry (Pound's *Cantos*), strict chronology aside, there may be some argument for seeing his first canto as a kind of manifesto for what has come to be known as modernist literature, that which has come to be associated with the writings of T. S. Eliot, James Joyce, Ernest Hemingway, and Pound himself around the time of World War I. The manifesto suggests that we can only retrieve the wholeness our civilization has lost by re-connecting with our past, and thereby feeling things anew—the very opposite of what the modernists saw as the cliché-ridden and orotund poetry prevalent prior to World War I.

What Pound does in *Canto I* is to provide his own tensely archaic translation of a sixteenth-century Latin translation of part of Book XI of Homer's *Odyssey*.[2] This book is the so-called Nekuia, the Book of the Dead—itself thought to be one of the earliest parts of the *Odyssey*. Already Pound is making a point. We see Homer (to the extent that we still do), as refracted through the lenses of twenty-five (or more) centuries of Homeric

---

[1] Ezra Pound, *The Cantos of Ezra Pound* (New York: New Directions Books, 1996). Pound's dates were 1885–1972. An American by birth, he lived much of his life in Europe. In the first half of the twentieth century he was one of the most influential figures in literature throughout the world, both because of his own poetry and because of his assistance to and promotion of others (including T. S. Eliot, Ernest Hemingway and James Joyce). His *Cantos* were a lifelong sequence of poems: although the first group were only actually published in 1934, he maintained that he began them in 1904–1905, and he was still working on them when he died. The *Cantos* (117 of them plus fragments) are an attempt to bind up in poetic form our (or Pound's) debt to the past where it really matters, and where, for the most part, it has been forgotten. All of Pound's obsessions are there—his admiration for Confucius and John Adams, his love of the Malatesta Temple in Rimini and of the *Odyssey*, his hatred of usury as the enemy of generative love and fertility, his (qualified) support for Mussolini. This last led to him broadcasting for Mussolini during the war, after which he was incarcerated by the Americans in a cage outside Pisa, and subsequently (until 1958) in a lunatic asylum in Washington DC. The *Pisan Cantos* recount what led to his disastrous decision to broadcast, and in poetry of a very high order, his descent into hell in Pisa and of his re-connection while he was in the cage with the natural and human worlds.

[2] The *First Canto* (appearing first in *A Draft of XXX Cantos*, originally published in 1934), is based on the 1538 (Latin) translation of the *Odyssey* by Andreas Divus Justinopolitanus, a copy of which Pound picked up in Paris around 1908, as he tells us.

reading and study and thought. But the meaning deepens when we consider the context of the Nekuia.

In the previous book of the *Odyssey*, Odysseus had been living in somewhat reluctant luxury with the enchantress Circe. Although his life with Circe is not without its pleasure, she is actually keeping him captive, when he what he really wants is to return to his home in Ithaca. Eventually Circe agrees to let him go, but Odysseus must first sail to the land of the Cimmerians, a sunless land of mist and fog. There he and his companions will find the entrance to Hades, the domain of the dead, and there Odysseus is to consult the dead prophet Tiresias on his chances of returning home. In Pound's own translation, in *Canto XLVII*, Circe says this:

> First must thou go the road
> to hell
> And to the bower of Ceres' daughter Proserpine,
> Through overhanging dark, to see Tiresias,
> Eyeless that was, a shade, that is in hell
> So full of knowing that the beefy men know less than he,
> Ere thou come to thy road's end.
> Knowledge the shade of a shade,
> Yet thou must sail after knowledge
> Knowing less than drugged beasts.

Circe forbears to mention that it is she who had turned Odysseus's men into drugged beasts, but what she does tell him is this: in order to find his *home*, which is what he really wants, Odysseus must consult one who has more wisdom than the living. For the living (including Odysseus himself at this point) are no more enlightened than drugged beasts; so he must consult one who is *dead*, the blind prophet Tiresias. And to get to the dead, he must travel a hard road, a *journey* distant in miles and in mentality from the intoxicating delights of Circe's palace and bed. He and his men must set sail again, on the ship Circe gives them.

> And then went down to the ship,
> Set keel to breakers, forth on the godly sea, and
> We set up mast and sail on that swart ship,
> Bore sheep aboard her, and our bodies also
> Heavy with weeping, and winds from sternward
> Bore us out onward with bellying canvas,
> Circe's this craft . . .

When, after carrying out due sacrifice and encountering one of their own dead companions, Odysseus does meet Tiresias, the news is not good. Odysseus has angered Poseidon, the god of the sea (because he blinded

Polyphemus, the Cyclops, who is Poseidon's son). So although Odysseus himself will return, due to Poseidon's spite, he will "lose all companions" (as, we might add, did Pound himself decades later, though no blame is due here to Poseidon; had he himself listened more closely to the dead, he might not have been so comprehensively seduced by Mussolini's characteristically modern propaganda and rhetoric. Pound, a drugged beast indeed). However, at the end of *Canto I* Pound does afford us a glimpse of Aphrodite "with golden girdles and breast bands, with dark eyelids bearing the golden bough" of Hermes (who is the guider of souls to the underworld). So, in the midst of death, perhaps, for those who go down into Hades and are reborn, there may be love and fertility and the gifts of the Cyprian goddess.

To say that there is a message here, in so many layered a narrative, would be ridiculous. But let us just reflect on the idea that home can only be found by talking to the dead, particularly after a difficult journey. Of course, Pound's own poetic enterprise was an attempt to listen to the dead, and indeed to get them to talk once more. We are drugged beasts otherwise, in thrall not to Circe but to the clamor and mindlessness of the present. Without a sense of our roots, cultural and otherwise, and a recognition of the timeless truths embedded there, we do not know who we are. We do not know where home is. Our minds and souls, and maybe our bodies too, are sterile. For all the ease we might find in our Circean palace, we are in a wasteland.

We have heard a lot about the supposed iniquity of university and other school courses being filled up with the works of dead white men. I was once attacked in print (by a professor of education, needless to say) for allegedly advocating a curriculum of the dead. The professor was, of course, following the injunction of philosopher John Dewey (1859–1952) in *Democracy and Education*,[3] to let the dead bury their dead. Dewey believed that any study of history which did not take as its starting point "some present situation with its problems" would be worthless. Actually if we follow Pound's and Homer's lead, what we should be advocating is exactly the opposite: a curriculum that puts us (and our children) in touch with those who have helped to form what we are, and with those who themselves have been in touch with truths transcending our time. We will learn little from the past if we insist on looking at it through the prism of the present, and as it might appear to relate to our current problems and perspectives. Most of us find it easy to sympathize with uprooted people who want to discover or rediscover their origins, when they are the descendents of slaves or of those fleeing famine or persecution—and rightly so. But a recapitulation of the common heritage of Western Civilization in and for itself is met all too often with disdain or worse.

---

[3] John Dewey, *Democracy and Education* (1916) (New York: Free Press, 1997), see chap. 16.

I have no wish to be polemical here, but simply wish to suggest that the most rewarding antidote to the mindlessness of the present is entry into the conversation which began with Homer, and which has continued (more or less) ever since, until perhaps now. Initially this may not be easy. The world of writers before our own time may seem strange and difficult to penetrate. These writers may have beliefs and practices alien to us, and even at times repugnant. Their world may not at first sight seem to have any bearing on our current problems; and to insist on looking at it through the prism of the present will almost certainly distort its true nature (as when we bring our prejudices about racism, feminism, and the like to analyze Greek or Roman society, for example, before we have tried to understand the meaning and dynamic of these societies on their own terms). We will have to undertake a journey of discovery in order to be in a position to listen to what the dead have to tell us.

In reading and discussing Greek tragedy and Plato, Virgil, Ovid, and Horace, to say nothing of Augustine, Dante, Chaucer, Shakespeare, and Milton, along with Camoes and Cervantes, and Racine and Goethe, we will enter worlds and experiences otherwise unimaginable in the twenty-first century. From these we could learn so much about ourselves, about our forbears, and about our true home—if we, like Odysseus, were prepared to listen to the dead. Moreover, as one does this, one discovers that one is participating in a conversation which has gone on for so many centuries—as we see with Pound, but not only with Pound—and with so much commentary back and forth. One begins to swim in a sea of wisdom, which if not actually timeless, is deeper and broader than any one time, and which affords a vantage point from which to judge momentary presents.

II. DEWEY AND DARWIN

John Dewey, among all modern thinkers, articulates most clearly and forcefully a vision of life and education antithetical to the one I have just outlined. Dewey believed that Darwin's theory of evolution was the greatest solvent of contemporary thought about old questions, a climax brought about in general terms by the scientific revolution but, as far as human affairs were concerned, most particularly by *The Origin of Species* (1859).[4] We can argue about the extent to which Darwin was a Social Darwinist (wanting the elimination of the unfit and so forth) and about the contradictions (or not) between his theory and religious belief, but, as important as these issues are, they may not represent the most profound effect

---

[4] John Dewey, "The Influence of Darwinism on Philosophy," in *The Influence of Darwinism on Philosophy and Other Essays in Contemporary Thought* (New York: Henry Holt and Co., 1951). In my analysis of Dewey, I have drawn on Bradley C. S. Watson, *Living Constitution, Dying Faith* (Wilmington, Delaware: ISI Books, 2009), chap. 3.

Darwin's theory has had on the modern mind. According to Dewey, Darwin sank "the sacred ark of permanency," that, under the influence of the Aristotelian notions of final causes and fixed species, had conditioned our thinking about ourselves. Post-Darwin, everything—morality, religion, politics—should be regarded as changeable, and up for revision as, in ever-changing circumstances, we face new dilemmas and construct for ourselves new goals.

Thinking of life in Darwinian terms will lead us to the ineluctable conclusion that over the course of millennia, thousands, if not millions, of species have evolved, and become extinct. Each species survives for the time it does because it solves its problems better than its competitors; but success here is always relative to the time and the problems posed at and by the time. Since new problems and new solutions, including new species, emerge all the time, a solution—and a successful species—at time t may be nothing of the sort at time t+1. Even if time t's species soldiers on through time t+1 and beyond, it will be in part, at least, because factors within its makeup and behavior suited it to the problems it had to face at t+1 rather than those which made it successful in relation to the challenges it had to face at t. Very often, as we know, time t's champion fails at time t+1; the fossil record is replete with traces of species which failed to make it through, despite (or even because of) their great successes and adaptability at earlier times. The history of evolution is predominantly that of species which have become extinct.

What Dewey did was to generalize the evolutionary story so as to include human history and human affairs. Growth is his guiding metaphor here, as elsewhere, and in human affairs growth basically means developing in such a way that one is able to produce new solutions to new problems. Life itself, for Dewey, is a continual and unending process of problem solving. In the human realm, the knowledge and culture of the past is predominantly the deposit of old solutions to the problems of yesterday, and earlier still in time. Quite consistently, his occasional nod to the great minds of the past notwithstanding, there is in Dewey's thinking a relentless focus on the modern, and on the demands of the present. Far from wanting us to savor the best that has been thought and said, Dewey insisted that what has been done and known is merely the deposit of yesterday's solutions to yesterday's problems.

The best analogue in human culture to the evolutionary method is science—that is, science regarded as a process of progressive problem solving, often of a practical, technological nature, in which the theories and technologies of the past are as dead as the fossils in some pre-Cambrian rock—historical curiosities, of antiquarian interest perhaps, but of no relevance to what we want to do today. After all, it would be urged, today's scientists do not have to know about Aristotle's biology, let alone his physics, or about Ptolemy's astronomy. These figures are the intellec-

tual equivalents, it would be said, of long extinct biological species, irrelevant to the problems of today.

Would it, though, take us too far in a Kuhnian direction to raise at least
an eyebrow here?[5] It is undoubtedly true that today's scientists are by
and large trained in ignorance of the work of their predecessors, but it
may nevertheless be the case that this itself is a product of an evolutionary approach to science and its methods which a) takes too much for
granted the absolute superiority of contemporary scientific theory over
past paradigms, and b) conspires to close the minds of today's scientists
to possibilities other than those enshrined in today's scientific theories
and practices. Maybe, even in Dewey's preferred area of activity, the
scientific, a strictly evolutionary attitude to scientific practice and education is not altogether healthy; but that was not a doubt in Dewey's own
mind.

III. Education for Democracy

So far, so Darwinian. Anyone attempting to follow Dewey in applying
his philosophy to education will, like Dewey himself, evince scant regard
for the achievements of the past. But there is to Dewey's thought an
idealistic, Hegelian aspect, over and above his Darwinism. Unlike Darwin,
and like Hegel and the idealists, Dewey believed strongly in human
society as a quasi-organic reality. Dewey saw social divisions and competitiveness as inherently harmful, as fracturing and subverting the wholes
which give individuals their meaning and in communion with which
they best flourish. One way in which this sort of community spirit is
broken up is by the differences of achievement which are so marked a
feature of traditional systems of education, with their grading and competitiveness. These devices for sifting people become particularly pernicious when, as Dewey believes is the case, the knowledge and skills being
tested are about things which interest only small and exclusive sections of
a society. Against arcane specialization of this sort, Dewey will insist that
a good education focuses on topics in which the whole community has an
interest, and problems which are of obvious practical import.

On these matters, in which all have a direct involvement and interest, everyone will have his or her point of view, and everyone should
be heard, not just as a matter of democratic decency, but also because
each different perspective will have something worthwhile to contribute. For Dewey and his followers, therefore, education should be an
exercise of democracy in miniature, with the teacher a leader of group

---

[5] I am referring here to Thomas Kuhn's argument in *The Structure of Scientific Revolutions*
(Chicago: Chicago University Press, 1961), passim, that the core premises of ruling scientific
models are never really refuted when the models in question are replaced, but only passed
over and forgotten—with the possibility of being revived in new forms in the future.

work and group discussions, rather than, in Dewey's own words, "an external boss or dictator" (as if *any* form of benign exercise of authority and wisdom on the part of a teacher is tantamount to political oppression as far as Dewey is concerned). And it is not just for the sake of what goes on in the school that participatory democracy should be the norm and mode of activity. Just as the topics to be analyzed and worked on (researched, in Dewey's terms) are to be those of relevance to the wider community in which the school exists, and for which it exists, so the practice of democratic involvement and negotiation within the school is a preparation for democratic activity outside the school when the pupils become adults and are ready to play their part in the democratic deliberations and decision-making of the wider, adult community, both in politics and in the work place.

The idea that education is important because it makes people ready for participation in democratic politics, and keen so to participate is taken for granted to such an extent nowadays, even by people espousing different and more traditional views of education than Dewey, that it is worth spending a little time analyzing its implications. In an era when public spending is under examination, and decisions on public spending must be justified in terms of their social and economic impact, the idea might seem attractive because it gives a rationale for spending public money on education. We need education because otherwise we will not have a population of individuals able effectively to exercise their democratic rights and duties. And this line of argument is frequently adduced in order to justify including in education areas of study, such as history, literature, and the classics, which may at first sight seem remote from narrowly economic or utilitarian concerns. Though this might not be Dewey's way here, it will be urged that this broad training of the mind is necessary in a society in which people are expected to play a role in politics and public life. Hence public spending on these things needs no further justification.

At a very basic level, any such argument, either in narrowly Deweyesque terms, or in a broader, more traditionalist form is an argument from cause to effect. The argument suggests that if people are educated in this way they will turn out to be mature democratic deliberators, and that this effect justifies public spending on education and, ultimately, education itself. Any such argument is thus vulnerable to empirical disproof. Disproof will occur if people who have been educated according to the required prescriptions turn out to have little interest in politics, or turn out simply to have a bundle of largely unexamined prejudices, rather than exercising that significant degree of independent judgment which an education for democracy is supposed to induce. It will also be, to say the least, unfortunate, if people educated in a Deweyesque spirit, or in some other mode whose supporters see it as contributing to the ideals of democracy, turn out to be indifferent to the political process or even hostile to it.

Although one imagines that followers of Dewey will insist that there are few educational systems anywhere in the world which enact enough of Dewey's prescriptions, to dispassionate observers of the state education systems in Britain and the United States, it will seem that they have not been untouched by the sorts of things which Dewey advocates, such as a stress on group work, on pupil activity and so-called "discovery" and "research," on "critical thinking," on multiculturalism and on a generally egalitarian and anti-elitist attitude to curricula and assessments. In any event, however, populations of high school graduates are being produced who are neither knowledgeable about democratic processes nor keen to participate in them. An enervating cynicism about politics and about much else besides seems far more prevalent even among university students, and even there among those who profess an interest in politics, the tendency is to follow left-liberal organs of public opinion which foster such attitudes. There is enough of Dewey in the mass education systems of Britain and the United States to make one doubtful that more of it will remedy the political apathy so prevalent in those countries.

If Deweyesque forms of education may not have the political effects their supporters intend and claim, for those hoping that education can be a stimulant to democratic activity, the picture is, if anything even more problematic in the case of traditional forms of education—at least it is, if one considers the levels of support among university teachers and students in Germany and Austria for the Third Reich during the 1920s and 1930s. No doubt there were plenty of other factors at work here, as in other cases where intelligentsia have supported tyranny. This in itself does not condemn the forms of education to which these people had been exposed (or at least, not until explicit indoctrination became a part of the education in question). But it does show that an education in the classics and the sciences did not in itself give its ex-pupils the sense or courage to resist what was going on in the wider society of their time, nor indeed does it necessarily fill its pupils with enthusiasm for the sorts of democratic arrangements favoured by today's political elites. The main conclusion I want to draw at this point, though, is simply that looking for a direct political result from a form of education is not just risky, empirically speaking; it is actually to look for the justification of a form of education in the wrong place, in its effects rather than in what it is in and for itself.

IV. A GOOD IN ITSELF

In the case of traditional liberal education, the claims of some of its defenders notwithstanding, this would be all to the good, for it is a form of education which—at least in the hands of Blessed John Henry Newman (1801–90), its most distinguished advocate—claims that the cultivation of the intellect is a good in itself, and that what is studied in it is worthwhile for its own sake.[6] Of course, people schooled in these things *may* turn out to be, in Newman's sense, gentlemen, that is, people with a mature generosity of judgment and intellectual patience and sophistication; but, equally they might end up running advertising agencies, populist political parties and relentlessly down-market television companies. (In Britain, this is just what some of the most successful of them do.) If, as Newman sometimes seems to claim, the *justification* of liberal education is that it turns out generations of gentlemen, we and he are doomed to disappointment. He and we should simply bite the bullet and insist on the intrinsic value of what is done in liberal education (knowing about the world, the soul and God, through studying the best that has been thought and known, and being thus enabled to develop the conversations into which we enter in and through that form of education).

However, invoking the intrinsic value of what is to be studied is just what the follower of Dewey cannot do in regard to his conception of education. For Dewey, education is a means to help the community collectively solve its problems and to encourage the type of community activism he sees as underpinning democratic problem solving. It is from this perspective that the initiatives associated with Dewey derive their rationale: group work, discussion, relevance, practical research devoted to the examination of perceived problems, "learning to learn" and the insistence on the value of pupils "discovering" things for themselves. It is also from this perspective that the sort of inclusiveness sought by Dewey becomes important, because he desires an approach to local and national government in which all participate in collective opinion forming and decision-making. Democracy, in Dewey's view, is more than a mode of government, or a means of getting rid of rulers regularly and peacefully; it is to be seen as what he calls a mode of "associated living," in which there is continuous readjustment of both individuals and the community as a whole in response to ever-changing problems and situations. And the onus is always on us, individually and collectively, to think out our solutions afresh in the light of ever-changing circumstances, eschewing dogma and authority as illusory crutches, and striving always to see what we regard as knowledge as analyzable mediately or immediately in terms of its practical effects. In the context of such a philosophy, education itself becomes intensely political, with the demand that it focuses on driving a highly political agenda responsive not to timeless or long-held wisdom, but to needs or perceived needs of the present sociopolitical situation.

[6] John Henry Newman, *The Idea of a University* (1858) (Indiana: University of Notre Dame Press, 1982) esp. chap. 5.

V. The Needs of the "People": Contemporary Politics

A fully comprehensive international analysis of contemporary state education is beyond the scope of this paper. Nevertheless, taking Britain as an example, the Deweyesque trends identified at the end of the last section (group work, problem solving, relevance, and so on) are increasingly dominant in state education. Given that similar trends are evident in other advanced democracies—which readers can verify for themselves—the conclusion must be that those who look to a different form of education (a classically centered liberal education, for example), are unlikely to find a home in a state system in the twenty-first century. State education *may*, in certain periods of the past, have tolerated or even fostered elements of a liberal education; but this was at a time when politicians were far more content to adopt a "hands off" attitude to education. In most advanced liberal democracies of today, it is taken for granted that politicians will actually run the systems of education they see themselves as funding, and run them in a way that emphasizes their own projects of utilitarian outcomes and social engineering. In practice this comes to mean that education systems are far more consonant with Deweyesque ideals than with anything approaching a liberal system of education. The latter takes for granted that certain subjects have been shown over time to be good in themselves and also that in these studies ability and achievement are very unequally distributed. Both of these assumptions run counter to the egalitarian "presentism" of the contemporary political mind.

The idea that state education ought to reflect contemporary political imperatives should come as no surprise to anyone who glances at the various ends to which it has been put since the nineteenth century, when modern states began to interest themselves in education. Thus, while state education, wherever and whenever it has existed, has always had as one of its aims the narrowly utilitarian one of preparing populations for work (whether manual or mental), it has also had the more local aims consonant with local political imperatives. These have included promoting evangelical Christianity against Catholicism (in the United States), nation building in general (in Prussia and Germany), promoting the values of the secular state (in France), and the preparing a cadre of young people apt for military service and the administration of an over-extended empire (Britain), to take four characteristic examples from the nineteenth century. In the twentieth century, in addition to some or all of these, education has been conceived by politicians as an agent of social mobility and for a more egalitarian society. This, together with a stress on contemporaneity and on economic needs, has tended to make politicians sympathetic to conceptions of education closer to Dewey than to Newman.

In each case the policy in question is defended by claiming that education is a social concern. As such, it should reflect social needs and values—or what politicians take those needs and values to be. Moreover, as the state funds education, it should have a direct interest in its administration and aims. (The fact that this funding is only possible because of taxation from individuals who might have very different ideas on education is normally overlooked at this point.) Further as societies have become more democratic and the state more intrusive and powerful, and democracy itself more populist, there have been moves to make education itself more egalitarian, shunning those aspects of the curriculum which cannot be shared by all, and avoiding elitism (as it would be called) in access to educational provision—both themes which would have resonated with Dewey, for whom what is now known as inclusiveness was the very touchstone of a healthy system of education.

We need not deny that education is in some sense a social concern, nor that society as a whole has an interest in seeing that its members are educated. But, as J. S. Mill argued in On Liberty,[7] saying that education is a social concern need not imply that the state has a paternalistic duty to see that children are educated. It does not follow from the social importance of education that the state itself should run, regulate or finance it. Indeed Mill argued, to the contrary, that a general state education would be little more than a "mere contrivance for moulding people to be exactly like one another," and that "in proportion as it is efficient and successful, it establishes a despotism over the mind leading by natural tendency to one over the body."[8] Dewey, by contrast, had no such doubts: As long ago as 1889, he averred that "what the best and wisest parent wants for his own child, that must the community want for all its children," adding that "any other ideal for our schools is narrow and unlovely; acted upon it destroys our community."[9] So, Dewey seems to think that democracy will be *destroyed* unless the community has a single system of education, predicated on the will of the best and wisest parent. Such a single system is just what Mill feared, in fact.

VI. ENGLAND AND ELSEWHERE

If the National Curriculum in England[10] under the New Labour government of 1997–2010 is a guide, the best and wisest parent turns out to have favored a child-centered and largely content-free curriculum, replete with new subjects such as "citizenship" and "personal, social, and health education." It is a curriculum that seems to want to address every perceived social problem, from obesity to smoking, from alcohol, drug abuse,

---

[7] J. S. Mill, *On Liberty* (1859) (as in *Utilitarianism*, ed., Mary Warnock, London: Collins/ Fontana), chap. 5.

[8] Ibid., 239–40.

[9] John Dewey, *The School and Society* (Chicago: University of Chicago Press, 1907), 19.

[10] England: because due to various constitutional complications, the National Curriculum voted on and approved by the UK Parliament, including MPs from Scotland, Wales, and Northern Ireland, applies only to England.

and teenage pregnancy to pedophilia, "homophobia," global warming, inequality, and racism—anything and everything that was part of that government's agenda of social engineering, and, therefore, anything and everything *except* concentrated and disinterested attention to the best that had been thought and known.

It will doubtless be pointed out that in England a national curriculum was not actually introduced by New Labour, but by a very different government, that of Mrs. Thatcher, who personally would have had little truck with any of the above. There are still, in conservative circles in Britain, politicians who cling to the dream of Mrs. Thatcher, that by central government decree a curriculum of a more traditional kind could be imposed on the country as a whole. The most basic reason why both Mrs. Thatcher and her followers were deluded in this matter is that it is not possible by central government edict to force some four hundred thousand state-certified and state trained teachers to do something many of them are temperamentally opposed to and intellectually unprepared for— for their formation has been in the hands of those more influenced by Dewey and Jean-Jacques Rousseau (1712–78)[11] than by Newman or Matthew Arnold (1822–88), of whom they have probably never heard.[12] And even the New Labour government of 1997–2010, to which the teachers and their unions were far closer in spirit, struggled to get teachers to carry out a couple of simple tests of reading and arithmetic in primary schools. Even if the teachers were more malleable than they are, however, there would still be the customary bureaucratic inertia to overcome in attempting what would have amounted to a sea-change in attitude, to say nothing of the downright opposition to such a change within what might be called the educational establishment: government officials, local administrators, teacher trainers, university departments of education, inspectors, teacher unions and the self-styled "subject associations." I know how prevalent the opposition is, because from 1993–1997 I was a member of the governmental advisory board charged with developing the national curriculum in England and Wales. Most of my time on it was spent attempting to outmaneuver and circumvent this establishment, to little avail during the period in question and ultimately to no avail at all. The 1997 change of government simply handed to our opponents the instruments of power the Conservatives had unwisely forged and put in place (the outcome I did predict in the late 1980s when the national curriculum was being set up).

The fundamental difficulty faced by defenders of liberal education in a state system of education is that such a system is bound, by its very nature, to favor statist or collectivist policies. What this means in practice

---

[11] Cf. Jean-Jacques Rousseau, *Emile or On Education*, trans. Christopher Kelly and Allan Bloom (1762; Dartmouth: Dartmouth College, 2009).
[12] Cf. Matthew Arnold, *Culture and Anarchy* (London: Smith Elder 1882).

in the early twenty-first century is that it will be bureaucratic in operation and socially leveling in aspiration. It will be bureaucratic because of the political demands for accountability in the spending of public money, which will inevitably lead to demands for managerially quantifiable results; it will be socially leveling in aspiration because it is very hard to argue in a populist democracy (which is paying for the system in question) that some things are intrinsically better than others, and that some of what is intrinsically better is going to be beyond the abilities or understanding of the majority.

So no one should be surprised to read in the preamble to the English National Curriculum that education is "a route to equality of opportunity for all, a healthy and just democracy, a productive economy and sustainable development, valuing diversity in our society and the environment in which we live." Given that any genuine equality of opportunity will involve a continuous discounting of unequal outcomes at any stage, and given that the politics of diversity amounts in practice to a refusal to admit differences of quality between say, the art of the graffito dauber or of a rapper and that of Rembrandt or Bach, as well as the idea that culture is one inclusive conversation, these are anything but neutral requirements.

Nor should we forget that the modern world and the politics of the modern state are aspects of what Plato called the "great beast." The great beast is the public world, which can be pulled in any direction by the force of public opinion, and in a populist democracy, public opinion is easily manipulated by propaganda and the mass media. Political leaders are almost by necessity demagogues, in thrall to all sorts of interests and powers, and above all bound to celebrate the contemporary and the new, for that is where success and celebrity are to be found, and any hint that there may be timeless or ancient truths or values will throw into question the whole project of modernity. So we should not be surprised that even with the change of government in Britain in 2010, there has been no significant questioning of education's egalitarian aspirations, and no real freeing up of education from the target setting practices and insistence on quantifiable outcomes which destroy the liberal spirit. Nor should we expect there to be such a freeing-up trend, given that all politicians are constrained in similar ways, and given too that few politicians will ever renounce powers that they have inherited.

VII. Conclusion

While I have focused on the example of England, there is no reason to suppose that similar ideological drifts are not occurring in state education systems elsewhere in the developed world. Policy and practice of the sort advocated by Dewey are well-nigh inevitable once we forget our roots and see ourselves and our world in an evolutionarily progressive light;

once progressivist evolutionism becomes the dominant force in a culture, the prospects for a form of education emphasizing timeless values are slim indeed. Actually, Dewey's evolutionism and his educational philosophy go together, and are mutually reinforcing, and, not coincidentally are the predominant ideology of the modern state (whether it is ostensibly conservative or left-liberal).

The conclusion is that those who wish to avoid the fate of the Homeric drugged beasts had best look outside the modern, progressivist state for forms of education congenial to them. This might mean schooling which is formally and technically independent (though even here, caution is recommended, as in Britain at least, progressivist and even statist ideas are not absent from the independent sector of education). But an independent sector of education within a system of predominantly state provision is always bound to be fighting a rearguard action against the ever-encroaching tentacles of state regulation and accreditation. It will also suffer from the charge that it is available only to a relatively privileged few. Whether this criticism is fair or not, such a charge is bound to be damaging to morale, and to put those against whom the charge is made inevitably on the defensive. Far better for those who value liberal education (and indeed other forms of education outside the collectivist norm) would be a system in which the state played no role in educational provision, such as Mill advocated. But would a state predicated on Deweyite progressivism ever countenance such a thing (through vouchers or tax credits, for example)? This is the crux on which advocates of liberal education are impaled, while the majority of the population—and nearly all politicians—cling to the illusion that improvements in education are merely a matter of implementing better policies. They do not see that, for liberal education anyway, the problem is the state itself. Whatever the rhetoric, and whatever the intentions of policymakers, in the modern world the whole dynamic of education is bound to be the opposite of liberal.[13,14]

Philosophy, University of Buckingham

---

[13] An interesting test of this claim will be the current situation in England, where there is a government vigorously implementing what it believes to be a liberal education agenda. But if I am right, the outcome will do little more than embed yet more deeply the grip the state has on the system—to the ultimate detriment of the present government's aims.

[14] The research for this paper was undertaken while the author was a Visiting Scholar at the Social Philosophy and Policy Center, Bowling Green State University.

INDEX

Ability, 101
Adaptation, 326
Africa, 139
Agency, 50, 82–85; secondary, 274
Agreement, 89, 100
Alcohol use, 332
Alexander the Great, 99
Altman, Andrew, 280–308
"Amy's Pup-in-the Tub," 5
Andersson, Anna-Karin, 114
Anscombe, G. E. M., 48
Aphrodite, 324
Aquinas, 243
Arendt, Hannah, 301, 304
Aristotle, 326
Arnold, Denis, 164
"Associated living," 330
Associations, 88
Assurance, 39
Atlantic Ocean, 93
Atrocity: mass, 299; Nazi, 306–7
Augustine, 325
Austin, John, 36, 39
Austria, 329
Authenticity, 20
Authority, 29, 34, 65, 328, 330; of law, 39
Autonomy, 17–20, 53, 75, 90, 240, 315, 320; and political liberties, 3
Autonomy Argument, the, 17
Axelworthy, Lloyd, 302

Background injustice, 155, 171–72
Barbie, Klaus, 302
Bargh, John, 255
Barry's Argument, 208
Bentham, Jeremy, 46
Bias, 23
Book of the Dead, 322
Bowie, Norman, 164
Brennan, Jason, 1–27
Brentano, Franz, 85
Bureaucracy, and education, 334

Calvinists, 274
Cameos, 325
Campaign, 15
Capital, 191
Capitalism, 63, 148, 158
Caplan, Bryan, 22–23
Cartesian dualism, 244

Causation, 14
Central government, 333
Cepalism, 139
Cervantes, 325
Chaucer, 325
Chalk, Frank, 294
Change: agent as source of, 82–83
Charity, 76
Charter of the International Military Tribunal (1945), 282
Charter of the United Nations, 280
Child support, 115
Children: transfer of as a feature of genocide, 297–98
China, 149
Christiano, Thomas, 12, 16
Christopher Heath Wellman, 213–32
Citizens, 65; deliberative, 24; participatory, 24
Citizenship: and political liberties, 9
Civic Humanist Argument, the, 4–5
Civil law, 316
Civil liberties, 2–3
Classical liberalism, 50, 57
Clemenceau, Georges, 235
Closed society, 28
Coercion, 32, 36, 64–65, 161, 175, 313, 315, 320; alternatives to, 41–42; and state power, 28–31; as secondary to authority, 40
Cohen, G. A., 101, 180–82, 243
Cohen, Joshua, 57
Commands, 36–37
Common Agricultural Policy, 133
Compensation, 101
Competition, 136, 327
Compliance: with law, 38
Confirmation bias, 22
Conflict, 30
Conscious will, 254
Consciousness, 241
Consent, 52, 89, 161, 309–311, 313–316, 318
Constitutive value: and political liberties, 4
Consumers, 133
Contracts, 309
Convention on the Prevention and Punishment of the Crime of Genocide, 286, 293, 297, 300
Conversion of property, 117
Cooperation, 31

337

340   INDEX

Landes, David, 148
Larmore, Charles, 31
Latin America, 139
Lauterpacht, Hersch, 282
Law, 34, 36–37
Legal moralism, 309, 312–13, 318
Legal positivism, 307–8
Legitimacy, 29, 47; and coercion, 64–65;
   political, 30
Leipzig, 283
Leisure time, 183
Lemkin, Raphael, 286, 296–97, 304
Levine, Andrew, 32
Liability, 174
Liberal democracy, 214, 331
Liberal education, 329, 333
Libertarianism, 29, 50, 58–59
Liberties, 53, 315, 321; basic, 67; political,
   63; restrictions on, 46
Liberty-limiting principles, 310, 313
Libet, Benjamin, 251
Lifetime Channel, 16
Locke, John, 64, 75–76, 84, 114; and human
   generation, 112–13; on ownership, 99;
   theory of acquisition, 98
Lockean proviso, 100
London Charter, 282–84

Mack, Eric, 57
Macleod, Christopher, 304–5
Majority, political, 16
Market democracy, 50–51; and economic
   liberty, 59; and injustice, 78; and Kant,
   76; and tax-funded social safety net
   programs, 77
Martens Clause, 282
Marxism, 32, 88, 158–59, 221
Mass murder, 297–99
Mass violence, 294
Maximin decision rule, 190, 193
Maximizing principle, 193
May, Larry, 302, 304
Mercantilism, 129–30
Meyers, Christopher, 169
Middle Ages, 237
Mill, J. S., 20–21, 42, 57, 92, 136, 315–16,
   310, 332, 335; and economic liberty, 58
Milton, John, 325
"Minimal liberalism," 311
Minimum wage, 74
Minorities, political, 17
"Moderate liberalism," 311, 315
Monopolies, 138; of force, 48–49
Monty Python, 115
Moore, Michael S., 233–80
Moral agency, 88, 92; as a natural kind, 89,
   104; mutual recognition of, 100
Moral character, 312

Moral paternalism, 312, 318
Moral responsibility, 101
Morris, Christopher W., 28–49
Morse, Stephen, 243
Multinational enterprises, 155, 162–63
Murphy, Liam, 60–62
Murray, Charles, 70–71
Musgrave, Richard, 195
Mussolini, 324
Mutz, Diana, 24

Nagel, Thomas, 29, 31, 48, 57, 60–62
Narveson, Jan, 57
Nation building, 331
Nation-states, 7
National Curriculum (in England), 332–33
NATO, 305
Natural law, 308
Natural rights, 81
Nazi Germany, 40, 280
Nazis, 282, 284, 296–97, 302–3, 306–7
Needs, 163
Nersessian, David, 295, 303–4
Neuroscience, 242–79
Newman, Blessed John Henry, 329–33
Nicaragua, 163
Nickel, James, 53–54
Non-harmful wrongs, 311
Non-wrongful harms, 311
Norms, 43
Nozick, Robert, 18–19, 29, 31, 51, 57, 112,
   123, 183, 202; and self-ownership, 113
Nuremburg trials, 282, 284, 306
Nussbaum, Martha, 57

O'Hear, Anthony, 322–35
Obesity, 332
Objects: as property, 109
Obligation, 37
Odyssey, 322
Offense principle, 309–10, 313–14
Okin, Susan Moller, 113, 123
Original Position, 214–15
Osysseus, 325
Otsuka, Michael, 100–1
Outcomes Argument, the, 10–13
Ovid, 325
Ownership, 54–57, 82, 90, 106; and self-
   authorship, 69; collective, 96; full lib-
   eral, 107–8; group, 104; of children,
   115; of personal property, 68–69; of
   sperm, 117–18,123–25; rights of, 76;
   state, 103

Pain, 311, 312
Pareto efficiency, 184, 194
Parfit, Derek, 202
Paris Peace Conference, 283

Participation: political, 14
Participatory democracy, 328
Paternalism, 310, 315, 320
Paternity, 116
Patriarchy, 11
Pauper-Labor Argument, 143–44
Pedophilia, 333
Peoples, 214–16
Perfectionism, 198
Person: political conception of, 84, 200
Persuasion, 34
Pets, 89
Phillips v. Irons, 117–18, 122
Physician-assisted suicide, 316–17
Pinker, Steven, 235
Plato, 325, 334
Pogge, Thomas, 147–49, 216
Political community: humanity as, 304
Political legitimacy, 66
Political liberties: and autonomy, 17; and enlightenment, 20; communicative function of, 26; value of, 1–19
Political office: value of right to run for, 11–12
Political participation: as an impediment to enlightenment, 21–22
Political power, 8; and moral status, 7; of individual citizens, 16
Polyphemus (the Cyclops), 323
Poor, the, 105; and competition, 152–53; and free trade, 131; and injustice, 126–27
Possession, 94
Posthumous reproduction, 119, 124
Pound, Ezra, 322, 324
Poverty, 76, 147, 163
Powell, Benjamin, 163
Powers, 37, 53
Practical rationality, 239
"Principle of effectiveness," 141–42
Progressivism, and education, 334–35
Prohibition of alcohol, 43
Propaganda, 334
Property, 58, 93–96, 107; as a legal convention, 60; personal, 54; rights of, 59
Property paradigm, the, 106, 109–10; and reproductive issues, 110–15
Property-owning democracy, 183
Protectionism, 126, 170; and injustice, 133
Prussia, 331
Ptolemy, 326
Public opinion, 334
Public policy: and ownership, 106
Public property, 103
Public spending, 328
Pufendorf, 114
Punishment, 290, 308

Racine, 325
Racism, 333

Rand, Ayn, 50
Rational irrationality, 23
Rational reconstruction, 180–81
Rationality, 38
Ratner, Steven, 288
Rawls, John, 28–29, 36, 50–51, 57, 73, 213–32; against thick conception of economic liberty, 62; and self-respect, 74; on economic liberties, 58–60; proponent of the *Status Argument*, 6
Raz, Joseph, 43
Read, Leonard, 51
Reasons for action, 43
Reciprocity, 185, 190, 202, 206
Redistribution, 220
Reductionism, 245
Religion, and education, 331
Republicans, 22, 24
Respect: and exploitation, 157; and political liberties, 6; for others as self-authors, 66
Responsibility, 160, 172–73; and personhood, 84
Rights, 7, 53, 81, 104–5, 311, 318, 320; and international trade, 144–46; and legitimacy, 66–67; as claims, 55; inalienable, 315–19; of property, 121; parental, 106, 110–11, 114; to run for office and vote, 8–27
Ripstein, Arthur, 47, 310, 316, 319
Rissee, Mathias, 143–44
Roemer, John, 171
Rome Statute, 287
Rousseau, Jean-Jacques, 333
Rule of law, 290
Rules, 37, 65
Russell, Bertrand, 293
Russia, 149
Rwanda, 300, 303
Rwandan genocide, 285

Sample, Ruth, 159–60, 171
Samuel Freeman, 78
Sanctions, 36, 38
Scale: of violence, and genocide, 292
Second-order desires, 86
Security, 69
Self-authorship, 65
Self-consciousness, 85
Self-ownership, 76, 90–92, 102
Self-respect, 6, 73, 195
Sellars, Wilfred, 321
Shakespeare, 325
Single system, of education, 332
Single-parenting, 124
Skarbek, David, 163
Slavery, 89, 315–16
Slye, Ronald, 289
Smith, Adam, 57

Smith, Kellie, 117
Smoking, 332
Snyder, Jeremy, 167–69, 172–73
Social construction, 8, 15; and political
  liberties, 3; of basic rights, 61
Social Construction Argument, the, 13–16
Social democracy, 70–71
Social engineering, 331
Social justice, 50
Social mobility, 331
Social pressure, 22
Social respect, 6
Social Security taxes, 46
Social status: and political liberties, 3
Socialism, 55, 63, 142
Sokolowski, Robert, 85
Sovereignty, 35–36
Sovereignty principle, 310, 316
Soviet Union, 40, 282
Specialization, 327
Species, 326
Sperm: as a gift, 117–18; evidentiary value
  regarding crime, 115; forensic use, 116
Spontaneous order, 50–51
Stagnation: in developing world, 148
Stalin, 294
State: as an agent, 102; concept of, 32–33;
  justification of, 31; unjust, 40–41
State education, 331
State of nature, 62
Status Argument, the, 6–7
Statute of the International Criminal
  Court, 282
Steinbock, Bonnie, 119–21
Structural exploitation, 158–59
Structural injustice, 159–61
Surplus, 129
Sweatshop: definition of, 161–92
Sweatshops, 154

Talent: distribution of, 207
"Tale of the Slave," 18–19
Taxes, 42, 56, 60, 309
Technology, 326
Teenage pregnancy, 333
Territoriality, 34
Tesón, Fernando R., 126–53, 218
Thatcher, Margaret, 333
Third Reich, 281, 283, 303, 307, 329
Threats, 37
Tocqueville, Alexis de, 20–21
Tomasi, John, 5, 50–80
Torts, 309
Trade barriers, 126; harms of, 129–30
Tragedy, Greek, 325
Transactional exploitation, 158
Transfer, voluntary: of sperm, 118
Tripartite soul, 238

Turkish massacres of Armenians, 283, 290–
  91, 296
Tyrrell, James, 111–12

UN General Assembly, 286
Unfairness, 178–79, 313
Unions: suppression of, 169–70
United Nations, 284, 305
United Nations Economic Commission for
  Latin America and the Carribean, 139
United States, 116, 162, 282, 305
Universal Declaration of Human Rights,
  280
Utility: of individual vote, 11–12

Value, 312; subjective, 2
Victims: of genocide, 296
Vietnam War: and genocide, 293
Violence, organized, 299
Virgil, 325
Vladman, Mikhail, 171
Volenti Principle, 309, 312, 315–17
Voluntariness, 88, 92, 315; and exploitation,
  156
Voluntary slavery, 319
Voting: instrumental value of, 10

Wages, 163
Waldron, Jeremy, 72, 109
Wales, 333
Wall, Steven, 180–212
Wallis, Peter, 117
Walzer, Michael, 16
War-nexus requirement, 284, 287
Wealth, 127, 196
Weber, Max, 32–34
Wegner, Daniel, 254
Welfare-state capitalism, 183
Wenar, Leif, 142–53
Wertheimer, Alan, 158, 166, 171
Westen, Drew, 23
Wolff, Jonathan, 32
Worker safety, 163
Working, 54
World Bank, 147
World Trade Organization, 146
World War I, 283, 322
World War II, 288, 300, 303, 307
Wrongful conduct, 310–14; and exploita-
  tion, 157; and genocide, 291, 298
Wrongful harm, 307

Yankee Stadium, 313
Young, Iris Marion, 172
Yugoslavia, 285, 300, 303

Zwolinski, Matt, 154–79

For EU product safety concerns, contact us at Calle de José Abascal, 56–1°,
28003 Madrid, Spain or eugpsr@cambridge.org.

www.ingramcontent.com/pod-product-compliance
Ingram Content Group UK Ltd.
Pitfield, Milton Keynes, MK11 3LW, UK
UKHW020807190625
459647UK00032B/2262